# VEHICULAR TRAFFIC SCIENCE

# VEHICULAR
# TRAFFIC SCIENCE

PROCEEDINGS OF THE THIRD INTERNATIONAL SYMPOSIUM ON
THE THEORY OF TRAFFIC FLOW
NEW YORK, JUNE 1965

HELD UNDER THE AUSPICES OF THE
TRANSPORTATION SCIENCE SECTION OF THE
OPERATIONS RESEARCH SOCIETY OF AMERICA

*Edited by*

### LESLIE C. EDIE

*The Research and Development Division*
*The Port of New York Authority*
*New York City*

*and*

### ROBERT HERMAN and RICHARD ROTHERY

*Department of Theoretical Physics*
*Research Laboratories, General Motors Corporation*
*Warren, Michigan*

## AMERICAN ELSEVIER PUBLISHING COMPANY, INC.

NEW YORK       1967

SOLE DISTRIBUTORS FOR GREAT BRITAIN
ELSEVIER PUBLISHING COMPANY, LTD.
*Barking, Essex, England*

SOLE DISTRIBUTORS FOR THE CONTINENT OF EUROPE
ELSEVIER PUBLISHING COMPANY
*Amsterdam, The Netherlands*

*Library of Congress Catalog Card Number: 67-16248*

# Preface

THIS VOLUME contains the Proceedings of The Third International Symposium on the Theory of Traffic Flow held under the auspices of the Transportation Science Section of the Operations Research Society of America. This Section of ORSA was formed in 1962 because of the growing interest and importance of the new field of research in transportation science. Vehicular traffic flow theory is perhaps the best developed and most rapidly growing part of the subject and has provided stimulus and inspiration for the application of scientific methods to air, sea, rail, and other transportation systems. Vehicular traffic theory which, in the past, was mainly focused on flow problems has continued to enlarge its scope and now encompasses broader fields of interest. To reflect this broader scope these Proceedings are entitled *Vehicular Traffic Science*.

The present symposium was conducted in the spirit of its two predecessors. The First Symposium on the Theory of Traffic Flow was organized by the General Motors Research Laboratories, and was held December, 1959, in Warren, Michigan. It initiated and catalyzed the present series of International Meetings. Fifteen technical papers were presented and published in Proceedings entitled *Theory of Traffic Flow*. The Second International Symposium on this subject, organized by the Road Research Laboratory, was held in London during June, 1963, and contributed to the international flavor of this series. Thirty-four papers were presented and published in the Proceedings of that meeting. The Third Symposium was organized by the Transportation Science Section of ORSA with the endorsement of the International Federation of Operations Research Societies.

The Third International Symposium on the Theory of Traffic Flow was held in New York City during June, 1965. Forty-five technical papers were presented, all of which are published in these Proceedings in full or in the form of summaries. They cover a variety of traffic phenomena relating to single-lane, two-lane, and multi-lane traffic flow; general theory and experiment; networks and intersections; pedestrian and vehicle gap acceptances; simulation; and economics and scheduling. The program of this meeting reflected a continuation and expansion of the fields of research which were covered in the first two symposia as well as the development of new ideas. The aim of the work is to develop an understanding of vehicular traffic which will contribute to the solution of the pressing problems of traffic congestion, delays, and accidents with their rising economic costs to Society as a whole, and their rising personal costs to individual members of Society in terms of human frustration and suffering.

The traffic theorist of today, whether engineer, physicist, or psychologist, has an ever increasing capacity to bring the widest range of technical skills to bear on these problems. While traffic problems in general are exceedingly complex, there are well defined aspects which can be dealt with theoretically in explicit mathematical form. Various papers published in this volume illustrate that this can be done in a meaningful way. There are also significant experiments which can be conducted to test the validity of theory as a description of real traffic situations; a number of papers deal with such experimental verifications. To the extent that theories are confirmed by experiments, they may sometimes be used as guides by traffic engineers and others to reduce congestion and solve various problems on operating roadways. Some of the theoretical and experimental work of the first two symposia is already contributing to improvements in traffic management and operations. Much of this earlier work has been included in the curricula of the leading universities throughout the world where traffic engineers and traffic scientists are receiving their academic training. Through the cooperative efforts of traffic engineers and traffic scientists a new science and technology is evolving for dealing with one of the World's major problems.

The success of the Third Symposium required the generous support of public-spirited organizations. On behalf of the Executive Committee and the symposium participants, we express our appreciation to the Alfred P. Sloan Foundation, Automotive Safety Foundation, Chrysler Corporation, The Ford Motor Company, General Motors Corporation, International Bridge Tunnel and Turnpike Association, International Business Machines Corporation, Operations Research Society of America, and The Port of New York Authority. But for them this meeting would not have been possible.

The work of conducting a scientific symposium requires the cooperation, assistance, and devotion of many individuals to carry out the planning and organization of the activities, including the review of papers offered for presentation. We thank all of those who have contributed to this work.

The Executive Committee, which handled Symposium matters large and small, consisted of Leslie C. Edie, Chairman; Denos C. Gazis, Vice Chairman; Richard Rothery, Secretary; Walter Helly, Treasurer and Arrangements Chairman; Robert Herman, Program Chairman.

LESLIE C. EDIE
ROBERT HERMAN
RICHARD ROTHERY

New York City
November, 1966

# Contents

# Testing the Applicability of the Theory of Continuity on Traffic Flow at Bottlenecks

W. LEUTZBACH

Technical University, Karlsruhe, Germany

## Abstract

Volume, speed, and density measurements have been carried out on a single lane of traffic over a highway section approximately one-half mile long. These measurements were obtained from four observation points, which permitted a reconstruction of vehicle movements through this section of roadway. This observational data has been used to test the theory of continuity by measuring the speed of propagation of density changes in the traffic stream.

THE THEORY of continuity[1] is treated in a great number of mathematical papers. There has been, however, only relatively limited research on its usefulness in describing actual traffic flow.[2,3] Therefore, a research program on the subject of single lane traffic flow included a further effort to test the theory. The following basic idea was applied:

When at a given point, $x_0$, the development of density in time is known (density pattern), and when the relationship between flow, $q$, and density, $k$, is known also from observations (fundamental diagram), the theory of continuity permits the evaluation of a straight line within the time-distance plane ($x$-$t$ plane) along which density is a constant. Where such straight lines intersect, shock waves occur. The speed of these shock waves can also be evaluated.[1]

When the $x$-$t$ plane has thus been filled with lines of equal density, the progress of density can be evaluated or even directly read for any other point $x_i$, provided the theory of continuity is valid, and provided that the fundamental diagram remains unaltered between the points of observation and $x_i$.

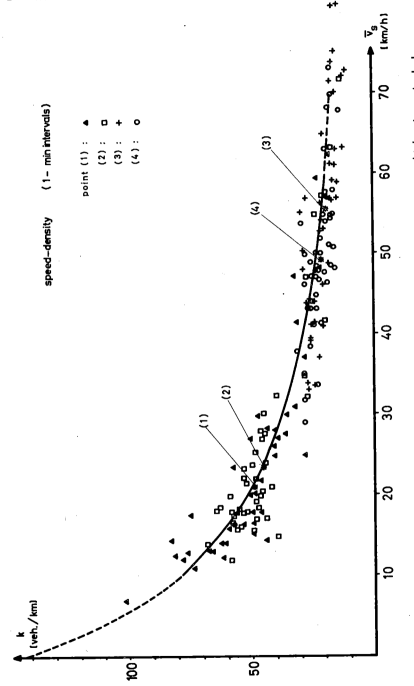

FIGURE I.  Density vs. speed calculated for I-min intervals from observations on vehicles in a single lane of one-way traffic.

Similar considerations apply in principle when the development of density is observed at a fixed point of time along a section of road, but it seems improbable that there are technical means which will permit the observation of sufficiently long road sections carrying sufficiently dense traffic.

To prove the aforementioned basic considerations, observations were carried out on the Karlsruhe Mannheim Autobahn (freeway).

Due to road repair, two of the four lanes were closed at the time of observation; traffic approaching on two lanes was consequently compressed into one lane in each direction.

The measurements were carried out by means of time-recorders. There were four observation points, each 300 meters (m) apart. At each point two pressure tubes were laid across the highway, 10 m apart. Thus it was possible to record the travel times, $t$, needed to traverse this road interval, $s$, and to record the movement of each vehicle within the entire observation section. Altogether a 13-minute time interval was analyzed.

To evaluate the fundamental diagram, the space-mean speed was calculated from successive 1-minute intervals:

$$\langle v_s \rangle = \frac{s}{\frac{1}{n}\sum t} \tag{1}$$

For the corresponding density,

$$k = \frac{q}{\langle v_s \rangle} \; ; \qquad\qquad k = \frac{60}{3.6} \cdot \frac{\sum t}{s} \tag{2}$$

$$k[\text{veh/km}], \qquad t[\text{sec}], \qquad s[\text{m}]$$

Only in very few cases may it be possible to plot the relation between $k$ and $v$ in an analytical form. In most cases the smoothed curve can only be approximated (Fig. 1). The fundamental diagram can then be plotted point by point from the rectangular areas beneath the $k$-$v$ graph,

$$q = k \cdot \langle v_s \rangle \tag{3}$$

The slope of the straight lines of equal density is then the tangent to the fundamental diagram

$$\frac{dx}{dt} = \frac{dq}{dk} \tag{4}$$

For each of the four points the observed density pattern was plotted from sliding 1-min intervals i.e., 1-min intervals taken every 5 sec. Then, by using the fundamental diagram (Fig. 2), the lines of equal density were plotted as described above. With increasing time, these lines go from point 2 to point 1, and from point 3 to point 4 (Fig. 3). As seen in Fig. 3 there are discrepancies between the theoretical and the observed density patterns.

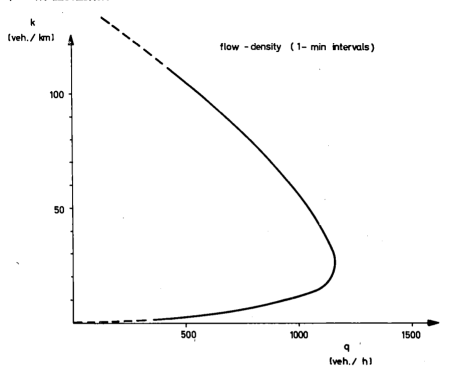

FIGURE 2.  Fundamental diagram, derived from the smooth curve in Fig. I.

To describe these discrepancies numerically, the areas

A   below the observed density pattern,
B   below the evaluated density pattern and
C   between the observed and evaluated density patterns

were measured (Fig. 4). Then:

$$a_1 = \frac{A - B}{A} \tag{5}$$

$$a_2 = \frac{C}{A} \tag{6}$$

At point 1,  $a_1 = 12.7\%$
$a_2 = 21.0\%$;
at point 4,  $a_1 = 19.1\%$ and
$a_2 = 20.8\%$.

The theory of continuity is based on a functional relationship between

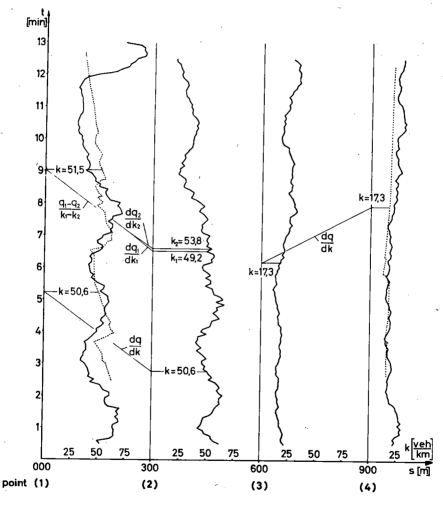

FIGURE 3. Observed density patterns (in 1-min intervals) at four observation points, compared with theoretical density patterns plotted by using the fundamental diagram in Fig. 2, and applying the theory of continuity.

density and speed, or volume and density. As seen in Fig. 1, however, the observation data from 1-min intervals are quite scattered. It seemed likely that, to some extent, this might be the reason for the discrepancies. There is no doubt that the postulations of the theory of continuity are better fulfilled the longer the observed period of time.

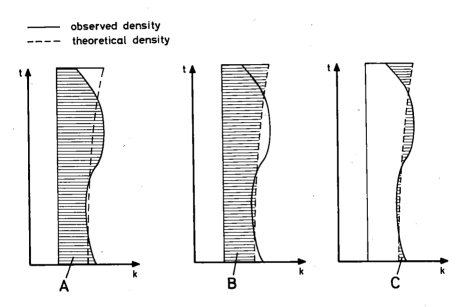

FIGURE 4.   Comparison of observed and theoretically calculated densities.

To prove this, the observational data used before were aggregated into sliding 5-min intervals (aggregation into independent intervals was not possible due to the limited total duration of observations). The procedure described above was repeated; the results are shown in Fig. 5. Comparison of the theoretical with the observed density pattern, however, was carried out only for point 1 (Fig. 6).

Now, $a_1 = 9.8\%$, and $a_2 = 10.8\%$. Both values were lower than in the first calculation.

By increasing the observation interval from 1 to 5 min, the density pattern was smoothed (compare Fig. 6 with Fig. 3). Any greater oscillations of density, if present in the traffic stream, are only again evident when the total duration of observations is increased.

Within certain limits, traffic flow was almost equal at all observation points during the entire observation period. This is, of course, natural since no vehicle was able to enter or leave the highway between points 1 and 4 and because approaching vehicles were forming a permanent queue.

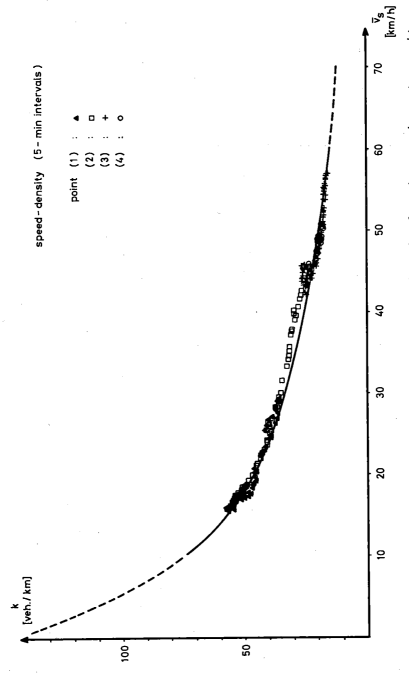

FIGURE 5.   Density *vs.* speed calculated for 5-min intervals; data taken from the same observations used in Fig. I.

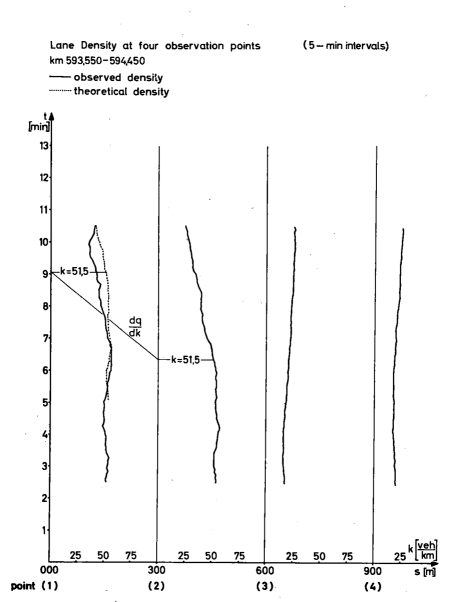

FIGURE 6. Observed density patterns in 5-min intervals, compared at point 1 with a theoretical density pattern at point 2, and applying the theory of continuity.

If with equal total flow at two observation points two different densities are observed, it is possible that these different densities might be connected to points on the two branches of only one fundamental diagram. They might, however, also belong to two different fundamental diagrams. When at three or more observation points with equal total flow there are at least three different densities, the latter case—possibly combined with the first—applies (Fig. 7a) except when the fundamental diagram is plotted as in Fig. 7b.

In the $k$-$v$ diagram, Fig. 8, contrary to Fig. 1, the central line was not plotted by visual estimate, but is the hyperbola describing the average flow at the four observation points during the observation period of 13 min.* The two edge lines are hyperbolae representing the observed minimum and maximum flow during a 1-min interval. As is seen, they also embrace almost all the flow-values at points 1 to 4; this is due to the similarity of flow at all observation points.

Whether only one fundamental diagram applies to the different observation points or whether there are several can probably be seen only from the position of each individual datum relative to its mean value (Fig. 9). Since, according to Fig. 8, there is at least a tendency for all data to be within the hyperbolic area, it is possible that only one fundamental diagram (as shown in Fig. 7b, for example) applies to all four observation points. To answer this question, either the sample size must be enlarged and/or the variance of the individual values be reduced by increasing the time intervals (compare Fig. 5 with Fig. 1).

Also, it could be suggested to use the mean flow hyperbola to evaluate the density propagation, since it roughly follows the relationship between $k$ and $\langle v_s \rangle$. Within the $q$-$k$ diagram the hyperbola used as a "fundamental diagram" is a parallel to the $k$-axis (Fig. 9), so that above the $s$-$t$ plane the corresponding lines of equal density will be parallel to the $t$-axis. This, however, means that from the density at one point, the densities at other points cannot be calculated.

As several factors need further attention, a final conclusion from the research work carried out so far can only be drawn with hesitation, i.e., out of the aforementioned reasons there is no definite answer to whether the theory of continuity can be used to describe actual traffic flow:

    a. In some cases the observed densities were close to the optimum point of the fundamental diagram, provided the latter was as shown in Fig. 2. Near this point, however, even small density oscillations (and thus also any inaccuracy of the fundamental diagram) may lead to relatively large alterations in the slope of lines of equal density.

    b. As is seen in Figs. 1 and 5 the observation data of the individual observation points are situated in two distinctly separate areas of the $k$-$v$-graph. From this it can be seen that the traffic after the bottleneck was

*$q = k \cdot \langle v_s \rangle = $ const.

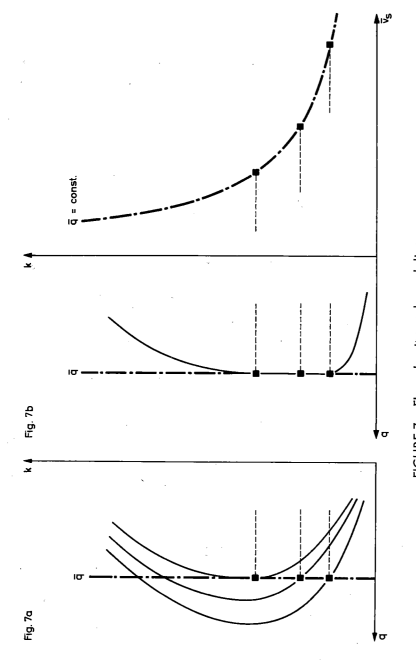

FIGURE 7.   Flow, density, and speed diagrams.

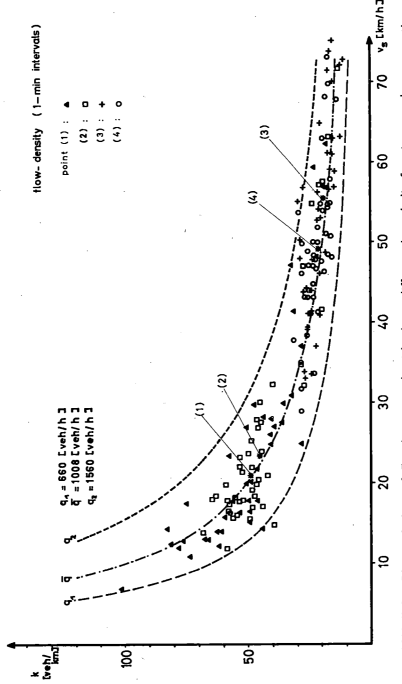

FIGURE 8. Observed data of Fig. I compared with three different hyperbolic functions, each representing a constant flow.

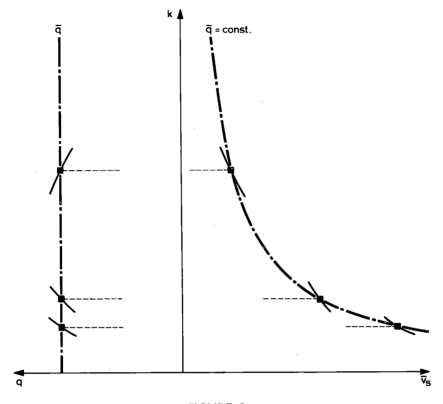

FIGURE 9.

obviously in a process of acceleration. It cannot, however, be definitely established whether there is one fundamental diagram valid at all observation points, or whether it varies within the observation area.

## Acknowledgement

The author is indebted to Mr. R. Ernst for helpful discussions and valuable contributions to the subject.

## References

1. M. J. Lighthill, and G. B. Witham, On Kinematic Waves, *Proc. Roy. Soc.*, Series A, **229,** No. 1178, 281–345 (May 1955).
2. G. M. Pacey, The Progress of a Bunch of Vehicles Released from a Traffic Signal, *Road Res. Lab.*, RN/2665/GMP (January 1956).

3. J. Foster, An Investigation of the Hydrodynamic Model for Traffic Flow with Particular Reference to the Effect of Various Speed-Density Relationships, *Proc. Australian Road Res. Board*, **1**, Part 1, 229–257 (1962).
4. P. I. Welding, Time Series Analysis as Applied to Traffic Flow, *Proc. Second Intern. Symp. on the Theory of Traffic Flow*, London 1963, published by OECD, Paris 1965.

# Propagation of Disturbances in Vehicular Platoons

ROBERT HERMAN and RICHARD ROTHERY

Theoretical Physics Department
Research Laboratories, General Motors Corporation
Warren, Michigan

**Abstract**

The results of a series of experiments carried out using an eleven vehicle platoon are analyzed within the framework of hydrodynamical models of traffic flow. Particular emphasis is focused on the speed of propagation of disturbances through this traffic stream.

## Introduction

A DECADE ago, in the Proceedings of the Royal Society, Lighthill and Whitham[1] published a paper entitled "A Theory of Traffic Flow on Long Crowded Roads." This publication was the first attempt to present a theoretical model for vehicular traffic using classical hydrodynamics. Several other papers along similar lines have followed. The most notable of these are by Richards,[2] Greenberg,[3] and Pipes.[4]

Common to all of this work are the main assumptions which form the theoretical foundation of this approach. The first of these assumptions is that vehicle number is conserved, that is, on any element of road the net change of the number of vehicles within is due to the net flow in and out of this section of roadway. The second assumption asserts that the number of vehicles passing any point on a section of roadway depends explicitly only on the concentration and positionally on the characteristics of the roadway facility, i.e.,

$$q = f(k, x) \tag{1}$$

14

From these assumptions one can derive the continuity equation, namely

$$\frac{\partial k}{\partial t} + \frac{\partial q}{\partial x} = 0 \qquad (2)$$

It follows from Eqs. 1 and 2 that a constant flow will be measured by an observer moving with respect to the ground with a speed $c$, where

$$c = \frac{\partial q}{\partial k}\bigg]_x \qquad (3)$$

or for a homogeneous road facility where the flow is assumed to be independent of position, we may write

$$c = \frac{dq}{dk} \qquad (4)$$

Since for the steady state we have

$$q = uk \qquad (5)$$

then from Eq. 4 we may write

$$c = u + k\frac{du}{dk} \qquad (6)$$

Experimentally the speed of the traffic stream is always found to be a decreasing function of concentration. Therefore, the second term of Eq. 6 is always negative, and $c$ is always less than the speed of the traffic stream. It is advantageous to use Eq. 6 to define a parameter $\lambda$, i.e., we rewrite Eq. 6 as

$$c = u - \lambda \qquad (6a)$$

where $\lambda$ is the speed of propagation of a disturbance back through a chain of vehicles as measured from the moving frame of reference of the traffic stream. For convenience we write

$$k\frac{du}{dk} = -\lambda \qquad (7)$$

In the paper by Greenberg, although it is not explicitly stated, the parameter $\lambda$ is assumed to be a constant,* and as Russel[5] has so succinctly stated, if we use Eq. 7 as our starting point, it is relatively easy to derive the equation of state for a traffic fluid, and from this vantage point, the physical meaning of the underlying assumptions remain clear. For example, if we assume that the total reaction time of a driver-vehicle unit is proportional to the intervehicle spacing, a not unreasonable assumption, then $\lambda$ is the coefficient of proportionality and we have from Eq. 7

$$u = \lambda \ln (k_j/k) \qquad (8)$$

and

$$q = \lambda k \ln (k_j/k) \qquad (9)$$

where $k_j$ is the integration constant and equal to the traffic stream concentration when the stream speed is zero.

It is interesting to point out that for this same assumption regarding the speed of propagation of a disturbance, an entirely different theoretical

* Unfortunately, $\lambda$ is denoted by $c$ in this reference.

description of a traffic stream yields the same results of Eqs. 8 and 9 for the steady state. This alternate description is the "car-following model of single lane traffic flow" which attempts to describe the detailed manner in which one vehicle follows another.*

It would appear then that the parameter $\lambda$, independent of any assumptions regarding its analytical form, plays an important role in so far as traffic is concerned. And yet, very little attention has been made in an effort to determine its value or functional dependence experimentally. One notable exception to this is the work by Foster,[7] reported in the Proceedings of the Australian Road Research Board. Here, the value of $\lambda$ was measured for starting waves generated by a queue of vehicles starting from a signalized intersection.

The results of this study, while based on a very limited number of runs, indicate that for starting platoons $\lambda$ was approximately a constant equal to 18 mph, a value not too different from the values obtained by the authors from car-following experiments carried out in three vehicular tunnels in New York City.[8] There, the range of values for $\lambda$ was 18–22 mph.

Indeed, it is rather surprising that there is such good agreement considering that completely different experimental techniques were used, not to mention the entirely different traffic environments and driver populations studied.

It is true that several authors, including ourselves, have attempted to measure this same parameter indirectly for different roadway environments and traffic conditions using data on average speed and concentration of a traffic stream and fitting it to Eq. 8. However, this is hardly any test of the theory, and until the theory is on solid foundations it certainly cannot be used as an estimate for the speed of propagation of a disturbance. To date there appears to be no direct measurement of this parameter for a moving traffic stream.† In an effort to begin to fill this void, the authors have carried out a series of experiments using platoons of automobiles on a test track facility. Information was obtained using instrumentation that would facilitate the determination of the speed of propagation of a disturbance and the simultaneous measurement of traffic stream parameters, in order that a direct comparison could be made.

In the next section we discuss the experimental techniques used in carrying out these experiments.

## Experimental Techniques

To determine the basic characteristics and simplify as much as possible the complexities of single lane traffic flow, a series of experiments was carried out using platoons of eleven vehicles, each of which was a production model

---

* See, e.g., Eq. 9 of Ref. 6.
† See, however, the papers of W. Leutzbach, and L. C. Edie and E. Baverez of these Proceedings.

(1965 LeSabre Buicks) and of a common performance class. As a measure of performance, each of these particular vehicles had the ability to accelerate from a standing start to 60 mph, in 11 to 12 sec. Again, in an effort to study a traffic flow situation as idealized as possible, the roadway used was a straight, wide, and level test track with no entrances, exits, or cross roads along its $2\frac{1}{2}$ mile length. This facility and these vehicles provided a means for studying the properties of a homogeneous traffic stream and simulates, in a sense, traffic flow on a limited access roadway.

Of the eleven vehicles used to form each platoon, three vehicles were equipped with instrumentation that provided information from which it was possible to construct each of these vehicle trajectories. These recordings for the three instrumented vehicles were made simultaneously on a single magnetic transport by telemetering the trajectory information from two of the instrumented vehicles to the third. The three instrumented vehicles were positioned in the platoon as the lead or first vehicle, $F$, a mid-vehicle, $M$, and the last vehicle, $L$. The significance of this instrumentation is that it allows one

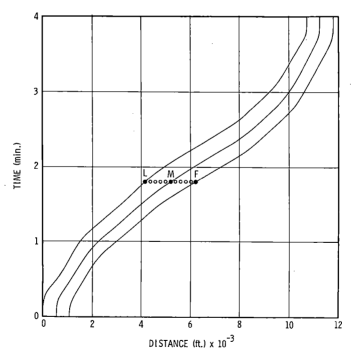

FIGURE I.  Vehicle trajectories for the first, $F$, middle, $M$, and last vehicle, $L$, of an eleven vehicle platoon. The driver of the first vehicle followed the programmed maneuver from a standing start of accelerating to 20, 40, 60, 40, and 20 mph before coming to a complete stop after traveling a distance of approximately 2 miles.

to study in detail the dynamical properties of a single lane of traffic spatially as well as a function of time, i.e., by knowing the initial positions of these three vehicles with respect to each other, the time and spatial history of each instrumented vehicle can be recorded. From this information the spatial configuration of the platoon can be calculated as well as the individual speed profiles. Relative distances and relative speeds between each of the instrumented vehicles is then also known.

A typical run is illustrated in Fig. 1 where the trajectories for three instrumented vehicles is shown. The trajectories in this particular case are that of

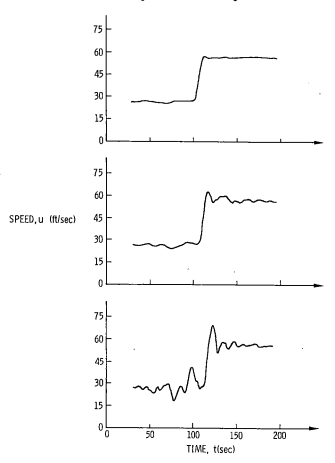

FIGURE 2.    One set of speed profiles for the three instrumented vehicles. The first vehicle (top graph) accelerated from one speed to another. The middle vehicle (center graph) and last vehicle (bottom graph) of the eleven vehicle platoon followed a comparable speed change but not without time lags and oscillations or "noise" added to the system.

the first, sixth, and eleventh vehicles in an eleven vehicle platoon. This test run extended over a 2 mile distance where the initial and final spacing between each successive instrumented vehicle was 0.1 mile. A set of speed profiles for a maneuver where the driver of the lead vehicle accelerated from one speed to another is shown in Fig. 2. The time lags between the first, middle,

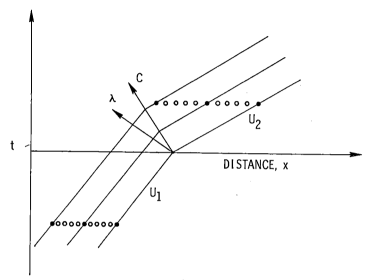

FIGURE 3. Idealized vehicle trajectories where the lead vehicle accelerates from a speed $U_1$ to $U_2$ instantaneously. A graphical representation of the propagation of this disturbance is shown both with respect to the roadway, c, and with respect to the moving traffic stream, $\lambda$.

and last vehicles of the platoon are clearly visible. The determination of these time lags together with the knowledge of the spatial configuration provide all the necessary information for the determination of the speed of propagation of so-called "shock waves" or disturbances with respect to the traffic stream or roadway. This is illustrated in Fig. 3 where the speed of the disturbance, with respect to the roadway, c, and the speed of the disturbance with respect to the vehicles, $\lambda$, is indicated for idealized trajectories. If real vehicular trajectories were as free of noise as is the case in Fig. 3, there would be little difficulty in the measuring of the response time of the system. Unfortunately, as can readily be seen from Fig. 2 the speed change of the following vehicles is not a simple step function.

To illustrate this point further with regard to "noise," we have plotted in Fig. 4 two cases, *A* and *B*, where the driver of the lead vehicle attempted to drive with a constant speed. The speed profile of the lead vehicle is seen to be relatively smooth. The noise added to the platoon by the following first five, and subsequently the next five drivers, is clearly seen in the speed profiles of the sixth and eleventh vehicles. It is interesting that in case $B$ where the lead

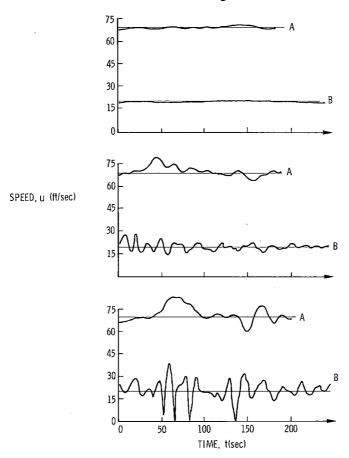

SPEED, u (ft/sec)

TIME, t(sec)

FIGURE 4.   Speed profiles recorded from two runs A and B for the three instrumented vehicles positioned as the first (top graph), middle (center graph) and last vehicle (bottom graph) of an eleven vehicle platoon.

vehicle maintained the relatively low but nearly constant speed of approximately 14 mph* enough noise was added to the system that the eleventh

* The statement that 14 mph is a relatively low speed is of course highly subjective, and clearly depends on the era. Historians have pointed out that during the early development of the railroads in the United States people proclaimed that the lifetime of this mode of transportation was limited since man biologically could not withstand the high and sustained speed of 12 mph. Today's newspaper men, tomorrow's historians, are now making the same proclamations, but for different reasons and, of course, for somewhat higher speeds.

vehicle came to a complete stop three times during this 4 min run. This property of noise as a function of platoon position has been reported earlier.[8,9] The experiments in the present paper are, however, unique in the sense that the input signal—in this case the speed profile of the lead vehicle—was known simultaneously along with the output or response signal, i.e., the

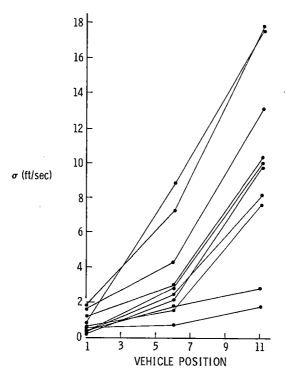

FIGURE 5.   Standard deviation of speed, $\sigma$ (ft/sec), vs. vehicle position for ten steady-state runs where the lead vehicle attempted to maintain a constant speed throughout each run.

speed profiles of one or more following vehicles. The increase of "speed noise" or "speed fluctuation" as a function of platoon position is strikingly demonstrated in Fig. 5 where the standard deviation of each speed profile for ten different test runs is plotted as a function of platoon position. The standard deviation of each speed profile increases for vehicles down the line. The small speed deviation of the lead vehicle is a reflection of the ability of the lead driver to maintain a nearly constant speed which was, in these runs, his assigned task. The significant relationship between speed noise and these experiments is that the amplitude of the disturbance or signal introduced as a change in speed by the lead driver necessarily could not be small, but instead it was necessary that the introduced disturbance was sufficiently large so that a reasonable signal-to-noise ratio could be maintained.

The degree to which the acceleration responses were amplified by the drivers of the platoon is shown in Fig. 6 where the initial acceleration of the

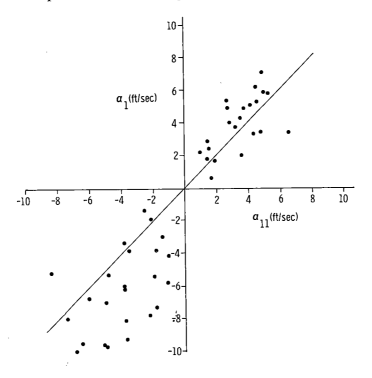

FIGURE 6.    Acceleration of the first vehicle, $a_1$(ft/sec²), vs. acceleration of the last or eleventh vehicle, $a_{11}$ (ft/sec²).

lead vehicle, $a_1$, is plotted vs. the initial acceleration response of the eleventh vehicle, $a_{11}$. In only 4 cases out of 24 is the amplitude of the acceleration disturbance amplified by the ten following drivers during deceleration, and in 6 cases out of 22 during accelerations. In those cases where the amplitude of the acceleration increases, the differences in the accelerations of the first and eleventh vehicles were less than 1.5 ft/sec² in all but three test runs.

## Results

The basic results of these experiments as they relate to the speed of propagation of a disturbance in a platoon of vehicles are summarized in Figs. 7 and 8. In Fig. 7 the experimentally obtained values for λ are plotted as a

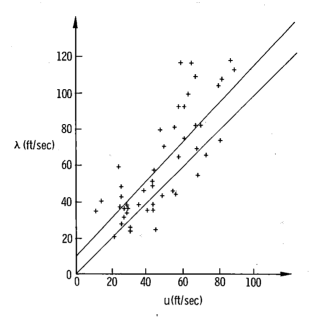

FIGURE 7.   Calculated values of the speed or propagation of a disturbance with respect to the traffic stream, λ (ft/sec), *vs.* the speed of the
traffic stream, *u*(ft/sec).

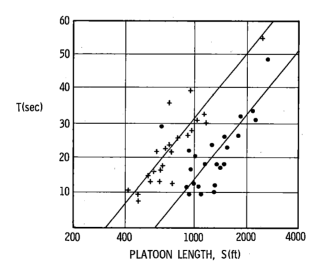

FIGURE 8.   Propagation time, *T* (sec), *vs.* platoon length, *S*(ft). The
platoon length has been plotted on a logarithmic scale. The solid dots
and crosses are for deceleration and acceleration maneuvers, respectively

function of the platoon speed. In addition to the 45° line, which differentiates the direction of the disturbance with regard to the roadway, there is also shown in Fig. 7 the linear "least squares" fit to the data. While this linear fit is a reasonable representation of the data up to a speed of 60 ft/sec, it does lead to difficulties. For example, if we let

$$\lambda = A + Bu \tag{10}$$

then from Eq. 7 we have

$$u = \frac{A}{B}\left\{\left(\frac{k_j}{k}\right)^B - 1\right\} \tag{11}$$

or more simply for our case where $B \approx 1$,

$$u = A\left\{\frac{k_j}{k} - 1\right\} \tag{12}$$

While the agreement between this equation and most experimental results can be made quite reasonable with a suitable choice of the parameter, $k_j$, Eq. 12 leads to the result that

$$q = A(k_j - k) \tag{13}$$

and this of course does not in general exhibit the known behavior that maximum flow occurs in a range of 40–60 vehicles/miles. On the other hand, if one attempts to take the nonlinearity of $\lambda$ vs. $u$ into account, e.g., by letting

$$\lambda = A + Bu^2 \tag{14}$$

one obtains, again using Eq. 7, the speed-concentration equation

$$u = \sqrt{\frac{A}{B}} \tan\left\{\sqrt{AB} \ln\left(\frac{k_j}{k}\right)\right\} \tag{15}$$

This has the undesirable feature that for the concentration range, $0 \leq k \leq k_m$, where $k_m$ is given by the equation

$$k_m = k_j e^{-\pi/2\sqrt{AB}} \tag{16}$$

the speed oscillates between plus and minus infinity. However, this range of concentration where Eq. 15 is unrealistic is relatively small compared to $k_j$ for those values of the parameters $A$ and $B$ in which a reasonable fit to the data is obtained. Similar results are obtained when one attempts to take the nonlinearity of $\lambda$ vs. $u$ into account by using an equation of the form

$$\lambda = A + Bu + Cu^2 \tag{17}$$

In this case, we obtain from Eq. 7:

$$u = \frac{1}{2C}\left\{\sqrt{\alpha} \tan\left(\frac{2}{\sqrt{\alpha}} \ln \frac{k_j}{k}\right) - B\right\} \tag{18}$$

where

$$\alpha = 4AC - B^2$$

It is not at all clear that any of these relationships or others that can be derived for speed and concentration or flow and concentration, in themselves, contribute to the theory of traffic flow even though they form a more consistent framework between these experiments and classical hydrodynamics as it is applied to traffic. The experimental findings, on the other hand, point to possible short comings of earlier work.

If as an alternative to developing steady-state flow relations, as in Fig. 8, we plot the experimentally obtained propagation times, $T$, as a function of the logarithm of platoon lengths, several interesting features relating to driver behavior emerge. First, there is a consistent and marked difference in the results for acceleration and deceleration disturbances. Then, independent of the type of disturbance, the logarithmic fit of propagation times $vs.$ platoon lengths appear excellent. Finally, there is a minimum propagation time of about 1 sec for each vehicle-driver interaction.

While the existence of the acceleration-deceleration dissymmetry has been pointed out in the literature, Fig. 8 clearly and effectively differentiates driver-behavior for these two classes of disturbances. The degree to which all or part of these complexities can be taken into account in car-following and/or hydrodynamical models will hopefully be the subject of future work.

## Acknowledgments

The authors acknowledge with pleasure Mr. George Gorday's assistance with instrumentation and data collection. We also thank Mr. Frank Lopez who did much of the initial work in the development of the telemetering system used in these experiments. Lastly, we thank Miss Sharon Smith who carried out the computer programming required in this work.

## References

1. M. J. Lighthill and G. R. Whitham, A Theory of Traffic Flow on Long Crowded Roads, *Proc. Roy. Soc.*, A **229,** 317 (1955).
2. P. I. Richards, Shock Waves on the Highway, *Operations Res.*, **4,** 42 (1956).
3. H. Greenberg, An Analysis of Traffic Flow, *Operations Res.*, **7,** 79 (1959).
4. L. A. Pipes, Wave Theories of Traffic Flow, *J. Franklin Inst.* **280,** 231 (1965).
5. H. Russel (Ohio State University), private communication.
6. D. C. Gazis, R. Herman, and R. Rothery, Nonlinear Follow-the-Leader Models of Traffic Flow, *Operations, Res.*, **9,** 545 (1961).
7. J. Foster, An Investigation of the Hydrodynamic Model for Traffic Flow with Particular Reference to the Effect of Various Speed-Density Relationships, *Proc. Austrailian Road Res Board.*, **1,** 229 (1962).
8. R. Herman and R. Rothery, Microscopic and Macroscopic Aspects of Single Lane Traffic Flow, *Operations Res.* (Japan), **5,** 74 (1962).
9. R. Rothery, R. Silver, R. Herman, and C. Torner, Analysis of Experiments on Single Lane Bus Flow, *Operations Res.*, **12,** 913 (1964).

# Generation and Propagation of Stop-Start Traffic Waves

LESLIE C. EDIE and ERIC BAVEREZ

The Port of New York Authority, New York

## Abstract

Stop-start traffic waves in tunnels are recurrent phenomena which reduce tunnel traffic production. They are studied by the analysis of two types of multipoint data. The pattern of their generation is disclosed by contours drawn on a space-time diagram giving average flow, concentration, and speed. Values for drawing such contours are taken from averages made jointly in both space and time using data from seven detectors in 600 feet. The propagation of stop-start waves is studied using data taken at five locations in 6000 feet. Values of wave speeds, wave amplitudes, and concentrations before, after, and during a stop-start wave are reported on. These analyses lead to a general picture of tunnel traffic behavior and explain the occurrence of periodic stop-start waves.

## Introduction

STUDIES[1-3] HAVE shown that a principal limitation on the productivity of a long tunnel like the Holland Tunnel is the periodic generation and propagation of stop-start waves. Two systems of control, using first an open loop and second a closed loop, have been tried to prevent the formation of such waves and to eradicate them when they form.[4] Although increased tunnel production has been realized by both control methods, the average increase has been only a few per cent and the closed-loop system has been shown to oscillate.[5] There is a need to understand better the generation and propagation of these waves in order to better control them.

The first theories dealing with the generation and propagation of stoppage waves, or shock waves, were the continuum theories based on fluid dynamics.[6-7] The theories, however, failed to explain the nature of the periodic

26

recurrence of stoppage waves in a tunnel. Newell modified continuum theory by assuming that the flow $q$ at a point on a roadway was not a unique function of the concentration $k$ but, instead, depended on two $q$-$k$ curves giving a different relationship following acceleration than following deceleration.[8] With this assumption, Newell showed how minor perturbations could become amplified and lead to periodic instabilities of the type observed.

Experimental observation and analysis to support the continuum theories has been limited. Notably lacking has been a detailed analysis of how changes in flow and concentration develop and propagate, and whether shock waves exist, and if so how they are created. In seeking answers to these questions two kinds of analyses have been made, one dealing with the generation and the other with the propagation of traffic waves.

## Generation of Waves

The first analysis consisted of constructing contours over space and time of average flow, concentration, and speed for a section of roadway about 600 ft long in the region of the bottleneck of the Holland Tunnel, located near the beginning of the upgrade. The location of the section studied is marked by arrows in Fig. 6, and is labeled *Bottleneck*. Such contours make clear the dynamic changes taking place in the traffic stream. The data for this analysis were collected several years ago by seven pressure-sensitive tapes installed

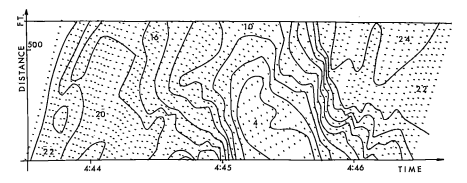

FIGURE I.   Space-time trajectories of individual vehicles and regions of equal speed. Speeds are given in miles per hour.

across the lane. The tapes were used to actuate a multi-pen recorder each time a vehicle wheel passed over one of them. The data were later transcribed to a space-time diagram and smooth curves of the trajectories of all vehicles observed were drawn, as illustrated by the dotted lines of Fig. 1. The solid lines in Fig. 1 are contours enclosing vehicles having the same speed.

Using the trajectories as data, the mean values of the continuum variables $q$ and $k$ at numerous sampled points, located in the space and time area shown, were measured using the measurement method suggested in the principal author's paper presented at the Second Symposium.[9] Averages were made in a rectangle having a length of 264 ft of space and a width of 18 sec of time. This amount of space and time is large enough to smooth out most random fluctuations and yet small enough to give a detailed picture of the dynamic changes taking place.

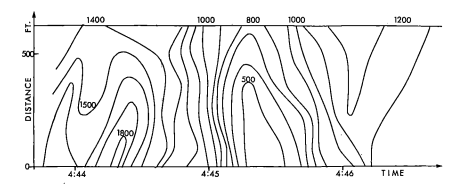

FIGURE 2.    Contour lines showing levels of equal average flow rate. The figures give the level of flow in vehicles per hour.

It will be observed in Fig. 1 that the initial steady-state condition of 22–24 mph rapidly deteriorates into unstable states of ever slower speeds. The slow-speed condition propagates backward in space passing out of the range of the observation at $4:45\frac{1}{2}$ p.m., following which the traffic stream returns to another steady state at the initial speed of about 22–24 mph. All of this occurs within a period of about three minutes. It is understandable that a macro cosmic theory, even though valid for dealing with many vehicles and long time periods, might not be applicable for describing such short-term transient phenomena.

What has taken place in this observation becomes fairly clear from a study of the flow, concentration, and speed contour maps in Figs. 2, 3, and 4, respectively. Referring to Fig. 2, one observes a relatively high flow rate into this section at 4:44 p.m. and shortly thereafter in the range of 1400–1800 vehicles/hour (vph). These flow rates, unable to penetrate this section, are turned back to form peak contour regions of higher than usual flow rates. This initial state is followed by a minute or so of declining flow rates, the contour lines of which are first vertical but later tend to close on themselves downstream; upstream they tend to remain open-ended and to propagate,

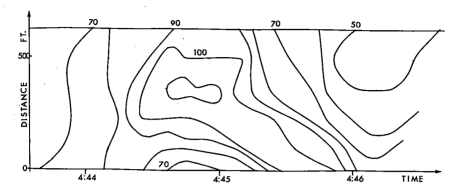

FIGURE 3.   Contour lines showing levels of equal average concentration. The figures give the concentration in vehicles per mile.

forming contour valleys of low flow. The lowest flow level contour shown encloses vehicles flowing at less than 500 vph and less than 5 mph.

With reference to Fig. 3, one observes that changes in concentration occurred in a considerably different contour pattern from changes in flow. As would be expected from the continuity equation, $dq/dx + dk/dt = 0$, when the flow gradient in space is zero, the concentration gradient in time is zero; and the contours are therefore orthogonal. In this example, a critical condition arises when high concentrations build up to about 100 vehicles per mile (vpm) and begin to propagate backwards. It is interesting to note that the contour lines of both $q$ and $k$ in Figs. 2 and 3, respectively, approach slopes approximately the same as the vehicle trajectories at the beginning and end of the observation. In this steady state changes in flow and concentration propagate at about the stream speed, a usual finding for relatively

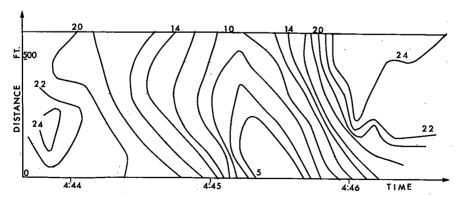

FIGURE 4.   Contour lines showing levels of equal average speed. The figures give the speed in miles per hour.

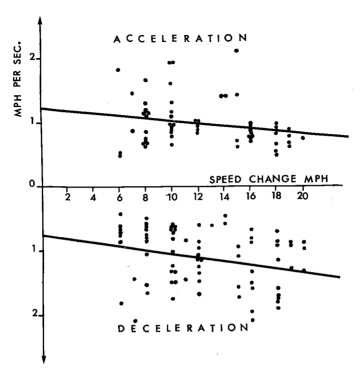

FIGURE 5. Average accelerations and decelerations of individual vehicles passing through slowdown-speed-up waves *vs.* the speed change involved. The lines are least-square fits to the data.

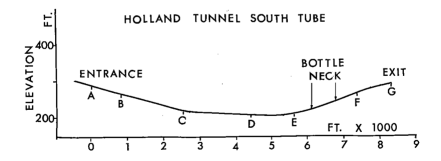

FIGURE 6. Profile of the Holland Tunnel South Tube showing observation points A through G for time-sequence experiments and the 600-ft bottleneck section where data for Figs. 1–5 were obtained.

constant-speed, steady-state conditions. This result suggests that for this scale of measurement, small changes in flow may not propagate at a speed equal to the slope of the tangent to a steady-state $q$-$k$ curve as suggested by the hydrodynamic wave theories of traffic flow. Instead, they are carried along at about stream speed or only slightly less than stream speed right up to saturation flows, at which level they suddenly reverse direction.

Figure 4 shows a contour of mean stream speed derived from the mean values of $q$ and $k$. A comparison with Fig. 1 shows it to have similar but smoothed gradients as compared to the individual vehicle speeds.

## Deceleration—Acceleration

Among the parameters needed to describe these features are the values of the decelerations and accelerations used by vehicles in slowdown-speedup maneuvers. Values have been measured for about 70 vehicles for each half of this maneuver (not always the same vehicle for both halves). The average deceleration and acceleration used by each vehicle was computed by taking the change in speed from 22 mph to the minimum speed. The results are plotted against the speed change in Fig. 5. It will be noted that accelerations and decelerations have approximately the same range, 0.5 to 2 mph/sec. The mean values are 1.1 mph/sec for deceleration and 1.0 mph/sec for acceleration. These values are about one-half those observed for bridge roadways and street intersections.[9]

It is interesting to note that as the speed change increases, the deceleration tends to increase but the acceleration tends to decrease. The rates tend to be approximately equal at a change of 9 mph for a traffic speed of 13 mph. This traffic speed is approximately that found for a type of steady-state condition observed at a tunnel bottleneck. Reference 2 gives evidence of this, particularly Fig. 6 and the discussion which identifies a steady-speed state occurring at 12 mph. This is the speed at which the expected speed of a following vehicle is the same as the speed of the vehicle ahead. Thus, at such speeds there is a tendency for a slow-speed wave to stand still at the bottleneck with the trajectories of vehicles passing through being symmetrical upstream and downstream. For this condition to persist without propagation it is also necessary for the reacceleration lag time to be equal to the headway time between vehicles.

## Propagation of Waves

It would be extremely pleasant to have detectors at approximately 100-ft intervals throughout a tunnel lane in order to study the changing structure of waves as they move backward and become amplified or attenuated, depending on whether the inflow from upstream exceeds or is less than the outflow downstream. Such a level of instrumentation has not yet been afforded. Fortunately, however, a good deal can be deduced about the speed of wave propagation and other features by merely counting vehicles *vs.* time at intervals about 2000 ft apart and plotting the counts as illustrated in Fig. 7. How this is done was explained in Reference 3. The slope of such curves

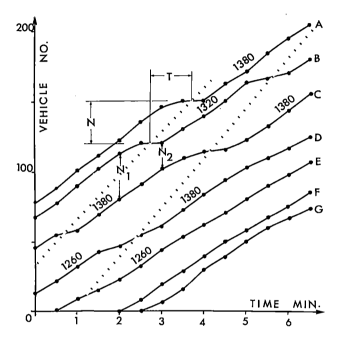

FIGURE 7. Time sequence data showing the arrival time of various vehicles at observers *A* through *G*. The slopes of the curves give the rates of flow and the figures following the slowdown waves (indicated by dotted lines) give flow rates in vehicles per hour.

gives the average rate of flow passing an observer during a counting period of 30 sec. For stoppage waves to be observed directly, giving a horizontal slope, they must, therefore, have a duration of at least 30 sec. However, when only a few vehicles pass in 30 sec during heavy congestion there is strong evidence of a stoppage for part of the counting period.

From these curves the following values may be read:

$N$ = the number of vehicles passing through a wave as it moves between two observers,

$T$ = the travel time of a wave between observers,

$N_1$ = the number of vehicles in a section just before a wave departs, and

$N_2$ = the number of vehicles in a section just after a wave departs.

TABLE 1. Wave Behavior in Section BC of Holland Tunnel (0.325 Mile in Length)

(Wave Identification No.)

| | 1 | 2 | 3 | 4 | 5 | 6 | 7 | 8 | 9 | 10 | 11 | 12 | Avg. |
|---|---|---|---|---|---|---|---|---|---|---|---|---|---|
| $k_j$ (vpm) | 206 | 194 | 194 | 191 | 194 | 188 | 194 | 203 | 160 | 142 | 191 | 191 | 188 |
| $k_1$ (vpm) | 89 | 123 | 126 | 101 | 89 | 77 | 108 | 96 | 126 | 55 | 96 | 80 | 96 |
| $k_2$ (vpm) | 75 | 75 | 49 | 52 | 71 | 62 | 71 | 59 | 83 | 37 | 71 | 55 | 62 |
| $r$ (sec) | 1.79 | 1.55 | 1.62 | 2.02 | 1.91 | 1.97 | 1.75 | 1.82 | 1.62 | 2.10 | 1.86 | 1.69 | 1.80 |
| $v$ (mph) | 9.8 | 11.9 | 11.5 | 9.4 | 9.8 | 9.8 | 10.6 | 9.8 | 13.9 | 12.7 | 10.2 | 11.1 | 10.7 |
| $a$ (veh) | 6 | 17 | 25 | 16 | 6 | 5 | 12 | 13 | 15 | 6 | 9 | 8 | 12 |

These values and the distance between observers, permit computation of the following variables:

$k_j$ = the jam concentration (vpm). Assuming that there is in fact a stoppage wave, it is $N/X$, where $X$ = length of the section in miles,

$k_1$ = the concentration in a section when a stoppage wave is present, namely $N_1/X$ (vpm),

$k_2$ = the concentration in a section after a stoppage wave, namely $N_2/X$ (vpm),

$r$ = the reacceleration response time following a stoppage wave, namely $N/T$ (sec),

$v$ = the speed of propagation of the stoppage wave, namely 3600 $X/r$ (mph), and

$a$ = the wave amplitude, $N_1 - N_2$ (vehicles).

Table I gives the values of these variables computed for 12 waves observed on a downgrade section of the Holland Tunnel 1700 ft long, extending 820 ft to 2520 ft from the entrance, a section where the greatest number of stoppage waves are observed. This is the section between observers $B$ and $C$ in Figs. 6 and 7.

The last 10 of the 12 waves in Table I occurred within 41 min. None appears to have been generated in section $BC$. The 12 shown were well formed by the time they were observed at the downstream end of Section $BC$. Five were apparently generated in the adjoining section $CD$, and 7 in the next section $DE$.

The average values for this and the other sections from the entrance to the bottleneck are given in Table II below:

Table II.   Average Wave Behavior in Four Sections of the Holland Tunnel

| Section | AB | BC | CD | DE |
|---|---|---|---|---|
| Length $X$ (miles) | 0.155 | 0.325 | 0.355 | 0.226 |
| $\langle k_j \rangle$ (vpm) | 207 | 188 | 197 | 186 |
| $\langle k_1 \rangle$ (vpm) | 139 | 96 | 99 | 106 |
| $\langle k_2 \rangle$ (vpm) | 70 | 62 | 73 | 84 |
| $\langle r \rangle$ (sec) | 2.04 | 1.80 | 1.87 | 1.83 |
| $\langle v \rangle$ (mph) | 8.5 | 10.7 | 9.8 | 10.6 |
| $\langle a \rangle$ (vehicles) | 11 | 12 | 9 | 5 |

It will be noted that Section $AB$ exhibits values of $\langle k_j \rangle$, $\langle r \rangle$ and $\langle v \rangle$ that are approximately 20% different from values in the other three sections. A conclusion that this entrance section has a character that much different from the other sections should be viewed with some question. An uncertainty, which could not be clarified, exists as to the exact location of the first observer. The length taken for $AB$ assumes he was at the tunnel portal; however, there is reason to believe he was stationed outside the tunnel on the entrance ramp.

A comment should be made about the method of computing the jam concentration $k_j$. An alternate assumption supporting this method is that flow rates in the stop-start waves are a linear function of concentration $k$. The number of vehicles $N$ observed by a wave in traversing a section of length $X$ is:

$$N = (k + q/v)X \tag{1}$$

If 

$$q = v(k_j - k), \tag{2}$$

then, 

$$k_j = N/X. \tag{3}$$

With regard to Eq. 2, Daou[11] has found high correlations for this relationship in platoons.

### Start-Up Flow Rates

A characteristic of fluid behavior which negates a kinematic explanation for recurring stoppage waves is that the release of a fluid from a stationary blocked state generates the maximum rate of flow possible in a given channel. Lighthill and Whitham, in their classic paper,[6] assumed the same characteristic existed for vehicular traffic. Thus, they concluded that the effect of oversaturation of a bottleneck section by a higher capacity roadway upstream was the propagation of a shock wave upstream which changed the state of the traffic upstream to a slow-speed crawl. The start-up flow from this crawl was always potentially higher than the bottleneck capacity and, therefore, a constant pressure was maintained on the bottleneck, thereby keeping its flow at a maximum.

With reference to Fig. 7, one can measure the start-up flows generated by stop-start waves by observing the slopes of the vehicles *vs.* time curves just following a wave. Some of these measurements have been noted on the curves in Fig. 7. The averages for all observations is given below.

|  | Location | | | | |
|---|---|---|---|---|---|
|  | A | B | C | D | E |
| No. observations | 8 | 10 | 10 | 8 | 3 |
| Avg start-up flow | 1360 | 1370 | 1340 | 1290 | 1240 |

It will be noted from the above and Table II that there is a rough relationship between start-up flow rates and wave amplitudes. The drop in start-up flow rates from $B$ to $E$ and the existence of maximum flow capabilities higher than the start-up flow rates are sufficient conditions to explain the recurrence of stoppage waves in the Holland Tunnel.

Once a stoppage wave is generated by the occurrence of a short pulse of high level flow (not followed by a significant gap to absorb it), it relieves some of the pressure on the bottleneck from whence it originated, and the concentration is temporarily reduced. However, as the starting wave moves backward it releases ever higher rates of flow causing the concentration to build back up to a critical level around 70–80 vpm. With such a concentration, a short pulse of high flow could again precipitate a stop-start wave.

Assuming a wave speed of about 15 fps and a traffic speed of about 30 fps the average distance covered by a stop-start wave and the vehicle which begins a second wave 4 min later would be $X/15 + X/30 = 240$, $X = 2400$ ft.

Thus oscillations of the right frequency could be set up over such an average distance. However, there is, of course, great variance in the time intervals between waves and in the distance covered by a wave before resurgent traffic precipitates the next wave.

The start-up flow gradient suggests two control arrangements which do not involve metering of traffic at the entrance portal, which is so far from the trouble sections $CD$ and $DE$. The first arrangement would be to move the control point inside the tunnel between points $B$ and $C$ where start-up flow rates are high. If traffic is slowed or stopped at this point, the subsequent loss in flow is 100 vph per lane less than between $D$ and $E$. The second arrangement would be to equalize the start-up flow rates by means of cones or other devices so that concentration would not build up again after a stop-start wave.

## Conclusion

The evolution of a stop-start wave in the Holland Tunnel has been studied in detail. Its generation resulted from the arrival of a pulse of high level flow at a time when the concentration was of the order of 70–80 vpm. Vehicles found themselves too close together in time and slowed successively to lower and lower speeds in an effort to reduce their mean time headways. In so doing, they used slightly increasing decelerations as their speed changes increased, but the increase was insufficient to reduce the average distance between vehicles; the concentration rose to 100–120 vpm. At this concentration a state of incompressibility was reached forcing vehicles to decelerate at points increasingly upstream; thus the compression wave began to propagate upstream. In emerging from the compression wave vehicles tended to use accelerations which decreased with speed change, and on the average were about 10% less in magnitude than decelerations. This resulted in an output from the starting wave that was less than the input to the stopping wave, and the amplitude of the stop-start wave increased as it propagated at about 10+ mph. The stopping speeds propagating slightly faster than the starting speeds.

Although only one specific case of wave generation has been shown here, and the number of different patterns resulting from the complicated inter-actions taking place is limitless, certain general principles have been brought out. With this general picture of stop-start wave generation and propagation it would appear feasible to develop an approximate quantitative model of tunnel traffic behavior useful as a process control model. However, more probably needs to be known of the structure of the stream as it approaches saturation conditions, and the probability distribution of high flow modes and their duration in order to predict with good reliability whether a stop-start wave will be generated. Messrs. Crowley and Foote have been studying this question and are reporting on some of their work at this symposium.[12]

## References

1. L. C. Edie, R. S. Foote, Effect of Shock Waves on Tunnel Traffic Flow, *Proc. Highway Research Board*, **39**, 492–505 (1960).
2. H. Greenberg, A. Daou, The Control of Traffic Flow to Increase the Flow. *Operations Res.* **8**, No. 4, 524–532 (1960).
3. L. C. Edie, R. S. Foote, "Experiments on Single Lane Fow in Tunnels." Theory of Traffic Flow, *Proc. Symp. on the Theory of Traffic Flow* (R. Herman, Ed.), Elsevier Publishing Co., Amsterdam, 1961, pp. 175–192.
4. R. S. Foote, Single-Lane Traffic Flow Control. *Proc. Second Intern. Symp. on the Theory of Road Traffic Flow*, J. Almond, Ed., O.E.C.D., Paris, (1965).
5. K. W. Crowley, I. Greenberg, Multiple Point Experimentation and Analysis in Single Lane Traffic, *Traffic Eng.* **35**, No. 6, 20–22, 38–41.
6. M. J. Lighthill, G. B. Whitham, On Kinematic Waves, II. A Theory of Traffic Flow on Long Crowded Roads, *Proc. Roy. Soc.* London, Series A, **229**, No. 1178, 1955, pp 317–345.
7. P. I. Richards, Shock Waves on the Highway, *Operations Res.* **4**, 42–51 (1956).
8. G. F. Newell, Theories of Instability in Dense Highway Traffic, *J. Operations Res. Soc. Japan*, **5**, No. 1, 9–54 (1962).
9. L. C. Edie, Discussion of Traffic Stream Measurement and Description, *Proc. Second Intern. Symp. on the Theory of Road Traffic Flow*, J. Almond, Ed., O.E.C.D., Paris (1965).
10. L. C. Edie, Car-Following and Steady-State Theory for Noncongested Traffic, *Operations Res.* **9**, No. 1, 66–76.
11. A. Daou, On the Flow Within Platoons, Twenty Fifth National Meeting of the Operations Res. Soc. of America, Montreal (May 27–29, 1964).
12. R. Foote, K. Crowley, Density-Speed-Flow Dyanmics in Single Lane Traffic Flow, *Third Intern. Symp. on the Theory of Traffic Flow*, New York City, 1965.

# Density-Speed-Flow Dynamics in Single Lane Traffic Flow

*ROBERT S. FOOTE and KENNETH W. CROWLEY*

**The Port of New York Authority, New York**

Traffic flowing through a 6000-ft length of single lane tunnel roadway, with a bottleneck at the output end, is observed simultaneously at the terminal points and four intermediate points under a variety of conditions. Output flow is observed to vary significantly, but as a consistent function of input flow, section density, and output speeds. A control on input flow based on output speeds, intended to maximize output flow, causes systematic oscillations in both input and output flow, section density, and output speed. A new control based on section density and input flow, as well as output speed, is being tested. The behavior of gaps is described and the distribution of headway times is discussed.

The first case is of exceptionally high production, followed by a transition to congested flow. Compared with a usual peak output of 21 vpmin, a period of 90 min is observed in which output flow averaged 22.6 vpmin. During the first 60 min, section densities averaged 42 vpmile, and output speed averaged 48 fps (32 mph). There were three instances, however, where density exceeded 53 vpmile, and each was followed by a drop in output speed to 43 fps (29.5 mph). Gaps occurred in the input flow naturally in each of these cases, and densities decreased and output speeds increased to the previous levels. Then, after an hour, densities went above 53 vpmile, and during the next 30 min rose gradually to 65 vpmile. Output speed dropped to 30 fps (20 mph) and output flow to 21.6 vpmin. For the final 30 min of the total 2-hour period observed, there were wide fluctuations in output speed, from 10 fps (6.7 mph) to 55 fps (37 mph), while section density remained more constant near 68 vpmile. Output flow averaged 21.2 vpmin, 6% below the average of the previous 90 min.

The second case might be described as a "pressurized" flow. Output is highly consistent, varying generally only one vehicle from the number counted the previous minute, but averaging only 20 vpmin. Section density during the 75 min of observation averaged 77 vpmile. Speeds fluctuated from 11 fps (7 mph) to 42 fps (29 mph), suggesting repeated shock waves.

The third case is one of morning traffic (rather than PM weekday peak as are the other cases), which is characterized by more commercial traffic. While densities averaging 40 vpmile are well below the critical levels found for PM traffic, output speeds are closer to critical. The average output speed during the 75 min observed is 36 fps (24 mph), but seven instances are observed where speeds dropped to 22 fps (15 mph). The output flow averages only 19 vpmin.

In the final case input flow is restricted whenever output speeds drop below 30 fps, which causes oscillations with a period of approximately 20 min. Four cycles are observed during 80 min. Input flow, section density, output speed, and output flow vary with nearly identical period and amplitude, but not in phase. Taking minimum output speed at $t = 0$, minimum input flow occurs at $t = 1.5$ min, minimum section density occurs at $t = 2.25$ min, and minimum output flow occurs at $t = 6$ min. In each case when output speed drops below 30 fps, output flow decreases. Output flow is observed to oscillate during the 80 min as follows: a high of 22 vpmin, followed by a low of 16 vpmin, 23 vpmin, 13 vpmin, 23 vpmin, 12 vpmin, 20 vpmin, 12 vpmin, and 22 vpmin. To damp these oscillations and stabilize output flow in the 22–23 vpmin range, input flow is to be controlled on the basis of input flow in the previous minute, section density and, finally, output speed.

# A Model of Car Following Derived Empirically by Piece-Wise Regression Analysis*

*A. HANKEN*

Georgia Institute of Technology, Atlanta, Georgia

*and*

*T. H. ROCKWELL*

The Ohio State University, Columbus, Ohio

The purpose of this study was to develop an empirically based model of car following which would predict following car acceleration (and change in acceleration) as a function of observed dynamic relationships with the lead car.

An experiment was performed on a level two-lane state highway with low traffic density. The lead car velocity was preprogrammed. Its speed varied between 20 and 60 mph; its acceleration between $+1.82$ and $-4.00$ mph/sec. Sensors and an automatic recorder were installed in the following car to record continuously the variables of interest. In this way the speed and acceleration of the lead car and the following car and the headway were determined at intervals of 0.5 sec.

A common procedure is to analyze these data by regression analysis. In this case the regression function is, however, completely unknown as no *a priori* model was postulated. A linear model may not be completely realistic as a number of previously proposed car following models are distinctly nonlinear.

To ascertain the nonlinear effect, a linear regression model was used as a first approximation over the entire data space $G_1$ (1200 data points). Next, $G_1$ was subdivided into two parts, $G_2$ and $G_3$, by a special (cutting) method and a linear regression model was postulated in each of the two subspaces. This procedure was repeated until the number of data points in each subspace $G_i$ was less than 100.

The regression coefficients were then determined by a least square fit in each subspace $G_i$ of the regression function

$$\ddot{x}_2(t + \tau) = \ddot{x}_{2m} + b_0[h(t) - h_m] + b_1[\dot{x}_1(t) - \dot{x}_{1m}] - b_2[\dot{x}_2(t) - \dot{x}_{2m}]$$

* This study was supported in part by the Ohio Department of Highways and Bureau of Public Roads.

where $\dot{x}_1(t)$, $\ddot{x}_1(t)$ are, respectively, the speed (mph) and acceleration (mph/sec) of the lead car at time $t$.

$\dot{x}_2(t)$, $\ddot{x}_2(t)$ are, respectively, the speed (mph) and acceleration (mph/sec) of the following car at time $t$.

$h(t)$ is the distance between the lead car and the following car.

$\tau$ is a time delay (sec).

$b_0$, $b_1$, $b_2$ are regression coefficients.

The index $m$ signifies the mean value of the variable over the considered data space. The "best" value of $\tau$, an adjusted parameter in the computer program, was determined by a least square method.

Typically, in $G_1$ (linear regression over the entire data space) the following equation was found:

$$\ddot{x}_2(t + 2.0) = 0.016 + 0.0058[h(t) - 134] + 0.498[\dot{x}_1(t) - 31.6]$$
$$- 0.546[\dot{x}_2(t) - 31.6]$$

Comparison of the regression equations in the subspaces $G_i$ gave the following results:

a. The effects of nonlinearity are not very important as the cutting procedure did not result in a substantial decrease of the residual variance.

b. The coefficient $b_0$ is usually small, positive, and independent of $h(t)$.

c. The coefficients $b_1$ and $b_2$ are positive; $b_2$ is usually larger than $b_1$, although the difference is rather small compared to their absolute value.

d. The coefficients $b_1$ and $b_2$ are independent of the headway $h(t)$ within the considered range (approx. 40–250 ft), e.g.,

in $G_2 : h_m = 115$ ft, $b_1 = 0.484$ sec$^{-1}$, $b_2 = 0.532$ sec$^{-1}$

in $G_3 : h_m = 156$ ft, $b_1 = 0.497$ sec$^{-1}$, $b_2 = 0.554$ sec$^{-1}$.

These results are compared with previously proposed models of car following. Extrapolation of this study to the concept of traffic flow theory is discussed.

# Single-Lane Traffic Flow on Circular and Straight Tracks

R. E. FRANKLIN

Oxford University Engineering Laboratory
Parks Road, Oxford, England

## Abstract

During the past few years, a large number of experiments on the flow of traffic in a single lane with no overtaking has been carried out at the Road Research Laboratory. These have been analysed, the objectives of the analysis being to discover what light is thrown on the questions of the flow-concentration relationship in steady and unsteady flow, the nature of flow in platoons, and the propagation of disturbances.

It seems likely that the flow-concentration relationship for "steady" flow is not a single curve but is divisible into three or four separate flow regimes; as the concentration increases these may be described as platooned flow, steady flow, quasi-steady congested flow, and unsteady high-concentration flow.

The results on platooned flow are clearly of only a preliminary nature; there is much research to be done into this question, particularly with regard to variations within platoons and the effect of platoon length on stability.

Experiments on the propagation of disturbances tend to confirm the conclusions about the nature of the steady-flow concentration diagram and suggest that, under changing conditions, the flow is rather less for a given concentration than for steady conditions.

## I. Introduction

IN THE last few years many controlled experiments on the flow of traffic in a single lane have been carried out at the Road Research Laboratory, and recently the author was given the opportunity of examining the accumulated data. Much of the work has already been reported by Wardrop,[1] but the mass of data is such that further analysis is possible, and this has been carried out.

42

Experiments were carried out both on closed, circular tracks (in an attempt to simulate an infinite road) and on a long straight section of a figure of eight track. In the former, experiments were carried out on tracks of radii 56, 106, 206, and 412 ft, and the speed of the traffic was measured by recording the passage times of vehicles between two timing points at opposite ends of diameters of the tracks; in the latter, either two timing points 1000 ft apart or four at spacings of $333\frac{1}{3}$ ft were used.

In preparing the present paper, besides the usual methods of determining flow and concentration, two other ideas have been used. The first is that when measurements are made with timing points it is possible to count the number of vehicles between timing points and plot it as a function of time. Consideration of the resulting graph allows one to comment on the nature of the flow. Secondly, with such plots and the original data it is possible to estimate the space-time average flow and concentration, quantities which in some ways are more satisfactory to deal with than the normally-defined ones.

The objects of the analysis were to see if light could be thrown on the flow-concentration relationship in a single lane, to examine the nature of flow in platoons, and to look at the way in which disturbances are propagated in a stream of traffic.

## 2. The Flow-Concentration Relationship

### 2.1. Flow on Circular Tracks

The data recorded in experiments on circular tracks are shown in Fig. 1, as computed by Wardrop.[1] If these are examined critically it does not seem reasonable to follow the usual practice and draw single curves through the points. Instead, it appears more likely that there are at least two distinct regimes of flow; for example, on the 106 ft radius track there seems to be one relationship for concentrations below 100 vehicles per mile and another for concentrations greater than this.

The reason for this is a simple, but important, one. As plotted in Fig. 1, the concentration is taken to be the number of vehicles on the track divided by the circumference of the track. Now if when the number of vehicles on the track is large it is reduced by taking off one or two vehicles, it may be expected that the remaining vehicles will increase their speed and spacing, causing a reduction in concentration, and perhaps a rise in the flow. However, if this is continued, the speed of the vehicles on the track will eventually rise to a value beyond which the drivers are not prepared to go. Further reduction in the number of vehicles cannot then cause an increase in speed; instead, gaps will appear, effectively forming the vehicles into one or more independent platoons, and because the speed remains unchanged, the flow will fall off linearly with reduction in average concentration.

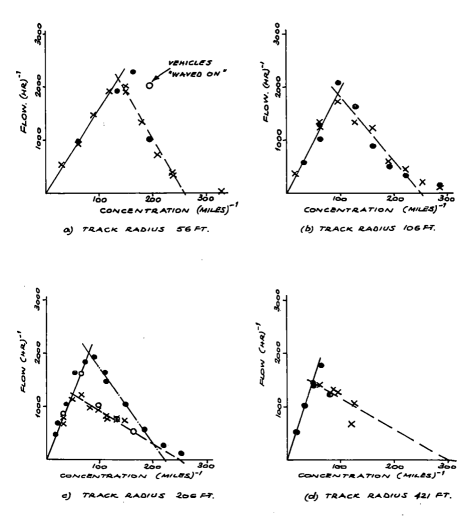

FIGURE I.    Flow-concentration data. Circular tracks.

Thus the interpretation of Fig. 1 is that when the average concentration falls below a certain value, gaps appear and platoons form. On the 106 ft radius track this critical concentration is about 100 vehicles per mile. Examination of the original data confirms this and also reveals that after platoons have formed and the vehicles move at a speed independent of the number of vehicles on the track, the concentration within platoons is usually roughly equal to the critical value, the exceptions being in very short platoons of two or four vehicles when it can be much higher.

The fact that in these tests the speed of the vehicles was measured by recording passage times between two timing points at opposite ends of a diameter of the track, permits a more detailed examination of the flow on the track. This not only illustrates the point above but reveals other interesting facts. If half the track circumference is regarded as a "test-length," the data may be used to plot a graph of the number of vehicles in the test-length as a function of time.* It then becomes possible to look at the way in which this number varies with time. One way of describing this is to calculate the correlation coefficient between successive changes in concentration.

If there is only one vehicle on the track, then each increase in concentration in the test-length is followed by a decrease, and the correlation between successive changes will be −1.00. For two vehicles close together, an increase may be followed with equal probability either by a further increase or by a decrease; the correlation coefficient is therefore zero. If a platoon of three vehicles is moving around the track the value becomes 0.33, and as the length of the platoon is increased, the correlation coefficient tends to the value of +1.00. At some average concentration, however, the length of the platoon will become greater than the test length, and thereafter the correlation coefficient falls rapidly with increase in concentration until the track is full. At this point, and for concentrations greater than this, the correlation coefficient will have a value near to −1.00, for on the average each increase is followed by a decrease.

The values of the correlation coefficient have been calculated for the 106 ft radius track on the assumption that twelve vehicles are sufficient to fill the track (this corresponds to a concentration of about 100 vehicles per mile), and the original data have been used to find the actual values. The results are shown in Fig. 2. It is seen that for eight vehicles and less the experimental values agree with those calculated, showing that for concentrations less than 100 vehicles per mile the vehicles were formed into platoons and not distributed around the track.

Further, it is to be noted that for numbers of vehicles equal to and greater than twelve, the correlation coefficient does not fall to −1.00 as it would if the vehicles were evenly spaced. Instead, it falls only to about −0.6 and then starts to rise again. There are two reasons which could account for the fact that the value −1.00 is not reached: either some drivers were holding much larger than average spacings, i.e., the stream was not homogeneous, or waves were traveling round the ring. The first is more likely because of the uniformity of the track and the data confirm that this was so. The tendency for the correlation to rise at higher concentrations is, however, an indication of disturbances traveling round the track, and corresponds to the observation made at the time of the experiments that at high concentrations only a few of the vehicles on the track were moving at any particular instant. The

---

* An example of such a graph may be found in Fig. 6a.

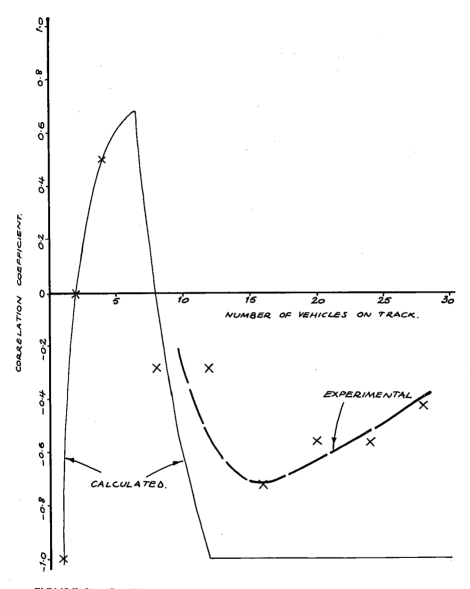

FIGURE 2.   Coefficient of correlation between successive changes in concentration on half the 106 ft radius track.

reason for this intermittent or unsteady flow is almost certainly the fact that at low speeds the sensitivity of a vehicle to throttle setting is high, and drivers find smooth control difficult.

It now seems clear that at least two types of flow are in fact possible on a circular track. The first of these occurs at low concentrations when the vehicles form into a platoon and travel at a speed independent of concentration. As the concentration is increased, a critical value is approached at which the length of the platoon becomes equal to the circumference of the track. If the concentration is increased beyond this value a second type of flow occurs in which the speed of the vehicles falls in such a way that the flow decreases linearly with concentration. However, one further interesting fact emerged from the experiments—on the 56 ft radius track it was found possible, at a fairly high concentration, to restore the flow almost to its maximum value by "waving-on" the drivers (see Fig. 1).

## 2.2. Flow on the Straight Track

In analysing the data from experiments on uniform flow on the straight track, the 1000 ft length of track between the timing points has been treated as a test length. Graphs were plotted of the number of vehicles in the test length as a function of time, and the space-time average concentration found for each run by averaging over a suitable time interval. The space-time average flow was estimated by averaging the flows at the inlet and outlet of the test length over the same period of time. Full details of these calculations are given in Reference 2; a graph of the resulting values of the space-time average flow and concentration is shown in Fig. 3.

Observations were limited to speeds equal to and less than 40 mph, and the free speed was not found. However, it was clear from the graphs of concentration vs. time that at 40 mph the stream of vehicles was beginning to split up into platoons, and it is likely that the free speed was not much greater than 40 mph.

Although the number of points is small, it seems probable that at concentrations greater than 100 vehicles per mile the flow-concentration relationship is similar to that found on the circular tracks, i.e., the flow falls linearly with increase in concentration. A difference appears, however, in that whereas for flow on the circular tracks the line on the flow-concentration graph representing the free speed intersects the line joining the data for higher concentrations, for flow on the straight track it does not. Instead, for those cases in which from the data the flow may be judged to be steady, the flow seems not to exceed about 2000 vehicles per hour. However, two points should be noted: first, a flow of 2000 vehicles per hour was reached only on the 56 ft radius track, and second, at high concentrations on this track it was possible to increase the flow to this value by waving on the drivers.

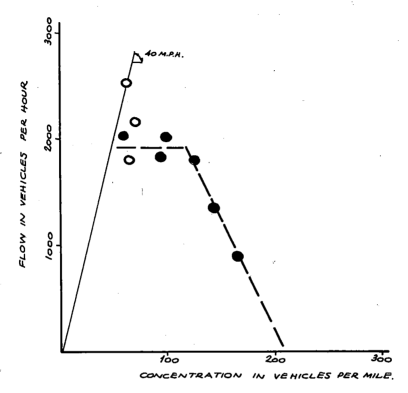

FIGURE 3.   Space-time average flow and concentration. Straight track.

## 2.3. Discussion

The experiments discussed in the two preceding sections throw considerable, light on the problem of the flow-concentration relationship and a general interpretation is given in the following paragraphs.

For any stretch of road there will be a speed above which, on the average, drivers will not go. If the stretch of road is long, this free speed may be determined by visibility, road curvature, road surface, or, perhaps, by an imposed speed limit; if it is short, it may also be influenced by the capacity of the entrance and exit sections and the acceleration characteristics of the vehicles. In the circular track experiments the free speeds were probably determined by the curvature and, in those on the straight track, by the facts that vehicles entered from a curve, accelerated into the test length, and left around another curve.

As the concentration on the road increases, vehicles tend to form into platoons because of the frequency at which they enter the road and variations between drivers. The flow at any particular concentration will depend on the extent to which platooning occurs. If the platoons are short, the speed of vehicles will not change appreciably and the concentration within platoons will be fixed only by the capabilities of following drivers and the confidence they have in the drivers of the vehicles ahead. Thus, in tests on the 106 ft radius track it was found that flows of over 3000 vehicles per hour were possible in short platoons of two or four vehicles. As the average concentration increases, however, platoons get longer, following drivers get more cautious, and the flow becomes less. The results of the experiments on the straight track suggests that when, because of increased concentration platoons merge, the flow is limited to something like 2000 vehicles per hour. It seems likely that at some concentration this steady flow breaks down. The indication is that as, in steady flow, the concentration increases, there is a point at which the spacing becomes too small for some drivers and they begin to hold larger than average spacings. Bunching now occurs and the flow begins to fall. The road may then be said to become congested and the speed variations of vehicles begin to increase until, when the average speed falls to a value at which speed control becomes difficult because of the high sensitivity to throttle setting, unsteady flow of the "stop-and-go" kind sets in. From the success of the single "waving-on" experiment, however, it also appears that when the flow becomes congested it is possible to restore the flow to its maximum value if drivers can be made to feel that the traffic will continue to move smoothly, and it is unlikely that they will be required suddenly to stop.

This interpretation of the flow-concentration relationship is necessarily a tentative one, but it reveals several points which, because of their relation to the important question of the control of traffic flow, might be the objects of future controlled experiments. Probably the two most important ones are the question of platooned flow and the possibility of delaying the onset of congestion. A preliminary study of the first of these is presented in the next section.

### 3. Flow in Platoons

The data from the experiments under discussion are not sufficient for a proper study of platooned flow, but there are enough for some preliminary work to be done. An analysis has been made of three experiments carried out on the circular track of 106 ft radius in which platoons of four, eight, and eleven vehicles formed.

In the first two cases two timing points at opposite ends of a diameter of the track were used. The results have been used to plot modified $x, t$ diagrams, the modification being that the diagrams were plotted to show the deviation of the actual times at which vehicles passed the observation points from those which would have been measured if the vehicles had been traveling at a constant speed. The diagram for the platoon of eight vehicles is given in Fig. 4, the points being joined by straight lines to emphasize the fact that only two timing points were used. In both cases the vehicles were clearly "following" in the sense that errors made by the leader affect all the other vehicles. But it is difficult to trace the $x, t$ path of a disturbance, partly because disturbances are modified by the following drivers and because of the uncertainty of the form of the graphs arising from the fact that the interval between observations is large. It was also found that both sets of data showed a very long wavelength disturbance which seemed to grow with distance down

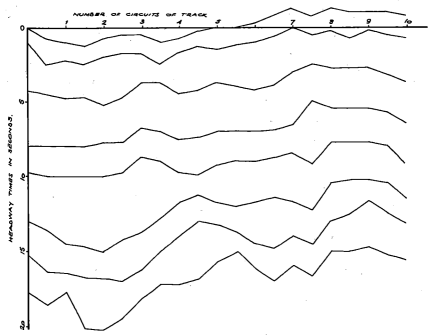

FIGURE 4.   Flow in platoons. Eight vehicles on 106 ft radius track.

the platoon. Small disturbances also seemed to be amplified, but it was difficult to be confident about this.

The variations between individual drivers were interesting. From Fig. 4 it is clear that two of the drivers in the platoon of eight vehicles were considerably more cautious than the others, a fact illustrated in another way in Fig. 5, for which 19 separate records of the passage of the platoon past the timing points have been used to plot the probability that a vehicle lay over the timing point at time $t$, given that the leader passed at time $t = 0$. From this graph it is clear that the drivers of cars 3 and 6 were following poorly, so that the drivers of cars 4 and 7 preferred to hold a larger than average spacing. It is also interesting to note that the variation of a car about its mean headway tends to increase down the platoon, confirming the suggestion that disturbances grow with distance along the platoon.

In the third experiment eight timing points were used and the leader was instructed to change his speed from 10 fps to 32 fps and back at more or less regular intervals throughout the run. With eight timing points it seemed reasonable to calculate velocities and plot velocity-time curves. This has been done[2] and it appeared that on the average the eleventh driver changed his speed about 7 sec after the leader had accelerated, indicating a rather short reaction time within the platoon of 0.7 sec per vehicle. Too much emphasis should not be placed on this, however, for it was noticeable that

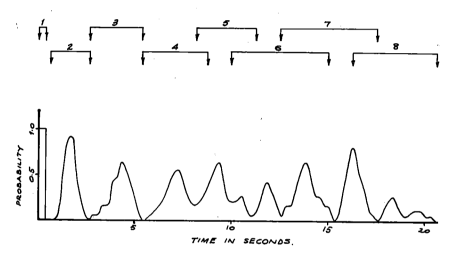

FIGURE 5.   Flow in platoons. Probability that a vehicle passes given that leader passed at $t = 0$. Eight vehicles on 106 ft radius track.

sometimes the eleventh driver responded almost immediately but with a lower acceleration, and it was this which resulted in his reaching the higher speed 6 or 7 sec after the leader. The average reaction time on deceleration was probably about the same, but here again the response was sometimes very quick and resulted in the eleventh driver overshooting to too low a speed and taking some time to settle down. The results showed clearly that there was a tendency for speed oscillations to grow, particularly at the lower speed, and it does seem possible that if the platoon had been longer, the vehicles at the tail may have been forced to stop.

## 4. The Propagation of Disturbances

The propagation of disturbances in a stream of traffic is of importance both because of the work of Lighthill and Whitham,[3] which shows that a relationship between flow and concentration implies that disturbances are

propagated as waves which can coalesce to form shock waves, and because
of the possibility that the flow-concentration relationship for unsteady flow
may be different from that for steady flow. Experiments were carried out on

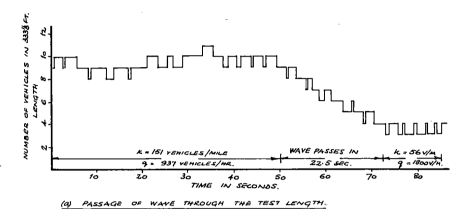

(a)  PASSAGE  OF  WAVE  THROUGH  THE  TEST  LENGTH.

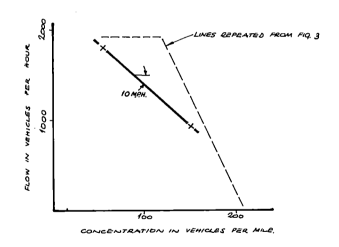

(b)  SPACE-TIME  FLOW  CONCENTRATION  RESULTS.

FIGURE 6.    Propagation of disturbances. Acceleration wave.

the straight track in which the speed was varied, and these will now be
discussed.

In the experiments four timing points were set up in the 1000 ft test-length,
thus dividing it into three sections of length $333\frac{1}{3}$ ft. The propagation of
disturbances may be examined in two ways, either by finding the time taken

for a disturbance to pass through one of the $333\frac{1}{3}$ ft lengths, or by plotting graphs of the numbers of vehicles which pass the timing points as a function of time. Both these methods have been used.

Figure 6a shows the variation with time of the number of vehicles in one of the short test-lengths during the passage of an acceleration wave. From

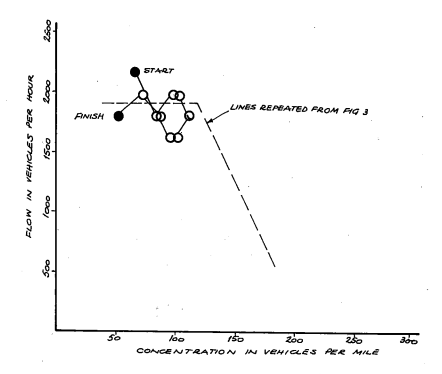

FIGURE 7. Propagation of disturbances. Short-time space-time average flow and concentration during a deceleration and acceleration.

this the time taken for the wave to pass over the section may be estimated and its speed deduced. The space-time average flow and concentration before and after the wave may also be found, and these are shown in Fig. 6b on a flow-concentration graph, together with a line representing the estimated wave speed. As is to be expected, the line joins the two points accurately.

Examples of the second method are to be found elsewhere in the literature (e.g., References 4, 2) and details will be omitted here.

Several runs have been analysed by both methods, and from these it seems that when the stream of traffic was accelerated and decelerated between the condition of maximum flow and congested flow, the disturbance was always propagated at a speed between 8 and 11 mph. This is considerably less than the speed represented by the slope of the line on the flow-concentration graph for congested flow.

More detailed investigations of disturbances have been made by plotting short-time, space-time average flows and concentrations in the test length during the passage of the disturbances. For the cases of acceleration and deceleration between no flow and maximum flow, it seems that the flow was almost constant and independent of concentration both when all the vehicles in the test-length were moving and when some were stationary. The flows were different by a factor of two, as is to be expected. Results similar to those obtained in the present work have been published by Edie[5] and it should be remarked that in such experiments the very rapid changes in flow as an acceleration or deceleration wave reaches the end of a test length suggest that both accelerations and decelerations are propagated as shocks. The results from a test in which the stream was first decelerated and then accelerated are shown in Fig. 7. It is seen here that the flow oscillates about a constant value. These oscillations are partly attributable to the short averaging time, and it is probably fair to say that during this test the flow through the test-length was constant. It appears, therefore, that these tests confirm the suggestion made earlier in this paper that there is a regime of steady flow in which the flow is constant and independent of concentration and, further, that this is very nearly independent of whether the flow is increasing or decreasing.

## 5. Conclusion

The experiments discussed in this paper have revealed several interesting features of the relationship between flow and concentration, which are of great interest both academically and from a practical point of view and merit careful attention in future controlled experiments.

## Acknowledgements

The author expresses his appreciation of the interest of Dr. R. J. Smeed and Mr. J. G. Wardrop, and the help they have given him, and his gratitude to the Director of Road Research for permission to present this paper.

## References

1. J. G. Wardrop, Experimental Speed/Flow Relations in a Single Lane. *Proc. Second Intern. Symp. on the Theory of Road Traffic Flow*, J. Almond, Ed., O.E.C.D., Paris (1965).
2. R. E. Franklin, Further Analysis of Some Experiments on Single-Lane Traffic. *Road Res. Lab.*, LN/829/REF (1965).

3. M. J. Lighthill and G. B. Whitham, On Kinematic Waves. *Proc. Roy. Soc.*, **A229** (1955).
4. L. C. Edie and R. S. Foote, "Experiments on Single-Lane Flow in Tunnels." Theory of Traffic Flow, R. Herman, Ed., Elsevier (1961).
5. L. C. Edie, Discussion of Traffic Stream Measurements and Definitions. *Proc. Second Intern. Symp. on the Theory of Road Traffic Flow*, J. Almond, Ed., O.E.C.D., Paris (1965).

# Acceleration Noise in a Congested Signalized Environment

WALTER HELLY and PHILIP G. BAKER

The Port of New York Authority, New York

## Abstract

Acceleration noise has been measured in a variety of mid-city traffic environments. The experiments, all in Manhattan, included travel on avenues, with and without progressive signalization, and on congested cross streets which intersect these avenues. It is shown that the signalization often is a more important contributor to acceleration noise than is the volume of traffic. In particular, streets without progressive signalization show little variation in acceleration noise with variation in volume; streets with progression have great variation with volume. Additionally, subjective observations suggest the conclusion that acceleration noise is not a very good measure of orderliness or smoothness of flow in signalized environments where traffic moves at a low average speed. An alternative measure of acceleration irregularity is proposed to partially compensate for the difficulties encountered.

## Introduction

THIS IS A REPORT on a series of acceleration noise, or dispersion, observations obtained in Manhattan, New York City, on streets subject to intense congestion and therefore controlled by very closely spaced traffic signals.

Acceleration noise, a traffic parameter first discussed by Herman et al.,[1] developed theoretically by Montroll,[2] and experimentally by Jones and Potts,[3] is defined as $\sigma_a$, the standard deviation over time of a car's acceleration. Thus

$$\sigma_a{}^2 = \frac{1}{T} \int_0^T [a(t) - \langle a(t) \rangle]^2 \, dt \tag{1}$$

Here, $T$ = time duration of journey, and $a(t) = $ acceleration with average value $\langle a(t) \rangle$. Since $\langle a(t) \rangle$ approaches zero for any prolonged journey, one normally calculates

$$\sigma_a{}^2 = \frac{1}{T} \int_0^T a(t)^2 \, dt \tag{1a}$$

The previous papers have demonstrated $\sigma_a$ to be a useful traffic parameter for stability analysis and for interrelating the effects of road, driver, and traffic conditions. However, these studies have been confined to country and suburban roads. It will be shown here that $\sigma_a$ is not always very sensitive to changing traffic conditions in a very congested environment, mainly because it fails to distinguish adequately differences between trips at very low speeds in dense traffic and faster trips with the same acceleration noise caused mainly by traffic signals. It would appear that instead of $\sigma_a$ one might try the modification

$$G = \frac{\sigma_a}{\langle v \rangle} \tag{2}$$

where $\langle v \rangle$ is the average velocity. This $G$ is a measure of the mean change in velocity per unit distance of the trip. We call it the "mean velocity gradient" and here apologize to semantic purists.

A similar, not strictly comparable approach was used by Greenshields,[4] who defined still another measure of irregularity, $Q$, as the "quality" of flow. Slightly changed for comparison, his formula is

$$\frac{1}{Q} = \sqrt{f} \left\{ \frac{\dfrac{1}{L} \displaystyle\int_0^L |a(x)| \, dx}{\langle v \rangle} \right\} \tag{3}$$

where $f =$ number of speed changes per unit distance (not otherwise defined but probably the number of acceleration sign reversals), $L =$ journey distance, and $a(x)$ is acceleration as a function of distance. Greenshields obtained $Q$ for several traffic environments, both in Manhattan and elsewhere. His values of $Q$ generally seem to be consistent with qualitative evaluations. However Formula 3 is awkward for data reduction. We have made some comparisons which indicate that it does not make a great numerical difference if one uses a time rather than a distance average of the root-mean-square rather than the mean absolute acceleration. Further, we do not see any advantage for the complication $\sqrt{f}$, nor does Greenshields make a strong case for it.

## Measurement and Data Reduction

The test car, a 1963 Valiant with automatic transmission, was fitted with a Kienzle TC08F Tachograph, the same device described in detail by Jones and Potts.[3] This provided a velocity *vs.* time chart, from which Eq. 1a was approximated by

$$\sigma_a{}^2 \cong \frac{1}{T} \sum \left( \frac{\Delta v}{\Delta t} \right)^2 \Delta t = \frac{(\Delta v)^2}{T} \sum \frac{1}{\Delta t} \tag{4}$$

The procedure followed was generally that of Reference 3, except that the summation was performed over the entire trip duration, not merely when the car was in motion. As pointed out in Reference 3, the inclusion of stopped time reduces the value of $\sigma_a$. However, the mean velocity gradient, $G$, logically is calculated from the overall mean velocity. Thus one is consistent in averaging both $\sigma_a$ and $G$ without omission of stopped time.

The results shown in the next section are averages of several test runs for each location and time period. Suppose these runs are over a distance $L$, that they are labeled $i = 1, 2, \ldots, n$, and that run $i$ takes a time $T_i$ and shows acceleration noise $\sigma_{ai}$. The averaging is performed by combining the $n$ runs into one over a distance $nL$, so that

$$\langle \sigma_a^2 \rangle = \frac{\sum\limits_{i=1}^{n} T_i \, \sigma_{ai}^2}{\sum\limits_{i=1}^{n} T_i} \tag{5a}$$

and

$$\langle G \rangle = \frac{\langle (\sigma_a^2) \rangle^{1/2}}{\langle v \rangle}, \quad \text{where} \quad \langle v \rangle = \frac{nL}{\sum\limits_{i=1}^{n} T_i} \tag{5b}$$

We also calculate $s(\sigma_a)$, an estimate of the standard deviation of $\sigma_a$ among the individual runs:

$$s^2(\sigma_a) = \frac{1}{n(n-1)} \left[ n \sum_{i=1}^{n} \sigma_{ai}^2 - \left( \sum_{i=1}^{n} \sigma_{ai} \right)^2 \right] \tag{5c}$$

### Experiments

The results are summarized in Table I. Unless indicated otherwise, each group of runs was performed by a single driver. All runs were made on business weekdays in the summer of 1964. The flow estimates are for rough comparison only because they were obtained on different days than those of the experiments, and because they were evaluated only at the approximate midpoints of the trajectories. Late afternoon flows were at much lower speeds than in the early afternoon.

1. *Park Avenue.* A wide two-way avenue with a central divider and signalized cross streets spaced 264 ft apart. The signals are stop-go (all signals red or all signals green) with 45 sec red and 45 sec green time. There are few trucks and no buses. As shown in the table, the acceleration noise $\sigma_a$ is actually larger at night without traffic than during the afternoon peak. The night $\sigma_a$ is almost entirely due to starting and stopping at signalized intersections. In contrast, the mean velocity gradient, $G$, does reflect the relative serenity and speed of the night runs.

The late afternoon traffic has a very large northbound commuter component. However, the southbound traffic showed no significant differences between the 2–4:30 p.m. and the 4:30–7 p.m. periods. Therefore the two periods were combined for the exhibited results.

TABLE I.    Acceleration Noise and Mean Velocity Gradient

| | Time | Flow vehicles per hour | No. of runs | Travel time/ mile (sec) | % of time stopped | Acceleration noise, $\langle \sigma_a^2 \rangle^{1/2}$ (ft/sec$^2$) | $s(\sigma_a)$ (ft/sec$^2$) | Mean velocity gradient $\langle G \rangle$ (sec)$^{-1}$ |
|---|---|---|---|---|---|---|---|---|
| *Park Ave.* | | | | | | | | |
| Northbound | 2–3 a.m. | 260 | 2 | 148 | 23.8 | 2.85 | 0.16 | 0.080 |
| Stop-go signals | 2–4:30 p.m. | 1540 | 6 | 238 | 33.6 | 2.46 | 0.33 | 0.111 |
| 48–96 St. | 4-30–7 p.m. | 1590 | 6 | 288 | 42.3 | 2.48 | 0.14 | 0.136 |
| 2.4 miles | | | | | | | | |
| *Park Ave.* | | | | | | | | |
| Southbound | 2–3 a.m. | 240 | 2 | 153 | 27.9 | 2.72 | 0.12 | 0.077 |
| Stop-go signals | 2–7 p.m. | 1520 | 12 | 258 | 44.8 | 2.47 | 0.14 | 0.120 |
| 95–47 St. | | | | | | | | |
| 2.4 miles | | | | | | | | |
| *36th St.* | | | | | | | | |
| Eastbound | 1–3 a.m. | 60 | 3 | 236 | 39.4 | 2.18 | 0.08 | 0.097 |
| Stop-go signals | 12–3 p.m. | 380 | 4 | 833 | 62.3 | 1.94 | 0.11 | 0.306 |
| 9–1 Avenues | | | | | | | | |
| 1.4 miles | | | | | | | | |
| *37th St.* | | | | | | | | |
| Westbound | 1–3 a.m. | 60 | 3 | 330 | 36.8 | 2.48 | 0.18 | 0.155 |
| Stop-go signals | 12–3 p.m. | 370 | 4 | 832 | 64.2 | 2.02 | 0.23 | 0.318 |
| 1–9 Avenues | | | | | | | | |
| 1.4 miles | | | | | | | | |
| *Eighth Ave.* | | | | | | | | |
| Northbound | 4–5 a.m. | 418 | 3 | 148 | 0 | 0.35 | 0.05 | 0.010 |
| Progressive | 12–3 p.m. | 1670 | 5 | 226 | 18.7 | 1.79 | 0.25 | 0.077 |
| signals | 3–6 p.m. | 1760 | 6 | 317 | 45.4 | 1.44 | 0.28 | 0.087 |
| Jane-55 St. | | | | | | | | |
| 2.25 miles | 1:30–3 p.m. | 1670 | 5[a] | 266 | 26.0 | 1.99 | 0.18 | 0.100 |
| *Ninth Avenue* | | | | | | | | |
| Southbound | 1–5 a.m. | 229 | 3 | 152 | 0 | 0.33 | 0.21 | 0.010 |
| Progressive | 12–3 p.m. | 1430 | 5 | 246 | 23.6 | 1.71 | 0.32 | 0.079 |
| signals | 3–6 p.m. | 1500 | 6 | 270 | 26.3 | 1.66 | 0.41 | 0.084 |
| 54–12 St. | | | | | | | | |
| 2.3 miles | 1:30–3 p.m. | 1430 | 5[a] | 242 | 25.9 | 1.69 | 0.30 | 0.077 |
| *West Side H'way* | | | | | | | | |
| *Northbound* | | | | | | | | |
| No signals | 9–12 a.m. | 2160 | 4 | 84 | 0 | 0.55 | 0.07 | 0.009 |
| 20-Dyckman St. | | | | | | | | |
| 9.5 miles | | | | | | | | |

[a] Five different drivers.

2. *36th and 37th Streets.* These are narrow one-way streets, with heavy commercial traffic and (often illegal) parking along both curbs. The test run of 1.4 miles crossed 10 signalized intersections. These signals are totally uncoordinated, having only the property that most give less than half of their cycle times to the traffic on 36th and 37th streets.

Again the acceleration noise is greater at night than during peak traffic because of the stop-go effects of the signals. Travel was very slow, even at night. The day values of $G$ were the highest observed anywhere.

3. *Eighth and Ninth Avenues.* These wide one-way avenues have progressive signals spaced 264 ft apart and timed for a fairly uniform speed of 24 m/hr ($= 35$ ft/sec). The night $\sigma_a$ and $G$ are both very low, evidencing the success of progressive signals at low traffic flows. The day values are lower than on Park avenue, but the advantage seems to be slight.

On each of these avenues, one series of runs was performed with five different drivers to check on the variation between them. Perhaps because all were adult white collar males, this variation, measured by $s(\sigma_a)$, is no larger than for several runs by one driver.

4. *West Side Highway.* A limited access, center divided, sixlane highway with no intersections, no trucks, and no buses. The first 2 miles of the route are on an elevated viaduct with sharp curves and no shoulders. The runs here were made for comparison to night traffic under the progressive signalization of Eighth and Ninth Avenues. It is seen that, while $\sigma_a$ is larger on the highway, $G$ is about the same in both environments.

Since all the exhibited results are based on calculations of $\sigma_a$ and $G$ over total trip times, without excision of stopped time, the alternative $\sigma_a$ was calculated for Eighth Avenue. The table shows $\sigma_a = 1.79$ for 12–3 p.m. and $\sigma_a = 1.44$ for the more congested 3–6 p.m. period. When the stopped ($v = 0$) time is not included, the corresponding values are 1.99 and 1.94. Thus, even though the values for the two time periods are brought closer together, the 3–6 p.m. period still does not show a greater $\sigma_a$.

## Discussion

1. A comparison of the results of Table I with the drivers' subjective reactions yields the following very approximate relationships:

| $G$ | Subjective Reaction |
|---|---|
| 0–0.02 | Comfortable, no irritation |
| 0.02–0.10 | Acceptable under urban conditions |
| 0.10–0.20 | Frustrating, very tiring |
| >0.20 | Beyond reasonable endurance |

2. The mean velocity gradient $G$ is better than the acceleration noise, $\sigma_a$, as a measure of traffic irregularity, because it conforms better to the degree of congestion, to the amount of speed changing occuring during a trip, and to subjective evaluations.

3. In some cases traffic signals can contribute more to acceleration noise than does the competing traffic.

4. With regard to $\sigma_a$ and $G$, progressive signals have little, if any, superiority over stop-go signals for dense traffic. However, their superiority for light traffic is affirmed once again.

5. The variation in $\sigma_a$ among drivers appears to be no greater than the variation between runs performed by one driver. This conclusion probably holds only in an environment so congested as to provide limited scope to individualism.

## Further Work

Similar experiments will be conducted in vehicular tunnels where an effort will be made to relate exhaust gas emission to acceleration noise or mean velocity gradient. If close correlation prevails, it will be both appropriate and practical to use these measures in working towards the reduction of atmospheric contamination.

## References

1. R. Herman, E. W. Montroll, R. B. Potts, and R. W. Rothery, Traffic Dynamics: Analysis of Stability in Car Following, *Operations Res.*, **7**, 86–106 (1959).
2. E. W. Montroll, "Acceleration Noise and Clustering Tendency," Theory of Traffic Flow, R. Herman, Ed., Elsevier (1961).
3. T. R. Jones and R. B. Potts, The Measurement of Acceleration Noise—A Traffic Parameter, *Operations Res.*, **10**, 745–763 (1962).
4. B. D. Greenshields, The Quality of Traffic Flow, "Quality and Theory of Traffic Flow," Bureau of Highway Traffic, Yale, pp. 3–40, 1961.

# Local Steady State Theory

# and Macroscopic Hydrodynamics

# of Traffic Flow

*I. PRIGOGINE*

Universite Libre of Brussels
Brussels, Belgium

*and*

*ROBERT HERMAN and ROBERT ANDERSON*

Research Laboratories
General Motors Corporation
Warren, Michigan

## Abstract

It is shown that if the conservation of cars is the only conservation law valid for the description of traffic flow, then the Lighthill-Whitham theory of kinematic waves is the only possible macroscopic hydrodynamical description. Further, in the case that the latter description is valid, the equation of motion of the traffic fluid is

$$\frac{d\langle v \rangle}{dt} = \Phi \frac{\partial c}{\partial x}$$

where

$$\Phi = -c \left( \frac{\partial \langle v \rangle}{\partial t} \right)^2 \leq 0,$$

$\langle v \rangle$ is the average speed, and $c$ is the concentration. A few general remarks are presented on the limits of validity of the macroscopic hydrodynamical description.

## Introduction

A VERY interesting macroscopic hydrodynamic description of traffic flow was introduced and discussed in detail by Lighthill and Whitham.[1] Their main result was the derivation of kinematic waves which satisfy a first order partial differential equation. The terminology *kinematic* waves was used by Lighthill and Whitham for the case in which the description of a system does not involve a detailed microscopic dynamical law, but rather it involves only an "equation of state" and the conservation of the number of cars. Richards[2] has, independently, considered what is a particular case of the Lighthill-Whitham Theory. Other investigators (see, for example, Greenberg[3]) have considered the application of classical hydrodynamics to traffic flow.

On the other hand, the authors[4] have developed a statistical approach to traffic flow which corresponds to that usually given in statistical mechanics. The most important single quantity in this approach is the one-car speed distribution function $f(x, v, t)$ which satisfies a kind of generalized Boltzmann equation

$$\frac{df}{dt} = \frac{\partial f}{\partial t} + v\frac{\partial f}{\partial x} = O(f). \tag{1.1}$$

In our approach we assumed that the r.h.s. of Eq. 1.1 is essentially the sum of two types of terms: a contribution representing relaxation processes describing the desire on the part of the drivers to return to some desired speed distribution, and the interaction processes that originate from various interactions between drivers.

More specifically, we assumed that the operator in the r.h.s. of Eq. 1.1 is of the form

$$O(f) = -\frac{f - f^0}{T} + c(\langle v \rangle - v)(1 - P)f, \tag{1.2}$$

where $f^0$ = one-car desired speed distribution function,

$T$ = relaxation time,

$$c = \int_0^\infty f\, dv = \int_0^\infty f^0\, dv = \text{concentration},$$

$$\langle v \rangle = 1/c \int_0^\infty vf\, dv = \text{average speed},$$

$P$ = probability of passing.

However, most of the discussion we shall present here is independent of the special form of Eq. 1.2. We shall only assume that $O(f)$ is the sum of two types of operators

$$O(f) = \mathscr{D}(f) + I(f) \tag{1.3}$$

where $\mathscr{D}(f)$ is a linear functional in $f$, similar to $-\dfrac{f-f^0}{T}$, and $I(f)$ a *nonlinear* functional in $f$ corresponding to various intrinsic processes.

It is clear that a statistical theory of traffic should lead to a clarification of the limits of validity of macroscopic hydrodynamical descriptions (i.e., descriptions which postulate an "equation of state" which relates the space-time behavior of average quantities) exactly as does statistical mechanics for fluid dynamics.

This will be the object of this as well as a subsequent paper (quoted as paper II). Here we wish to present a few general remarks; in the next paper we shall present a detailed study based on the explicit form Eq. 1.2 of the traffic flow operator $O(f)$.

## 2. Invariants

The operator $O(f)$ is necessarily such as to preserve the total number of cars. Therefore, it has to satisfy the identity

$$\int_0^\infty dv\, O(f) = 0. \tag{2.1}$$

As a consequence of Eq. 2.1 and of the normalization condition

$$\int_0^\infty dv\, f = c, \tag{2.2}$$

Eq. 1.1 leads to the conservation equation

$$\frac{\partial c}{\partial t} + \frac{\partial}{\partial x}(c\langle v\rangle) = 0. \tag{2.3}$$

However, there is no reason to expect that characteristics of the car distribution other than their number should be conserved. The conservation of energy and momentum can be ruled out in the general case because of the existence of the well-known situation in which a fast car closing in on a slow car is unable to pass, and adopts the speed of the slow car. Both energy and momentum are not conserved in such a process. For example, the special choice Eq. 1.2 gives us

$$\int_0^\infty dv\, v O(f) = -\frac{c[\langle v\rangle - \langle v^0\rangle]}{T} + (1-P)c[(\langle v\rangle)^2 - \langle v^2\rangle], \tag{2.4}$$

which is equal to the rate of change of the average velocity due to relaxation and interaction processes.

We shall therefore assume that Eq. 2.1 is the only integral identity imposed on $O(f)$. This is in sharp contrast with the kinetic gas equation (the "real" Boltzmann equation)

$$\frac{df}{dt} = \frac{\partial f}{\partial t} + v\frac{\partial f}{\partial x} + \mathscr{F}\frac{\partial f}{\partial v} = C(f), \tag{2.5}$$

where the collision operator $C(f)$ now satisfies the conditions (conservation of number, momentum, and energy through collisions)

$$\int d\mathbf{v}\, C(f) = 0,$$

$$\int d\mathbf{v}\, \mathbf{v}\, C(f) = 0, \tag{2.6}$$

and

$$\int d\mathbf{v}\, v^2\, C(f) = 0.$$

As a consequence, the most general equilibrium solution of Eq. 2.5 describing a homogeneous time-independent system contains the five conserved quantities

$$c, \mathbf{V}, T, \tag{2.7}$$

corresponding, respectively, to the concentration

$$\int d\mathbf{v}\, f = c, \tag{2.8}$$

to the average velocity

$$\frac{1}{c}\int d\mathbf{v}\, \mathbf{v} f = \mathbf{V}, \tag{2.9}$$

and to the temperature

$$\tfrac{1}{2}\int d\mathbf{v}\, m(\mathbf{v} - \mathbf{V})^2 f = \tfrac{3}{2}kT. \tag{2.10}$$

The most general macroscopic hydrodynamical description of a system involves the assumption that the system is in local equilibrium. By local equilibrium it is meant that the quantities which characterize the system are varying sufficiently slowly with respect to space and time, so that the same description holds as in the case of the homogeneous time-independent case, but with the local values of the quantities. Hence, the statistical theory will produce the macroscopic theory when we impose the condition of local equilibrium. More precisely, the most general local equilibrium solution of Eq. 2.5 contains the five functions

$$c(\mathbf{x}, t), \mathbf{V}(\mathbf{x}, t), T(\mathbf{x}, t). \tag{2.11}$$

In other words we may, in the gas kinetic case, prescribe independently five moments of the distribution function. On the contrary, in the traffic flow case we may prescribe only the single moment, Eq. 2.2.

To the local equilibrium solution of kinetic theory

$$f = f[c(\mathbf{x}, t), \mathbf{V}(\mathbf{x}, t), T(\mathbf{x}, t), \mathbf{v}], \tag{2.12}$$

corresponds in the traffic case local steady state solutions*

$$f = f(c(\mathbf{x}, t), \mathbf{v}),\tag{2.13}$$

in which the space time behavior of $f$ appears only through the local concentration. As a consequence of Eq. 2.13 the local average velocity becomes a functional of $c(x, t)$,

$$\langle v(x, t)\rangle = \frac{1}{c(x, t)} \int_0^\infty dv\, vf(c(x, t), v) = \langle v[c(x, t)]\rangle.\tag{2.14}$$

Let us now discuss the physical meaning of the local steady state solution.

## 3. Local Steady States

The time independent homogeneous solution of Eqs. 1.1 and 1.2 satisfies the nonlinear integral equation

$$\mathscr{D}(f) + I(f) = 0,\tag{3.1}$$

which contains the concentration $c$ as a parameter. Let us write this solution in the form

$$f = F(c, v).\tag{3.2}$$

In the inhomogeneous case we may follow the same method as is used in the gas theory (Chapman-Enskog method). Indeed, if the time scale associated with the operators $\mathscr{D}$ and $I$ is sufficiently short (which means that the characteristic times appearing in Eq. 1.2 are much smaller than the characteristic times associated with the inhomogeneity), the first approximation to the distribution function, Eq. 3.2, will be still given by Eq. 3.2 but *with the local value of the concentration.*

$$f = F(c(x, t), v).\tag{3.3}$$

A scheme for successive approximations starting with Eq. 3.3 can be worked out. But since we shall not use it here, we will not go into details. A special simple formulation of the condition of validity of the local steady state solution of Eq. 3.3 can be given if the sum of the operators in Eq. 3.1 is written as

$$\mathscr{D}(f) + I(f) = -\frac{f - F}{\tau_{eff}},\tag{3.4}$$

where $\tau_{eff}$ is an effective relaxation time. The local steady state solution will be a good approximation whenever $\tau_{eff}$ may be considered negligible with respect to all other time scales involved.

It should be noted that the steady state solution of Eq. 3.3 does not correspond to an "equilibrium" situation in the usual sense. Indeed, for

---

* The reason why we speak in the case of traffic, of local *steady state* instead of local *equilibrium* will be made clear in Section 3.

each of the two operators we have

$$\mathscr{D}(F) \neq 0, \qquad I(F) \neq 0, \tag{3.5}$$

with

$$\mathscr{D}(F) = -I(F), \tag{3.6}$$

while equilibrium would correspond to the stronger requirement

$$\mathscr{D}(F) = I(F) = 0. \tag{3.7}$$

This is only possible in the limit of low concentrations where $F$ (see Eq. 1.2) reduces to the desired velocity distribution

$$F \to f^0. \tag{3.8}$$

The nearest gas kinetic analogy is obtained by writing Eq. 2.4 in the form

$$\frac{\partial f}{\partial t} + v \frac{\partial f}{\partial x} = C(f) - \mathscr{F} \frac{\partial f}{\partial v}. \tag{3.9}$$

The local steady state solution $F$ corresponds to a velocity distribution in which the effect of the collisions is compensated by the effect of the external field in such a way that

$$C(F) - \mathscr{F} \frac{\partial F}{\partial v} = 0, \tag{3.10}$$

## 4. Macroscopic Hydrodynamics of Traffic Flow

Kinematic waves as introduced by Lighthill and Whitham are direct consequences of the local steady state solutions. Indeed, in the conservation Eq. 2.3 the average speed $\langle v \rangle$ is now to be considered as a functional of $c$ in accordance with Eq. 2.14.

Therefore, we have also

$$\frac{\partial c}{\partial t} + \frac{\partial(c\langle v \rangle)}{\partial c} \frac{\partial c}{\partial x} = 0. \tag{4.1}$$

The general solution of this equation is found by standard methods to be

$$c = c\left(x - \frac{\partial(c\langle v \rangle)}{\partial c} t\right).$$

This corresponds to a wave propagation with the kinematic wave velocity

$$v_{\text{kin}} = \frac{\partial(c\langle v \rangle)}{\partial c} = \langle v \rangle + c \frac{\partial \langle v \rangle}{\partial c}. \tag{4.2}$$

The consequences of Eq. 4.1 have been discussed in various papers.[1,2]

It is essential to note that kinematic waves are consequences of *strong coherence* (short time scales) of the "traffic fluid." From this point of view there exists a nice analogy with other wave propagation phenomena studied in recent years in various fields of physics such as plasma waves, and phonons. The strong coherence in the case of traffic includes the will of the drivers to relax to a well defined desired speed distribution function, as well as the effect of interaction between drivers.

Another consequence of the local steady state situation is the existence of a well defined relation between the average acceleration of an element of the traffic fluid and the concentration gradient. Indeed, from Eq. 2.14 we have for the average acceleration for an observer moving with the average speed of the traffic fluid

$$\frac{d\langle v \rangle}{dt} = \frac{\partial \langle v \rangle}{\partial c} \frac{\partial c}{\partial t} + \frac{\partial \langle v \rangle}{\partial c} \frac{\partial c}{\partial x} \langle v \rangle. \tag{4.3}$$

Combining the conservation of cars as expressed in the form of Eq. 4.1 with Eq. 4.3 yields for the average acceleration

$$\frac{d\langle v \rangle}{dt} = \Phi \frac{\partial c}{\partial x}, \tag{4.4}$$

where

$$\Phi(c) = -c\left(\frac{\partial \langle v \rangle}{\partial c}\right)^2 \leq 0.$$

We note that Eq. 4.4 is the equation of motion of the traffic fluid and could serve as a convenient point for the comparison of the traffic fluid and a classical fluid. The "friction coefficient" $\Phi$ is a negative quantity and shows that the average acceleration for an observer moving with the average speed of the traffic fluid is positive when moving into a less dense region of traffic and negative when moving into a denser region of traffic. Some authors have postulated equations of the form of Eq. 4.4, whereas here it is evident that this type of equation is a direct consequence of number conservation and the steady state assumption.

We now introduce a second "friction coefficient" which relates the average acceleration for an observer stationed at a fixed position of the roadway to the concentration gradient. Indeed, from Eq. 2.14 we have

$$\frac{\partial \langle v \rangle}{\partial t} = \frac{\partial \langle v \rangle}{\partial c} \frac{\partial c}{\partial t}, \tag{4.5}$$

which we can combine with Eq. 4.1 to obtain

$$\frac{\partial \langle v \rangle}{\partial t} = \varphi \frac{\partial c}{\partial x}, \tag{4.6}$$

where

$$\varphi = - \frac{\partial \langle v \rangle}{\partial c} \frac{\partial (c\langle v \rangle)}{\partial c} = - \frac{\partial \langle v \rangle}{\partial c}\left(\langle v \rangle + c\frac{\partial \langle v \rangle}{\partial c}\right) = \Phi + \langle v \rangle\left(-\frac{\partial \langle v \rangle}{\partial c}\right).$$

A schematic representation of the "friction coefficient" $\varphi$ is given in Fig. 1. It should be noted that $\varphi$ starts out at zero because for low concentrations $\partial \langle v \rangle / \partial c \sim 0$. This follows because one would expect that $\langle v \rangle$ would start out at some $\langle v \rangle^0$ plus a term of order at least $c^2$ because of binary interactions between drivers. Then, $\varphi$ increases to a maximum and vanishes again at $c_m$, the concentration at which the flow curve presents a maximum. Hence, for an

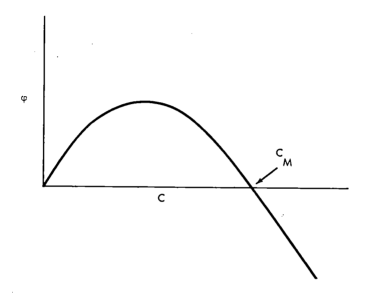

FIGURE I.

observer at a fixed point on the roadway, $c < c_{max}$, we have corresponding to a positive concentration gradient an increase of the average speed. This is an unavoidable consequence of the steady state assumption which shows that in this region $\partial c / \partial t$ and $\partial c / \partial x$ are of opposite sign.

It may be of interest to relate the macroscopic speed obtained from the follow-the-leader traffic theory[5] to the present discussion. For this model

$$\langle v \rangle = -\alpha \ln c + \text{constant}, \qquad (4.7)$$

where $\alpha$ is the speed at maximum flow. For this model we find that

$$\Phi = -\frac{\alpha^2}{c}, \qquad (4.8)$$

and

$$\varphi = \frac{\alpha}{c}(\langle v \rangle - \alpha). \qquad (4.9)$$

We can see from comparing Eq. 4.9 with the general required behavior of $\varphi$ that Eq. 4.9, as previously noted, does not have the correct limiting behavior as $c \to 0$.

The above serves to further illustrate the difference in structure between macroscopic hydrodynamics of fluids and of traffic flow. In the case of fluids we have to supplement the information given by thermodynamics (equation of state ...) by five supplementary independent equations (for the simplest case of reversible motion). In traffic flow we have to supplement the information given by the study of homogeneous time independent situations $[O(F) = 0]$ by only *one* supplementary equation. However, these statements require that the local steady state theory is a valid description. Therefore, it seems appropriate to add a few remarks on the limitations of this description for the case of traffic.

## 5. Limitations of the Local Steady State Theory

A detailed discussion of the limitations of the steady state theory can be made only on the basis of a detailed model such as specified in Eq. 1.2. While this will be discussed in paper II, we should like, however, to present a few general remarks here:

### a. Size of the Inhomogeneity

If the characteristic time scale associated with the operator $O(f)$ is $\tau_{\text{eff}}$ and the average speed is $\langle v \rangle$, we obtain a characteristic length

$$L_{\text{eff}} = \tau_{\text{eff}} \langle v \rangle. \tag{5.1}$$

We require that the characteristic length of the inhomogeneity be such that

$$L_{\text{inh}} \gg L_{\text{eff}}, \tag{5.2}$$

in order that a local steady state can be established in the traffic fluid. An order of magnitude for $L_{\text{eff}}$ can be obtained for the linear desired speed distribution function $f^0$ model studied in a subsequent paper. For this model, for instance,

$$L_{\text{eff}} \sim 10^2 \text{ ft} \quad \text{for} \quad c \sim 0.02 \text{ cars/ft}. \tag{5.3}$$

### b. Time Scale

If deviations from the local steady state theory are taken into account, Eq. 4.1 has to be replaced by an equation of the form

$$\frac{\partial c}{\partial t} + v_g \frac{\partial c}{\partial x} = D \frac{\partial^2 c}{\partial x^2}, \tag{5.4}$$

where $v_g$ is a characteristic wave speed and $D$ an effective diffusion coefficient.

Such an equation will be discussed in more detail in II. Therefore, Eq. 4.1 will lead to reliable results only if

$$t \ll \frac{L_{inh}^2}{D},\qquad(5.5)$$

If the inequality of Eq. 5.5 is not satisfied, the deformation of waves, associated with a concentration inhomogeneity, by diffusion becomes important. For example, we show for the simple model referred to in Section 5a, that

$$D_{max} \sim 10^3 \text{ ft}^2/\text{sec} \quad \text{for} \quad c \cong 0.02 \text{ cars/ft}.\qquad(5.6)$$

Therefore, the local steady state theory is not, in general, a long time theory, but is, in fact, a short time theory for various concentration ranges and inhomogeneity sizes.

### c. Instabilities

As we have seen, the local steady state theory is based on an *exact* cancellation of the effect of the two operators $\mathscr{D}$ and $I$ (see Eq. 3.6).

However, from our knowledge of similar situations in statistical theory of transport processes we may expect that this cancellation cannot be exact at high concentration. For example, similarly the cancellation in Eq. 3.10 does not occur at high fields. Then, runaway solutions have to be considered and an *exact time independent description breaks down.*

A similar behavior is likely to appear in the case of traffic theory. Then, the flow curve would have a systematic time average component plus oscillatory time dependent contributions. This situation will be investigated in detail in a future paper.

### References

1. M. J. Lighthill and G. R. Whitham, *Proc. Roy. Soc.*, **A229,** 317 (1955).
2. P. I. Richards, *Operations Res.*, **4:1,** 42 (1956).
3. H. Greenberg, *Operations Res.*, **7:1,** 79 (1959).
4. I. Prigogine, "Theory of Traffic Flow," R. Herman, Ed., Elsevier (1961).
5. D. C. Gazis, R. Herman, and R. B. Potts, *Operations Res.* **7:4,** 499 (1959).

# Statistical Hydrodynamics of Traffic Flow

R. BALESCU and I. PRIGOGINE

Universite Libre of Brussels
Brussels, Belgium

and

ROBERT HERMAN and ROBERT ANDERSON

Research Laboratories
General Motors Corporation
Warren, Michigan

## Abstract

The dispersion and absorption of perturbation waves is studied by analyzing the behavior of a homogeneous time-independent traffic "fluid" under the influence of small perturbations. We have shown that employing our Boltzmann-like approach, the undamped kinematic waves of the Lighthill-Whitham macroscopic theory correspond to perturbation waves characterized by long wavelengths, in fact, rigorously they correspond only to infinite wavelengths. The main result, shown in detail for a particular model, is that the long wavelength perturbation waves are the first to go unstable as one increases the concentration of the unperturbed system. The first deviation from the Lighthill-Whitham theory can be described with a diffusion-type equation. Hence, the onset of instability can be analyzed in terms of an effective diffusion coefficient. Further, the system is inherently unstable to all perturbation waves in what we have termed the collective flow regime of our earlier work. Based on the above we suggest that this latter behavior, i.e., instability of the collective regime, concentrations greater than the critical concentration, would account qualitatively for the observed limit of $C$, approximately 50 cars/mile beyond which steady-state flow has a relatively low probability of being observed.

## I. Introduction

IN A preceding paper[1] (quoted as paper I) we have studied the relation between the macroscopic hydrodynamic description of traffic flow and the statistical approach as based on a generalized kinetic equation. We have shown that a local steady-state theory leads directly to the undamped kinematic waves of the Lighthill-Whitham macroscopic hydrodynamic description.[2] Such a local steady-state approach can, however, in general be valid only in the limit of perturbations characterized by a sufficiently large characteristic length (see I, Section 5). We may then speak of the local steady-state theory as a long wavelength theory.

We would like now to discuss the space-time behavior of traffic flow for the whole relevant range of wavelengths from the average distance between cars up to infinity. In other words, we would like to present a discussion of the dispersion and absorption of the perturbation waves by analyzing the behavior of the traffic flow under the influence of small perturbations. This is, of course, only possible on the basis of a statistical model. We hope, however, that the features we shall derive are of a generality which goes beyond the special model we shall use, exactly as many fundamental features of the phonon or the plasmon spectrum in physics do not depend on the details of the statistical assumptions.

Closely related to the problem of the absorption of perturbation waves is the question of stability of traffic flow. Indeed, a positive absorption coefficient means the amplification of initially present inhomogeneities. Therefore, our paper presents also a new alternate approach to the problem of stability of traffic flow under circumstances in which an approach based on the "follow the leader" type theory[3] is not applicable since in the latter theory passing is not allowed, while in our approach it is the dominant relaxation mechanism.

We start as before with the generalized Boltzmann equation

$$\frac{\partial f}{\partial t} + v \frac{\partial f}{\partial x} = O(f), \tag{1.1}$$

where $O(f)$ is the basic statistical traffic operator which includes all the mechanisms which lead to a modification of the velocity distribution function of the cars. Next we take

$$f(x, v; t) = F(v) + \hat{f}(x, v; t), \tag{1.2}$$

and similarly for the concentration and flow

$$c(x; t) = C + \hat{c}(x; t),$$
$$q(x; t) = c(x; t)\langle v(x, t) \rangle = CU + \hat{q}(x; t), \tag{1.3}$$

where $F$ satisfies the equation

$$O(F) = 0, \tag{1.4}$$

which corresponds to a time and space independent solution of Eq. 1.1 appropriate to a given concentration $C$ of cars. In Section 3 we present a method for the study of $f$ based on the special form of $O(f)$ we used in our preceding work and appropriate to the case when $f$ may be considered as a small perturbation.

We use an elementary Fourier-Laplace transform technique to determine an expression for the Fourier-Laplace transform $v_k(z)$ of $\hat{c}(x; t)$. Through the inverse Laplace transform, the behavior of $\hat{c}(x; t)$ will be determined by the nature and the location of the singularities of $v_k(z)$. Employing standard techniques we find in general that the contributions to $\hat{c}(x; t)$ arise from the poles of $v_k(z)$ and the branch cuts associated with $v_k(z)$.

The interesting feature is that we may express $v_k(z)$ as

$$v_k(z) = \frac{\Omega_k^{(1)}(z) + \Omega_k^{(2)}(z)}{\epsilon_k(z)}, \tag{1.5}$$

where $k$ is the wavenumber of the disturbance and $z$ is a complex frequency. The function $\epsilon_k(z)$ plays an important role in the theory, and by analogy with similar terminology in physics it may be called the dispersion function.[4] The important point is that the singularities of $\epsilon_k^{-1}(z)$ and $\Omega_k^{(2)}(z)$ are determined entirely by the form of the operator $O(f)$ and depend, therefore, only on the properties of the unperturbed traffic flow. Whereas, the singularities of $\Omega_k^{(1)}(z)$ depend on both the initial form of the perturbation and the parameters of the unperturbed traffic flow. Hence, there is a nontrivial separation of the investigation of stability of the traffic flow system into two areas of study. One is the study of a "characteristic" stability of the system—contributions which arise from $\epsilon_k(z)$ and $\Omega_k^{(2)}(z)$ and are determined only by the properties of the unperturbed traffic flow. These correspond to modes of the system which are illicited by any and all perturbations of the system if the wavelength associated with the mode is present in the perturbation. The stability of the mode is independent of the nature of the perturbation. The other is the study of a "perturbation dependent" stability of the system—contributions which arise from $\Omega_k^{(1)}(z)$ and are related intimately to the nature of the initial perturbation as well as depending upon the parameters of the unperturbed traffic flow.

The singularities of $\epsilon_k^{-1}(z)$, $\Omega_k^{(1)}(z)$, and $\Omega_k^{(2)}(z)$ found in our calculation are poles and branch cuts. Each pole contributes a term of the form

$$(amplitude) \cdot (e^{-iz_0(k)t}),$$

where the amplitude is the residue of a pole, while the contribution from a branch point $z_b$ leads to damped terms of the asymptotic form $t^{-\alpha}e^{-iz_b t}$ where $\alpha > 0$.

We can always split $z_0$ into a real and an imaginary part, and a positive value of the imaginary part means amplification of initially present inhomogenieties. There are two possibilities; either

$$Im\ z_0(k) \underset{k \to 0}{\to} 0,$$

or

$$Im\ z_0(k) \underset{k \to 0}{=} \text{finite.}$$

In the first case or the long wavelength limit we have undamped wave propagation. As we shall see this behavior is characteristic of the singularities arising from the dispersion function. The corresponding waves are precisely the kinematic waves of traffic hydrodynamics. On the contrary, the singularities which arise from $\Omega(z)\ |_{k=0}$ are damped rapidly, assuming stability, in times of the order of the relaxation time $T$. As a consequence they do not contribute to the long time behavior of the traffic fluid.

Before we proceed let us give a qualitative description of the dispersion and absorption of kinematic waves.

## 2. Dispersion and Absorption of Perturbation Waves—Qualitative Discussion

Here we discuss the behavior of the singularities arising from the zeros of the dispersion function. Let us call these zeros

$$z_0(k) = \omega(k) + i\gamma(k), \tag{2.1}$$

then $\omega(k)$ gives us the dispersion of the kinematic waves and $\gamma(k)$ their absorption. As expected, we find in the long wavelength limit

$$\omega(k) = v_g k + O(k^3), \tag{2.2}$$

$$\gamma(k) = -Dk^2 + O(k^3). \tag{2.3}$$

Therefore, in the limit of long wavelengths for which we may neglect $\gamma(k)$ we have the undamped kinematic waves of Lighthill and Whitham propagating with the velocity $v_g$.

Before we go into the discussion of the dispersion and absorption of the kinematic waves let us summarize the qualitative behavior of the flow vs. concentration curve (see Fig. 1) for the homogeneous time-independent traffic situation. This curve is characterized by the occurrence of the remarkable points $C_M$ and $C_{\text{critical}}$. One corresponds to the maximum of the flow curve, the other to the transition from the individual to the collective regime.[6] We have drawn Fig. 1 for the case in which

$$C_M < C_{\text{critical}}. \tag{2.4}$$

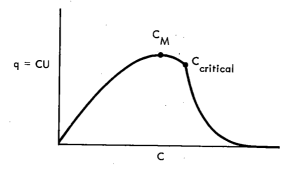

FIGURE I.   Schematic representation of the flow $q$ vs. concentration curve for the case $C_M < C_{\text{crit}}$.

However, this inequality is not general. We would, in the opposite case, obtain Fig. 2 in which $C_M$ lies on the extrapolated part of the individual flow curve. In the subsequent discussion for the sake of simplicity we suppose that Fig. 1. applies. The reader may easily modify our statements to include the case of Fig. 2.

From the macroscopic study of kinematic waves, we know that for kinematic waves the speed of propagation is related to the flow curve through the equation

$$v_g = \frac{\partial(CU)}{\partial C} .$$

(2.5)

We therefore obtain the form shown in Fig. 3 for $v_g$ as a function of concentration. This is precisely what may be derived from the detailed theory

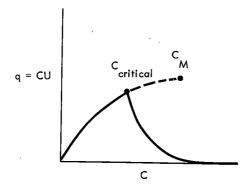

FIGURE 2.   Schematic representation of the flow $q$ vs. concentration for the case $C_M > C_{\text{crit}}$.

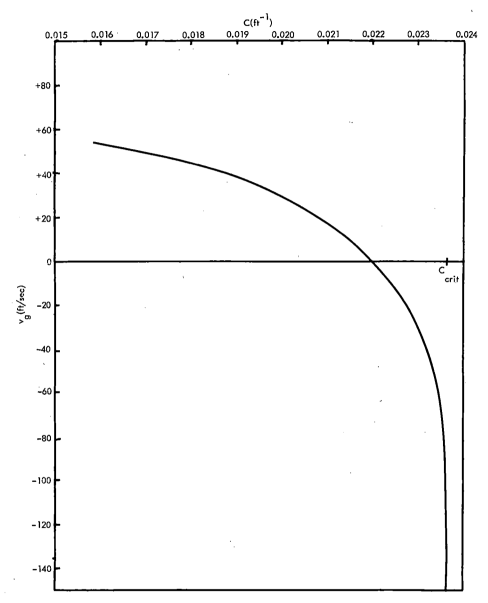

FIGURE 3. The group velocity $v_g$ vs. the concentration $C$ for the linear desired speed model specified by Eqs. 7.1–7.4.

in Section 7. The group velocity for infinite wavelengths is positive for $C < C_M$, vanishes for $C \to C_M$, i.e.,

$$\frac{\partial \omega}{\partial k}\bigg|_{k=0} \to 0 \qquad \text{for } C \to C_M, \tag{2.6}$$

and becomes negative for $C > C_M$.

Let us now consider the behavior of the diffusion coefficient $D$ defined in paper I in order to account for the first deviation from the macroscopic theory. For the simple model investigated in detail in Paragraph 7 it has the behavior shown in Fig. 4. The most unusual features are the following:

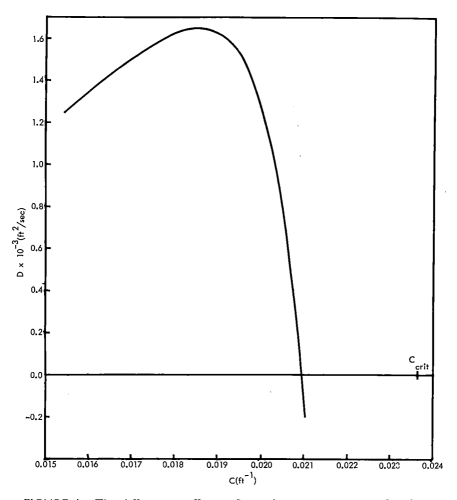

FIGURE 4.    The diffusion coefficient $D$ vs. the concentration $C$ for the linear desired speed model specified by Eqs. 7.1–7.4.

for low concentrations we find

$$D \to 0 \quad \text{for} \quad C \to 0. \tag{2.7}$$

Moreover, not only does the diffusion coefficient vanish but in general for $C \to 0$

$$\begin{cases} \gamma = 0 \\ \omega = v_g k \text{ for all values of } k. \end{cases} \tag{2.8}$$

In other words, in the limit of vanishingly small concentrations there is no absorption of perturbation waves, and the macroscopic theory of kinematic waves becomes exact for *all wavelengths*. This is very natural and is a feature which is model independent. Indeed the relaxation time $T$ then goes to zero (see Section 6 and the remarks accompanying Eq. 6.15). Note that we neglect all relaxation times which are not related to passing. Therefore at every moment the distribution function is maintained in the neighborhood of the desired speed distribution. No time delays and no irreversible processes appear at all.

Another remarkable feature is that the diffusion coefficient increases with concentration, goes through a maximum, vanishes for some concentration $C_D$ (which is in the model we treat in Section 7 slightly smaller than $C_{\text{critical}}$), and then becomes negative. This change indicates the beginning of the breakdown of the simple hydrodynamical theory (based on a local theory steady-state solution), because beyond $C_D$ perturbations of sufficiently long wavelengths are amplified instead of damped.

This behavior can be observed if we study the absorption coefficient $\gamma(k)$ as a function of $k$ for different values of the concentration (see Fig. 6.) This is studied in detail in Section 8. For the very low concentration $C_1$, $\gamma$ is negative for all wavelengths, the perturbations are always damped; for $C_2$ we are below $C_D$ and the damping is larger than for $C_1$; for $C_5$ we are just beyond $C_D$ and perturbations of sufficiently long wavelengths become unstable. This reversal in the damping with increasing concentration can be accounted for completely in terms of the maximum of the diffusion coefficient (see the discussion in Section 7). For $C_6$ the domain of instability has grown; for $C_7$ the system is unstable with respect to all perturbations because the curve lies in the upper half-plane for all pertinent values of $k$. In the model we have studied in detail (see Section 8) instability with respect to all wavelengths occurs precisely at $C_{\text{critical}}$, that is, in the collective flow regime.

The occurrence of this instability probably indicates that the distribution function now becomes explicitly a function of time, and the unperturbed function $F$ (see Eq. 1.2) no longer gives a correct starting point. The macroscopic hydrodynamic theory as discussed in our paper I is no longer valid. Broadly speaking, the distribution function is at some moment more influenced by the desires of the drivers and at the next moment by the interactions between the drivers. It is a fundamental problem of traffic hydrodynamics to obtain explicit time dependent solutions of the basic kinetic equation. We hope to achieve this in the near future through the use of an extended variational technique developed recently by one of the authors (I. P.) and his coworkers.[5]

## 3. Exact Solution of the Linearized Traffic Equation

In this section we present the exact solution of the kinetic Eq. 1.1 subject to the conditions given by Eqs. 1.2–4, where we consider $\hat{f}(x, v; t)$ as a small perturbation of the steady state solution $F(C, v)$. We take for $O(f)$ an operator which attributes the time evolution of the speed distribution function $f$ to "collision" and relaxation processes. Specifically,

$$
O(f) = \left(\frac{\partial f}{\partial t}\right)_{\text{collision}} + \left(\frac{\partial f}{\partial t}\right)_{\text{relaxation}}
$$
$$
= (1 - P)c(\langle v \rangle - v)f - \frac{f - f^0}{T} \, ; \tag{3.1}
$$

where $P = $ probability of passing,

$\langle v \rangle = 1/c \int_0^\infty dv \, vf \doteq$ average speed,

$f^0 = $ desired speed distribution function,

$T = $ relaxation time.

and $T$ and $P$ are taken to be functions of the concentration $c$ only. This is the same operator that has been discussed in previous work.

To linearize the kinetic Eq. 1.1, all quantities appearing in Eqs. 1.1 and 3.1 must be expanded to first order in the perturbed quantities. In all subsequent remarks careted quantities correspond to small spatial and temporal perturbations of the steady-state solution Eq. 1.4 and its moments. Proceeding we find, because of Eqs. 1.2–4 and the assumption that $T$ and $P$ are functions of $c$ only, that to first order in $\hat{c}$

$$
T = T_C + \left(\frac{\partial T}{\partial c}\right)_C \hat{c} = T_c + T_c'\hat{c},
$$
$$
P = P_C + \left(\frac{\partial P}{\partial c}\right)_C \hat{c} = P_c + P_c'\hat{c}, \tag{3.2}
$$

and because of the definition of the desired speed distribution function $f^0$, i.e., the desired distribution of speeds is the same at all concentrations,

$$
f^0 = (C + \hat{c})f^0,
$$

and

$$
\int_0^\infty dv f^0(v) = 1. \tag{3.3}
$$

Substituting Eqs. 1.2–4 and Eqs. 3.1–3 into the kinetic Eq. 1.1 yields

$$\frac{\partial f}{\partial t} + v\frac{\partial f}{\partial x} = -\frac{(F + f - (C + \hat{c})f^0)}{T_c\left(1 + \frac{T_c'}{T_c}\hat{c}\right)}$$

$$+ (1 - P_c - P_c'\hat{c})[CU + \hat{q} - Cv - \hat{c}v](F + f). \quad (3.4)$$

Equating like orders of the perturbed quantities, we obtain the zeroth order equation:

$$0 = -\frac{F - Cf^0}{T_c} + (1 - P_c)C(U - v)F, \quad (3.5)$$

which is just a restatement of Eq. 1.4, and the *first order equation or linearized kinetic equation:*

$$\frac{\partial f}{\partial t} + v\frac{\partial f}{\partial x} = -\frac{(f - \hat{c}f^0)}{T_c} + (F - Cf^0)\frac{T_c'}{T_c^2}\hat{c} + (1 - P_c)C(U - v)f$$

$$+ [(1 - P_c)(\hat{q} - \hat{c}v) - P_c'C(U - v)\hat{c}]F. \quad (3.6)$$

We now introduce the Fourier-Laplace transforms* corresponding to the various perturbed quantities:

$$\hat{f}(x, v; t) = \frac{1}{2\pi}\int dz e^{-izt}\int_{-\infty}^{\infty} dk e^{ikx} \rho_k(v; z),$$

$$\hat{c}(x; t) = \frac{1}{2\pi}\int dz e^{-izt}\int_{-\infty}^{\infty} dk e^{ikx} v_k(z), \quad (3.7)$$

$$\hat{q}(x; t) = \frac{1}{2\pi}\int dz e^{-izt}\int_{-\infty}^{\infty} dk e^{izx} \omega_k(z),$$

and specify the initial value problem for the linearized kinetic Eq. 3.6 by assuming that

$$\hat{f}(x, v; 0) = \int_{-\infty}^{\infty} dk e^{ikx} f_k(v; 0). \quad (3.8)$$

Employing Eqs. 3.7 and 3.8, and noting that the Fourier-Laplace transform of $\partial \hat{f}/\partial t$ is

$$\mathscr{L}\left(\frac{\partial f}{\partial t}\right) = -\frac{1}{2\pi}\int_{-\infty}^{\infty} dk e^{ikx} f_k(v; 0) - \frac{iz}{2\pi}\int_{-\infty}^{\infty} dk e^{ikx} \rho_k(v; z), \quad (3.9)$$

we obtain from the linearized kinetic Eq. 3.6,

$$\rho_k(v; z) =$$

$$\frac{f_k + (1 - P_c)F\omega_k - \left[(1 - P_c)U + \left\{P_c' - \frac{T_c'}{T_c}(1 - P_c)\right\}C(U - v) - \frac{1}{T_cC}\right]Fv_k}{[ik + (1 - P_c)C]v - (1 - P_c)CU - iz + \frac{1}{T_c}}$$

$$(3.10)$$

<hr>

* The complex variable $iz$ used here is usually denoted by $-s$ in the literature on Laplace transforms.

In obtaining Eq. 3.10 we have eliminated $f^0$ in terms of $F$ using the zeroth order Eq. 3.5.

Since

$$\int_0^\infty dv\, \rho_k(v; z) = \nu_k(z),$$

and

$$\int_0^\infty dv\, v\, \rho_k(v; z) = \omega_k(z), \tag{3.11}$$

a set of two simultaneous equations for $\nu_k(z)$ and $\omega_k(z)$ can be obtained by first integrating Eq. 3.10 over all speeds and then by multiplying Eq. 3.10 by the speed $v$ and then integrating over all speeds. Let us introduce the notation

$$\begin{Bmatrix} A_n \\ \alpha_n \end{Bmatrix} = \int_0^\infty dv\, v^n \frac{\begin{Bmatrix} \hat{f}_k(v; 0) \\ F(c, v) \end{Bmatrix}}{[ik + (1 - P_c)C]v - (1 - P_c)CU - iz + \dfrac{1}{T_c}} \tag{3.12}$$

There are simple recursion relations for the $A_n$'s and $\alpha_n$'s which can be obtained by the method of partial fractions

$$\begin{Bmatrix} A_{n+1} \\ \alpha_{n+1} \end{Bmatrix} = \int_0^\infty dv\, v^n \frac{\begin{Bmatrix} \hat{f}_k(v; 0) \\ F(C, v) \end{Bmatrix}}{[ik + (1 - P_c)C]} + \begin{Bmatrix} A_n \\ \alpha_n \end{Bmatrix} \left[ (1 - P_c)CU + iz - \frac{1}{T_c} \right]. \tag{3.13}$$

An integration of Eq. 3.10 over all speeds yields

$$\nu_k \left[ 1 + \left\{ (1 - P_c)U + \left( P_c' - \frac{T_c'}{T_c}(1 - P_c) \right)CU - \frac{1}{CT_c} \right\}\alpha_0 \right.$$
$$\left. - \left\{ P_c' - \frac{T_c'}{T_c}(1 - P_c) \right\}C\alpha_1 \right] - \omega_k(1 - P_c)\alpha = A_0, \tag{3.14}$$

and multiplication of Eq. 3.10 by a speed $vs$. followed by integration over all speeds yields

$$\nu_k \left[ \left\{ (1 - P_c)U + \left( P_c' - \frac{T_c'}{T_c}(1 - P_c) \right)CU - \frac{1}{CT_c} \right\}\alpha_1 \right.$$
$$\left. - \left\{ P_c' - \frac{T_c'}{T_c}(1 - P_c) \right\}C\alpha_2 \right] + \omega_k[1 - (1 - P_c)\alpha_1] = A_1. \tag{3.15}$$

The determinant of the system of two simultaneous Eqs. 3.14 and 3.15 is $\nu_k$ and $\omega_k$ is what we called in Section 1 the dispersion function $\epsilon_k(z)$ and is found to be

$$\epsilon_k(z) = 1 - \left[ (1 - P_c)\left( 1 - \frac{T_c'}{T_c}C \right) + P_c'C \right](\alpha_1 - U\alpha_0) - \frac{\alpha_0}{CT_c}$$
$$+ (1 - P_c)\left[ P_c' - \frac{T_c'}{T_c}(1 - P_c) \right]C(\alpha_1{}^2 - \alpha_0\alpha_2). \tag{3.16}$$

The dispersion function can be reduced to a linear form in $\alpha_0$ by employing Eq. 3.13

$$\epsilon_k(z) = 1 - \left\{ \frac{\left( [1 - P_c]\left[ 1 - \frac{T_c'}{T_c} C \right] + P_c'C \right)ik + [1 - P_c]^2 C}{[ik + (1 - P_c)C]^2} \right.$$

$$\left. \times \left\{ C + \left[ -\frac{1}{T_c} + iz - ikU \right]\alpha_0 \right\} - \frac{\alpha_0}{CT_c} \right. \quad (3.17)$$

It is important to observe that the dispersion Eq. 3.17 is determined only by the properties of the unperturbed steady-state distribution $F(C, v)$.

We find that the Fourier-Laplace transform $v_k(x)$ of the concentration perturbation $c(x; t)$ is given by

$$v_k(z) = \frac{\Omega_k(z)}{\epsilon_k(z)}, \quad (3.18)$$

where

$$\Omega_k(z) = \begin{vmatrix} A_0 & -(1 - P_c)\alpha_0 \\ A_1 & 1 - (1 - P_c)\alpha_1 \end{vmatrix} = \Omega_k^{(1)}(z) + \Omega_k^{(2)}(z),$$

which can be reduced by the method of partial fractions to

$$\Omega_k^{(1)}(z) = ikA_0, \quad (3.19)$$

$$\Omega_k^{(2)}(z) = (1 - P_c)\hat{c}_k\alpha_0,$$

where

$$\hat{c}(x; 0) = \int_{-\infty}^{\infty} dk e^{ikx}\hat{c}_k.$$

We make the important observation here that the singularities of $\epsilon_k^{-1}(z)$ and $\Omega_k^{(2)}(z)$ are determined entirely by the properties of the unperturbed traffic flow, whereas the singularities of $\Omega_k^{(1)}(z)$ depend on both the initial perturbation and the parameters of the unperturbed traffic flow. Now the behavior of $\hat{c}(x; t)$ will be determined by the nature and location of these singularities, hence we are led to the remarks made in the introduction about the separation of the stability investigation into consideration of "characteristic" and "perturbation-dependent" stability.

## 4. "Characteristic" Stability of a Traffic Convoy

The characteristic stability of a traffic convoy will be investigated in this section to illustrate the formalism developed in Section 3. For the purpose of this discussion, a traffic convoy is taken as a system of vehicle-drivers in which all drivers desire to travel at the same speed, say $U$, i.e.

$$f^0 = C \delta(v - U). \quad (4.1)$$

Hence, it follows from Eqs. 1.1 and 3.1 that the steady-state solution is given by

$$F(c, v) = C \, \delta(v - U). \tag{4.2}$$

In this case the dispersion function, Eq. 3.17 takes the simple form

$$\epsilon_k(z) = 1 - \frac{\alpha_0}{CT_c}, \tag{4.3}$$

with

$$\alpha_0 = \frac{C}{ikU - iz + T_c^{-1}}$$

Therefore, the zeros of $\epsilon_k(z)$ correspond to simple poles of $\nu_k(z)$ which are located at

$$z_0(k) = kU, \tag{4.4}$$

and correspond to kinematic waves without dispersion and absorption.

Let us now consider the singularities of $\Omega_k^{(2)}(z)$. They correspond to the singularities of $\alpha_0$ which correspond to simple poles of $\nu_k(z)$, located at

$$z_0(k) = kU - \frac{i}{T_c}. \tag{4.5}$$

Thus we see that these poles display no dispersion, but correspond to strong damping in a time the order of the relaxation time $T_c$. We see here that the long time behavior contributions from the dispersion function $\epsilon_k(z)$ dominates those of $\Omega_k^{(2)}(z)$. Hence, we have the interesting result that the analysis of the "characteristic" stability of a traffic convoy leads to contributions to $\hat{c}(x, t)$ which are stable for all concentrations.

## 5. Comments on "perturbation dependent" stability

As remarked in the introduction, we mean by "perturbation dependent" those contributions which arise from the term $\Omega_k^{(1)}$ which is given by Eq. 3.19. These contributions are related intimately to the nature of the initial perturbation as well as depending upon the parameters of the unperturbed traffic flow. Here we shall confine our comments to the mathematically simple but physically non-trivial case of a velocity "spike" initial perturbation at the speed $u$; i.e.,

$$f(x, v; 0) = \hat{c}(x; 0) \, \delta(v - u), \tag{5.1}$$

where $\delta(\xi)$ is the Dirac delta function.

An examination of Eq. 3.19 leads to the result that the contributions associated with $\Omega_k^{(1)}(z)$ are simple pole contributions which are located at

$$z_0(k) = ku - i \left[ (1 - P)C(u - U) + \frac{1}{T} \right] \tag{5.2}$$

Therefore, again we find no dispersion of the kinematic waves but absorption. For small concentrations these contributions are damped in a time of the order of the relaxation time $T$. More precisely, from arguments given in a previous paper[6] we know that

$$(1 - P)C(v_{\min_F} - U) + \frac{1}{T} \geq 0, \tag{5.3}$$

for all unperturbed concentrations $0 \leq C \leq C_P$,* where $v_{\min_F}$ is the minimum speed associated with the unperturbed flow. It should also be noted that $v_{\min_F} = v_{\min_{f_0}}$, an expression of the fact that the lowest speed permitted in the unperturbed flow is the lowest desired speed. Hence, the poles given by Eq. 5.2 correspond to damped oscillations for all concentrations if

$$u \geq v_{\min_F}, \tag{5.4}$$

whereas, instability occurs if

$$u < v_{\min_F}, \tag{5.5}$$

at concentrations which depend on the difference $(v_{\min_F} - u)$. The physical interpretation of this type of instability, i.e., Eq. 5.5 holds, is that the collisions are successful in preventing the system from relaxing back to $F$ which is a distribution of higher speeds than $(F + \hat{f})$.

In Section 7 the argument and the results of Eqs. 7.6 and 7.7 are also applicable to the case that $f$ can be written as

$$\hat{f}(x, v; 0) = \hat{c}(x; 0) \times \text{polynomial in } v, \tag{5.6}$$

with the modification that the effect of $v_{\min_{\hat{f}}}$ and $v_{\max_{\hat{f}}}$ as they differ from $v_{\min_F}$ and $v_{\max_F}$ must be taken into account.

## 6. Long Wavelength Behavior of Kinematic Waves and Diffusion Equation

We are interested in the behavior of the zeros $z_0$ of the dispersion function†

$$\epsilon_k(z) = 1 - \left\{ \frac{aik + (1 - P_c)^2 C}{[ik + (1 - P_c)C]^2} \right\} \left\{ C + \left[ -\frac{1}{T_c} + iz - ik\langle v \rangle \right] \alpha_0 \right\} - \frac{\alpha_0}{CT_c}, \tag{6.1}$$

in the neighborhood of the zero(s) corresponding to $k = 0$. To obtain their behavior we first note that

$$\epsilon_k(z)\big|_{k=0} = 0, \tag{6.2}$$

* The quantity $C_P$ is the limiting concentration beyond which cars can no longer pass.

† Note      $a = (1 - P_c)\left(1 - \frac{T_c'}{T_c} C\right) + P_c C,$

and

$$\alpha_0 = \int_0^\infty dv \, \frac{F(C, v)}{[ik + (1 - P_c)C]v - (1 - P_c)C\langle v \rangle - iz + \frac{1}{T_c}}.$$

implies that

$$z_0(k = 0)\alpha_0 \big|_{k=0} = 0. \tag{6.3}$$

Now, it follows from general arguments, that $z_0(k = 0)$ is finite, hence we conclude that

$$z_0(k = 0) = 0. \tag{6.4}$$

From continuity arguments and 6.4, we can expand $z_0(k)$ as a power series in $k$ in the neighborhood of $k = 0$,

$$z_0(k) = \sum_{n=1}^{\infty} \frac{\partial^n z_0}{\partial k^n}\bigg|_{k=0} k^n. \tag{6.5}$$

A determination of $z_0(k)$ can be obtained by substituting Eq. 6.5 into Eq. 6.2, rearranging this in a power series in $k$, and then invoking the condition that the coefficient of $k^m$ for all $m$ must vanish identically. It is sufficient for our purposes to examine the linear and quadratic terms in this series.

From the coefficient of $k$ we obtain

$$0 = \frac{i}{(1 - P_c)^2 C} [-2(1 - P_c) + a] - i \frac{\partial z_0}{\partial k}\bigg|_{k=0} \frac{T_c}{C} I_{1;0}$$

$$+ i\left\{\left[\frac{2(1 - P_c) + a}{(1 - P_c)^2 C^2}\right] + U \frac{T_c}{C}\right\} I_{1;0} \tag{6.6}$$

where we define

$$I_{n;\rho} = \int_0^\infty dv \frac{v^\rho F(C, v)}{[\Gamma(v + \beta)]^n}, \tag{6.7}$$

and

$$\Gamma = T_c(1 - P_c)C,$$

$$\beta = \frac{1}{\Gamma} - U.$$

Remembering that

$$z_0 = \omega + i\gamma \tag{6.8}$$

and setting the real and imaginary parts of Eq. 6.6 separately equal to zero we find

$$v_g = \frac{\partial \omega}{\partial k}\bigg|_{k=0} = U - \left(2 + \frac{a}{(1 - P_c)}\right)\frac{1}{(1 - P_c)CT_c}\left[1 - \frac{C}{I_{1;0}}\right], \tag{6.9}$$

and

$$\frac{\partial \gamma}{\partial k}\bigg|_{k=0} = 0.$$

From the coefficient of $k^2$ we find that

$$
\begin{aligned}
0 = {} & \frac{-2}{(1-P_c)^2 C^2}\left[-3 + \frac{2a}{(1-P_c)}\right] - i\left.\frac{\partial^2 z_0}{\partial k^2}\right|_{k=0} \frac{T_c}{C} I_{1;0} \\
& + 2i\left(U - \left.\frac{\partial z_0}{\partial k}\right|_{k=0}\right)\left\{iT_c\left.\frac{\partial z_0}{\partial k}\right|_{k=0} I_{2;0}\right. \\
& + i\frac{[-2(1-P_c)+a]}{(1-P_c)^2 C^2} T_c I_{1;0} - \left.i\frac{T_c^2}{C} I_{2;1}\right\} \\
& + \frac{\left[-3 + \dfrac{2a}{1-P_c}\right]}{(1-P_c)^2 C^2} \frac{2I_{1;0}}{C} - \frac{2i^2 T_c}{(1-P_c)^2 C^2}[-2(1-P_c)+a]I_{2;1}.
\end{aligned}
\tag{6.10}
$$

Employing Eqs. 6.8 and 6.9 and setting the real and imaginary parts of Eq. 6.10 separately equal to zero we obtain

$$
\left.\frac{\partial^2 \omega}{\partial k^2}\right|_{k=0} = 0,
\tag{6.11}
$$

and

$$
\begin{aligned}
D = {} & -\left.\frac{\partial^2 \gamma}{\partial k^2}\right|_{k=0} = \left(\frac{C}{T_c} I_{1;0}\right)\left[\frac{-2}{(1-P_c)^2 C^2}\left[-3 + \frac{2a}{(1-P_c)}\right]\left[1 - \frac{I_{1;0}}{C}\right]\right. \\
& + 2(v_g - U)\left\{\frac{T_c^2}{C} v_g I_{2;0} + \frac{[-2(1-P_c)+a]}{(1-P_c)^2 C^2} T_c I_{1;0} - \frac{T_c^2}{C} I_{2;1}\right\} \\
& + \left.\frac{2T_c}{(1-P_c)^2 C^2}[-2(1-P_c)+a]I_{2;1}\right]
\end{aligned}
$$

Hence we find that to lowest order in $k$

$$
\begin{aligned}
Re z_0(k) &= \omega(k) = v_g k + 0(k^3), \\
Im z_0(k) &= \gamma(k) = -Dk^2 + 0(k^3).
\end{aligned}
\tag{6.12}
$$

Equation 6.12 implies that the long wavelength contributions to $\hat{c}(x, t)$ from the poles of $\epsilon_k^{-1}(z)$ satisfy the diffusion equation

$$
\frac{\partial \hat{c}}{\partial t} + v_g \frac{\partial \hat{c}}{\partial x} = D \frac{\partial^2 \hat{c}}{\partial x^2}
\tag{6.13}
$$

Since

$$
c(x; t) = C + \hat{c}(x; t),
\tag{6.14}
$$

where $C$ is independent of $x$ and $t$, Eq. 6.13 can be written as

$$
\frac{\partial c}{\partial t} + v_g \frac{\partial c}{\partial x} = D \frac{\partial^2 c}{\partial x^2},
\tag{6.15}
$$

to $O(k^2)$ or

$$\frac{\partial c}{\partial t} + v_g \frac{\partial c}{\partial x} = 0. \tag{6.16}$$

for $k = 0$. The latter equation, Eq. 6.16, corresponds to the description of the Lighthill-Whitman undamped kinematic waves.

## 7. Concentration Dependence of the Long Wave-Length Behavior

To obtain further results we have taken as a model, which illustrates the type of information that can be obtained, a linear desired speed distribution function

$$f^0 = \begin{cases} 2cv/v_L^2 & 0 \leq v \leq v_L. \\ 0 & v_L < v \end{cases} \tag{7.1}$$

We adopt our usual forms for the probability of passing $P$ and the relaxation time $T$, i.e.,

$$P = \begin{cases} 1 - c/c_P & 0 \leq c \leq c_P, \\ 0 & c_P < c \end{cases} \tag{7.2}$$

and

$$T = \tau(1 - P)/P,$$
$$\tau = \text{constant}. \tag{7.3}$$

We refer the reader to an earlier paper[7] for a discussion of the motivation for the above choice in particular, the discussion accompanying Eqs. 3 and 4 in this cited paper. For the purpose of numerical computation we set

$$v_L = 100 \text{ ft/sec},$$
$$C_P = 0.05 \text{ cars/ft}, \tag{7.4}$$
$$\tau = 2 \text{ sec}.$$

The flow curve for this particular model can be found in this same paper[7] and will not be reproduced here.

We will now present the numerical results for this model for the long wavelength behavior. Figures 3 and 4 show, respectively, the group velocity $v_g$ and the diffusion coefficient $D$ as a function of concentration. Examining Fig. 3 we see that $v_g$ starts out at zero concentration with the value of the average desired speed $\langle v^0 \rangle$ and then decreases as a function of concentration. At a concentration of 0.022 car/ft, $v_g$ changes sign; i.e., just beyond this concentration the kinematic waves propagate in a direction opposite to the direction of flow for an observer stationed at the side of the roadway. The zero of $v_g$, corresponds to the concentration at which the flow is a maximum, which is a general result.

Figure 4 reveals several interesting features. First, and one of the most significant results, is the fact that the diffusion coefficient becomes negative beyond $C = 0.21$ car/ft, i.e., the long wavelength perturbations are not damped out in time. Thus, the steady-state solutions are unstable for long wavelength perturbations beyond $C = 0.021$ car/ft. Further on in this section we shall see that the long wavelength perturbations are the first perturbations to result in instability, i.e., the steady-state solutions are stable to all wavelength perturbations for concentrations less than $C = 0.021$ car/ft.

A second interesting feature is the existence of a maximum in this $D$ versus $C$ curve. This is a result of the fact that independent of the exact form for $f^0$

$$D|_{c=0} = 0, \tag{7.5}$$

and the first feature discussed in the previous paragraph. The significance of this result can only be satisfactorily discussed in the next section on the short wavelength behavior.

The contributions from $\Omega_k^{(2)}(z)$ are in general model dependent for all $k$. But for an $f^0$ which is expressable as a polynomial in $v$ we find that the singularities are branch points located at $z_b^{(1)}$ and $z_b^{(2)}$

$$z_b^{(1)} = kv_{\min} - i\left[\frac{1}{T_c} - C(1 - P_c)U\right], \tag{7.6}$$

$$z_b^{(2)} = kv_{\max} - i\left[C(1 - P_c)v_L + \frac{1}{T_c} - C(1 - P_c)U\right], \tag{7.7}$$

and $v_{\min} \leq v \leq v_{\max}$. We shall find that the damping associated with $\Omega_k^{(2)}(z)$ for the long wavelength behavior is larger than that associated with $\epsilon_k(z)$ for the particular model we have considered and, hence, the long-time behavior for long wavelengths arises from the behavior of the diffusion coefficient $D$. We point out again, as at the end of Section 5, that the above results are also applicable to the evaluation of the "perturbation dependent" term $\Omega_k^{(1)}(z)$ for the case that

$$f = \hat{c}(x; 0) \times \text{polynomial in } v, \tag{7.8}$$

with the modification that the effect of $v_{\min_f}$ and $v_{\max_f}$ must be taken into account.

## 8. "Characteristic" Stability (Intermediate and Short Wavelength Behavior)

In this section we consider the whole range of relevant wavelengths. This range is determined by the requirement that the wavelength $\lambda$ associated with the perturbation must be greater than or of the order of the average distance between cars $1/C$. Hence, since

$$k = 2\pi/\lambda, \tag{8.1}$$

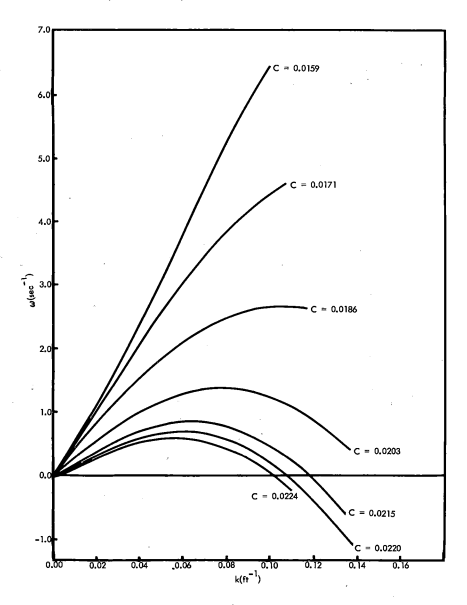

FIGURE 5. The real part $\omega$ of the zero $z_0$ of the dispersion function $\varepsilon_k(z)$ vs. the wave number $k$ for various concentrations $C$ for the linear desired speed model specified by Eqs. 7.1–7.4.

we find that in terms of the wave number $k$

$$0 \leq k < 2\pi c \tag{8.2}$$

In the previous section we focused our attention on the case $k \sim 0$ and we found general results, i.e., results independent of $f^0$. But even to fully discuss that limiting case we had to turn to a specific model for $f^0$. Here we wish to consider the intermediate and short wavelengths and we must employ a specific model for $f^0$ because of the complicated form for $\epsilon_k(z)$.

Figure 5 shows $\omega(Re \ z_0)$ as a function of the wave number $k$ for a constant concentration $C$. The expected feature here is the increase in dispersion for increasing concentration.

In Fig. 6 $\gamma(Im \ z_0)$ is plotted as a function of $k$ for a constant concentration $C$. We see that starting at $\gamma = 0$ for all $k$ for $C = 0$ and proceeding to higher concentrations, that first the trend is to higher damping until we reach a concentration of $C \sim 0.0186$ car/ft and then there is a reversal to smaller damping.

This reversal can be completely explained in terms of the maximum of the diffusion coefficient $D$ and the long wavelength behavior of $\gamma$. In particular, an examination of

$$\gamma = -Dk^2, \tag{8.3}$$

in the vicinity of $D_{\max}$ completely accounts for the reversal. As we proceed beyond $C_{D_{\max}}$ the steady state solutions are stable to all wavelengths until we reach $C = 0.021$ car/ft. At this point we find that the long wavelength perturbations being to be unstable. It is important to again note that this is the point at which $D$ begins to go negative. As we proceed to even higher concentrations the solutions become unstable to a larger range of wavelengths. When we reach $C_{\text{critical}}$ we find that the solution is unstable to all wavelengths. Hence, an important result for this model is the fact that the collective flow regime is completely unstable.

Figure 7 shows $\gamma$ versus $C$ for constant $k$ and vividly shows the effect of $D$ changing sign at $C \sim 0.021$ car/ft.

We refer the reader to Section 2 where a qualitative discussion of these results is given.

## 9. Conclusions

We have shown that there exist a certain number of types of perturbation waves coming from the different singularities of $\Omega_k^{(1)}(z)$, $\Omega_k^{(2)}(z)$, and $\epsilon_k(z)$. Between these perturbation waves we have identified the kinematic waves of the Lighthill-Whitham macroscopic theory with the poles of the dispersion function $\epsilon_k(z)$. These have an especially simple long wavelength behavior as their damping goes strictly to zero in this limit. Even these waves correspond to a complicated long time behavior. For higher concentrations they are

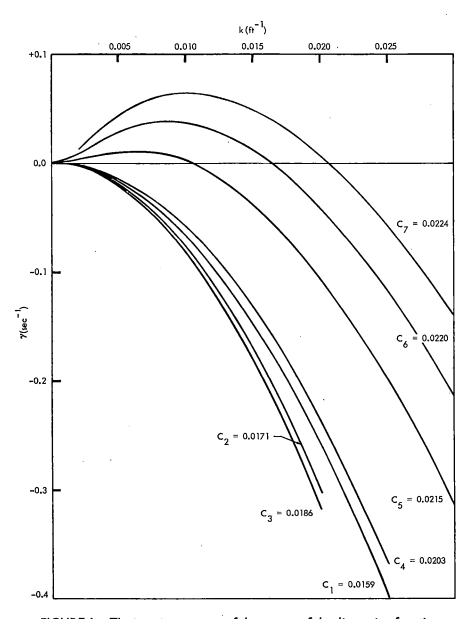

FIGURE 6.   The imaginary part $\gamma$ of the zero $z_0$ of the dispersion function $\varepsilon_k(z)$ the wave number $k$ for various concentrations $C$ for the linear desired speed model specified by Eqs. 7.1–7.4.

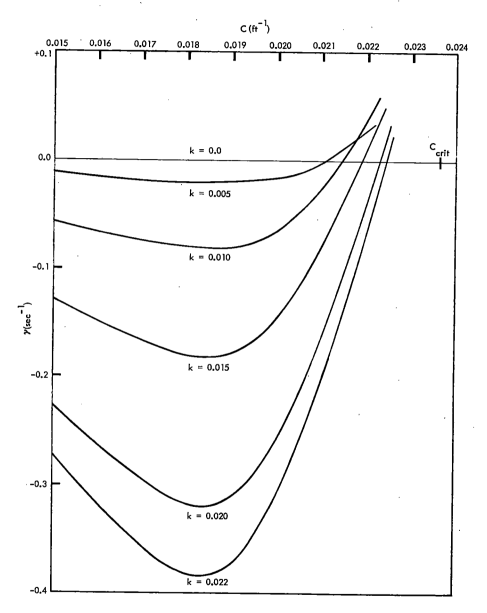

FIGURE 7.   The imaginary part $\gamma$ of the zero $z_0$ of the dispersion function $\varepsilon_k(z)$ vs. the concentration $C$ for various $k$ for the linear desired speed model specified by Eqs. 7.1–7.4.

amplified and therefore the time-independent hydrodynamical description becomes inadequate.

This transition from stability to instability is most directly seen by studying the diffusion coefficient. We have given the expression for the diffusion coefficient $D$ in terms of the parameters of the nonperturbed kinetic equation.

The first deviations from the Lighthill and Whitham theory are given by a diffusion equation which is accurate to $0(k^2)$. Further, the stability of the long wavelengths can be ascertained from the sign of the effective diffusion coefficient, i.e., $D > 0$ implies stability. Now an extremely important result is shown for the desired speed distribution function $f^0$ we have considered in Section 7. Namely, that the long wavelength perturbation waves are the first to become unstable as one increases the concentration. Hence, the presence of inherent instability in the system is detected by the behavior of $D$, i.e., whenever $D$ becomes negative instabilities appear.

We can see here, in more detail, the conclusion, given in paper I, that the local steady state theory as well as the macroscopic hydrodynamical theory is not in general a long-time theory. Indeed, as shown in Section 6, the macroscopic description has been obtained in the limit of long wavelength phenomena. On the other hand, those are precisely the phenomena which first exhibit instability. Hence, the macroscopic description is valid only for times short compared to the inverse rate of growth. Another particular result is that for this $f^0$ the traffic "fluid" is inherently unstable to all perturbation waves beyond $C_{critical}$. This gives a possible further insight into the characterization of the collective flow regime.

Based on the above we suggest that this latter behavior, i.e., instability of the collective regime (all $C > C_c$), would account qualitatively for the observed limit of $C \sim 50$ cars/mile beyond which there is no steady flow observed.

One of the authors (R. L. A.) would like to thank Dr. George H. Weiss, National Institutes of Health, for helpful discussion of certain mathematical aspects of this paper, and Dr. Robert Silver, General Motors Research Laboratories, for helpful discussions.

## References

1. I. Prigogine, R. Herman, and R. Anderson, *Proc. Third Intern. Symp on the Theory of Traffic Flow*, American Elsevier (1966).
2. M. J. Lighthill and G. B. Whitham, *Proc. Roy. Soc.*, A229, 317 (1955).
3. D. C. Gazis, R. Herman, and R. B. Potts, *Operations Res.*, 7:4, 499 (1959).
4. R. Balescu, "Statistical Mechanics of Charged Particles" John Wiley & Sons, New York, 1963.
5. I. Prigogine, *Proc. of the Non-Equilibrium Thermodynamics and Stability Symp.* The University of Chicago Press, Chicago, 1965.
6. I. Prigogine, R. Herman, and R. L. Anderson, *Bull. Cl. Sci. Acad. Roy. Belg.*, Series 5, XLVIII, 792 (1962).
7. R. L. Anderson, R. Herman, and I. Prigogine, *Operations Res.*, 10, 180 (1962).

# Markov Renewal Models in Traffic Flow Theory

WILLIAM S. JEWELL

Operations Research Center &
Department of Industrial Engineering
University of California, Berkeley, California

The use of renewal-process models is well established in traffic flow theory, particularly for those problems which do not require isolation of individual behavior, as in car-following models, but which need more "discreteness" of the individual vehicle than is provided by classical flow-density analogies.

On the other hand, the basic assumption of the renewal-theoretic approach—that successive headways in a traffic stream are independently and identically distributed—tends to break down in heavy traffic, as has been noted experimentally. For specific problems, such as finite-length vehicles, or traveling platoons of vehicles, the theory can be adjusted on an *ad hoc* basis, but a more general approach is needed which will be both physically "modelable," and mathematically "maleable," and, naturally, experimentally verifiable. The suggestion of Haight that successive headways might have a general joint distribution function does not seem to be promising on either of the first two counts.

The purpose of this paper is to explore, in a preliminary fashion, the possible extensions to existing traffic flow models under the assumption that the traffic stream is a Markov-renewal (or semi-Markov) process. Although this idea was advanced as early as 1960 by Weiss and Maradudin, the author feels that it has not received the attention it deserves.

The primary advantages of this new model are: (1) the "types" of different vehicles in an inhomogeneous traffic stream, and the "correlation" between successive headways is introduced in a natural way; (2) the additional mathematical labor in formulating and solving a given problem is almost negligible; (3) most of the average-behavior formulas and the large-sample results of current road-traffic theory carry over with trivial modification; and (4) the model appears to have wide applicability to different traffic phenomena.

After a review of basic Markov renewal terminology, the paper[1] presents selected

1. Report ORC 65-24, Operations Research Center, University of California, Berkeley, California.

mathematical results, including asymptotic counting formulae. As an example of application, the theoretical correlation between successive headways in a traffic stream with traveling platoons is developed.

The results of a limited experimental program undertaken at the University of California, Berkeley are also presented, but the time-varying nature of the data and the small sample size make inferences difficult.

# Interchange Spacing and Driver Behavior Effects on Freeway Operation*

*T. W. FORBES, JAMES J. MULLIN, and MILES E. SIMPSON*

Department of
Psychology and Division of Engineering Research
Michigan State University, East Lansing, Michigan

## Abstract

Measurements of traffic flow characteristics were obtained from samples of heavy urban freeway traffic flow. A technique previously described used 35-millimeter air photos and correction and calculation of quantities by means of an electronic computer.

Six sections of freeway with different on-and-off ramp spacing were compared in terms of traffic volumes, spot speeds, densities, weaves, slow downs, and stoppages. Evidence of interference with flow was found on a highway section with short spacing between two on-ramps and one off-ramp, but less apparent interference on two other sections with short on-and-off ramp spacings. Volume density curves for most sections showed the picture described in many previous studies of a maximum point at intermediate densities followed by a lower volume at still higher densities. But one section never showed this self-limiting characteristic. Thus, different volume-density relationships were shown on different sections of the same urban freeway.

## I. Introduction

VARIOUS RESEARCH approaches have been used to seek factual information on the effects of interchange spacing and driver behavior on freeway operation. In this project a special sweep-sampling 35 mm air photo technique, using a light airplane, was used to record traffic flow during morning and afternoon traffic peaks on three sections of an urban freeway in Detroit. Twelve flights

* The research reported was carried out under contract with U.S. Department of Commerce, Bureau of Public Roads.

each obtained photographic records sampling about 40 min of peak hour morning or afternoon traffic. Approximately 72 orbits (144 sweeps) and 22,000 individual pictures resulted. For statistical comparisons, eight of the weekday records (four morning and four afternoon) were selected for completeness of sampling. Each yielded approximately 100 samples or a total of about 800.

Systematic procedures were developed for measuring in selected samples of pictures the positions of individual cars, correcting for slant range, and calculating volume, speed, time headway and space headway, and acceleration. Samples of up to 5 cars per lane were followed and their positions measured for 5 sec.

The method showed good correspondence with ground volume records and although a somewhat larger total sample would be desirable, statistically reliable comparisons were obtained. On the six highway sections (three in each direction), a lower average speed and more actual slow downs and stoppages occurred in Section 2 under (outbound) peak traffic conditions. This indicated interference with flow because of the relatively close spacing of two on-ramps and an off-ramp in this section as compared to one on-ramp and two off-ramps on the opposite side of the highway, and to greater spacings in other sections studied. Section 4 showed the second lowest average speed, apparently related to its close on-off-ramp spacing in combination with double heavy right and left on-ramps feeding it.

Differing flow-density relationships were found for the first time on different sections of the same freeway. Further analysis of these data was prevented by time limitations.

## II. Objectives

The objectives of this research were, first, to try out and evaluate the sweep-sampling air photo technique and, second, to carry out a pilot study on effects of interchange spacing on driver behavior and freeway operation on three areas of an urban freeway. The various problems met in development and evaluation of the method were satisfactorily overcome. The method proved satisfactory for the purposes of the study.

## III. Experimental Highway Sections

To compare effects on traffic flow, comparisons were made of three locations on the Lodge Freeway in Detroit. The first location was in the downtown section, the second through a business district farther out, and the third through a semi-residential area. The experimental sections were numbered 1, 2, and 3 for the outbound direction and 4, 5, and 6 inbound (see Fig. 1).

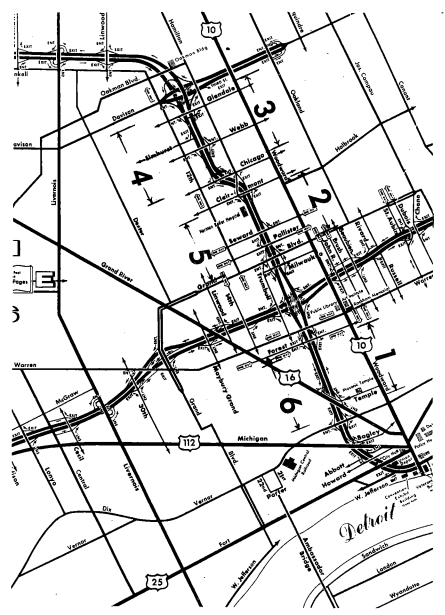

FIGURE I. Map of John Lodge Freeway extending northwest from downtown Detroit. Experimental Sections 1, 2, and 3 for outbound traffic; 4, 5, and 6 for inbound traffic.

Sections 2 and 5 were four lanes wide and had the closest spacing of on and off ramps. The other four were three lane sections with greater on- and off-ramp spacings, except for Section 4. Table I summarizes these characteristics.

TABLE I.   Interchange Spacings.

| Section | Between | Ramp spacing (ft) | No. of on-ramps | No. of off-ramps |
|---------|---------|-------------------|-----------------|------------------|
| 1 | Grand River Avenue and | 3350 | 1 | 1 |
| 6 | Forrest Avenue | 3325 | 1 | 1 |
| 2 | West Grand Blvd. and | 1750 | 2 | 1 |
| 5 | Clairmont Avenue | 2225 | 1 | 2 |
| 3 | Webb Avenue and | 1850 | 1 | 2 |
| 4 | Glendale Avenue | 1200 | 2 | 1 |

## Flow Measurements Used

The measurements of traffic flow were estimates of volume, counts of density, and measurement of velocity, time headway, space headway, and vehicle acceleration. These were calculated by electronic computer using measurements of pictures obtained by the 35 mm sweep sampling air photo technique as previously described.[1] Measurements were first corrected for slant range. Then rear-to-rear distances between cars gave space headways, distance moved per second gave velocities, calculated time past a known point gave time headways, calculated number of cars passing a point gave a volume estimate, and vehicles in a known distance were counted to give density.

## Method of Analysis

Eight records were complete enough for comparisons, four during morning and four during afternoon peak traffic—about 40 min each.

Before making various calculations, frequency distributions and average values by orbit and by time of day were plotted for each section. Examples of these were published in the previous description of the technique.

Arithmetic means by lane for each section for four afternoon peak hour records and for four morning peak hour records were calculated. Differences between these means by lane for different highway sections were compared and tested statistically by Fisher's "$t$" function to determine statistical significance.

Finally, volume-density plots were made for different sections by lanes.

## IV. Results

### Volume Comparisons

Traffic volume between the different highway sections did not show statistically significant differences except that, as expected, afternoon volumes outbound were higher than inbound, and the reverse for the morning peak hour. Figure 2 shows a summary of the traffic volume relationships for the different sections for morning and afternoon peak hours.

### Velocity

In line with the well known traffic flow characteristics, average spot speeds were lower during high volume traffic. In addition, average speeds in Section 2 were lower than those in Sections 1 and 3, and slightly lower than Section 4. Sections 5 and 6 were somewhat higher. (See Fig. 3.) Velocity differences between the six sections were for the most part statistically significant during peak hour traffic when compared along the highway. Comparisons of average velocity across the highway were statistically significant for Section 5 during a.m. and Section 2 during p.m. (peak flow in each case).

The speed measurements were "time slice" measurements over a 1 sec interval between successive frames of the air photo record. The arithmetic means of these represent "spot speeds" taken in succeeding 5 sec samples. For the most part, four samples per highway section per orbit of the plane were averaged to give a section average. Together with those from succeeding orbits these gave an overall section average. These average "time-slice" velocities cannot be used to calculate travel time but should serve for comparison of section flows with validity.

If harmonic means were to be calculated for determining travel time, the low speed values would be weighted more heavily. The range of speeds should be increased thereby and, therefore, differences probably would be increased.

### Density

Density counts were made from the films by observing the number of cars within the 500 foot section used for selecting the sample. The total count for four samples (2000 ft) in a given highway section and orbit were then summed and converted to vehicles per thousand feet.

### Volume versus Density Relationships

Volume was plotted against density for Lane 2 for the different highway sections using averages by orbit. These plots exhibited the general characteristic widely described in the literature, i.e., linearly increasing volume and density to a certain point, and then a maximum volume with either no increase or a slight drop in volume as density further increased.

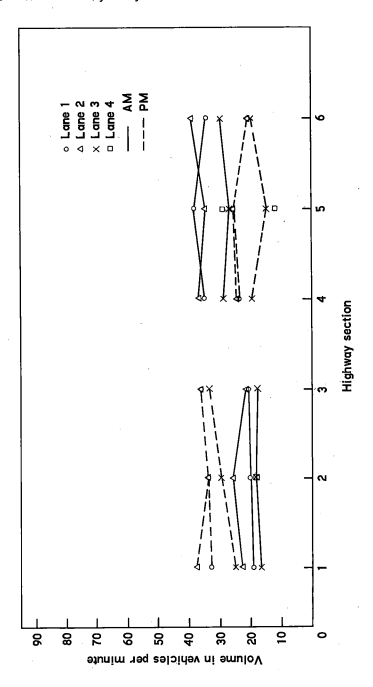

FIGURE 2.   Average volume levels by lane and section during four a.m. and four p.m. peak hours, cars passing a point in each sample totaled for a given lane, section and orbit, averaged for 14 to 16 orbits.

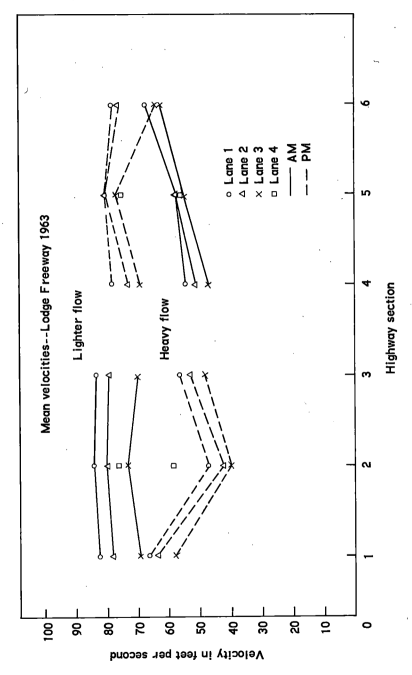

FIGURE 3. Average velocities by lane and section. "Time-slice" velocities calculated for each vehicle averaged by lane and section for 14 to 16 orbits.

The plots for Sections 2 and 4 included densities up to 16 or 17 vehicles per thousand feet, Section 3 and 5 up to 13 vehicles, and Sections 1 and 6 up to 11 vehicles per thousand feet (except for two points).

Maximum volumes reached 45 cars per minute in all, except for Sections 1 and 5 which leveled off at about 40 vehicles per minute. Figure 4 shows the plots for Sections 2 and 6.

In the plot for Section 2 there were two low-volume points suggesting a slowdown at densities of 10.5 and 13 vehicles per thousand feet. Section 4 also showed two such points at 13 vehicles per thousand feet.

Note that the plot for Section 6 did not show a definite leveling off in volume. Therefore, the results indicate a different type of volume density curve for different sections of the same highway for the first time.

## Low Velocity Cutting Points

Certain velocity and volume-density mean values showed a lower level than most of the others. A quality control technique was therefore used to test whether any points were lower than would be expected by chance. This involves calculating the standard deviation of the group of values and determining from this a cutoff point below which values would be expected only 5 times in 100. Any point below the 0.05 line was then viewed as possibly greater than expected. Total points below the line for 14 to 16 orbits ranged from 1 to 3 for all sections except Sections 2 and 4. These showed 5 and 4, respectively, in the afternoon peak. Although not inconsistent with other indices, these could not be considered statistically significant differences.

## Time and Space Headways

Time and space headways (time and distance between cars front to front or rear to rear) for each lane in the various sections were plotted by orbit and time of day (see Reference 1, Fig. 11C and 11D). Considerable variability in these was indicated. No obvious differences between sections appeared and no further analysis was possible in the time available.

## Vehicle Acceleration

Vehicle acceleration within the 5 sec interval was calculated and arithmetic means by orbit were plotted for each lane and section by time of day. Variability of acceleration values was greater under low traffic volume conditions than under heavy traffic conditions during the peak hours. Therefore, differences appeared between highway sections in opposite peak traffic, e.g., Sections 2 and 5 at p.m. peak. Although certain very large decelerations did occur, variations of velocity under lighter traffic volume were probably responsible rather than slowdowns and stoppages.

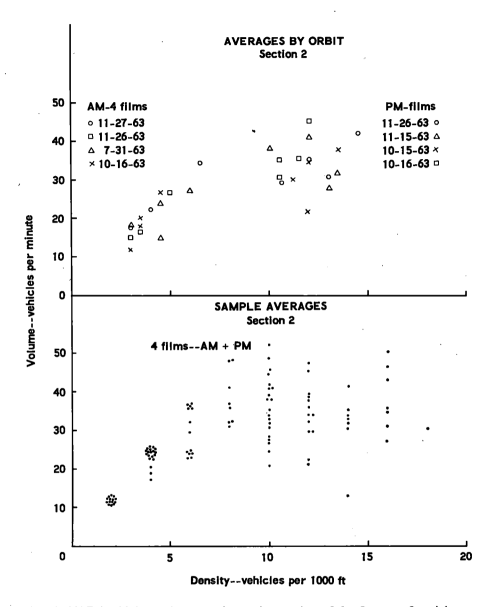

FIGURE 4.   Volume-density relationships in Lane 2 for Sections 2 and 6 for four a.m. and four p.m. peak hour records. Each point is total volume and density for the 3 or 4 samples in a given lane, section, and orbit.

## Observed Slow Downs and Stoppages

The procedure for data reduction from the film records required indication by the operator when a stoppage was observed. These stoppages were tabulated and treated separately in analysis of the records. This was necessary because the electronic computer calculation program would have become unduly complex to handle the special case of zero velocities. Also, average velocities might have been unduly reduced by a simple stoppage if these had been included.

Section 2 showed a markedly greater number of stoppages than the other sections, some of them involving more than one lane at a time. Only stoppages of the self-limiting "accordion flow type" were included. Where any evidence of a disabled vehicle was found, the stoppage was not included.

The number of weaving vehicles was observed by the operator. The number of weaves varied between lanes and sections, the largest number being shown by Section 5 in inbound morning peak traffic. A relatively high number of weaves did not necessarily go with either a high number of stoppages or lowest average speed.

## Discussion

Section 2 showed more observed stoppages, lower average velocities, and possibly more velocity values lower than the 0.05 cutoff line.

On the other hand, Section 5, at the same location but with inbound traffic with heavy flow in the morning hour, showed almost no stoppages and less slowing. Under peak conditions it nevertheless carried about as high lane volumes. More weaving vehicles were recorded here, probably because of off-ramps to the crossing Ford expressway at the downstream end of this section. Thus more weaving with few stoppages and slowdowns can actually be an index of efficient operation of the highway.

Sections 2 and 5 both have close spacing of ramps but Section 2 has two on-ramps and one off-ramp while Section 5 has one on-ramp and two off-ramps. It seems probable, therefore, that close spacing of two on-ramps has more interfering effect with traffic flow than close spacing of two off-ramps, or the spacing between on-ramp and nearest off-ramp. However, there may have been effects of other conditions differing between the two sections such as location of heavy input just upstream of Section 2.

Metering of inbound traffic in the morning occurred automatically at the Davison Interchange where right and left on-ramps enter. Section 4, just downstream from this point, has the closest on-off ramp spacing. It also showed, as a whole, the lowest average peak hour velocity of the three inbound sections. But once cars were under way, there were very few observed slowdowns. The same metering condition from right and left on-ramps occurred in the morning peak for Section 6 (just downstream from the major interchange at the Ford-Lodge connection). However, four off-ramps from this section and the open end of the freeway feed into downtown streets. Average peak hour (a.m.) speeds and volumes remained high on this section (see Fig. 4).

Metering of outbound afternoon traffic occurred from back-ups on left- and right-hand on-ramps from the Ford Expressway just upstream from Section 2. Much less distance was available for stabilization of flow before reaching Section 2 where two additional heavily used on-ramps entered. A different effect on driver behavior, therefore, is not surprising, i.e., more slowing than on Section 5.

The differing volume-density relationships on different sections are believed to be the first reported from different sections of the same highway showing such differences. Further analysis of these data was impossible in this project because of time limitations.

Such differing flow-density relations on different parts of the same highway during peak traffic are of importance for traffic flow theory, simulation, and control procedures since they indicate the effect of driver reactions to varying conditions on specific highway sections.

## References

1. T. W. Forbes, J. J. Mullin, and M. E. Simpson, Traffic Data Acquisition from Air Photos by Modified Conventional Methods, Proc. 1964 Conf. on Traffic Surveillance, Simulation and Control, U.S. Bureau of Public Roads, Washington, D.C., September 14, 1964.

## Appendix

### Derived Traffic Flow Characteristics (from Reference I)

Programs for the Michigan State University CDC 3600 Computer were prepared to derive from the corrected car positions in each frame the following traffic flow values:

1. Volume — $q$ = estimate of vehicle per min calculated by Eq. 2

2. Distance headway (in ft) — $S_h = (x_n - x_{n+1})$ where $x$ is distance of the rear of a vehicle from the zero reference

3. Velocity of each vehicle (in ft per sec) — $u = \dfrac{x_{n,f+1} - x_{n,f}}{t_{f+1} - t_f}$ where $f$ = frame number. Time between frames was 1 sec.

4. Acceleration (in ft per sec$^2$)

$$a = (u_{n_{5th\ sec}} - u_{n_{1st\ sec}})/5$$

5. Time headway (in sec)

$t_h = (t_{n+1} - t_n)$ at which vehicle $n + 1$ and vehicle $n$ passed a known reference, $r_1$.

6. Density (in vehicles per 1000 ft)

$k =$ vehicles between 500 ft reference marks, summed for 3 or 4 samples in one lane per orbit $\div \frac{3}{2}$ or 2, respectively.

Headway values are defined as distance or time between vehicles, front to front or rear to rear bumper. Distance headways were obtained directly by subtraction between vehicles in the same frame; velocities were obtained by subtraction of the location of a vehicle from one film frame to the next. Because frames were 1 sec apart, velocities were directly obtained in ft per sec.

In each case the time headway was calculated from the time one vehicle passed a given reference point until the next one passed the same point. The reference point ahead of each sample was used.

In the case of weaving vehicles the location of the vehicle from one frame to the next was more difficult to program since the position in the previous frame must be compared with that in the next frame, but in a different lane.

Volume in vehicles per min past a reference mark was estimated in each case from the number of cars passing in the 5 sec sample period. Estimates of volume for each sample were obtained by the computer program which counted the number of cars past the 500 ft reference point in each sample, and added the proportion of the next time headway remaining in the 5 sec. That is,

$$\frac{500 - x_n}{u_n} = t_n = \text{time for vehicle } n \text{ to pass the 500 ft mark,}$$

where $u_n$ is the vehicle velocity in ft/sec assumed constant.

$$\text{volume} = q(\text{est.}) = 12m = \text{vehicles/min}$$

where $m =$ number of vehicles for which $5 - t_n = 0$.

For example, in a case where $n = 3$

$$m = 3 + \frac{5 - t_3}{t_4 - t_3}$$

# A Contribution to the Statistical Analysis of Speed Distributions

J. LINDNER

Institute of Highway Engineering and Transportation
Technical University of Berlin, Berlin, Germany

In 1962 speed observations were performed on different types of roads in Berlin, and speed distributions were analysed.[1] An approximation by the normal distribution was possible only in a few cases. For the representation of the "non-normal" distribution by a function, a method was applied that permitted to approximate the distribution by an expansion series with successive derivations of the normal distribution. Besides arithmetic mean and variance, skewness and excess of the observed distributions were used as parameters.

Generally, there is the possibility to describe each distribution by a sequence of its statistics. Such suitable statistics are the cumulants $k_r$, or derived from these the $\gamma$-statistics (skewness and excess).[2] Mathematical advantages can be attained by using a function with the statistics of the observed distribution as parameters. Such a function can be represented by an expansion of basic functions in series similar to the Fourier analysis. As a suitable basic function for this expansion the normal distribution has been found.[3]

The differences of any distribution from the normal distribution as a basic function can be expanded as a series of successive derivations of the normal distribution.

The result of this expansion series is the following:[4]

For a density function $f(\lambda)$ it can be written

$$f(\lambda) = \rho(\lambda) - \frac{\gamma_1}{3!}\rho^{(3)}(\lambda) + \frac{\gamma_2}{4!}\rho^{(4)}(\lambda) - \frac{\gamma_3}{5!}\rho^{(5)}(\lambda) + \ldots$$

$f(\lambda)$ = density function that is to be approximated

$$\rho(\lambda) = \frac{1}{\sqrt{2\pi}}\,e^{-\lambda^2/2} \qquad \rho^{(i)}(\lambda) = i\text{th derivative of } \rho(\lambda)$$

$\gamma_i$ = $\gamma$-statistics, as for instance $\gamma_1$ = skewness of first order, $\gamma_2$ = excess of first order, $\gamma_3$ = skewness of second order.

There is a corresponding expansion for the distribution function $F(\lambda)$.

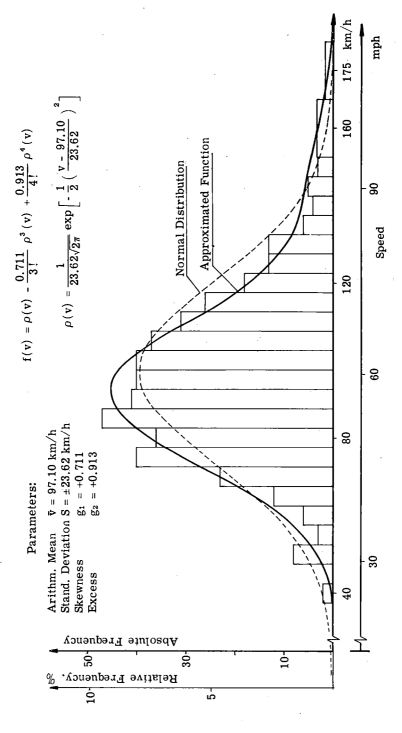

FIGURE I.  Approximation of an observed speed distribution by an expansion series.

The following relations between the derivatives of the normal distribution $\rho(\lambda)$ exist:

$$\rho^{(i)}(\lambda) = \rho(\lambda) \cdot P_i(\lambda)$$

where $P_i(\lambda)$ is a polynomial of the degree $i$ and can be found recurrently by

$$P_i(\lambda) = -\lambda P_{i-1}(\lambda) + P_{i-1}^1(\lambda)$$

$$P_{i-1}^1(\lambda) = -(i - 1) \cdot P_{i-2}(\lambda)$$

with

$$P_0(\lambda) = 1$$

Using the polynomials $P_i(\lambda)$ and the tabulated values of the normal distributions it is possible to calculate the derivatives of the normal density function $\rho^{(i)}(\lambda)$ (table in Reference 4).

Cramér indicates that the expansion series of $f(\lambda)$ converges and that for practical applications it will be sufficient to consider only those terms which include the skewness $\gamma_1$ and the excess $\gamma_2$.

Example of an Observed Speed Distribution: AVUS-Autobahn in Berlin (see Fig. 1). This observed speed distribution is significantly different from the normal distribution. On the other hand the use of the first three terms of the expansion series gives a rather good approximation to the observed speed distribution.

## References

1. J. Lindner, Master thesis at the Institute of Highway Engineering and Transportation of the Technical University of Berlin, 1962–1963.
2. M. G. Kendall, "The advanced Theory of Statistics," Vol. I and II. Charles Griffin Company Limited, London, 1951.
3. R. von Mises, "Vorlesungen aus dem Gebiete der angewandten Mathematik," Band I. Franz Deuticke, Leipzig und Wien, 1931.
4. H. Cramér, "Mathematical Methods of Statistics." Princeton University Press, 1951.
5. P. Egert, and W. Leutzbach, Geschwindigkeiten im Straßenverkehr außerhalb geschlossener Ortschaften. Forschungsbericht im Auftrage des Ministeriums für Wirtschaft und Verkehr des Landes Nordrhein-Westfalen.

# A Statistical Analysis of

# Speed-Density Hypotheses

*J. DRAKE, J. SCHOFER, and A. MAY\**

Northwestern University, Evanston, Illinois

A number of hypotheses that have been proposed to describe the relationships between basic stream characteristics are compared, using a common set of data. The ability of the various functions to predict flow parameters over the range of operating conditions is evaluated, using statistical techniques.

DURING RECENT years a number of hypotheses have been proposed to describe the relationships between basic stream flow characteristics.[1-4] To the authors' knowledge no attempt has been made to perform an objective comparison of these hypotheses using a common set of data. It was the purpose of this investigation to accomplish such a comparison using data collected on a modern freeway. The ability of the various functions to predict flow parameters over the entire range of operating conditions was evaluated using rigorous statistical techniques; where these failed, sound judgment was applied.

The tests were performed by regressing average speed *vs.* average density, since in this form all of the relations could be transformed into linear functions. The volume-density and speed-volume relationships were verified visually.

Observations were conducted on the Eisenhower Expressway in Chicago, using the Pilot Detection System of the Chicago Area Expressway Surveillance Project. During four weekday afternoons, between 1:00 and 6:00 p.m., a series of 1224 1-min observations were collected during normal traffic and weather conditions.

To avoid biasing the analysis in favor of any one hypothesis, the original observations were sampled at a uniform rate over the density scale. Thus any given value of density between 14 and 118 veh/mi had an equal probability of being in the sample. Although the fundamental relation $q = uk$ is defined

---

\* Present address: I.T.T.E., U. of California, Berkeley, California.

for space-mean speed, time-mean speed was employed in the analysis, consequent to an extensive substudy which gave considerable justification to this approximation.

To permit a meaningful comparison of the seven alternative speed-density hypotheses selected for consideration (see Fig. 1 and Table I), the analysis

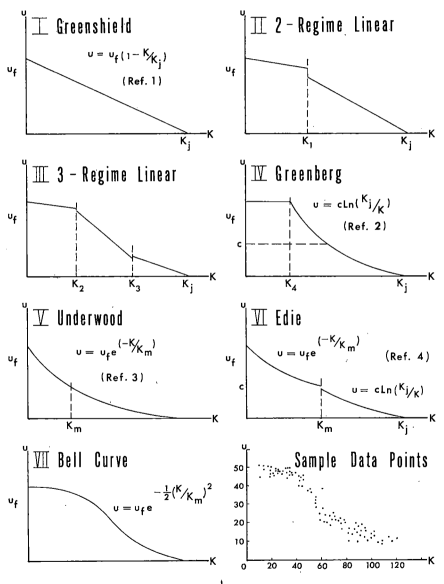

FIGURE I.  Speed-density hypotheses.

TABLE I.   Summary of Results

| Hypothesis | Equation | Coefficient of determination $r^2$ | Standard error $S_e$ | F-ratio test of significance values of "F"[a] | Slope vs. zero values of "t"[b] | $U_f$ prediction values of "t"[c] | Multi-regime vs. single | Mean free speed $U_f$ | Jam density $k_j$ | Optimum density $k_m$ | Optimum speed $c$ | Maximum flow $q_{max}$ |
|---|---|---|---|---|---|---|---|---|---|---|---|---|
| I Greenshields | $U = 58.6 - 0.468k$ | 0.896 | 4.648 | 1005 | 31.8 | 1.57 | — | 58.6 | 125 | 62.5 | 29.3 | 1830 |
| II 2-Regime Linear | $U = 60.9 - 0.515k$ $(k \leq 65)$; $U = 40 - 0.265k$ $(k \geq 65)$ | 0.685 | 4.158 | 250 | A 11.2; B 11.7 | 7.46 | ** | 60.9 | 151 | 59.2 | 30.4 | 1800 |
| III 3-Regime Linear | $U = 50 - 0.098k$ $(k \leq 40)$; $U = 81.4 - 0.913k$ $(40 \leq k \leq 65)$; $U = 40.0 - 0.265k$ $(k \geq 65)$ | 0.590 | 3.556 | 167 | A 6.9; B 35.8; C 11.7 | 22.6 | * | 50.0 | 151 | 44.6 | 40.7 | 1815 |
| IV Modified Greenberg | $U = 48.0$ $(k \leq 35)$; $U = 32.8 \ln \dfrac{145.5}{k}$ $(k \geq 35)$ | 0.866 | 3.867 | 745 | A 2.1; B 28.8 | 26.3 | * | 48.0 | 146 | 53.7 | 32.8 | 1760 |
| V Underwood | $U = 76.8 e^{-k/56.9}$ | 0.901 | 5.076 | 1050 | 32.4 | 40.4 | — | 76.8 | — | 56.9 | 28.3 | 1610 |
| VI Edie | $U = 54.9 e^{-k/163.9}$ $(k \leq 50)$; $U = 26.8 \ln \dfrac{162.5}{k}$ $(k \geq 50)$ | 0.681 | 3.550 | 245 | A 5.3; B 15.4 | 8.59 | * | 54.9 | 162 | 50.0 | 40.5 | 2025 |
| VII Bell Curve | $U = 48.6 e^{-0.0013k^2}$ | 0.884 | 4.571 | 872 | 29.5 | 21.2 | — | 48.6 | — | 62.0 | 29.5 | 1830 |

[a] Significance at 1% level requires "F" greater than 6.85.
[b] Significance at 1% level requires "t" greater than 2.36.
[c] Significance at 1% level requires "t" greater than 2.33.
** No significant difference
* Significant difference

.was structured into a series of rigorous statistical tests. While certain indicators of "goodness of fit" are customarily quoted from a regression analysis (e.g., $r^2$ or $s_e$), such measures constitute no basis for exacting binary conclusions. The series of tests described herein were formulated in strictly falsifiable terms. The general criterion guiding the entire research effort was the ability of the various functions to predict the entire range of flow characteristics, and the tests were designed to cover this range. The rejection philosophy underlying the research therefore dictated the rejection of an entire hypothesis if it failed just one of the tests.

Four hypotheses (two linear regimes, three linear regimes, modified Greenberg, and Edie) were discontinuous relationships, and required the location of the appropriate breakpoint(s) between regimes. That location selected was the data point which maximized the likelihood function of the entire sample, formed by multiplying together the frequency functions of the error variances for each regime.[5] Of course, the likelihood function varied for each hypothesis. Maximization was accomplished by elaborate successive approximation techniques.

Having established these breakpoints, the appropriate regression analyses were conducted for all seven hypotheses, and the discontinuous hypotheses were examined ($F$-test)[6] for significant differences between the proposed regimes on the assumption that strict continuity prevailed. The hypothesis of two linear regimes failed this test at the 0.025, 0.010, etc., levels of confidence, and was therefore rejected.

All hypotheses were then tested for a slope significantly different from zero. Nonlinear hypotheses were so tested in the context of the appropriate transformation to linearity. Each regime of discontinuous relationships was tested separately. The only hypothesis to exhibit a slope not significantly greater than zero was the modified Greenberg equation (low-density regime). However, this situation was forced upon the hypothesis in establishing the breakpoint, and actually gave support, rather than reason for rejection, of a mean free-speed "hat" concept.*

Each hypothesis was then subjected to an $F$-test for significance of the composite regression. Having established optimal breakpoints for discontinuous forms, statistics were developed for each discontinuous relationship by expressing appropriate formulas in terms of the dependent variables only. The values for $r^2$ and $s_e$ in Table I were computed in this fashion. All seven hypotheses exhibited significant regressions at all levels considered (see $F$-values in Table I).

The ability of each hypothesis to predict the (Lane 2) mean free speed of the facility was examined by a test for significant difference between the value

* The optimal breakpoint for the modified Greenberg form indicated that interaction between vehicles began at an average density of 35 vehicles per mile (an average spacing of 150 ft).

predicted by each regression and a value derived independently from an analysis of 16 100-vehicle samples all having average densities of less than 10 veh/lane-mile. All hypotheses except the Greenshields' relationship failed this test (see $t$-values in Table I), a result which defied the rejection structure of the research design. Ignoring the critical "$t$" values, the actual "$t$" values suggested that the Edie hypothesis and the two linear regime hypothesis were considerably less inaccurate than other hypotheses (except Greenshields' relation) on a relative basis.

Because the various hypotheses endured these tests with so little differentiation, there remained considerable latitude for judgment on more directly intuitive grounds. While the reader is encouraged toward self-interpretation, it seems appropriate to point out the more obvious deficiencies in the various hypotheses outside of the context of a strict test structure:

    1. The value of mean free speed (76.8 mi/hr) predicted by the Underwood curve was considerably high, particularly since one purpose for the formulation of this hypothesis was to improve the realism of the Greenberg relation at low densities.

    2. Previous experience with the operation of the study location and inspection of speed-volume plots of data points indicated an optimum speed in the vicinity of 40 mph. Except for the three linear regimes hypothesis and the relationship advanced by Edie, the various values for optimum speed were rather low.

    3. The jam density value (125 veh/lane-mi) predicted by the Greenshields hypothesis was very low.

Considering these observations in a "rejection" context, it became evident that the Edie form (and perhaps the three linear regimes hypothesis) warranted further attention. Three further observations were of interest in this connection:

    1. These two hypotheses yielded the highest estimates for maximum flow;**

    2. They furthermore yielded the highest (finite) estimates for jam density;

    3. Although they resulted in the two lowest values for $r^2$, they yielded the two lowest values for the standard error of estimate.

That a flow of 1815 to 2025 veh/lane-hour is possible on a three-lane urban freeway is not an unreasonable contention. Indeed, within some upper bound a high value is most appealing since this parameter estimates maximum *possible* flow. Similarly, the highest values of jam density would seem to warrant most attention, particularly since it is conceivable that a density of roughly 300 veh/lane-mi is potentially measurable (bumper-to-bumper conditions for a length of 1 mile). The nature of the composite $r^2$ statistic used

---

** It should be emphasized that the maximum flow predicted by the Edie form was not a local maximum, but rather a boundary value of the free-flow regime. The extension of this curve yielded an optimum density (of interest as a parameter only) of 164 veh/lane-mile.

was shown during the course of analysis to be somewhat conservative in cases where it was inaccurate for reasons too complex to permit elaboration in this summary.

Thus, the results tended to support these two hypotheses above all others tested. From the standpoint of logical theoretical consistency, the Edie hypothesis certainly excels in comparison to the three linear regimes alternative. From the less elegant standpoint of application, however, all hypotheses (except the two linear regimes) performed well enough to warrant continued use.

## References

1. B. D. Greenshields, A Study in Highway Capacity, *Proc. Highway Res. Board*, **14**, 468f (1935).
2. H. Greenberg, An Analysis of Traffic Flow, *Operations Res.* **7**, 79–85 (1959).
3. R. T. Underwood, Speed, Volume and Density Relationships, *Quality and Theory of Traffic flow*, Yale Bureau of Highway Traffic, 141–188 (1961).
4. L. C. Edie, Car Following and Steady-State Theory for Non-Congested Traffic, *Operations Res.* **9**, 66–76 (1961).
5. R. E. Quandt, The Estimation of the Parameters of a Linear Regression System Obeying Two Separate Regimes, *J. Am. Statistical Assoc.* **58**, 873–880 (1958).
6. R. E. Quandt, Tests of the Hypothesis that a Linear Regression System Obeys Two Separate Regimes, *J. Am. Statistical Assoc.* **55**, 324–330 (1960).

# On the Stability of Vehicular Traffic Flow—A Phenomenological Viewpoint[*]

## DAVID H. EVANS

Research Laboratories, General Motors Corporation
Warren, Michigan

The purpose of this investigation is to explain the scatter of the data points obtained when flow of vehicular traffic as a function of concentration is measured. A schematic representation of data and the curve fitted to the data is shown in the Fig. 1. Typically, such data comes from measurements of single lane flow in tunnels

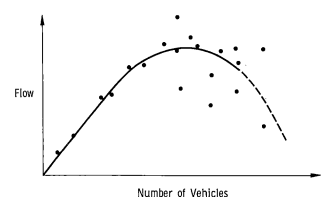

Flow

Number of Vehicles

FIGURE 1.

and multi-lane flow on freeways. The scatter of the data is small for concentrations less than the concentration at maximum flow, i.e., in the unsaturated flow regime. For higher concentrations the flow at first decreases and then breaks up, resulting in wide data scatter in this saturated flow regime. It is this scatter that this paper attempts to explain by showing the instability which exists if the flow-concentration relationship is given by a convex curve resembling the line shown in the figure. In particular the assumptions of the model are that the system under examination

* D. H. Evans, *J. Op. Res. Jap.* **8**, 134 (1966).

has an arbitrary inflow $q(t)$, given as a function of the time $t$, and if the number of cars in the system is $N(t)$ the outflow is proportional to $N(2M - N)$; thus $N$ satisfies the differential equation $dN/dt = q - \gamma N(2M - N)$, where $M$ and $\gamma$ are constants. The results of analysis are:

(1) For an initial unsaturated flow a step function change in input, which is not too large, causes the flow to transform exponentially to a new steady state unsaturated flow. If the initial flow is in the saturated regime a step function increase causes the flow to decrease and grind to a halt (the model breaks down in process); a decrease causes the flow to go from a saturated to an unsaturated flow. Similar results obtain for an infinitesimal pulse change in the input.

(2) For infinitesimal oscillatory variations in the input the flow is unstable if the mean is the maximum steady state flow; otherwise, the flow can always be stable.

(3) For finite oscillations in the inflow, the stability criterion is obtained. Generally, large stable oscillations may exist in either the saturated or unsaturated regimes; some, but not all, oscillations between the two are unstable.

# The Application of Erlang's Theory to the Calculation of Road Traffic Capacity

*TOM RALLIS*

Department for Road Construction, Traffic Engineering and
Town Planning
The Technical University of Denmark, Copenhagen, Denmark

On the basis of the theory of Telephone Traffic, and with the aid of Erlang's rejection formula, the probability of disturbances to road traffic is calculated.

The traffic load $A$ depends partly on the number of cars per unit of time $N$, and partly on the time $b$ during which each car occupies the safety distance $L$ between two cars, or the speed $v = L/b$.

To calculate the rejection probability $B$ for a road with $n$ lanes used by a traffic load $A = Nb$, it is assumed that the arrivals are in accordance with the Poisson distribution.

Theoretically, it is always easy to calculate the probability of rejection on the strength of Erlang's rejection formula, without regard to the separation (headway) time distribution and without making assumptions as to the distribution of traffic over the different lanes.

It is shown that the notions of "basic capacity" and "practical capacity" used in the 1950 edition of the *Highway Capacity Manual* are based on 40 and 22% disturbed cars (rejected from desired speed), respectively, to two lane traffic in one direction on a rural highway free from intersections.

In keeping with the results shown in the new edition of the *Highway Capacity Manual*, it is shown that four lanes with a traffic volume of 5000 vehicles per hour in one direction have the same degree of disturbance ("service degree"), 31%, as three lanes with 3340 vehicles per hour or two lanes with 1880 vehicles per hour, or one lane with 560 vehicles per hour. It is pointed out that it is difficult to apply Erlang's waiting time theory proper, but in certain cases, where the application of the rejection theory is too inaccurate, the attempt should be made to supplement with the theory of delays for systems $M/M/n$, $M/D/n$, or $D/M/n$.

The probability for delay is however always higher than the probability for rejection.

In the case of heavy traffic on roads without intersections, the rejection formula will, therefore, always understate the degree of disturbance; even so, the results are useful for purposes of comparison.

It would thus be possible, in road traffic, to compare capacity data with the aid of a common criterion, i.e., the passing rejection percentage, so that different installations can be designed on the basis of the same rejection criteria. Design work can be placed on a rational basis by comparing the improvement in the rejection percentage due to an increase in the number of lanes with the additional capital expenditure required for the new lane (Moe's principle).

# Queueing in Rural Traffic

ALAN J. MILLER

Institute of Highway and Traffic Research
University of New South Wales, Australia

## Abstract

In the first part of this paper, some applications are given of a model for queueing in rural traffic when limited overtaking is possible. The applications make use of an empirical relationship between the overtaking rate and the opposing traffic flow, and use a relationship between means and standard deviations of speed distributions.

Queueing, when overtaking is impossible, is discussed in the latter part of the paper. Vehicles are assumed to enter a length of road at random. Mean queue lengths and speeds at different distances along the road have been calculated for different flows and speed distributions.

THERE ARE many factors which influence the extent of queueing in rural traffic, including the flow (volume) of vehicles, the opposing flow on undivided roads, gradients, sight distances, speeds, traffic composition, width of carriageway and shoulders, type of driver, etc. To study the effects of these factors entirely empirically would be almost impossible because of the large number of variables involved. For instance, to infer the effect of carriageway width upon queueing and speeds, it would be necessary to compare data from a number of different sites, probably on different roads. Each road would have different flows, traffic composition, sight distances, etc., and it would be extremely easy to mistakenly attribute the effect of one factor to another.

The two basic operations of queueing are catching-up and overtaking. If we first understand the relative importance of the rates of catching-up and overtaking, by relating these rates to the factors just listed, we are in a much better position to appreciate their complex effects and interactions than if the task is treated entirely empirically.

Models for queueing when limited overtaking is possible, have been proposed,[1,2,3] and some applications of the first model will be given.

When overtaking is possible, it is possible for an equilibrium to exist between catching-up and overtaking so that average queue lengths, speeds, etc., fluctuate about some constant level. When no overtaking is possible, queues increase steadily in length. This case is considered in the latter part of this paper.

## Queueing on Two-Lane Roads when Limited Overtaking is Possible

O. K. Normann[4] showed that the rate at which vehicles desire to pass a slow vehicle is found by taking the concentration of vehicles traveling at each speed faster than the slow vehicle and multiplying by the speed difference. For instance, if we have one slow vehicle traveling at speed $u$, the concentration of vehicles is $k$, and a proportion $h(v)\,dv$ of the vehicles have speeds in the infinitesimal range $(v, v + dv)$ then, the rate at which vehicles desire to overtake the slow vehicle is

$$k \int_u^\infty (v - u)h(v)\,dv \qquad (1)$$

Normann expressed this result in the form of a sum rather than an integral.

The total desired rate of overtakings (or passings, in American usage) is then obtained by taking the concentration of slow vehicles of each speed and multiplying by the value of Eq. 1. The desired rate of overtakings is then

$$k^2 \int_0^\infty \int_u^\infty (v - u)h(v)h(u)\,dv\,du \qquad (2)$$

The usual statistic for describing differences or the spread of vehicle speeds is the standard deviation. Wardrop[5] showed that if speeds are normally distributed, the value of the double integral is $\sigma/\sqrt{\pi}$ or $0.5642\sigma$, where $\sigma$ is the standard deviation. The total desired rate of overtakings can, for practical purposes, be taken as

$$0.56\sigma k^2 \qquad (3)$$

In practice, under fairly free-flowing conditions, the standard deviation has been found to be approximately 18% of the mean speed.[6,7,8] Substituting $\sigma = 0.18\langle v \rangle$ in Eq. 3, where $\langle v \rangle$ is the mean speed, and converting to flows (volumes, in American usage), gives the total desired rate of overtakings as approximately

$$0.1q^2/\langle v \rangle \qquad (4)$$

where $q$ is the flow. If the units of distance and time are miles and hours, respectively, the total desired rate of overtakings will be in units of overtakings per hour per mile of road. The means and standard deviations are of the *space* speed-distribution.

When overtaking is limited, vehicles form into bunches and the formulae above can be applied to the bunches rather than to individual vehicles. This has the advantage that whereas differences in speed between consecutive vehicles fall off fairly rapidly as bunch sizes increase, speed differences between consecutive bunches can be expected to change much more slowly.

A bunch is defined as one or more vehicles traveling together at about the same speed, but including in the bunch any overtaking vehicles which have caught up the last vehicle but not completed overtaking the slow vehicle heading the bunch. The practical problem of discriminating between bunches has been considered by Underwood,[9] Buckley,[10] Daou,[11] and Miller.[12]

Miller[1] proposed a model in which overtakings occurred at an average rate $\lambda$ per unit time from bunches containing more than one vehicle. One overtaking consisted of one or more vehicles overtaking from a bunch and themselves traveling together as a bunch afterwards. If, though, three vehicles overtook a slow vehicle in rapid succession, but the second of the three was the slowest so that the first vehicle left the other two behind, then two overtakings were considered to have occurred.

In this model, queue lengths were expressed in terms of the parameter

$$z = 0.56\sigma k/\lambda(1 - x) \tag{5}$$

or

$$z = 0.1q/\lambda(1 - x) \tag{6}$$

if the assumption that the standard deviation of bunch speeds equals 18 % of the mean speed, is used. $k$ and $q$ are the concentration and flow of vehicles, respectively. $x$ is the proportion of the road "occupied" by vehicles. If $\langle d \rangle$ is the average distance between consecutive vehicles within bunches (measured between corresponding parts of the vehicles), then $x$ is defined as $k\langle d \rangle$.

Queue lengths were found from large samples of data from England and Sweden to have distributions very closely approximated by the Borel-Tanner distributions. Figure 1 shows the relationship which was deduced between mean queue lengths and the parameter $z$. For $z > 1$, the relationship is almost linear and the mean queue length $\langle r \rangle$ is given approximately by

$$\langle r \rangle = (1 + ze)/(e - 1)$$
$$= 0.58 + 1.58z \tag{7}$$

Overtaking rates were estimated and related to the opposing flow for a straight two-lane rural road in Sweden. Using the method of least squares, the regression formula below was obtained. $Q$ is the opposing flow in vph.

$$\lambda = 2750Q^{-0.62} \text{ overtakings per hour} \tag{8}$$

This crude model showed the relative importance of the quantity of traffic and the ease of overtaking. For light traffic, average bunch sizes increase approximately linearly with the flow in the direction considered. As the road becomes more crowded, that is, as $x$ approaches 100%, average bunch sizes increase very much more rapidly until there is just one bunch stretching the entire length of the road. If there are large differences in speed due to, say, a high proportion of commercial vehicles, bunches will be larger, whereas a strictly enforced upper limit on speeds may result in a low standard deviation and, hence, relatively short bunches. If the model is anywhere near realistic,

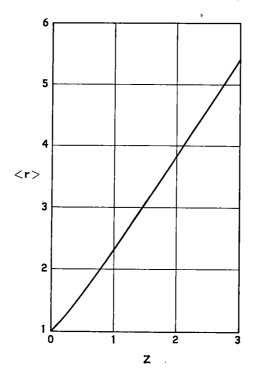

FIGURE I.   Mean bunch size $\langle r \rangle$ against $Z$.

average bunch sizes can be expected to decrease inversely as the overtaking rate. If the results of the analysis of the Swedish data are applicable on other roads in other countries, average bunch sizes can be expected to increase a little more rapidly than the square root of the opposing flow (i.e., as $Q^{0.62}$). That is, the opposing traffic has proportionately less effect than the flow in the direction considered. A similar result was found by Normann[13] by finding the regression of average speed upon the flows in the two directions.

The quantity $x$ has been defined as the proportion of the length of road occupied by vehicles at any time. Each vehicle is considered to occupy a length of road equal to its own length plus the distance the driver chooses to leave between himself and the rear of a vehicle ahead when he is following in a bunch. Each vehicle is assumed to occupy this length of road whether or not it is actually within a bunch when observed. At a random time, the probability that a particular point on a road is occupied is then $x$. Hence at any point, $x$ is the proportion of time during which vehicles are passing the point. That is, $x$ is the proportion of the time during which there is saturation flow at any point or, in Webster's terminology[14], $x$ is the degree of saturation at any point.

### Some Applications of the Model

Using the formula for the average overtaking rate derived from the Swedish data, mean bunch sizes have been calculated for a range of flows in the direction considered, and for opposing flows of 100, 300, and 600 vph. An average headway of 2.4 sec between vehicles within bunches has been used in calculating the values of $x$. Fortunately, for the range of speeds in which we are likely to be interested, the average separation in time changes very slowly though the separation in distance increases rapidly with speed. The calculated mean bunch sizes are shown in Fig. 2.

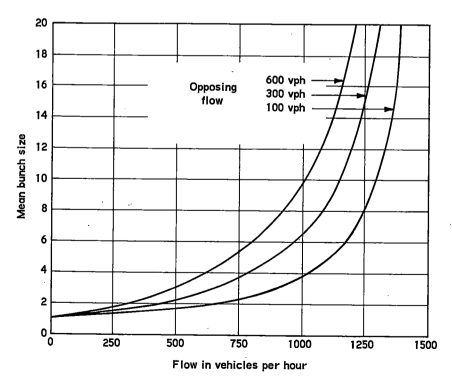

FIGURE 2.   Mean bunch size *vs*. flow is for three opposing flows and unrestricted sight distances.

If a desirable limit to the average bunch size is arbitrarily chosen as, say, three, then this limit is reached for flows of about 900, 650, and 500 vph in the direction considered, when the opposing flows are 100, 300, and 600 vph, respectively. Notice that the total flows are all in the neighborhood of 1000 vph. If bunch sizes have Borel-Tanner[15] distributions, when the mean bunch

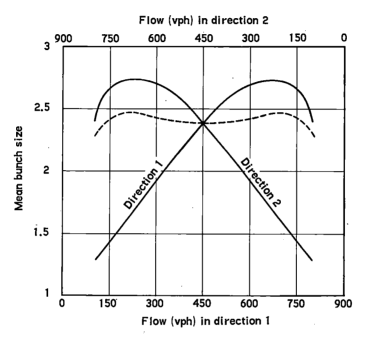

FIGURE 3.   Mean bunch sizes on a two-lane rural road with unrestricted overtaking sight distances when the sum of the flows in both directions is 900 vph. The broken line is the mean for both directions, weighted in proportion to the flows.

size is three vehicles, 10% of the bunches will be of 7 or more vehicles, 5% will be of 11 or more vehicles and 1% will be of 22 or more vehicles.

The U.S. Highway Capacity Manual[16] quotes practical capacities of two-lane rural roads which are independent of the distribution of the traffic between the two directions. To see whether this is realistic, a total two-direction flow of 900 vph was taken and divided between the two directions in varying proportions. Again, the overtaking rate, Eq. 8, was used and 2·4 sec average headways within bunches. Figure 3 shows the results.

The interesting feature of Fig. 3 is that there is a proportional split between the two directions at which the mean bunch size for *one* direction reaches a maximum. In direction 1 the mean bunch size decreases when the flow is increased $\frac{1}{7}$, from 700 to 800 vph, because at the same time the opposing

traffic flow is halved from 200 to 100 vph, and the much greater ease in overtaking more than compensates for the increase in catching-up rate. The
weighted average of the mean bunch sizes remains roughly constant up to a
5:1 split between the two directions. This gives some justification to the
assumption in the *Highway Capacity Manual* that directional split is im-
material.

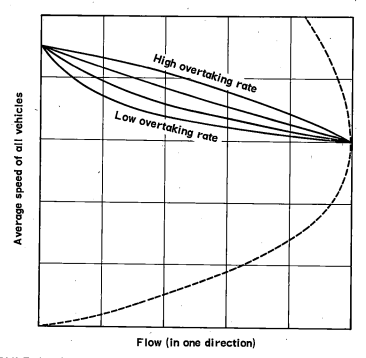

F low (in one direction)

FIGURE 4. Average speed against flow for four different overtaking
rates. Broken line represents a speed-flow relationship between
vehicles within bunches.

It is interesting to note that in O. K. Normann's[12] early work he looked at
the separate flows in each direction and obtained the linear regression formula

$$\langle v_1 \rangle = 44.92 - 0.01044 q_1 - 0.00719 q_2, \tag{9}$$

where $\langle v_1 \rangle$ is the average speed in direction 1 and $q_1, q_2$ are the flows in directions 1 and 2, respectively. If the total flow $Q = q_1 + q_2$ is kept constant, the
weighted average speed for all vehicles is a parabolic function of $q_1$ (or $q_2$)
with a maximum at $q_1 = q_2 = \frac{1}{2}Q$.

No mention has so far been made of the relationship between average
speeds, and flows and overtaking rates. This is because it appears necessary

to use much more complex models[15,2,3] than the one used in this paper. One of the difficulties is that the overtaking rate is a function of speed, and results obtained for, say, the distribution of bunch speeds, depend critically upon the function of speed used for the overtaking rate. There is more discussion on this subject later.

As an approximation we could assume that for any road there is one distribution for the speeds of vehicles leading bunches (including bunches of only one vehicle), and one speed distribution for vehicles within bunches. The average speed of all vehicles is then linearly related to the proportion of vehicles leading bunches. This proportion is simply the reciprocal of the mean bunch size as there is one leader per bunch and an average or $\langle r \rangle$ vehicles per bunch. Figure 4 shows the family of curves obtained for speed against flow if these assumptions are used. To calculate these curves it was assumed that the standard deviation of bunch speeds was 18% of the mean speed of all vehicles. Each curve represents a different overtaking rate.

### Queueing Behind Individual Slow Vehicles on Two-Lane Roads

Let us consider one vehicle traveling at speed $u$, which is sufficiently slow for it to rarely catch up other vehicles. The rate at which it is caught up by faster vehicles is given by Eq. 1. The slower the vehicle, the greater the rate at which it is caught up by other vehicles. On the other hand, the slower the vehicle, the easier it is to overtake—at least, when sight distances do not restrict overtaking.

The time taken to complete the overtaking of one vehicle, starting at the speed of that vehicle, increases with speed and appears to be about 0.25 sec for every 1 mph of speed of the overtaken vehicle under ideal test track conditions. This number has been obtained from miscellaneous tests of new cars over the speed range 30–60 mph reported in journals for motorists. In practice, overtaking maneuvers probably take appreciably longer. Let us assume that the average time required to overtake is related linearly to the speed of the overtaken vehicle.

Let $q_1$ be the flow of vehicles in the direction of the slow vehicle considered, and let $q_2$ be the flow in the opposite direction. The flow of traffic in the opposite direction relative to the vehicle traveling at speed $u$ is then $q_2(1 + u/\langle v_2 \rangle)$, where $\langle v_2 \rangle$ is the space-mean speed of vehicles traveling in the opposite direction. Adams[17] showed that the average waiting time for a gap of $\tau$ seconds in a random flow of $Q$ vph is

$$W = \frac{1}{Q}(e^{Q\tau} - Q\tau - 1) \tag{10}$$

$$\approx \tfrac{1}{2}Q\tau^2 \quad \text{provided } Q \ll 1 \tag{11}$$

Substituting $Q = q_2(1 + u/\langle v_2 \rangle)$ and $\tau = au$ where $a$ is an unknown constant, the average waiting time for the first vehicle waiting to overtake the "$u$-vehicle" is approximately

$$\tfrac{1}{2}q_2(1 + u/\langle v_2 \rangle)a^2 u^2 \tag{12}$$

If we further assume that the waiting times of consecutive vehicles overtaking the "$u$-vehicle" are independent, then the ratio of catching-up rate to overtaking rate is the product of Eq. 1 and 12.

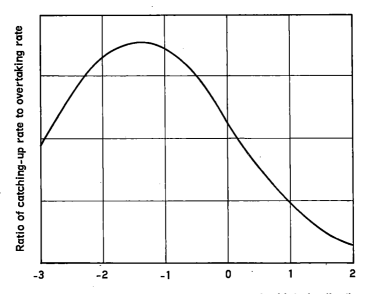

Speed, in standard deviations from the mean, of vehicle leading bunch

FIGURE 5.   Ratios of catching-up rate to overtaking rate against bunch speed, on roads with unrestricted sight distances. The approximate form of Adam's formula has been used. The vertical scale depends upon the flows.

The speed at which the ratio of catching-up rate to overtaking rate is a maximum is then found by solving

$$\frac{d}{du}\left\{ u^2\left(1 + \frac{u}{\langle v_2 \rangle}\right) \int_u^\infty h(v)(v - u)\, dv \right\} = 0 \tag{13}$$

or

$$\frac{\displaystyle\int_u^\infty h(v)v\, dv}{\displaystyle\int_u^\infty h(v)\, dv} = u\,\frac{3 + 4(u/\langle v_2 \rangle)}{2 + 3(u/\langle v_2 \rangle)} \tag{14}$$

The left-hand side is the average speed of all vehicles with speed greater than $u$. If the average speed of vehicles is the same in both directions and this average speed, call it $\langle v \rangle$, is substituted for the left-hand side of Eq. 14 and for $\langle v_2 \rangle$ in the right-hand side, then the simple solution

$$u = \langle v \rangle / \sqrt{2} \tag{15}$$

is obtained for Eq. 14. Equation 14 has been solved numerically for a normal distribution of speeds with a standard deviation equal to 18% of the mean speed, and in this case the solution is

$$u = 0.725 \langle v \rangle \tag{16}$$

This suggests that the longest queues can be expected to form behind vehicles traveling at about 70–75% of the average speed and that shorter queues can be expected behind both faster and slower vehicles. This result only applies when sight distances do not restrict overtaking. Figure 5 shows the ratio of catching-up to overtaking rates plotted against the speed of the overtaken vehicle.

## Queueing when Overtaking is Impossible

The simple model used in the early part of this paper is suitable for describing the macroscopic behavior of traffic over lengths of rural road with fairly uniform conditions. It is not satisfactory, though, for roads with few or no overtaking opportunities. When no overtaking is possible, there is no equilibrium for queue lengths which increase steadily as the length of the section on which overtaking is impossible increases. The distance from the last point where overtaking was possible is then an essential parameter. It seems barely necessary to mention this. Yet empirical studies of bunching in such circumstances which have been reported have usually not given the position of this observation point with respect to the last overtaking place.

Let us find the distribution of bunch sizes and speeds at the end of a length of road $X$ on which no overtaking is possible. Let us assume that vehicles enter the length of road at random, except that there is a minimum distance $\langle d \rangle$ between any two vehicles measured between corresponding points on the two vehicles. This distance is, as before, the average distance between consecutive vehicles within bunches. Since it is the distances strictly between vehicles which are important in catching up, let us, to simplify the mathematics, subtract the distance $\langle d \rangle$ from the distance between each pair of vehicles (i.e., between corresponding points) and consider two vehicles as being in a bunch when they occupy, simultaneously, the same point on the road. If vehicles enter the length of road a distance $\langle d \rangle$ closer together but with speeds unaltered, the flow is scaled up. If $q$ is the flow of vehicles in the simulated case, then $q' = q/(1 - x)$ is the flow in the model when there are no distances between vehicles in bunches. $x$ has the same meaning as previously.

Let $h_t(v)$ be the probability density function of the journey speeds $v$ of vehicles over the length $X$ if the vehicles do not catch-up slower vehicles. The suffix $t$ is used to denote that it is the distribution for all those vehicles passing a fixed point over a period of time. All speeds referred to are journey speeds over the length $X$.

The probability that a bunch of exactly $n$ vehicles with the speed of the leader in the infinitesimally small range $(u, u + du)$ reaches the end of the length $X$ during the infinitesimally small time period $(t, t + dt)$ is then the product of three terms $A$, $B$, and $C$ where

$A(u) \, du \, dt$ = the probability that a vehicle with the necessary journey speed entered the length of road between the times $(t - X/u)$ and $(t + dt - X/u)$,

$B(u)$ = the probability that no slower vehicle which the $u$-vehicle" could catch up, entered the length of road shortly before the "$u$-vehicle", and

$C(n, u)$ = the probability that the next $(n - 1)$ vehicles to enter the length of road after the "$u$-vehicle" were all traveling sufficiently fast to catch it up within the distance $X$.

The value of the first term is, by definition

$$A(u) \, du \, dt = q' h_t(u) \, du \, dt \tag{17}$$

A vehicle with speed between $v$ and $(v + dv)$, where $v$ is less than $u$, would have had to have entered the length of road between $(t - X/v)$ and $(t - X/u)$ for the "$u$-vehicle" to catch it up. The probability of this is

$$q' h_t(v) \left[ \left( t - \frac{X}{u} \right) - \left( t - \frac{X}{v} \right) \right] dv \tag{18}$$

The probability that no slower vehicle which the "$u$-vehicle" could catch up, entered the length of road ahead of the "$u$-vehicle" is then

$$B(u) = \exp \left\{ -q' X \int_0^u \left( \frac{1}{v} - \frac{1}{u} \right) h_t(v) \, dv \right\} \tag{19}$$

Converting to concentrations $k' = k/(1 - x)$ and space-speed distributions gives

$$B(u) = \exp \left\{ -\frac{k' X}{u} \int_0^u (u - v) h_s(v) \, dv \right\} \tag{20}$$

[Note: Here $k$ is the concentration obtained by using the *desired* journey speeds rather than the actual speeds.]

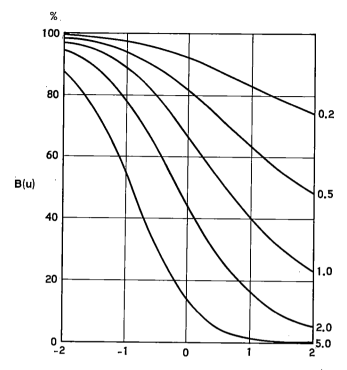

Speed of vehicle in standard deviations away from the mean

FIGURE 6. Probability of a vehicle of given speed not catching up a slower vehicle. Values of $k'X\sigma/\langle v\rangle$ for each curve are given at the right-hand side.

This form has been preferred to Eq. 19 as it contains a similar integral to Eq. 1.

Figure 6 shows the probability $B(u)$ that a vehicle with an undelayed journey speed $u$ reaches the end of the length $X$ without catching up a slower vehicle. The curves are for a range of values of the quantity $k'X\sigma/\langle v\rangle$ or $0.18k'X$ if we again take the standard deviation equal to 18% of the mean speed. Notice that $kX$ is the average number of vehicles which would be on the length of road $X$ if there were free overtaking, and $k'X$ is equal to $kX/(1-x)$. A gamma distribution with a coefficient of variation of 18% was used for the journey speed distribution.

The calculation of the term $C$ is complicated, While the "$u$-vehicle" is traveling the length $X$, another slow vehicle may enter the length of road and hold back vehicles which might otherwise have caught up the "$u$-vehicle". In Fig. 7, vehicle 3 would have caught up the "$u$-vehicle" if vehicle 2 had not been between them.

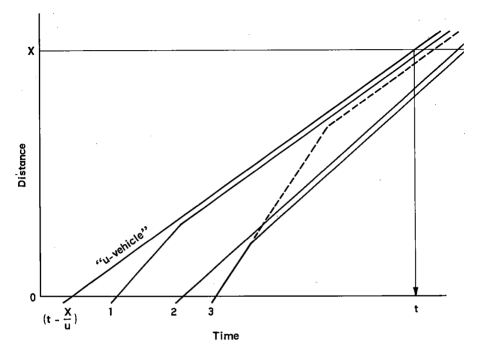

**FIGURE 7.** A distance-time diagram to illustrate a point in the text.

The probability that there is a "vehicle 2" in the infinitesimally small time interval

$$\left( t - \frac{X}{u} + s, \, t - \frac{X}{u} + s + ds \right)$$

and that it is the first vehicle which cannot catch-up the "$u$-vehicle" in the length $X$, is

$$g(s, u) \, ds = q' \int_0^{u'} h_t(v) \, dv \exp\left\{ -q' \int_0^s \int_0^{u''} h_t(v) \, dv \, ds' \right\} ds \tag{21}$$

$u'$ is the speed at which "vehicle 2" just fails to catch-up the "$u$-vehicle" in the length $X$, and similarly for $u$ and $v$. That is,

$$u' = X \Big/ \left( \frac{X}{u} - s \right) = u \Big/ \left( 1 - \frac{su}{X} \right) \tag{22}$$

The exponential term in Eq. 21 is the probability that no other vehicle with any speed $v$ which could not catch-up the "$u$-vehicle" entered the length of road at any time $[(t - (X/u) + s')]$ where $s' < s$. Hence from Eq. 21 the probability that there is no "vehicle 2" is

$$G(u) = \exp\left\{-q'\int_0^{X/u}\int_0^{u'} h_t(v)\, dv\, ds'\right\}$$  (23)

The probability that $(n - 1)$ vehicles catch up the "'$u$-vehicle" is then the Poisson probability that $(n - 1)$ vehicles with sufficient speed entered the road within a time $X/u$ or $s$, whichever is shorter, after the "$u$-vehicle". Hence

$$C(n, u) = G(u)\frac{m^{n-1}}{(n-1)!}\, e^{-m}$$

$$+ \int_0^{X/u} \frac{[m(s)]^{n-1}}{(n-1)!}\, e^{-m(s)} g(s, u)\, ds$$  (24)

where  $$m = \frac{k'X}{u}\int_u^\infty (v - u)h_s(v)\, dv$$  (25)

and  $$m(s) = \frac{k'X}{u}\int_u^{u'} (v - u)h_s(v)\, dv + q's\int_{u'}^\infty h_t(v)\, dv$$  (26)

The desired probability, call it $p_n(u)\, du\, dt$, that a bunch of vehicles with speed in the range $(u, u + du)$ reaches the end of the length $X$ between times $t$ and $t + dt$ is then given by the product of Eqs. 17, 20, and 24.

## Some Numerical Results

Values of the mean bunch size $\langle r\rangle$ and the drop in mean speed have been computed for a range of values of $y = k'X\sigma/\langle v\rangle$ and for three speed distributions. These distributions were gamma distributions with coefficients of variation of $12\frac{1}{2}\%$, $18\%$, and $25\%$ for the time-speeds.

Figure 8 shows $\langle r\rangle$ plotted against $y$ for the "middle" distribution, i.e., the one with $18\%$ coefficient of variation. Except for high values of $y$, the curves were indistinguishable. For $y = 5$, the values of $\langle r\rangle$ were found to be 4.10, 4.31, and 4.60 for the coefficients of variation of $12\frac{1}{2}\%$, $18\%$, and $25\%$. As can be seen, the relationship is nearly linear.

Figure 9 shows the number of standard deviations drop in speed plotted against the reciprocal of the mean bunch size. This relationship is also nearly linear. Again, only the "middle" curve is shown. For $y = 5$, the drops in mean speed were 1.37, 1.38, and 1.38 standard deviations.

Over the range of values plotted, good numerical approximations are given by

$$\langle r\rangle = 1 + 0.65y$$  (27)

$$\langle u\rangle = \langle v\rangle - 1.15\sigma y/(1 + 0.65y)$$  (28)

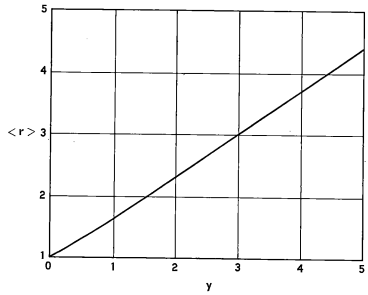

FIGURE 8.   Mean bunch size $\langle r \rangle$ at different points along a road plotted against $y = k'X\sigma/\langle v \rangle$, when overtaking is impossible.

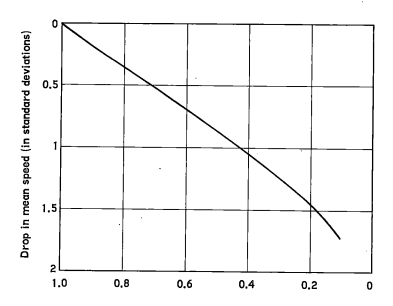

FIGURE 9.   Drop in speed in standard deviations of the free-speed distribution plotted against the reciprocal of mean bunch size, when overtaking is impossible.

## Acknowledgments

I gratefully acknowledge my thanks to the organizing committee for this symposium, the Australian Road Research Board, and the University of New South Wales for making it possible for me to attend the symposium and present this paper.

## References

1. A. J. Miller, Analysis of Bunching in Rural Two-Lane Traffic, *Operations Res.*, **11**, 236 (1963).
2. I. Prigogine, and F. C. Andrews, A Boltzmann-like Approach for Traffic Flow, *Operations Res.* **8**, 789 (1960).
3. A. J. Miller, Road Traffic Flow Considered as a Stochastic Process, *Proc. Camb. Phil. Soc.*, **58**, 312 (1962)
4. O. K. Normann, Results of Highway Capacity Studies, *Public Roads*, **23**, 57 (June 1942).
5. J. G. Wardrop, Some Theoretical Aspects of Road Traffic Research, *Proc. Instn. Civ. Engnrs.*, **2**, 325–362 (1952).
6. J. Almond, Speed Measurements at Rural Census Points, *Traffic Engng. & Control*, **5**, 290 (1963).
7. H. M. Taylor, Analysis of Some Rural Speed Data, in *Res. Bull.* 1963, Dept. of Transportation, Birmingham Univ.
8. R. B. Potts, R. W. Rothery, and R. Herman, Behaviour of Traffic Leaving a Signallized Intersection, *Traffic Engng. & Control*, **5**, 529 (1964).
9. R. T. Underwood, Traffic Flow and Bunching, *J. Australian Rd. Res.*, **1** (6), 8 (1963).
10. D. J. Buckley, Road Traffic Headway Distributions, *Proc. Australian Rd. Res. Bd.*, **1** (1), 153 (1962).
11. A. Daou, On flow within platoons, Unpublished res. report, Port of New York Authority, 1964.
12. A. J. Miller, A queueing Model for Road Traffic Flow, *J. Roy. Statist. Soc.*, Series B, **23**, 64 (1961).
13. O. K. Normann, Preliminary Results of Highway Capacity Studies, *Public Roads*, **19**, 225 (Feb. 1939).
14. F. V. Webster, Traffic Signal Settings, *Rd. Res. Tech. Paper 39*, H.M.S.O., London, 1958.
15. J. C. Tanner, Delays on a Two-Lane Road, *J. Roy. Statist. Soc.*, Series B, **23**, 38 (1961).
16. Highway Capacity Manual. Bureau of Public Roads, Washington, 1950.
17. W. F. Adams, Traffic Considered as a Random Series, *J. Instn. Civ. Engnrs.*, **4**, 121 (1936).

# A Model for Overtaking on a Two-Lane Road with Limited Visibility*

*JAN GUSTAVSSON†*

Division of Mathematical Statistics
Royal Institute of Technology, Stockholm, Sweden

## Abstract

A vehicle which travels on a two-lane road is able to overtake a slower one only if the traffic in the opposite direction is sparse enough, and if the sight conditions are good enough, to allow the driver to decide if that is the case. The paper deals with the distribution of the distance a vehicle has to travel behind a slower one until an overtaking becomes possible when the other traffic is of a simple kind and the sight varies in a special way along the road. A numerical example of the average speed and some empirical results about the sight on actual roads are given.

## Introduction

THE TRAFFIC on a two-lane road is characterized by the traffic in one direction of the road being influenced by the traffic in the opposite direction. In order that a vehicle shall be able to overtake a slower one, it has to travel a certain distance in the other lane. An overtaking, therefore, can be undertaken only if the traffic in the opposite direction is sparse enough to make it possible for the overtaking vehicle to travel the required distance in the other lane. Further the structure of the road influences the traffic. The occurrence of, for example, bends and hills reduces the visibility and can thereby make an overtaking impossible. If the traffic is dense also, the other vehicles in the same direction

* This work was supported by the Official Swedish Council on Road Safety Research.
† Present address: Institute of Mathematical Statistics, University of Stockholm, Stockholm, Sweden.

have an effect upon the possibilities to overtake. And if there are intersections on the road, turning maneuvers as well as vehicles entering or leaving the road influence the structure of the traffic.

This paper deals with how a vehicle traveling along a two-lane road is influenced by the simplified and idealized type of traffic supposed to frequent the road in question. The other traffic in the direction of the vehicle under consideration is supposed to consist of a stream of vehicles all of which are traveling at a constant speed $v_1$, and where the distances between consecutive such vehicles are independent random variables, identically distributed with the distribution function

$$F_1(x) = \begin{cases} 1 - e^{-\lambda_1 x} & \text{if} \quad x \geq 0 \\ 0 & \text{if} \quad x < 0. \end{cases}$$

Also, the traffic in the opposite direction consists of a stream of the same kind, that is, the distances between consecutive vehicles are independent and identically distributed with the distribution function

$$F_2(x) = \begin{cases} 1 - e^{-\lambda_2 x} & \text{if} \quad x \geq 0 \\ 0 & \text{if} \quad x < 0, \end{cases}$$

and all the vehicles are traveling at a constant speed $v_2$. The vehicle we consider is supposed to travel at the speed $V$, greater than $v_1$, as far as it is not prevented from overtaking a slower vehicle. Furthermore, we shall assume that the free sightdistances along the road in the direction of the faster vehicle vary in a special way. To make an overtaking possible we shall require that on one hand there is a large enough distance to the nearest oncoming vehicle, and on the other hand that also the sight distance is large enough. Consequently, an overtaking can become impossible either because of too short a sight distance or too short a distance to the nearest oncoming vehicle, or for both reasons. When the faster vehicle catches up a slower one it overtakes it at once, if the oncoming traffic and the sight conditions allow. Otherwise, it reduces its speed instantaneously to $v_1$ and travels with that speed a certain waiting distance behind the slower vehicle until an overtaking becomes possible, and then increases its speed instantaneously to $V$. The vehicles forming the traffic streams described above are supposed not to be able to leave the road, and no other to enter it. The length of all vehicles is further assumed to be zero.

Tanner[3] has studied the average speed of a faster vehicle which travels along a two-lane road, where the other traffic consists of two streams of the kind described above, but where only the oncoming stream determines if it is possible to overtake or not. Tanner,[4] as well as Yeo,[5] has also studied the average speed of the faster vehicle when the single vehicles in the two streams are substituted by queues of vehicles, and where there has to be a greater gap to overtake a queue with many vehicles than one with a few.

## The Sight Function

In the present model we shall study the distribution of the waiting distance the faster vehicle has to travel behind a slower one until an overtaking becomes possible when a new factor is introduced, by taking explicitly into regard the sight conditions.

Along the road there are supposed to be hilltops and bends which conceal the sight. Suppose that a vehicle travels up a steep hill. The driver will then, on the whole, not be able to see beyond the top of the hill until it is passed. The driver's free sight distance will then decrease linearly while the vehicle

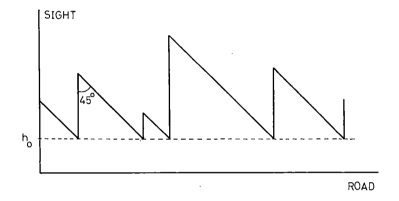

FIGURE I.   The variation of the sight distances along the road, according to the model.

approaches the top of the hill. When the top is reached, the sight may at once increase. The situation remains the same if the vehicle, instead, was approaching a sharp bend with hidden sight. We shall here assume that on the road there is a certain minimum sight distance. The sight above this is assumed to decrease linearly up to the minimum as the vehicle travels up to the top of a hill or up to a bend. It is then assumed to increase with a jump and to decrease linearly again to the minimum as the vehicle travels up to the next hilltop or bend. The sight distances are, hence, supposed to vary along the road as in Fig. 1, where $h_0$ is the minimum sight.

Further, the distances between the jumps are supposed to be independent random variables, identically distributed with the distribution function

$$W(x) = \begin{cases} 1 - e^{-wx} & \text{if } x \geq 0 \\ 0 & \text{if } x < 0. \end{cases}$$

In practice, the sight function is more rounded off. In Fig. 2 is shown a part of a diagram on the sight distances along an actual road. To make an overtaking possible we shall require that the distance to the nearest oncoming vehicle exceeds a certain constant $g$, which depends on the speeds $v_1$, $v_2$, and $V$, and also that the driver of the faster vehicle can see far enough along the road to decide if there is such a distance free from oncoming vehicles. More precisely, we shall require that the sight above the minimum sight exceeds a

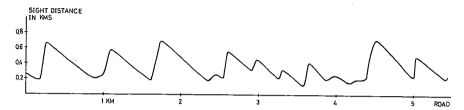

FIGURE 2.   The variation of the sight distances along a section of an actual road.

constant $h$. The two traffic streams in the opposite directions are supposed to be independent of each other and of the sight function described above. The course can be illustrated in a time-road diagram as in Fig. 3, where the thick broken line represents the faster vehicle. An overtaking is impossible in a distance $h$ before every point where the sight function has a jump, and in a distance $g$ before every oncoming vehicle, that is, in every shadowed area in the diagram.

## The Waiting Distance at an Overtaking with Regard to the Sight Distance and the Oncoming Traffic

Let us consider the following situation. The faster vehicle is assumed just to have caught up a vehicle in the slower stream. The distances between consecutive oncoming vehicles, as also the distance up to the first oncoming one, are all independent and identically distributed with the distribution function $F_2(x)$. The sight distance, above the minimum sight, is independent of and has the same distribution function $W(x)$ as the following distances between the jumps in the sight function. The streams of slower and oncoming vehicles are independent of each other and of the sight function.

When we, in the following, are dealing with sight distances we mean, unless the contrary is stated, sight above the minimum sight.

Let $T$ denote the waiting distance the faster vehicle has to travel behind the slower one until an overtaking becomes possible. Let, further, $T_{ij}$, $i, j = 1, 2$ denote the waiting distances for the four possible combinations of large

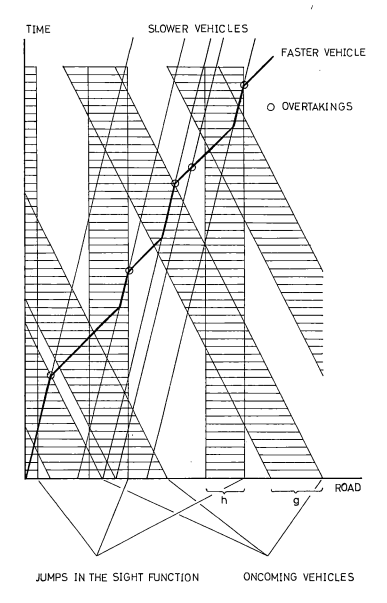

FIGURE 3.  A time-road diagram on the movements of the different vehicles.

enough sight or not, and large enough distance gap, to the nearest oncoming vehicle, or not. That is,

$$
\begin{aligned}
T &= T_{11} & &\text{if the sight} \le h \text{ and the gap} \le g \\
&= T_{12} & &\text{if the sight} \le h \text{ and the gap} > g \\
&= T_{21} & &\text{if the sight} > h \text{ and the gap} \le g \\
&= T_{22} & &\text{if the sight} > h \text{ and the gap} > g
\end{aligned}
$$

The case $T = T_{ij}$ will, in the following, be denoted by the case $(ij)$, $i, j = 1, 2$.

Let further $T$ have the distribution function $G(x)$ with the Laplace Stieltjes transform

$$
\gamma(s) = \int_0^\infty e^{-sx}\, dG(x)
$$

and the variables $T_{ij}$ have the distribution functions $G_{ij}$ with the transforms $\gamma_{ij}$.

From the assumptions about distributions and independence we get the following relation

$$
\begin{aligned}
G(x) = {}&W(h)F_2(g)G_{11}(x) + W(h)[1 - F_2(g)]G_{12}(x) \\
&+ [1 - W(h)]F_2(g)G_{21}(x) + [1 - W(h)][1 - F_2(g)]G_{22}(x)
\end{aligned} \tag{1}
$$

and by forming the Laplace Stieltjes transform of Eq. 1 we get the corresponding relation for the transforms.

As we shall indicate below the distributions of the variables $T_{ij}$ can be expressed by the aid of the distribution of $T$ by a decomposition of these variables into independent components. This, together with the above, gives a relation from which $\gamma(s)$ can be determined.

Introduce the following notations:

$X =$ the sight distance
$c = v_1/(v_1 + v_2)$
$Y =$ the traveling distance, at the speed $v_1$, up to the nearest oncoming vehicle $= c$ (the distance to the nearest oncoming vehicle)
$X_1 =$ the sight distance above $h = X - h$ if $X > h$
$m = \min(h, cg)$

*The case* (11)

In this case neither the sight nor the distance to the first oncoming vehicle is large enough to permit an overtaking.

$X$ has the distribution function $\dfrac{W(x)}{W(h)} = \begin{cases} 0 & \text{if } x < 0 \\ \dfrac{1 - e^{-wx}}{1 - e^{-wh}} & \text{if } 0 \le x < h \\ 1 & \text{if } h < x \end{cases}$

$Y$ has the distribution function $\dfrac{F_2\left(\dfrac{x}{c}\right)}{F_2(g)} = \begin{cases} 0 & \text{if } x < 0 \\ \dfrac{1 - e^{-(\lambda_2/c)x}}{1 - e^{-\lambda_2 g}} & \text{if } 0 \le x \le cg \\ 1 & \text{if } cg < x \end{cases}$

The faster vehicle has, to begin with, to travel behind the slower vehicle a distance equal to the longest of the distances $X$ and $Y$. After having done this the situation is the same as the original one in the sense that there is no information left about either the sight or the gap. The relation to the processes formed by the vehicles in the oncoming stream, and the points where the sight function has jumps, is the same as the original one. The sight and the distance to the first oncoming vehicle are exponentially distributed with the distribution function $W(x)$ and $F_2(x)$, respectively. This is evidently true in relation to one of the two processes, and from the properties of a Poisson process it follows that it is also true in relation to the other. The further waiting distance will therefore have the distribution function $G$ for which reason we denote it by $T$. The waiting distance $T_{11}$ can then be written as

$$T_{11} = \max(X, Y) + T$$

From this we get that $\gamma_{11}(s)$ can be written as

$$
\gamma_{11}(s) = \left\{ \int_0^m e^{-sx}\, \frac{W(x)\, dF_2(x/c)}{W(h)F_2(g)} + \int_0^m e^{-sx}\, \frac{F_2(x/c)\, dW(x)}{F_2(g)W(h)} \right. \\
\left. + \int_m^h e^{-sx}\, \frac{dW(x)}{W(h)} + \int_m^{cg} e^{-sx}\, \frac{dF_2(x/c)}{F_2(g)} \right\} \gamma(s)
$$

(2)

Here, $dF_2(x/c)$ stands for differentiation with respect to $x$ (not to $x/c$).

*The case* (21)

In this case the sight exceeds $h$ but the gap is not large enough.

$X$ has the distribution function $\dfrac{W(x) - W(h)}{1 - W(h)} = \begin{cases} 1 - e^{-w(x-h)} & \text{if} \quad x \ge h \\ 0 & \text{if} \quad x < h \end{cases}$

$Y$ has the distribution function $\dfrac{F_2(x/c)}{F_2(g)}$

$X_1$ has the distribution function $W(x)$

To begin with, we have to distinguish here between different cases as to whether the traveling distance to the first oncoming vehicle exceeds $h$.

1. $Y > h$

This can happen only if $m = h$. When the faster vehicle has traveled the distance $Y$ behind the slower one the further waiting distance will, as in Case 11, have the distribution function $G$, for which reason we denote it by $T$. The waiting distance can therefore be written as

$$T_{21} = Y + T$$

2. $Y \le h$

Then, the traveling distance $Y$ to the first oncoming vehicle does not exceed $h$, and we have to distinguish further between two cases, namely, if the sight above $h$ exceeds $Y$.

## 2.1 $X_1 \leq Y$

When the faster vehicle has traveled the distance $Y$ behind the slower one, the sight is $h + X_1 - Y$, which in this case does not exceed $h$. The faster vehicle, therefore, has to travel behind the slower one at least the distance $h + X_1$. The further waiting distance we denote by $T$ as it, by the same arguments as before, has the distribution function $G$. In this case $T_{21}$ can be written as

$$T_{21} = h + X_1 + T$$

## 2.2 $X_1 > Y$

In this case the sight exceeds $h$ when the faster vehicle meets the first oncoming one. We have to distinguish between the cases whether the gap to the next oncoming vehicle then exceeds $g$.

2.2.1   The gap to the next oncoming vehicle $> g$. When the faster vehicle has traveled the distance $Y$ behind the slower one, the sight as well as the gap is large enough to permit an overtaking, and in this case we therefore have that

$$T_{21} = Y$$

2.2.2   The gap to the next oncoming vehicle $\leq g$. When the faster vehicle has traveled the distance $Y$ behind the slower one the assumptions are precisely the same as those we have supposed in Case 21, which we are now dealing with. The further waiting distance, which we denote by $T_{21}'$, will therefore have the distribution function $G_{21}$, and $T_{21}$ can in this case be written as

$$T_{21} = Y + T_{21}'$$

By summarizing the different cases above we get that $\gamma_{21}(s)$ can be written as

$$\gamma_{21}(s) = \left\{ F_2(g) \left[ 1 - \int_0^m e^{-sx}[1 - W(x)]dF_2\left(\frac{x}{c}\right) \right] \right\}^{-1} \left\{ [1 - F_2(g)] \right.$$

$$\times \int_0^m e^{-sx}[1 - W(x)] \, dF_2\left(\frac{x}{c}\right) \qquad (3)$$

$$\left. + \gamma(s) \left\{ \int_m^{cg} e^{-sx} \, dF_2\left(\frac{x}{c}\right) + \int_0^m e^{-s(m+x)} \left[ F_2\left(\frac{m}{c}\right) - F_2\left(\frac{x}{c}\right) \right] dW(x) \right\} \right\}$$

Case 12 gives rise to an expression for $\gamma_{12}$ quite analogous to the one for $\gamma_{21}$ given above. In Case 22 the sight as well as the distance to the first oncoming vehicle is large enough to permit an overtaking, that is, $T_{22} = 0$ and $\gamma_{22}(s) = 1$.

The four cases above give together with Eq. 1 a relation which determines $\gamma(s)$, which can be written in the form

$$\gamma(s) = e^{-wh - \lambda_2 g} \Bigg\{ 1 - \frac{w}{s + w}(1 - e^{-wh - (\lambda_2/c)m - sh}) - \frac{\dfrac{\lambda_2}{c}}{s + \dfrac{\lambda_2}{c}}(1 - e^{-wm - \lambda_2 g - scg})$$

$$+ \frac{w\dfrac{\lambda_2}{c}}{s + w + \dfrac{\lambda_2}{c}}\left(\frac{1}{s + w} + \frac{1}{s + \dfrac{\lambda_2}{c}}\right)(1 - e^{-m(s + w + \lambda_2/c)})\Bigg\}^{-1} \tag{4}$$

If, specifically, $h = cg = m$, then the expression for $\gamma(s)$ reduces to

$$\gamma(s) = \frac{\left(s + w + \dfrac{\lambda_2}{c}\right)e^{-m(w + \lambda_2/c)}}{s + \left(w + \dfrac{\lambda_2}{c}\right)e^{-m(s + w + \lambda_2/c)}} \tag{5}$$

which has the same form as the expression we should have got if there was no oncoming traffic but the sight, above minimum sight, had to exceed $m$ and the distances between the jumps were exponentially distributed with the parameter $w + (\lambda_2/c)$.

From Eq. 4 we get the moments of the distribution for the waiting distance by calculating the derivatives of $\gamma(s)$ at $s = 0$. The mean waiting distance is given by

$$-\gamma'(0) = m - h - cg + e^{wh + \lambda_2 g}\Bigg\{\frac{e^{-(\lambda_2/c)m}[e^{-wm} - e^{-wh}]}{w}$$

$$+ \frac{e^{-wm}[e^{-(\lambda_2/c)m} - e^{-\lambda_2 g}]}{\lambda_2/c} + \frac{1 - e^{-m(w + \lambda_2/c)}}{w + \lambda_2/c}\Bigg\} \tag{6}$$

In the above problem of determining the distribution of the waiting distance which the faster vehicle had to travel behind the slower one, the sight above minimum sight, and the gap, were assumed to be distributed according to the negative exponential distributions $W(x)$ and $F_2(x)$, respectively, when the slower vehicle was caught up.

Let us now consider the situation that the faster vehicle has just overtaken a vehicle in the slower stream. Denote by $\langle T \rangle$ the waiting distance the faster vehicle has to travel behind the next slow vehicle until an overtaking becomes possible, and let $\langle T \rangle$ have the distribution function $\langle G(x) \rangle$ with the Laplace Stieltjes transform $\langle \gamma(s) \rangle$. The problem of determining the distribution of the waiting distance $\langle T \rangle$ can be brought back on the preceding one by using the same technique and the same type of arguments. When an overtaking is just accomplished there is, however, some information on the one hand about the sight above minimum sight, and on the other about the distance to the nearest oncoming vehicle, namely that they exceed $h$ and $g$, respectively. When the faster vehicle travels a distance $\xi$ relative to the slower stream it travels a distance $K \cdot \xi$ along the road, where $K = V/(V - v_1)$. Since the distances between consecutive slower vehicles have the distribution function $F_1(x)$, the traveling distance to the next slow vehicle has the distribution function $F_1(x/K)$. We have to distinguish here between if, when the next slower vehicle is caught up, there remains some information about the sight and gap. When the faster vehicle travels a distance $g$ at the higher speed relative to the oncoming stream it travels a distance $c'g$ along the road where $c' = V/(V + v_2)$. Dependent on whether the traveling distance to the next slow vehicle is greater or less than $h$ and $c'g$, and the relation between these, the situation is somewhat different.

Suppose that $h \geq c'g$. Since $c' > c$ we then also have that $h > cg$. In this case $\langle \gamma \rangle(s)$ can be written as

$$\langle \gamma \rangle(s) = \int_0^{c'g} [1 - W(\xi)] \left[ 1 - F_2\left(\frac{\xi}{c'}\right) \right] dF_1\left(\frac{\xi}{K}\right) + \gamma(s)\varphi(s) \tag{7}$$

where $\gamma(s)$ is given by Eq. 4 with $m = cg$, and $\varphi(s)$ can be written as

$$\varphi(s) = 1 - F_1\left(\frac{h}{K}\right) + \int_{c'g}^h \frac{se^{w(h-\xi)} + we^{-s(h-\xi)}}{s + w} dF_1\left(\frac{\xi}{K}\right)$$

$$+ \int_0^{c'g} \left\{ \frac{s\dfrac{\lambda_2}{c}}{(s + w)\left(s + w + \dfrac{\lambda_2}{c}\right)} e^{wh - cg(s+w)} [e^{\xi(cs/c' - w(1 - c/c'))} \right. \tag{8}$$

$$\left. - e^{-\xi(w+\lambda_2/c')}] + \frac{w}{s + w} e^{-sh}e[\xi s - e^{-\xi(w+\lambda_2/c')}] \right\} dF_1\left(\frac{\xi}{K}\right)$$

From Eq. 7 we get the moments of the distribution of the waiting distance by calculating the derivatives of $\langle \gamma \rangle(s)$ at $s = 0$. The mean waiting distance is given by

$$-\langle\gamma'\rangle(0) = \frac{-1}{\frac{\lambda_1}{K}} + \frac{w}{\frac{\lambda_1}{K}\left(w + \frac{\lambda_1}{K}\right)}e^{-(\lambda_1/K)h} + \frac{w + \frac{\lambda_2}{c'}}{\left(w + \frac{\lambda_2}{c}\right)\left(\frac{\lambda_1}{K} + w + \frac{\lambda_2}{c'}\right)}e^{wh + \lambda_2 g}$$

$$+ \frac{\frac{\lambda_2}{c}\left(1 - \frac{c}{c'}\right)}{\left(w + \frac{\lambda_2}{c}\right)\left[\frac{\lambda_1}{K} + w\left(1 - \frac{c}{c'}\right)\right]}e^{w(h - cg)} \tag{9}$$

$$+ \frac{\frac{c}{c'}\frac{\lambda_2}{c'}\frac{\lambda_1}{K}}{\left(w + \frac{\lambda_1}{K}\right)\left[\frac{\lambda_1}{K} + w\left(1 - \frac{c}{c'}\right)\right]\left(\frac{\lambda_1}{K} + w + \frac{\lambda_2}{c'}\right)}e^{-(\lambda_1/K)c'g + w(h - c'g)}$$

The cases that $cg \le h \le c'g$ and $h \le cg$ give rise to corresponding expressions for $\langle\gamma\rangle(s)$ and the mean waiting distance. By putting $w = 0$ in the formulas above we get the corresponding expressions for the case in which only the oncoming traffic determines if an overtaking is possible or not (compare Tanner).

### The Average Speed of the Faster Vehicle

In order that the faster vehicle shall be able to overtake a slower one, the sight above the minimum sight $h_0$ has to exceed $h$, and the gap in the oncoming stream has to exceed $g$. We shall here assume that $g$ is given by

$$g = \frac{a(V + v_2)}{V - v_1}$$

This corresponds to the case that the overtaking vehicle has to travel a certain distance $a$, relative to the overtaken one, in the opposite lane. In the model the slower vehicles are, however, assumed to be overtaken one at a time and the faster vehicle can enter the gap between any two of them. We shall further assume that the total required sight is equal to the required gap, that is,

$$h_0 + h = g = \frac{a(V + v_2)}{V - v_1}$$

Let $y(t)$ denote the speed of the faster vehicle at time $t$. If the distances the faster vehicles travel while waiting behind the slower ones are independent and identically distributed with mean $\alpha$, and independent of the sequence of the slower vehicles, it can be shown that

$$\lim_{t \to \infty} E\{y(t)\} = v_1 + \frac{V - v_1}{1 + \alpha\lambda_1\frac{V - v_1}{v_1}}$$

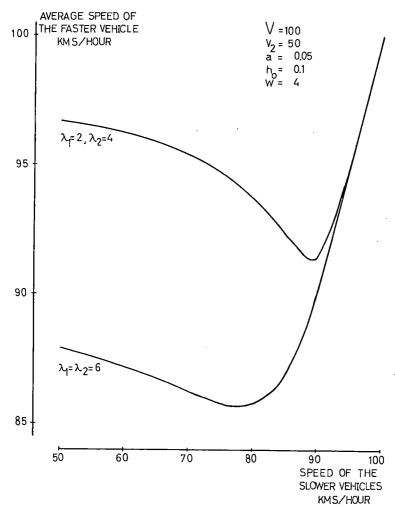

FIGURE 4.   The average speed of the faster vehicle over a long journey in the case when its desired speed is 100 kms/hr.

Further,

$$\frac{1}{\tau}\int_0^\tau y(t)\, dt$$

converges in quadratic mean and thus also in probability to the same limit when $\tau \to \infty$. The integral represents an average speed of the faster vehicle over a journey of duration $\tau$. By using the above formula with $\alpha$ replaced by the mean waiting distance $-\langle \gamma' \rangle(0)$ we get an expression for the average speed of the faster vehicle over a long journey. In Fig. 4 is illustrated how this average speed varies with the speed of the slower vehicles $(v_1)$, in the case the

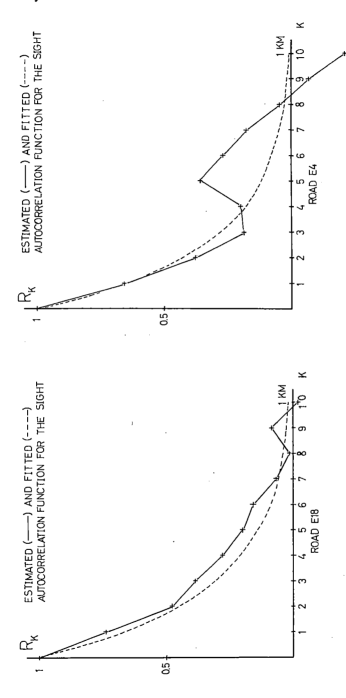

FIGURE 6. Estimated and fitted autocorrelation functions for the sight on a section of an actual road.

FIGURE 5. Estimated and fitted autocorrelation functions for the sight on a section of an actual road.

speed of the faster vehicle $(V)$ is 100 km/hr. Further in this example the speed of the oncoming vehicles $(v_2)$ is 50 km/hr. The relative overtaking distance $(a)$ is 0.05 km and the minimum sight $(h_0)$ 0.1 km. The density of the jumps in the sight function $(w)$ is 4 jumps/km. The average speed is given for two different pairs of densities for the slower and oncoming vehicles $(\lambda_1$ and $\lambda_2)$— on one hand 2 and 4 vehicles/km, and on the other 6 vehicles/km in each direction. For these values of the parameters $h < cg$ for $v_1 < 68.3$ and $cg \leq h \leq c'g$ for $68.3 \leq v_1 \leq 75$, and $h > c'g$ for $v_1 > 75$.

## The Sight on Actual Roads

For the sight function assumed in the model, the correlation between the sight distances at the points $x$ and $x + \xi$ is equal to $e^{-w\xi}$, that is, the correlation between the sight distances at $x$ and $x + \xi$ decreases exponentially with the distance between the points.

For the main roads in Sweden there are available diagrams on the sight distances along the road. A part of such a diagram in one direction is shown in Fig. 2. For some road sections we have estimated the autocorrelation function for the sight in 10 points. The estimates are based on samples of 50 observations $x_1, \ldots, x_{50}$ from the diagrams, one for every 100th meter, and are computed according to the formula

$$R_K = \frac{\dfrac{1}{50 - K} \displaystyle\sum_{i=1}^{50-K} (x_i - \langle x \rangle)(x_{i+K} - \langle x \rangle)}{S^2} \quad \text{for} \quad K = 1, \ldots, 10$$

where

$$\langle x \rangle = \frac{1}{50} \sum_{i=1}^{50} x_i \quad \text{and} \quad S^2 = \frac{1}{50} \sum_{i=1}^{50} (x_i - \langle x \rangle)^2.$$

The result from two different road sections is shown in Figs. 5 and 6. From the same roads samples are also taken where the observations are 600 meters apart and treated as independent. The observed and expected frequencies have been compared but are not given here. The fitted autocorrelation functions plotted in the figures are based on these samples.

Both types of samples are fairly small. They, however, indicate that for certain roads, or sections of roads, the model might well describe the actual sight while for others the agreement is not so good. These circumstances indicate that further investigations would be of interest.

## Acknowledgments

For valuable discussions in connection with this work the author wishes to express his gratitude to Professors B. J. Andersson and C. G. Esseen at the Royal Institute of Technology, Professor U. Grenander at the University of Stockholm, and Professor L. Carleson at the University of Uppsala.

# A Mathematical Model for Traffic on a Two-Lane Road

*SVEN ERLANDER*

University of Stockholm, Stockholm, Sweden

## Abstract

In this paper we shall discuss a simple model for traffic on a two-lane road. We shall assume that the road is infinitely long and that there are no crossings. We shall investigate the mean speed of vehicles with a given desired speed, assuming that the traffic conditions along the road are homogeneous. Vehicles are not allowed to leave or enter the road. Every vehicle is assumed to travel at its desired speed until it catches up with another vehicle. Upon catching up it immediately assumes the speed of the slower vehicle and follows this vehicle a certain distance, depending upon the oncoming traffic and the sight conditions, before it can move into the opposing lane and pass. When passing becomes possible the passing vehicle immediately resumes its desired speed, which it maintains until it catches up with another vehicle. A distribution of desired speeds will be assumed to be given. The sight conditions and the oncoming traffic will be described in very general terms. A nonlinear integral equation for the mean speed of a vehicle with given desired speed will be derived, and various aspects of this equation will be investigated. The relationship of this model to other models for traffic on two-lane roads will be discussed briefly. Finally, a few numerical examples will be given.

## I. The Theoretical Model

CONSIDER AN infinitely long two-lane road without crossings but with horizontal and vertical curves. Assume that traffic conditions are homogeneous along the road and stationary in time. Vehicles are not allowed to leave or enter the road. We make the following assumptions:

1.1.  Consider one of the lanes, say lane $A$. Let the density of vehicles in this lane be $a$, so that there are on the average $a$ vehicles per unit length.

Assume that every vehicle has a desired speed $x$, which it maintains when it is not delayed behind another vehicle. We shall refer to a vehicle with desired speed $x$ as an $x$-vehicle or as a vehicle $x$. Let $x$ be a random variable with distribution function $K(x)$, so that the density of vehicles with desired speed $x$ along the road is $adK(x)$. To avoid trivial complications we assume that all vehicles have a desired speed greater than zero. In fact, we assume that all points of increase of $K(x)$ lie in the interval $[\delta, \gamma]$, $0 < \delta \leq \gamma < \infty$, so that there is also an upper bound of the desired speeds. The restriction of the distribution $K(x)$ to a certain interval $[\delta, \gamma]$ does not, of course, prevent us from studying the behavior of single vehicles with desired speed outside of this interval. We also assume that $a$ and $K(x)$ are constant in time and constant along the road.

It should be noticed that $K(x)$ is, in general, not equal to the distribution of desired speeds for vehicles passing a certain point at the road, and $a$ is, in general, not equal to the average number of vehicles passing a certain point on the road per unit time. Whether the definitions of density and desired speed distribution are made to refer to space or time is of course to some extent arbitrary.

1.2. Consider now the opposing lane. Let the mean speed of the vehicles in this lane be $\mu$, and let their density be $\alpha$ vehicles per unit length. We shall not attempt to describe in detail the structure of the traffic in this lane. We shall assume only that, from the point of view of a vehicle in lane $A$, the vehicles appear as if almost all of them traveled at the speed $\mu$ and as if the distances between oncoming vehicles were independent random variables with a negative exponential distribution. These assumptions are helpful when we later obtain an expression for the average distance a vehicle in lane $A$ travels at a lower speed behind a slower vehicle before passing. The assumptions can, of course, be changed or avoided if an expression for this "waiting" distance can be obtained by other means.

1.3. In general, the vehicles in lane $A$ will to some extent be delayed because when catching up with a slower vehicle they will travel behind the slower vehicle until passing becomes possible. The passing maneuver requires a certain space in the opposing lane. Thus passing is possible only when a long enough distance in the opposing lane is free of oncoming vehicles and when the sight distance viewed from the passing vehicle permits the driver to see at least over the distance in question. Thus it is desirable to take the sight conditions into consideration. One way to describe how the sight varies along the road is the ingenious method suggested by Gustavsson.[3,4]

Let us assume that when moving along the road the sight decreases linearly until at a certain point the sight increases instantaneously to a higher level. Then the sight decreases again until there is another jump to a higher level, and so on. Assume that there is a lowest possible level beneath which the sight distance will never fall.

Assume now that the successive jumps above the minimum sight distance $h$ are independent random variables with distribution function $F(x) = 1 - e^{-\lambda x}$.

1.4.   A vehicle $x$ will maintain its desired speed $x$ as long as it is undisturbed by other vehicles. When catching up with a slower vehicle it will change its speed instantaneously to that of the slower vehicle and maintain this lower speed until passing becomes possible. At this time it immediately resumes its desired speed, which it maintains until it catches up with another slower vehicle. Let the average speed of a vehicle with desired speed $x$ be $m(x)$.

1.5.   When a vehicle with desired speed $x$ passes a vehicle with desired speed $y < x$ a certain relative distance $c$ is required in the opposing lane for the passing maneuver. Thus the distance that the $x$-vehicle will travel in passing the $y$-vehicle is

$$g_0 = \frac{cx}{x - m(y)},$$

where we assume that the $y$-vehicle travels at its average speed $m(y)$.

In this paper we do not intend to describe the traffic in the opposing lane in any detail. However, we know that in actual traffic not all vehicles in the opposing lane travel at the average speed $\mu$. The distance $g_0$ is not large enough to always guarantee a safe passing maneuver. In addition to the distance $g_0$ that the vehicle $x$ will actually be traveling in the opposing lane, a safety distance $g_1$ is required, as shown in Fig. 1. This safety distance shall be sufficiently long as to make sure that a vehicle in the opposing lane moving at high speed can not collide with the vehicle $x$ during the passing maneuver. The time taken by the vehicle $x$ in traveling over the distance $g_0$ is $c/(x - m(y))$. Thus, if we assume that the highest possible speed of vehicles in the opposing lane is $\mu_1$, we obtain

$$g_1 = \frac{c\mu_1}{x - m(y)},$$

and the total required distance free of vehicles in the opposing lane is

$$g = g_0 + g_1 = \frac{c(x + \mu_1)}{x - m(y)}. \tag{1}$$

To summarize, a vehicle $x$ with desired speed $x$ requires a gap in the oncoming traffic stream of at least length $g$ to pass a vehicle $y$ with desired speed $y$.

1.6.   Passing is possible only if the distance to the next jump (that is the distance to the next bend or top of a hill) of the sightfunction exceeds $(g - h)$. In that case the driver of the $x$-vehicle can see far enough to decide whether there is a gap $g$ in the oncoming traffic stream.

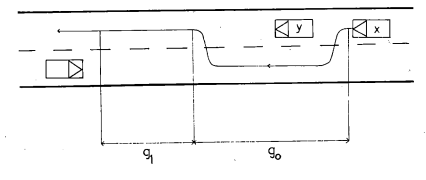

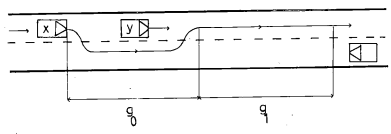

FIGURE I.    The $x$-vehicle travels the distance $g_0$ in the opposing lane and requires a safety distance $g_1$.

1.7.    When a vehicle $x$ with desired speed $x$ catches up with a vehicle $y$ with desired speed $y < x$ it has to travel on the average a distance $s(g)$ at the lower speed $m(y)$ before it can pass and resume its desired speed $x$. This means that the speed of the slower vehicle is assumed to be constant during the time it takes from the moment of catching up until vehicle $x$ has completed the passing maneuver. A more realistic approach would be to assume that the speed of the slower vehicle is a random variable $Y$ with expectation $EY = m(y)$. However, the assumptions made above mean that we substitute the expectation $EY$ for the random variable $Y$. This is, of course, rigorously inadmissible, but it is reasonable when the speed $Y$ of the overtaken vehicle does not vary too much during the time the $x$-vehicle is delayed behind it.

1.8.    The above assumptions regarding the passing maneuver to some extent takes into consideration the possibility of interaction of cars in the form of queues of vehicles traveling behind slower vehicles, waiting for an opportunity to pass. This is done by assuming that the overtaken vehicle $y$ maintains its average speed $m(y)$ and not its desired speed $y$. Thus, the $y$-vehicle may already be delayed when the $x$-vehicle catches up with it. On the other hand, the derivation of the basic integral equation below will be made under the assumption that every passing maneuver requires on the average the "waiting" distance $s(g)$. This assumption does not explicitly take into account the possibility that the same gap in the oncoming traffic may be used for several passing maneuvers. Only experimental data can show whether this is a serious drawback of the model. Also, the vehicles are treated as mathematical points in that no account is made of the physical space that they would occupy in reality. In dense traffic one has, of course, to take into consideration that on a finite stretch of road only a finite number of vehicles can travel simultaneously.

## 2. The Average Speed of a Vehicle with Desired Speed x

### 2.1. The Basic Integral Equation

We shall now derive an integral equation for the average speed $m(x)$ of a vehicle with desired speed $x$. At this point we shall make use of the assumptions in Sections 1.1, 1.4, and 1.7 leaving a more detailed discussion of $s(g)$ to the next section. The density of vehicles $y$ with desired speed $y$ along the road is

$$a \, dK(y).$$

On the average a vehicle $x$ with desired speed $x$ travels a distance $[m(x) - m(y)]$ relative to the $y$-vehicles during one unit of time, and thus the $x$-vehicle overtakes on the average

$$[m(x) - m(y)]a \, dK(y)$$

$y$-vehicles per unit time.

According to assumption (1.7) the $x$-vehicle has to travel on the average a distance $s(g)$ at the speed $m(y)$ before it can pass. Thus, the $x$-vehicle will travel at speed $m(y)$ for an average time per unit time of

$$\frac{s(g)}{m(y)} [m(x) - m(y)]a \, dK(y).$$

This means that in one unit of time the $x$-vehicle will on the average travel the time

$$\int_\delta^x \frac{(sg)}{m(y)} [m(x) - m(y)]a \, dK(y)$$

at reduced speed, and the time

$$1 - \int_\delta^x \frac{s(g)}{m(y)} [m(x) - m(y)]a \, dK(y)$$

at its desired speed $x$. Thus the total distance traveled in one unit of time will on the average be

$$m(x) = x - x\int_\delta^x \frac{s(g)}{m(y)} [m(x) - m(y)]a \, dK(y)$$

$$+ \int_\delta^x s(g)[m(x) - m(y)]a \, dK(y).$$

We therefore obtain the following integral equation for the average speed $m(x)$:

$$m(x) = x - \int_\delta^x s(g)[m(x) - m(y)]\left[\frac{x}{m(y)} - 1\right] a \, dK(y). \tag{2}$$

This equation is very similar to Carleson's[2] basic equation and, indeed, we have used almost the same arguments in deriving it. However, there are differences, the most important one being that we have defined $K(y)$ as the distribution of desired speeds along the road. This will be discussed in more detail in Section 5.

## 2.2. An Expression for $s(g)$

Let us now investigate in more detail the average distance $s(g)$ that a vehicle $x$ has to travel at reduced speed $m(y)$ before passing becomes possible. We shall now make use also of the assumptions 1.2, 1.3, 1.5, and 1.6. These assumptions are exactly the same as those used by Gustavsson.[3,4] This means that the oncoming traffic and the jumps in the sightfunction appear to the $x$-vehicle as two independent Poisson streams. The $x$-vehicle can pass only if there is a gap at least of size $g$ in the oncoming traffic stream and if at the same time the distance to the next jump of the sightfunction exceeds $(g - h)$.

Consider now the situation when the $x$-vehicle has just completed a passing maneuver. At this moment we know that the distance to the next oncoming vehicle is at least $g$ and the distance to the next jump of the sightfunction exceeds $(g - h)$ so that the two streams are no longer Poisson streams. However, when the $x$-vehicle has traveled far enough to have met the next oncoming vehicle and to have passed the next jump of the sightfunction it is again traveling in two independent Poisson streams.

The latter case was solved by Gustavsson.[4] In case the distances traveled between successive overtakings are long enough so that almost all overtakings occur under the assumptions used by Gustavsson[4] in deriving $\gamma(s)$ we can apply Gustavsson's formula[4] (6). We shall approximate this formula by expanding in series to the second power of $g$ and $(g - h)$. The approximation will not be good for large values of $g$ or in cases where the parameter values seldom permit passing. However, we want to use the expression for $s(g)$ in Eq. 2, and the most important thing is that the expression for $s(g)$ grows fast enough to practically stop all passing when this should be the case. The exact formulas for $s(g)$ involve exponential functions of $g$ and the parameters in question so that $s(g)$ will grow very rapidly for large values of $g$. However, it is believed that the expansion of those exponential functions up to the second power will take care of this growth to an acceptable degree in the interesting ranges. This model is supposed to be applicable only when traffic is not to dense. And besides, when $g$ exceeds a certain level passing becomes practically impossible and the exact behavior of $s(g)$ for larger values of $g$ is of no consequence as long as $s(g)$ fulfills some very general requirements. We obtain

$$s(g) = \frac{\alpha}{2} \frac{1}{1 + \dfrac{\mu}{m(y)}} g^2 + \frac{\lambda}{2} [\max\{g - h, 0\}]^2 \tag{3}$$

## 3. Solution of the Integral Equation

The integral equation, Eq. 2, cannot in general be solved by simple methods. Here we shall discuss an approximative method, which also works when we use other expressions for $s(g)$. However, we shall not specify $s(g)$ at this point; we must bear in mind that $s(g)$ is a function of $x$, $m(y)$ and all the parameters. In that case where $K(y)$ is a step function this method will give an exact solution.

The two mainsteps in this approximation method are the following.

1: Approximate the integral by a sum over a large but finite number of intervals. In this way the desired speed distribution $K(y)$ is approximated by a discrete distribution. In the case where $K(y)$ is a step function, the integral is a sum, and the second step can be carried out at once.

2: If the mass points are $\delta = y_0 < y_1 < \ldots < y_n = \gamma$ proceed from below and let $x = y_i$, $i = 0, \ldots, n$ in Eq. 2. In this way $m(y_i)$, $i = 0, \ldots, n$, are successively obtained and finally $m(x)$ is obtained for $x \geq \delta$. By making the partition of the interval $[\delta, \gamma]$ smaller, by letting $n$ increase, the integral can be approximated arbitrarily well.

Let $\{y_i\}$ be a partition of the interval $(\delta, \gamma)$ so that

$$\delta = y_0 < y_1 < \ldots < y_n = \gamma$$

and let $K(y_0) = p_0,$

$$K(y_i) - K(y_{i-1}) = p_i, \qquad i = 1, \ldots, n.$$

Move all mass points in the interval $(y_{i-1}, y_i]$ to the single point $y_i$, $i = 1, \ldots, n$. For this new distribution Eq. 2 gives for $y_{i-1} \leq x < y_i$

$$m(x) = x - \sum_{v=0}^{i-1} s(x, m(y_v))[m(x) - m(y_v)]\left[\frac{x}{m(y_v)} - 1\right] a p_v, \; i = 1, \ldots, n \tag{4}$$

where we have written $s(x, m(y_v))$ instead of $s(g)$ to stress the fact that $s(g)$ is a function of $x$ and $m(y)$. This can also be written:

$$m(x) = \frac{x + a \sum\limits_{v=0}^{i-1} s(x, m(y_v)) m(y_v) \left[\dfrac{x}{m(y_v)} - 1\right] p_v}{1 + a \sum\limits_{v=0}^{i-1} s(x, m(y_v)) \left[\dfrac{x}{m(y_v)} - 1\right] p_v} \tag{5}$$

For $x = y_{i-1}$, $i = 1, \ldots, n$, this gives

$$m(y_{i-1}) = \frac{y_{i-1} + a \sum_{v=0}^{i-1} s(y_{i-1}, m(y_v))m(y_v)\left[\dfrac{y_{i-1}}{m(y_v)} - 1\right]p_v}{1 + a \int_\delta^x s(y_{i-1}, m(y_v))\left[\dfrac{y_{i-1}}{m(y_v)} - 1\right]p_v} \tag{6}$$

This means that by using Eq. 6 for $i = 1, \ldots, n$ the values $m(y_v)$, $v = 0, \ldots, n - 1$, can successively be obtained and therefore by substituting those values into Eq. 5 we obtain an expression for $m(x)$ for every possible value of $x$.

## 4. Some Properties of the solutions

The basic equation can be written

$$m(x) = \frac{x + a \int_\delta^x s(g)[x - m(y)]\,dK(y)}{1 + a \int_\delta^x s(g)\dfrac{x - m(y)}{m(y)}\,dK(y)} \quad ; \quad x > \delta \tag{7}$$

For $x = \delta$ we always have $m(\delta) = \delta$. Let us now investigate the solutions for some special cases.

4.1.   What happens if the $x$-vehicle desires to drive very fast? Let $x \to \infty$. From Eq. 1 it follows that

$$\lim_{x \to \infty} g = c$$

It then follows from Eq. 3 that $\lim_{x \to \infty} s(g)$ exist and is given by

$$\lim_{x \to \infty} s(g) = \frac{\frac{1}{2}(\alpha c^2)}{1 + \dfrac{\mu}{m(y)}} + \frac{\lambda}{2}(\max[c - h, 0])^2$$

We thus obtain

$$\lim_{x \to \infty} m(x) = \frac{1 + a \int_\delta^\gamma \dfrac{m(y)}{\nu\mu + m(y)}\frac{1}{2}(\alpha c^2)\,dK(y) + a\frac{\lambda}{2}(\max[c - h, 0])^2}{a \int_\delta^\gamma \dfrac{1}{\mu + m(y)}\frac{1}{2}\alpha c^2\,dK(y) + a\frac{\lambda}{2}(\max[c - h, 0])^2\int_\delta^\gamma \dfrac{1}{m(y)}\,dK(y)}$$

We will in most cases have $c < h$ so that this can be simplified

$$\lim_{x \to \infty} m(x) = \frac{1 + \frac{1}{2}a\alpha c^2\int_\delta^\gamma \dfrac{m(y)}{\mu + m(y)}\,dK(y)}{\frac{1}{2}a\alpha c^2\int_\delta^\gamma \dfrac{m(y)}{\mu + m(y)}\,dK(y)} = \text{a constant}$$

This means that a vehicle, which desires to travel infinitely fast, will in effect obtain a constant average speed. The value of this constant average speed depends on the various parameters. An upper bound is given by

$$\lim_{x \to \infty} m(x) \leq \frac{2\mu}{a\alpha c^2} + \gamma \left( 1 + \frac{.2}{a\alpha c^2} \right)$$

where we have used $m(y) \leq \gamma$.

4.2.   Let us now investigate the behavior of the average speed $m(x)$, when traffic conditions become "jammed," even though the model was never intended to describe this kind of traffic. In spite of this it is of interest to see whether the model nevertheless behaves in a natural way.

Let the density of vehicles tend to infinity, that is, let either $a \to \infty$ or $\alpha \to \infty$, or let both $a$ and $\alpha$ tend to infinity simultaneously. One would expect the same result in both cases, and indeed Eq. 7 now becomes

$$m(x) = \frac{\int_{\delta}^{x} s(g)[x - m(y)]\, dK(y)}{\int_{\delta}^{x} s(g) \frac{x - m(y)}{m(y)}\, dK(y)} \tag{8}$$

This can also be written

$$\int_{\delta}^{x} s(g)[x - m(y)] \frac{m(x) - m(y)}{m(y)}\, dK(y) = 0$$

We now have

$$m(y) \leq y$$

so that for $y < x$ we obtain

$$m(y) < x$$

that is

$$x - m(y) > 0 \quad \text{for} \quad y < x.$$

The function $s(g)$ is positive for all non-trivial cases, so that the integral can be zero only if $m(x) = m(y)$ for every point of increase of the distribution function $K(y)$. Thus, $m(y) = $ a constant for all points $y < x$ of increase of $K(y)$. Since $m(\delta) = \delta$ and $m(y)$ is a non-decreasing function of $y$, this means that $m(y) = \delta$ for $\delta \leq y \leq y_0$, where $y_0$ is the largest point of increase of $K(y)$ in the interval $[\delta, x]$. But this holds for arbitrary $x$, so that for $x > \gamma$ we obtain that $m(y) = \delta$ for $\delta \leq y \leq \gamma$. It now follows immediately from Eq. 8 that $m(y) = \delta$ also for $y > \gamma$. Thus, we obtain

$$\lim_{a \to \infty} m(x) = \lim_{\alpha \to \infty} m(x) = \delta \tag{9}$$

that is, in this case all vehicles will travel at the lowest possible speed $\delta$.

4.3.   Similar results hold if the sight conditions become such that passing becomes impossible. Let $\lambda \to \infty$. Then the sight will approach the constant value $h$. Let now $h \to 0$. The sight will then tend to zero and passing becomes impossible, and one would expect the solution $m(x) = \delta$ as in the previous section. This is also the case. Indeed, we obtain Eq. 8, so that the final result is given by

$$\lim_{\substack{\lambda \to \infty \\ h \to 0}} m(x) = \delta \tag{10}$$

4.4.   Let us now investigate the case when the distribution function $K(y)$ has only one point of increase. Specifically, let us assume that almost all vehicles have desired speed $V$ so that

$$K(y) = \begin{cases} 0 & \text{for} \quad y < V \\ 1 & \text{for} \quad y \geq V \end{cases}$$

We then obtain $m(V) = V$ and for $x > V$

$$m(x) = \frac{x + as(g)(x - V)}{1 + \dfrac{as(g)(x - V)}{V}} = V + \frac{x - V}{1 + as(g)\dfrac{(x - V)}{V}} \tag{11}$$

Equation 11 illustrates in a simple way some of the properties discussed above. For instance, when $x$ tends towards infinity we obtain (if $c < h$):

$$\lim_{x \to \infty} m(x) = \frac{1 + \tfrac{1}{2}a\alpha c^2 \dfrac{V}{V + \mu}}{\tfrac{1}{2}a\alpha c^2 \dfrac{1}{V + \mu}}$$

For the various cases of "jammed" traffic we obtain $m(x) \to V$.

4.5.   Various other relations can be obtained by means of the model. We shall give the expressions for the average number of overtakings and the speed distribution of vehicles passing a certain point along the road. Let $n$ denote the average number of overtakings per road length and per unit time. One $x$-vehicle overtakes on the average

$$\int_\delta^x a[m(x) - m(y)] \, dK(y)$$

$y$-vehicles per unit time.

The density of $x$-vehicles along the road is $a \, dK(x)$, so that the average number of overtakings per unit length and per unit time is given by

$$n = a^2 \int_\delta^y \int_\delta^x [m(x) - m(y)] \, dK(y) \, dK(x) \tag{12}$$

Let now $H(x)$ be the desired speed distribution function for vehicles passing a certain point along the road. The density of $y$-vehicles with desired speed $y$

along the road is $a\,dK(y)$. Those vehicles approach the point with the average speed $m(y)$ so that $H(x)$ will be given by

$$H(x) = \frac{\displaystyle\int_{\delta}^{x} m(y)\,dK(y)}{\displaystyle\int_{\delta}^{\gamma} m(y)\,dK(y)} \tag{13}$$

Let now $G(x)$ be the distribution function of the average speed for vehicles passing a certain point along the road. We then have

$$G(x) = \frac{\displaystyle\int_{\delta}^{m^{-1}(x)} m(y)\,dK(y)}{\displaystyle\int_{\delta}^{\gamma} m(y)\,dK(y)} \tag{14}$$

where $m^{-1}(x)$ is a value $y$ for which $x = m(y)$.

## 5. Other Models

An integral equation approach to this problem was used for the first time by Newell.[8] Others, namely Tanner,[9,10] Yeo,[12] and Gustavsson[3,4] have used another technique. Basically, they consider one fast vehicle moving in a Poisson type stream of vehicles which all travel at the same (lower) speed. The traffic in the opposite lane is similarly characterized. Tanner and Yeo consider an infinitely long straight road, where the sight is always sufficient to allow passing, whereas Gustavsson takes the varying sight conditions into consideration. Miller[5-7] studies two lane traffic in terms of random bunches of vehicles. Wardrop[11] gave a formula for the number of overtakings for the case $m(x) = x$, that is, overtakings can be made without any delay. In this paper we have closely followed the approach used by Carleson[2] and Andersson,[1] the basic difference being that we have used the desired speed distribution "along the road," $K(x)$, whereas Carleson and Andersson use the desired speed distribution for vehicles passing a certain point, $H(x)$. The relation between those distributions is given by Eq. 13. Another difference is that we have made use of Gustavsson's results in obtaining an expression for the average distance a vehicle travels before passing becomes possible. Thus, we have obtained a model which not only takes into consideration the traffic in the two streams but also the sight conditions. Gustavsson's results was, of course, derived under very special assumptions about the traffic in the two lanes, but his solution may nevertheless to an acceptable degree describe the behavior of the average waiting distance in more complicated traffic situations.

## 6. Some Numerical Examples

6.1.  We shall give only a few numerical examples. Let us first consider the case when $K(x)$ has only one point of increase. The average speed of a faster vehicle will then be given by Eq. 11. This case is similar to that studied by Gustavsson,[3,4] that is, one faster vehicle is moving in a slower stream of vehicles which all travel at the same speed $V$. The distances between those vehicles are independent random variables with a negative exponential distribution function. The vehicles in the opposite lane also form a Poisson stream and the same holds for the sight above a certain minimum sight. Specifically, let the speed $x = 100$ km/hr, and let the speed of the oncoming traffic $\mu = 100$ km/hr, so that $\mu_1 = 100$ km/hr. Let the constant $c = 0.05$ km and the minimum sight $h = 0.1$ km. Let the average number of jumps in the sight function be $\lambda = 4$, and let the densities of vehicles in the two lanes be $a = \alpha = 2$ vehicles per km. Then, the average speed $m(x)$ is given for various values of $V$ by the following table:

| $V$ | 50 | 60 | 70 | 80 | 90 | 100 |
|------|------|------|------|------|------|------|
| $m(x)$ | 97.0 | 96.7 | 96.5 | 96.5 | 96.8 | 100.0 |

6.2.  Numerical values for real traffic are not easy to find. However, we shall give one example which is at least closely related to actual traffic as reported in a technical report from the Swedish Road Institute. From this report and from Gustavsson's investigations[4] it is possible to find values on the parameters which are, if not estimates of the real world parameters, at least not too far from being realistic.  Let us assume the following values of the parameters:

average speed of oncoming traffic $\mu\ = 80$ km/h
top speed of oncoming traffic $\qquad \mu_1 = 130$  km/h
relative passing distance $\qquad\qquad c = 0.05$ km
minimum sight $\qquad\qquad\qquad\quad h = 0.1$ km
average number of jumps of the sight function $\lambda = 4$ jumps/km
density of vehicles $\qquad\qquad\qquad\qquad a = 1.5$ vehicles/km
density of vehicles in the opposite lane $\qquad \alpha = 1$ vehicle/km
desired speed distribution $K(x)$:

| $x_v$ | 50 | 60 | 70 | 80 | 90 | 100 | 110 | 120 | 130 |
|-------|------|------|------|------|------|------|------|------|------|
| $p_v$ | 0.05 | 0.15 | 0.15 | 0.10 | 0.15 | 0.20 | 0.10 | 0.05 | 0.05 |

Then we obtain the following average speed function:

| $x$ | 50 | 60 | 70 | 80 | 90 | 100 | 110 | 120 | 130 |
|------|------|------|------|------|------|------|------|------|------|
| $m(x)$ | 50 | 60 | 69 | 79 | 88 | 98 | 107 | 117 | 127 |

The resulting distribution of average speed of vehicles passing a certain point along the road, $G(x)$, is given by the following table:

| $x_v$ | 50 | 60 | 69 | 79 | 88 | 98 | 107 | 117 | 127 |
|---|---|---|---|---|---|---|---|---|---|
| $p_v$ | 0.03 | 0.11 | 0.12 | 0.09 | 0.16 | 0.23 | 0.13 | 0.07 | 0.07 |

The average number of vehicles passing a certain point along the road in the studied lane is 128 vehicles/hr, and the average number of overtakings per unit time and per road unit length is
n = 26 overtakings/hr and km
The resulting distribution of desired speed of vehicles passing a certain point along the road, $H(x)$, is given by the following table;

| $x_v$ | 50 | 60 | 70 | 80 | 90 | 100 | 110 | 120 | 130 |
|---|---|---|---|---|---|---|---|---|---|
| $p_v$ | 0.03 | 0.11 | 0.12 | 0.09 | 0.16 | 0.23 | 0.13 | 0.07 | 0.07 |

7.2.1. Let us now investigate how the introduction of a speed limit would in this special case change the situation. Specifically, let us assume that the speed limit is 90 km/hr and let us also assume that all vehicles with desired speed greater than 90 km/hr will change their desired speed to 90 km/hr. The desired speed distribution $K(x)$ becomes

| $x_v$ | 50 | 60 | 70 | 80 | 90 |
|---|---|---|---|---|---|
| $p_v$ | 0.05 | 0.15 | 0.15 | 0.10 | 0.55 |

and we obtain the following average speed function:

| $x$ | 50 | 60 | 70 | 80 | 90 |
|---|---|---|---|---|---|
| $m(x)$ | 50 | 60 | 69 | 79 | 88 |

The resulting distribution of average speed at a certain point along the road, $G(x)$, becomes:

| $x_v$ | 50 | 60 | 69 | 79 | 88 |
|---|---|---|---|---|---|
| $p_v$ | 0.03 | 0.11 | 0.13 | 0.10 | 0.62 |

The average number of vehicles passing a certain point along the road in the studied lane is 117 vehicles/hr, and the average number of overtakings is
n = 10 overtakings/hr and km

7.2.2.    Let us also give one example of the influence of the density parameters $a$ and $\alpha$ in this special case. Let the densities in both lanes increase by a factor of 5, so that we obtain
    $a = 7.5$ vehicles/km and
    $\alpha = 5$ vehicles/km.
We then obtain the following average speed function:

| $x$ | 50 | 60 | 70 | 80 | 90 | 100 | 110 | 120 | 130 |
|------|----|----|----|----|----|-----|-----|-----|-----|
| $m(x)$ | 50 | 59 | 66 | 73 | 81 | 88 | 96 | 103 | 111 |

The resulting distribution of average speed of vehicles passing a certain point along the road, $G(x)$, is given by the following table:

| $x_v$ | 50 | 59 | 66 | 73 | 81 | 88 | 96 | 103 | 111 |
|------|------|------|------|------|------|------|------|------|------|
| $p_v$ | 0.03 | 0.11 | 0.13 | 0.09 | 0.15 | 0.22 | 0.12 | 0.07 | 0.07 |

The average number of vehicles passing a certain point along the road in the studied lane is 589 vehicles/hr, and the average number of overtakings is
    $n = 69$ overtakings/hr and km
The resulting distribution of desired speed of vehicles passing a certain point along the road, $H(x)$, is the following:

| $x_v$ | 50 | 60 | 70 | 80 | 90 | 100 | 110 | 120 | 130 |
|------|------|------|------|------|------|------|------|------|------|
| $p_v$ | 0.03 | 0.11 | 0.13 | 0.09 | 0.15 | 0.22 | 0.12 | 0.07 | 0.07 |

## Acknowledgement

The author wishes to express his deep gratitude towards Jan Gustavsson at the Royal Institute of Technology for many inspiring discussions about traffic models from which the author has largely benefited, and also for generously making available his unpublished material and for a great number of valuable suggestions. The Official Swedish Council on Road Safety Research supported the numerical calculations and made possible the presentation at the Third International Symposium on the Theory of Traffic Flow.

## References

1. B. J. Andersson, Carlesons trafikmodel. Unpublished.
2. L. Carleson, En matematisk modell for landsvagstrafik. *Nord. matematisk tidskrift,* Band **5**, 175–180 (1957).
3. J. Gustavsson, Trafikmodell med hansyn till siktstrackans variation. (1961) Unpublished.

4. J. Gustavsson, A Model for Overtaking on a Two-Lane Road with Limited Visibility. Third International Symposium on the Theory of Traffic Flow (1965).
5. A. J. Miller, A Queueing Model for Road Traffic Flow. *J. Roy. Stat. Soc.*, Series B, **23**, 64–75 (1961).
6. A. J. Miller, Road Traffic Flow Considered as a Stochastic Process. *Proc. Cambridge Phil. Soc.*, **58**, Part 2, 312–325 (1962).
7. A. J. Miller, Analysis of Bunching in Rural Two-Lane Traffic. *V. Oper. Res.*, **11**, 236–247 (1963).
8. G. F. Newell, Mathematical Models for Freely Flowing Highway Traffic. *J. Oper. Res. Soc. Am.*, **3**, 176–186 (1955).
9. J. C. Tanner, A Simplified Model for Delays in Overtaking on a Two-Lane Road. *J. Roy. Stat. Soc.*, Series B, **20**, 408–414 (1958).
10. J. C. Tanner, Delays on a Two-Lane Road, *J. Roy. Stat. Soc.*, Series B, **23**, 38–63 (1961).
11. J. G. Wardrop, Some Theoretical Aspects of Road Traffic Research. *Proc. Inst. Civ. Eng.*, Part II, **1, 2**, 325–362 (1952).
12. G. F. Yeo, Traffic Delays on a Two-Lane Road, *Biometrika*, **51**, 11–15 (1964).

# Convergence and Invariance Questions for Road Traffic with Free Overtaking

*TORBJÖRN THEDÉEN*

Division of Mathematical Statistics
Royal Institute of Technology
Stockholm, Sweden

The following simple model is studied:

The cars are considered as points on an infinite road with no intersections. They can overtake each other without delay and will forever maintain their once chosen speeds. The trajectories in the road-time diagram will thus be lines. The initial speeds are independent and identically distributed random variables, and they are also independent of the initial positions of the cars. We shall call these assumptions the independence conditions. The following problems are considered:

1. It is known that under rather weak conditions the spatial distribution of the cars will tend to that of a generalized Poisson process as the time $t \to \infty$. (See Breiman,[1] Dobrushin,[2] and Thedéen[5].) It is shown that the independence conditions are fulfilled even in the limit ($t \to \infty$). The corresponding asymptotic results hold on the time axis and even for an arbitrary line in the road-time diagram.

2. Under the assumption of independent motions of its points, a generalized Poisson process will conserve its distribution for all times $t$ (see Dobrushin[2] and Doob[3]). For the traffic model in question it is shown that if the independence conditions are supposed to hold for all $t$, and the distribution function for the speed is nondegenerate, then the only point process which will conserve its distribution for all $t$ is the generalized Poisson process.

3. If the spatial distribution of the cars is that of a Poisson process, and the independence conditions are fulfilled, then for any fixed point on the road the time positions of the cars will also form a Poisson process (compare Haight[4]). The same conclusion holds for the points obtained as the intersections between any fixed line and the trajectory-lines in the road-time diagram. Any of these points is obtained from its initial position $x$ by means of a transformation linear in $x$. It is shown that for transformations of the initial points which are monotonic in $x$, this linearity (in $x$) is also a necessary condition for the conservation of a Poisson process (but not necessary with the same intensity) and the independence conditions.

4. The number of overtakings in an interval on the road during the time $T$, under the assumption that the initial positions form a Poisson process, is shown to be asymptotically normally distributed as the time $T \to \infty$.

## References

1. L. Breiman, The Poisson Tendency in Traffic Distribution, *Ann. Math. Statist*, **34,** 308–311 (1963).
2. R. Dobrushin, On the Poisson law for Distributions of Points in Space, *Ukrain. Mat. Z.,* **8,** 127–134 (1956) (Russian).
3. J. L. Doob, "Stochastic Processes." Wiley, New York. 404–407. 1953.
4. F. Haight, "Mathematical Theories of Traffic Flow." Academic Press, New York. 117–121. 1963.
5. T. Thedéen, A Note on the Poisson Tendency in Traffic Distribution, *Ann. Math. Statist.* **35,** 1823–1824 (1964).

# Statistical Experiments with a
# Two-Lane Flow Model

*ROBERT M. OLIVER and TENNY LAM*

University of California
Berkeley, California

## Abstract

A series of observations of traffic on the Nimitz Freeway in California is analyzed within the framework of a hydrodynamic model for lane changing between two or more lanes. An experimental verification for the choice of the lane changing functions is also given.

## I. Introduction

IN A RECENT paper[4] one of the authors has discussed a theoretical model for lane changing when two or more lanes of traffic are traveling in the same direction, and passing and lane changing is allowed. In that paper the author assumed that the traffic stream could be identified as a compressible fluid obeying the equation of continuity.

$$\frac{\partial k_1}{\partial t} + \frac{\partial q_1}{\partial x} = P_{21}(x, t) - P_{12}(x, t) \tag{1a}$$

$$\frac{\partial k_2}{\partial t} + \frac{\partial q_2}{\partial x} = P_{12}(x, t) - P_{21}(x, t) \tag{1b}$$

In this model $P_{12}(x, t)$ and $P_{21}(x, t)$ are the lane-changing functions which describe the transfer of vehicles from lane 1 to 2 and lane 2 to 1, respectively. It was assumed that the lane changing functions could be written in the form

$$P_{12}(x, t) = \alpha k_1^2(x, t)(k_{2j} - k_2(x, t)) \tag{2a}$$

$$P_{21}(x, t) = \beta k_2^2(x, t)(k_{1j} - k_1(x, t)) \tag{2b}$$

and that the equations of state $q_1 = k_1 v_1$ and $q_2 = k_2 v_2$ hold in each lane. $k_{1j}$ and $k_{2j}$ are upper bounds for densities in lane 1 and lane 2, respectively. A theoretical justification of Eq. 2 and solution of Eq. 1 are the subject of the earlier paper; it is the purpose of this paper to give some experimental verification for the choice of the lane changing functions in Eq. 2.

Before we discuss our experiments we should mention that the model was originally proposed for high-velocity, low-density travel in two adjoining lanes of a four-lane freeway where vehicles were essentially unrestricted in making passing maneuvers and lane changes. While these situations can lead to high lane flow rates the number of lane changes made in a short length of roadway may be relatively small compared to the flow rate. One soon finds that a deterministic model, such as that suggested in Eqs. 1 and 2, does not easily lend itself to a situation where statistical samples are difficult and expensive to obtain, and where the time periods over which such data can be collected do not insure that the laws of large numbers will give stable and meaningful averages.

Consequently, we decided that we should experiment with a probabilistic model in which vehicle numbers play the key role and in which the number of vehicles in a small length of roadway is a random variable selected from a probability distribution which is stationary in time and space. We assume moreover that vehicle velocities are random variables independently selected from a common stationary probability distribution. The trajectory of each vehicle in a space-time diagram is assumed to have a constant slope, and it is this slope which is the random variable we have just described.

There are essentially two ways in which our lane-changing model could be tested experimentally. The first would be to use the results of one test site to estimate the parameters $\alpha$ and $\beta$, and then further use these values to estimate flow rates and lane changing functions at a new test site. The new theoretical estimates and the experimental values of lane-changes could be compared for goodness of fit.

A second way of using the experimental data is to compare results with predictions of a statistical model of Eq. 2 which is independent of the scale parameters $\alpha$ and $\beta$. The stochastic equilibrium model proposed in Sec. 2 was developed with this purpose in mind. Section 3 describes the site and physical characteristics of the traffic experiments. Section 4 discusses certain procedures followed in estimating space-mean speeds and coefficients of variation of stream velocities and flow rates. Section 5 is a summary of the results which we have obtained.

## 2. A Stochastic Equilibrium Model

We assume that the measurable quantities in our experiments, i.e., flow rates, number of lane changes and speeds, are random variables. To test the validity of the lane-changing model we study a version of Eq. 2 which incorporates statistical properties we feel are relevant to the process.

Let $\Delta X$ be defined as the fractional deviation from a mean value of the random variable $X$. Then, every quantity of the model can be redefined as follows:

$$K_1 = \langle K_1 \rangle (1 + \Delta K_1); \qquad K_2 = \langle K_2 \rangle (1 + \Delta K_2)$$
$$P_{12} = \langle P_{12} \rangle (1 + \Delta P_{12}); \qquad P_{21} = \langle P_{21} \rangle (1 + \Delta P_{21})$$
$$Q_1 = \langle Q_1 \rangle (1 + \Delta Q_1); \qquad Q_2 = \langle Q_2 \rangle (1 + \Delta Q_2)$$
$$V_1 = \langle V_1 \rangle (1 + \Delta V_1); \qquad V_2 = \langle V_2 \rangle (1 + \Delta V_2) \tag{3}$$

With this notation, $\langle K_1 \rangle$, $\langle Q_1 \rangle$, $\langle P_{21} \rangle$, $\langle V_1 \rangle$, etc., are expectations while $\Delta K_1$, $\Delta Q_1$, $\Delta P_{21}$, $\Delta V_1$, etc., are random variables having zero expectation and non-negative variance. We now assume that the lane changing functions

$$P_{12} = \alpha K_1^2 (K_{2j} - K_2) \tag{4a}$$

$$P_{21} = \beta K_2^2 (K_{1j} - K_1) \tag{4b}$$

and the fluid flow equations

$$Q_1 = V_1 K_1 \quad ; \quad Q_2 = V_2 K_2 \tag{5a, b}$$

are independent of position or time. In other words, we assume an equilibrium condition on a long flat road free of entrances and exits.

If the fractional changes in densities and flow rates are small and we can neglect $\Delta K_1$, $\Delta K_2$ $\Delta K_1^2$, $\Delta K_2^2$ and higher-order terms we obtain

$$P_{21} = \beta K_2^2 (K_{1j} - K_1) = \beta \langle K_2^2 \rangle (1 + \Delta K_2)^2 (K_{1j} - \langle K_1 \rangle (1 + \Delta K_1))$$

$$= \beta \langle K_2^2 \rangle (K_1 - \langle K_{1j} \rangle)(1 + 2\Delta K_2) - \beta \langle K_2^2 \rangle \langle K_1 \rangle \, \Delta K_1 + \text{higher-order terms}$$

$$\cong \beta \langle K_2^2 \rangle (K_{1j} - \langle K_1 \rangle)(1 + 2\Delta K_2) - \beta \langle K_2^2 \rangle \langle K_1 \rangle \, \Delta K_1 \tag{6}$$

Taking expectations and variances of both sides gives

$$E[P_{21}] = \langle P_{21} \rangle = \beta \langle K_2^2 \rangle (K_{1j} - \langle K_1 \rangle) \tag{7a}$$

$$\text{Var}\,[P_{21}] = 4\beta^2 \langle K_2^4 \rangle (K_{1j} - \langle K_1 \rangle)^2 \, \text{Var}\,[\Delta K_2] + \beta^2 \langle K_2^4 \rangle \langle K_1^2 \rangle \, \text{Var}\,\Delta K_1 \tag{7b}$$

$$- 4\beta^2 \langle K_2^4 \rangle \langle K_1 \rangle (K_{1j} - \langle K_1 \rangle) \, \text{Cov}\,[\Delta K_1, \Delta K_2]$$

Since $\text{Var}\,[\Delta P_{21}] = (\langle P_{21} \rangle)^{-2} \, \text{Var}\,[P_{21}]$, we can divide both sides of Eq. 7b by $\langle P_{21}^2 \rangle$ to obtain

$$E[\Delta P_{21}^2] = \text{Var}\,[\Delta P_{21}]$$

$$= 4\,\text{Var}\,[\Delta K_2] + \frac{\langle K_1^2 \rangle}{(K_{1j} - \langle K_1 \rangle)^2}\,\text{Var}\,[\Delta K_1] - 4\,\frac{\langle K_1 \rangle}{(K_{1j} - K_1)}\,\text{Cov}\,[\Delta K_1, \Delta K_2] \tag{8a}$$

The variance of lane changes from 1 to 2 are given by the similar expression

$$E[\Delta P_{12}^2] = \text{Var}\,[\Delta P_{12}]$$

$$= 4\,\text{Var}\,[\Delta K_1] + \frac{\langle K_2^2 \rangle}{(K_{2j} - \langle K_2 \rangle)^2}\,\text{Var}\,[\Delta K_2] - 4\,\frac{\langle K_2 \rangle}{(K_{2j} - \langle K_2 \rangle)}\,\text{Cov}\,[\Delta K_1, \Delta K_2] \tag{8b}$$

At this point we have related small statistical fluctuations in lane changes to fluctuations in lane densities. It now remains to find expressions for lane density fluctuations in terms of velocity and flow rate fluctuations. If the speed of each vehicle is assumed to be constant but distributed over $(0, \infty)$ with expectations $\langle V_1 \rangle$, $\langle V_2 \rangle$, and variances Var $(V_1)$ and Var $(V_2)$, then

$$E[K_1] = \langle K_1 \rangle = E\left[\frac{Q_1}{V_1}\right]; \text{ Var } [K_1] = \text{Var}\left[\frac{Q_1}{V_1}\right]$$

By assuming small fluctuations about their respective mean values we have

$$K_1 = \langle K_1 \rangle(1 + \Delta K_1) = \frac{\langle Q_1 \rangle(1 + \Delta Q)}{\langle V_1 \rangle(1 + \Delta V_1)} \cong \frac{\langle Q_1 \rangle}{\langle V_1 \rangle}(1 + \Delta Q_1 - \Delta V_1) + 0(\Delta Q_1, \Delta V_1)$$

Squaring both sides and taking expectations gives

$$E[\Delta K_1^2] = \text{Var } [\Delta K_1] = \text{Var } [\Delta Q_1] + \text{Var } [\Delta V_1] - 2 \text{ Cov } [\Delta Q_1, \Delta V_1] \quad (9a)$$

Similarly for lane 2 densities,

$$\text{Var } [\Delta K_2] = \text{Var } [\Delta Q_2] + \text{Var } [\Delta V_2] - 2 \text{ Cov } [\Delta Q_2, \Delta V_2] \quad (9b)$$

The variance of lane changing flow rates can now be obtained by substituting these expressions for Var $[\Delta K_1]$, Var $[\Delta K_2]$ and Cov $[\Delta K_1, \Delta K_2]$ into Eqs. 8a and 8b. The result we obtain is

$$\text{Var } [\Delta P_{21}] = \{4 \text{ Var } [\Delta Q_2] + 4 \text{ Var } [\Delta V_2] - 8 \text{ Cov } [\Delta Q_2, \Delta V_2]\}$$

$$+ \frac{\langle K_1^2 \rangle}{(K_{1j} - \langle K_1 \rangle)^2} \{\text{Var } [\Delta Q_1] + \text{Var } [\Delta V_1] - 2 \text{ Cov } [\Delta Q_1, \Delta V_1]\}$$

$$- \frac{4\langle K_1 \rangle}{K_{1j} - \langle K_1 \rangle} \{\text{Cov } [\Delta Q_1, \Delta Q_2] - \text{Cov } [\Delta Q_2, \Delta V_1]$$

$$- \text{Cov } [\Delta Q_1, \Delta V_2] + \text{Cov } [\Delta V_1, \Delta V_2]\} \quad (10)$$

In equilibrium, we expect the terms involving variances of flow rates and speeds as well as Cov $[\Delta Q_1, \Delta Q_2]$, Cov $[\Delta Q_1, \Delta V_1]$, Cov $[\Delta Q_2, \Delta V_2]$ and Cov $[\Delta V_1, \Delta V_2]$ to be large. On the other hand, vehicle densities are small compared to $K_{1j}$ and we expect small values for Cov $[\Delta Q_1, \Delta V_2]$, Cov $[\Delta Q_2, \Delta V_1]$. Neglecting terms involving $[\langle K_1 \rangle/(K_{1j} - \langle K_1 \rangle)]^2$ and Cov $[\Delta Q_1, \Delta V_2]$ and Cov $[\Delta Q_2, \Delta V_1]$ we obtain the approximate expression

$$\text{Var } [\Delta P_{21}] \cong \{4 \text{ Var } [\Delta Q_2] + 4 \text{ Var } [\Delta V_2] - 8 \text{ Cov } [\Delta Q_2, \Delta V_2]$$

$$- \frac{4\langle K_1 \rangle}{K_{1j} - \langle K_1 \rangle} (\text{Cov } [\Delta Q_1, \Delta Q_2] + \text{Cov } [\Delta V_1, \Delta V_2])\} \quad (11a)$$

Similarly,

$$\text{Var } [\Delta P_{12}] \cong \{4 \text{ Var } [\Delta Q_1] + 4 \text{ Var } [\Delta V_1] - 8 \text{ Cov } [\Delta Q_1, \Delta V_1]$$

$$- \frac{4\langle K_2 \rangle}{K_{1j} - \langle K_2 \rangle} (\text{Cov } [\Delta Q_1, \Delta Q_2] + \text{Cov } [\Delta V_1, \Delta V_2])\} \quad (11b)$$

An important aspect of Eqs. 10 and 11a,b is that they are independent of the constants of proportionality $\alpha$ and $\beta$. In other words, it is possible to test the specific functional assumptions made in Eq. 4 without having to obtain numerical estimates of the unknown parameters $\alpha$ and $\beta$.

### 3. Experimental Sites and Collection of Data

To test the models proposed above, an experiment was made on December 14, 1964, on the Nimitz Freeway (State Route 17) near San Leandro, California. The Nimitz Freeway is a four-lane divided freeway, and is nearly flat at the chosen site. The southbound direction was used so that the test site could be located at reasonable distances from entrances and exits. We felt that the Nimitz Freeway location represented equilibrium conditions.

The experiment used manual observations mainly, because previous attempts to use mechanical detection and recording equipment proved unsatisfactory. Student observers were employed as temporary help. Although none of them had had previous traffic counting experience, we spent some time explaining the nature of the experiments and the need for accurate counts. We made every effort to check the consistency of flow data; for example, several observers were asked to record independently the same data. The observers, using hand tally counters, counted 15-minute lane flow volumes and 15-minute lane changes. For the purpose of obtaining lane changing flow rates, the test site was divided into small observation sections, each of which was approximately 0.25 mile long. The lengths of the observation sections were intended to be small enough for stationarity assumptions to hold, yet large enough to give meaningful sample sizes. However, the precise location was largely controlled by the availability of large natural objects, such as traffic signs, for the identification of the section.

The experimental site was divided into three sections of 0.22 mile 0.28 mile and 0.33 mile, respectively. Data collected during the experiments were punched on cards and processed on an IBM 1620 computer. For purposes of computer coding, time periods are numbered 1–15. The time at the beginning of the period is indicated in column 2 of Table I. Vehicle counts were made at location $A$ to estimate lane flow rates in time periods 3–15. These data are coded in Table I, columns 3–9. Lane changes were counted in all three sections in time periods 1–15. These are recorded in columns 14–19 where the arrow head indicates direction of transfer. For example, $1 \rightarrow 2$ signifies those vehicles transferring from lane 1 to 2. It was assumed that a vehicle transferred at that point in space and time when all wheels crossed the lane line.

Spot speeds were obtained by two speed radars, each used to obtain speeds in one lane. Speeds were measured at $A$; the average and variance of the space-mean speeds are recorded in columns 10–13 of Table I. We assumed that vehicle velocities were constant for all three sections.

TABLE I.  Traffic Data Collected on Nimitz Freeway (December 14, 1964)

| No. | 15 minute time periods Beginning | Vehicle counts at A Lane 1 Cars | Lane 1 Truck | Lane 1 Total | Lane 2 Cars | Lane 2 Truck | Lane 2 Total | Total lanes 1 & 2 | Space mean speeds (miles per hour) Lane 1 Av | Lane 1 Var | Lane 2 Av | Lane 2 Var | Lane changing counts Section 1 1 → 2 | Section 1 2 → 1 | Section 2 1 → 2 | Section 2 2 → 1 | Section 3 1 → 2 | Section 3 2 → 1 |
|---|---|---|---|---|---|---|---|---|---|---|---|---|---|---|---|---|---|---|
| 1 | 10:15 a.m. | — | — | — | — | — | — | — | — | — | — | — | 21 | 12 | 27 | 21 | 34 | 31 |
| 2 | 10:30 a.m. | — | — | — | — | — | — | — | — | — | — | — | 15 | 20 | 29 | 30 | 15 | 28 |
| 3 | 10:45 a.m. | 280 | 19 | 299 | 133 | 57 | 190 | 489 | 55.01 | 36.70 | 46.99 | 61.67 | 18 | 15 | 27 | 25 | 26 | 47 |
| 4 | 11:00 a.m. | 328 | 18 | 346 | 146 | 72 | 218 | 564 | 54.94 | 32.30 | 45.73 | 63.26 | 19 | 16 | 28 | 28 | 18 | 18 |
| 5 | 11:30 a.m. | 311 | 16 | 327 | 173 | 54 | 227 | 554 | 55.51 | 32.67 | 47.21 | 39.51 | 16 | 16 | 37 | 27 | 22 | 31 |
| 6 | 11:45 a.m. | 354 | 16 | 370 | 176 | 70 | 246 | 616 | 54.69 | 36.32 | 44.90 | 62.69 | 18 | 12 | 17 | 22 | 20 | 24 |
| 7 | 12:00 a.m. | 279 | 12 | 291 | 161 | 43 | 204 | 495 | 56.16 | 36.59 | 46.55 | 76.49 | 17 | 18 | 25 | 18 | 20 | 31 |
| 8 | 12:15 p.m. | 275 | 13 | 288 | 154 | 42 | 196 | 484 | 56.24 | 33.00 | 46.87 | 47.88 | 29 | 10 | 30 | 30 | 25 | 31 |
| 9 | 1:15 p.m. | 260 | 11 | 271 | 153 | 69 | 222 | 493 | 56.64 | 26.49 | 43.80 | 58.07 | 14 | 16 | — | — | — | — |
| 10 | 1:30 p.m. | 298 | 16 | 314 | 144 | 54 | 198 | 512 | 57.17 | 16.26 | 46.03 | 52.35 | 19 | 14 | — | — | — | — |
| 11 | 1:45 p.m. | 351 | 9 | 360 | 152 | 69 | 221 | 581 | 56.12 | 26.89 | 43.35 | 102.19 | 16 | 10 | 26 | 18 | — | — |
| 12 | 2:15 p.m. | 365 | 21 | 386 | 185 | 63 | 248 | 634 | 54.63 | 30.90 | 41.36 | 58.49 | 24 | 18 | 27 | 9 | 20 | 24 |
| 13 | 2:30 p.m. | 366 | 17 | 383 | 158 | 62 | 220 | 603 | 55.91 | 35.87 | 46.03 | 68.12 | 21 | 17 | 27 | 22 | 28 | 28 |
| 14 | 2:45 p.m. | 393 | 22 | 405 | 218 | 56 | 274 | 679 | 50.61 | 72.34 | 41.54 | 54.52 | 15 | 19 | 19 | 15 | 15 | 21 |
| 15 | 3:00 p.m. | 429 | 15 | 444 | 208 | 50 | 258 | 702 | 56.25 | 14.85 | 44.00 | 31.57 | 12 | 8 | 21 | 20 | 18 | 36 |

At no point in the experiment were densities measured directly. Flow rate and velocities of each lane were used to estimate a point density value through the state equation $q = kv$. The density value for a section was the average of the two point density estimates at the beginning and end of each section. In Sec. 1, for example, the estimate for $\langle K_2 \rangle$ of Eq. 3 is given by

$$\hat{K}_2 = \tfrac{1}{2}(\hat{K}_2(A) + \hat{K}_2(B)) = \tfrac{1}{2}\left( \frac{\hat{Q}_2(A)}{\hat{V}_2(A)} + \frac{\hat{Q}_2(B)}{\hat{V}_2(B)} \right)$$

where we use the convention $\hat{X}(A)$ to denote the estimate of $\langle X \rangle$ at point $A$. To obtain values for lane flow rates at the end of each section, a cumulative count of lane flow was made at the beginning of the section and added to the net transfers within the section.

Although we do not distinguish between the effects of cars and trucks in this report, the data was collected in such a form that separate vehicle counts were made. Since this may prove to be of some value to later investigators we have decided to report the data as it was collected. However, we stress the fact that only total vehicle counts were used to compute flow rate, densities, and lane changes in this report.

## 4. Statistical Analysis of Data

The models used in this study require the estimation of sample means, variances, and covariances. One of the first problems which arises is estimating the space-mean speeds of vehicles from data which measures their time speeds. As we have already mentioned, we used radar devices to measure the time it takes each vehicle to traverse a small fixed distance at a known location. However, the speeds used in our model should be found by measuring the distance each vehicle moves in a small time interval. It is well known (Eqs. 1, 2) that the expectation and variance of time (subscript $t$) and space (subscript $s$) speeds are related as follows

$$E_s[V] = \left( E_t\left[ \frac{1}{V} \right] \right)^{-1} \tag{12a}$$

$$\mathrm{Var}_s[V] = E_s[V]E_t[V] - (E_s[V])^2$$

$$= E_t[V]\left( E_t\left[ \frac{1}{V} \right] \right)^{-1} - \left( E_t\left[ \frac{1}{V} \right] \right)^{-2} \tag{12b}$$

$(E[1/X])^{-1}$ is known as the harmonic mean of the random variable $X$. It follows from discussions in the following paragraphs that if we obtain samples of the time $t_i(i = 1, 2, \ldots, n)$ for the $i$th vehicle to traverse a unit distance we use an estimator ($\,\hat{}\,$ notation)

$$\hat{V}_t = \frac{1}{n} \sum_{i=1}^{n} \frac{1}{t_i} \tag{13a}$$

$$\hat{V}_s = \left( \frac{1}{n} \sum_{i=1}^{n} t_i \right)^{-1} \tag{13b}$$

for the time and space mean speeds. Before we discuss our choice of statistical estimators for other traffic variables we should mention that there is no attempt to demonstrate that they are unbiased. Rather, we chose what on intuitive grounds seem to be simple but good estimators.

Let $X$ be a random variable with expectation $E[X] = \langle X \rangle$. We have defined $\Delta X$ by $\Delta X = [(X/\langle X \rangle) - 1]$ (Eq. 3). Therefore, $\Delta X$ is also a random variable with zero expectation and variance,

$$\text{Var } [\Delta X] = E[\Delta X^2] = (\langle X \rangle)^{-2} \text{Var } [X] = C_x^2, \tag{14a}$$

where $C_x$ is known as the coefficient of variation of $X$. If $Y$ is another random variable following some other unknown statistical distribution, and $\Delta Y$ is defined in the same was as $\Delta X$, we also know that

$$\text{Cov } [\Delta X, \Delta Y] = E[\Delta X \, \Delta Y] = (\langle XY \rangle)^{-1} \text{Cov } [X, Y] \tag{14b}$$

In this paper we used the following estimators for expectation, variance, and covariance:

$$\hat{X} = \frac{1}{n} \sum_{i=1}^{n} X_i \tag{15a}$$

$$\hat{\sigma}_x^2 = \frac{1}{n-1} \sum_{i=1}^{n} (X_i - \hat{X})^2 \tag{15b}$$

$$\hat{\sigma}_{xy} = \frac{1}{n-1} \sum_{i=1}^{n} (X_i - \hat{X})(Y_i - \hat{Y}) \tag{15c}$$

$\hat{X}$ is the estimator for the mean, $\hat{\sigma}_x^2$ is the estimator for the variance, and $\hat{\sigma}_{xy}$ is the estimator for covariance. $X_i$ and $Y_i$ are the $i$th observations of the random variables $X$ and $Y$, and $n$ denotes the sample size.

Because the true population mean $\langle X \rangle$ is unknown, $\Delta X$ was redefined in our experiments as

$$\Delta X = \frac{X}{\hat{X}} - 1. \tag{16}$$

Although the sample mean of $\Delta X$ is zero, the expectation of $\Delta X$ defined in this way may not be equal to zero. For the calculation of $\hat{\sigma}_{\Delta x}^2$, we used the estimator:

$$\hat{\sigma}_{\Delta x}^2 = \hat{C}_x^2 = \frac{\hat{\sigma}_x^2}{\hat{X}^2} = \left( \frac{1}{\hat{X}} \right)^2 \frac{\sum_{i=1}^{n} (X_i - \hat{X})^2}{n-1} = \frac{\sum_{i=1}^{n} \Delta X^2}{n-1} \tag{17}$$

where $\hat{C}_x$ is the estimate of the coefficient of variation. To estimate Cov $[\Delta X \Delta Y]$, we used the estimator

$$\hat{\sigma}_{\Delta x \Delta y} = \frac{\hat{\sigma}_{xy}}{\hat{X}\hat{Y}} = \frac{1}{\hat{X}\hat{Y}(n-1)} \sum_{i=1}^{n} (X_i - \hat{X})(Y_i - \hat{Y})$$

## 5. Experimental Results and Conclusions

The data collected in periods 3–11 of Table I were used to verify Eqs. 11a, b. Since speeds were measured only at location $A$, the comparison of theoretical and experimental values for lane changes were made only in Sec. 1. The lane flow rates of Sec. 1 (periods 3–11) were found by averaging the flow rates measured at locations $A$ and $B$. The estimates for means, variances, and covariances for all traffic parameters listed in Table I were obtained as described in Sec. 4. These estimates appear in Tables IIa, b. We substituted the

TABLE IIa.    Estimates for Means and Variances

| | Section 1 (Periods 3–11) | | |
|---|---|---|---|
| $X$ | $\hat{X}$ | $\hat{\sigma}_X^2$ | $\hat{\sigma}_{\Delta X}^2$ |
| $Q_1$ | $1264.89 \frac{\text{veh}}{\text{hr}}$ | $19115.13 \left(\frac{\text{veh}}{\text{hr}}\right)^2$ | 0.011947 |
| $Q_2$ | $863.11 \frac{\text{veh}}{\text{hr}}$ | $4815.13 \left(\frac{\text{veh}}{\text{hr}}\right)^2$ | 0.006464 |
| $V_1$ | $55.83 \frac{\text{mi}}{\text{hr}}$ | $0.7132 \left(\frac{\text{mi}}{\text{hr}}\right)^2$ | 0.000229 |
| $V_2$ | $45.71 \frac{\text{mi}}{\text{hr}}$ | $1.9905 \left(\frac{\text{mi}}{\text{h}}\right)^2$ | 0.000952 |
| $P_{21}$ | $256.57 \frac{\text{veh}}{\text{mi-hr}}$ | $2680.99 \left(\frac{\text{veh}}{\text{mi-hr}}\right)^2$ | 0.040734 |
| $P_{12}$ | $335.27 \left(\frac{\text{veh}}{\text{mi-hr}}\right)$ | $6102.48 \left(\frac{\text{veh}}{\text{mi-hr}}\right)^2$ | 0.053727 |
| $K_1$ | $22.66 \left(\frac{\text{veh}}{\text{mi}}\right)$ | — | — |
| $K_2$ | $18.88 \left(\frac{\text{veh}}{\text{mi}}\right)$ | — | — |

TABLE IIb.    Estimates for Covariances

| Section I (Periods 3–11) | |
| --- | --- |
| Cov $(\Delta Q_1, \Delta Q_2) = 0.005902$ | Cov $(\Delta Q_2, \Delta V_2) = -0.001228$ |
| Cov $(\Delta V_1, \Delta V_2) = -0.000084$ | Cov $(\Delta Q_1, \Delta V_2) = -0.000464$ |
| Cov $(\Delta Q_1, \Delta V_1) = -0.000885$ | Cov $(\Delta Q_2, \Delta V_1) = -0.000988$ |

appropriate expressions for velocity and flow rates in Eqs. 11a, b to obtain the theoretical estimates Var $[\Delta P_{21}] = 0.03651$ and Var $[\Delta P_{12}] = 0.05267$. Using the observed data for actual lane changes in Table I, we obtained estimates:

$$\text{Var } [\Delta P_{21}] = 0.04073 \quad \text{and} \quad \text{Var } [\Delta P_{12}] = 0.05373.$$

Furthermore, the terms we had decided to neglect in Eqs. 11a, b turned out to be small in comparison to these variance terms. Based on these results we believe that the proposed relation, Eqs. 2a, b, between lane changes and vehicle densities is confirmed for low to medium densities.

To further test the two lane model, the constants $\alpha$ and $\beta$ used in the lane changing model were estimated for Sec. 1. Knowing that the right-hand sides of Eqs. 1a, b equals 0 in equilibrium,[4] we have

$$\alpha K_1^2(K_{2j} - K_2) = \beta K_2^2(K_{1j} - K_1) \tag{18a}$$

independent of position or time. Equation 18a, together with the equation for the conservation of flow,

$$Q_1 + Q_2 = V_1 K_1 + V_2 K_2 = \text{constant} \tag{18b}$$

can be used to solve a cubic equation for $K_1$ and $K_2$. Multiplying $K_1$ by $V_1$ and $K_2$ by $V_2$, we obtained the equilibrium flow rates $Q_1$ and $Q_2$. These equilibrium flow rates can then be compared with the actual flow rates of Sec. 1. For the total constant flow rate of 2128 vph, it was estimated that the equilibrium flow rates were 1214 vap in lane 1 and 914 vph in lane 2, for $\alpha = 0.004587$ mi²/(veh²-hr), $\beta = 0.00425$ mi²/veh²-hr), $K_{1j} = 200$ veh/mile and $K_{2j} = 160$ veh/mile. If this result is compared with the lane flow rate in Sec. 1 of the Nimitz Freeway, it can be seen that Sec. 1 was indeed quite close to its predicted equilibrium split.

As mentioned in an earlier paper, the absolute values of $\alpha$ and $\beta$ are probably not significant, but their ratio $\gamma = \beta/\alpha$ is an indicator of lane preference. In particular, if $\gamma = 1$, drivers find lanes equally preferable; if $\gamma < 1$, lane 2 is preferable to lane 1, and vice versa if $\gamma > 1$. The values of $\alpha$ and $\beta$ calculated from the Nimitz experiments give a ratio $\gamma = 0.927$, which indicates a slight preference for the outer lane (2).

In the low- to medium-density stream conditions that we observed we believe that lane changing maneuvers belong to the class of rare events. If this is true it is possible to have observation sections of length $\delta x$, and observation periods of length $\delta t$, small enough so that

$$\lim_{\delta x, \delta t \to 0} \text{Prob} \{P > j \mid \delta x, \delta t\} \to 0$$

where $P$ is the number of lane changes in such a section during the time period of length $\delta t$. Let $q$ be the probability that there is one lane change, and $1 - q$ the probability that there is no lane change. Then

$$q = Pr\{P = 1 \mid \delta x, \delta t\}; \qquad 1 - q = Pr\{P = 0 \mid \delta x, \delta t\}$$

When the number of lane changes depends on the length of highway and the length of the observation time, $\lim q \to 0$ as $\delta x, \delta t \to 0$. If the length of a

TABLE III.   Mean and Variance of Lane Changes (Time period 1–13)

| 15 min lane-change volume | Section 1 | | | Section 2 | | | Section 3 | | |
|---|---|---|---|---|---|---|---|---|---|
| | Mean | Variance | $\dfrac{Variance}{Mean}$ | Mean | Variance | $\dfrac{Variance}{Mean}$ | Mean | Variance | $\dfrac{Variance}{Mean}$ |
| $P_{21}$ | 14.93 | 10.81 | 0.728 | 27.73 | 39.43 | 1.735 | 29.30 | 56.90 | 1.942 |
| $P_{12}$ | 19.00 | 16.50 | 0.868 | 27.27 | 21.98 | 0.806 | 22.80 | 30.62 | 1.343 |

highway section is $x$ and the number of lane changes in it is to be observed for a period of time $t$, then it is possible to divide the highway of length $x$ into $n = x/\delta x$ small observation sections, and the time $t$ into $m = t/\delta t$ small observation periods. The total number of lane changes will be the sum of the outcomes of these $n \times m$ samples. If the probability of this total number of lane changes is binomially distributed, as $\delta x, \delta t \to 0$, $nm \to \infty$, the distribution of the number of lane changes approaches the Poisson distribution having the well known property that the variance to mean ratio is one. In Table III we have shown the variance to mean ratios of lane changes and, while we have not attempted to test the significance of these ratios, we feel that the agreement is good.

## References

1. F. Haight: "Mathematical Theories of Traffic Flow." Academic Press; New York. 1963.
2. J. G. Wardrop, Some Theoretical Aspects of Road Traffic Research, *Proc. Inst. Civ. Eng.*, Part II, **1,2**, 325–362 (1952).
3. L. Edie, Discussion of Traffic Stream Measurements and Definitions, Proc. Second Intern. Symp. on the Theory of Road Traffic Flow, J. Almond, Ed., O.E.C.D., Paris (1965).
4. R. M. Oliver, A Two-Lane Traffic Mod 1. ORC Report 64-34, University of California, Berkeley. February 1965. (To appear in *Operations Res.*)

# Optimum Assignment of a Reversible Lane in an Oversaturated Two-Way Traffic Link

*DENOS C. GAZIS*

IBM Watson Research Center
Yorktown Heights, New York

## Abstract

It is assumed that a two-way traffic link such as the Lincoln Tunnel of New York City is oversaturated both ways during a rush period. A reversible lane exists which involves a fixed penalty of idle time during the process of reversal of the direction of traffic. A method is given for finding the assignment of this lane, during the rush period, which minimizes the total delay to the users of the tunnel who queue up in both directions. The influence of constraints on the permissible size of one of the queues is also discussed, as well as possible adaptive features which may account for fluctuations of the demands over the expected design input.

## I. Introduction

CERTAIN TRAFFIC systems can be operated in many *modes*, i.e., combinations of various parameters which define them. For example, the flow of traffic along an artery through many signalized intersections may be controlled by one of many different progression designs, which generally handle well different traffic situations. Another example is a traffic link such as a tunnel or expressway in which one or more lanes may be reversed.

The optimization of the operation of a multimode system requires knowledge of the performance of each mode at different levels of the system's traffic demands, and the penalties of switching from one mode to another. Both are rather difficult to define and monitor. In present multimode systems the transition from one mode to another is effected, empirically, either at fixed times during the day or upon detection of changes in measurable qualities of traffic, such as density and speed at key points in the systems.

In this paper we treat the relatively simple problem of assignment of a reversible lane in a tunnel such as the Lincoln Tunnel of New York City. We first distinguish between the unsaturated and oversaturated cases. In the former, both Eastbound and Westbound traffic can be handled with any assignment of the reversible lanes. Some gain may be obtained by an optimum assignment of lanes which reduces the aggregate delay, or travel time, to the users of the tunnel. The unsaturated case is of no interest in the case of Lincoln Tunnel, where no lanes are reversed except during the period of oversaturation. During this latter period both the Eastbound and Westbound demands are heavy and result in queueing. Of the six available lanes of the tunnel two are assigned permanently for Eastbound traffic, two for Westbound traffic, and two are reversible. In practice, only one lane is reversed during the evening rush period. A proper lane assignment must accomplish one or all of the following things: minimize the delay of the users, exhaust the queues as early as possible, and minimize spill-back into the Manhattan streets. A preliminary discussion of the problem has been given by Greenberg.[1] In what follows the problem is formulated, using the approach given in two previous papers[2,3] for the treatment of oversaturated intersections. Explicit formulas are given for the optimum time of reversal, and the end of the rush period, in terms of parameters describing the asymptotic behavior of the cumulative demand near the end of this period. The numerical data of Greenberg are then used for a sample design.

## 2. General Solution

The assumptions used here are those also used by Greenberg, namely:

a. There exists a known history of demand which exceeds the service capability of the tunnel during a "rush-period."
b. One lane is reversible.
c. Reversal of this lane entails a fixed penalty which is equivalent to having this lane idle for a fixed period of reversal, $E$.
d. The throughput of each lane can be maintained at some high constant level as long as there is a queue waiting to be served.
e. The reversible lane increases the service rates, over the levels provided by the fixed ones, by different amounts in the two directions.

The objective of lane reversal is to minimize the delay to the users of the tunnel, in both directions, subject, perhaps, to some constraints regarding the maximum size of queue permissible on the Manhattan side of the tunnel.

The formulation and solution of the problem is shown in Fig. 1. The cumulative demand and service (CDS) diagram is plotted for both directions 1 and 2, and for their sum. The CDS diagram of Fig. 1 differs from that of References 2 and 3 in that only the excess of cumulative demand and service over the minimum cumulative service is shown. In the CDS diagram the area

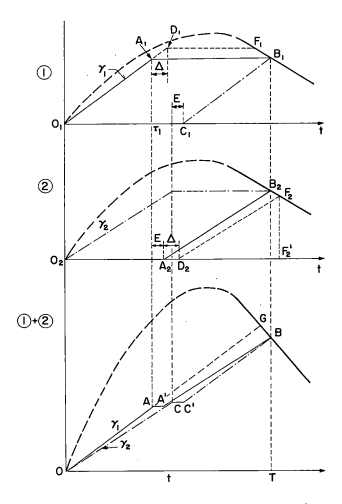

FIGURE 1.   General solution of the problem of optimum lane reversal of an oversaturated two-way traffic link.

between the demand and service curves is a measure of the delay to the users. The time $t = 0$ is the onset of oversaturation, when at least one of the queues starts forming. Utilization of the reversible lane increases the service rates by amounts $\gamma_1$ and $\gamma_2$, and it is assumed that $\gamma_1 > \gamma_2$. Furthermore, we assume that at the end of the rush period the rates of demand are approximately constant. Hence, the cumulative demand curves may be approximated by the straight lines

$$Q_i + b_i t = c_i, \qquad (i = 1, 2) \tag{1}$$

where $Q_i$ are the cumulative demands, $t$ is the time, and $b_i$, $c_i$ are constants. The detailed behavior of the $Q$-curves near the beginning of the rush period is not considered at this moment.

Let us observe the lower diagram, i.e., the sum diagram, of Fig. 1. The service curve has a slope $\gamma_1$ or $\gamma_2$, depending on whether the reversible lane is assigned to stream 1 or stream 2. Any service curve must lie below the line $OG$. If the single assignment $OG$ of the reversible lane exhausts both queues simultaneously, it certainly is the optimum assignment. Otherwise, a lane reversal may be required. The mathematical formulation of the optimization problem is as follows: the queue sizes, $x_i$, in the two directions satisfy the differential equations

$$\frac{dx_1}{dt} = -b_1 - \gamma_1 \min_{\tau \epsilon W} [u(\tau)]$$

$$\frac{dx_2}{dt} = -b_2 - \gamma_2 \min_{\tau \epsilon W} [1 - u(\tau)] \tag{2}$$

where $u$ is the control variable which takes the value 0 or 1, and the time interval $W$ is $t - E \leq \tau \leq t$. It is required to minimize the delay

$$f_0 = \int_0^T (x_1 + x_2) \, dt \tag{3}$$

by choosing appropriately $u(t)$ from the onset of oversaturation to the end of the rush period, $T$.

There are some similarities and some differences between the above problem and that of the oversaturated intersection treated in References 2 and 3. The differences are due mainly to the existence of a penalty in switching which introduces a memory effect, as it were, in the differential equations (2). Nevertheless, the optimal policy involves, in general, one switching just as in the case of oversaturated intersections, provided that the corresponding cumulative service curves remain below the demand curves.

The optimal policy which exhausts both queues as early as possible corresponds to the service curves $O_1 A_1 B_1$ and $O_2 A_2 B_2$, or $OAA'B$ in the sum diagram of Fig. 1. The end of the rush period, $T$, and the time of lane reversal, $\tau_{12}$, are given by

$$T = (c_1 \gamma_2 + c_2 \gamma_1 + \gamma_1 \gamma_2 E)/d$$

$$\tau_{12} = [c_1 b_2 - c_2 b_1 + \gamma_2 (c_1 - b_1 E)]/d \tag{4}$$

where
$$d = \gamma_1 b_2 + \gamma_2 b_1 + \gamma_1 \gamma_2. \tag{5}$$

If we must start the rush period with the reversible lane assigned to stream 2, we can still exhaust both queues at $T$ by reversing the lane at time $\tau_{21}$, which is obtained from the second of Eqs. 4 by an interchange of the subscripts 1 and 2. This policy corresponds to the service curves $O_1C_1B_1$, $O_2B_2C_2$, and $OCC'B$. In comparison with the optimum policy, it produces some additional delay equal to the area of the polygon $OAA'BC'CO$. If $\gamma_1$ is sufficiently larger than $\gamma_2$, this area may be large enough to warrant a check against a policy involving a second lane reversal. This does not appear to be the case for the Lincoln tunnel.

The total delay may be further reduced below the value produced by the above optimal policy if we are willing to extend the rush period for one of the streams. By a reasoning similar to that employed for the single intersection in Reference 2, we see that the total delay has a stationary value if we adopt a policy given by the service curves $O_1D_1F_1$ and $O_2D_2F_2$. This policy is obtained by extending the assignment of the reversible lane to stream 1 past the time $\tau_1$, so that the second legs of the service curves have durations which satisfy the relationship

$$\frac{(D_1F_1)}{(D_2F_2')} = \frac{\gamma_2}{\gamma_1}. \tag{6}$$

A small change of this policy is seen to give a zero change in total delay. The new switchover time is found to be

$$\tau_{12}' = \frac{c_1\gamma_1(b_2 + \gamma_2) - c_2\gamma_2b_1 + b_1b_2\gamma_2E}{\gamma_1(b_2 + \gamma_2)(b_1 + \gamma_1) - b_1b_2\gamma_2}. \tag{7}$$

Similarly, if we must start the rush period with the reversible lane assigned to stream 2, we can minimize the total delay by reversing the lane at time $\tau_{21}'$, obtained from Eq. 7 by interchanging the indices 1 and 2.

### 3. Design Example

The input values used by Greenberg[1] will be used here in a design example. It is assumed that the demand rates vary linearly between the points given in Table I. The last values given are assumed to be maintained indefinitely after the end of the rush period. The minimum service rates are 42 cars/min

TABLE I. Traffic Demand Rates at Lincoln Tunnel During a Typical Evening Rush Period (in cars/min)

| Time | 1 (Westbound) | 2 (Eastbound) |
|---|---|---|
| 4:00 p.m. | 50 | 45 |
| 4:30 p.m. | 60 | 75 |
| 4:45 p.m. |  | 60 |
| 5:15 p.m. | 95 |  |
| 5:30 p.m. | 60 | 60 |
| 5:45 p.m. | 50 |  |
| 6:00 p.m. |  | 30 |

Eastbound, provided by two lanes, and 62 cars/min Westbound, provided by three lanes. A sixth, reversible lane increases the service rate Eastbound by $\gamma_2 = 18$ cars/min, or the service rate Westbound by $\gamma_1 = 19$ cars/min.

The *CDS* diagram is shown in Fig. 2. It is seen that the minimum service capacity is first exceeded Eastbound at 4:15 p.m., which is taken as the onset

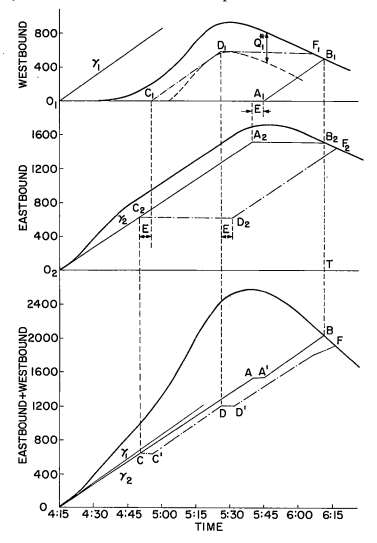

FIGURE 2.   Design example of optimum lane reversal for the over-saturated Lincoln Tunnel of New York City. The input values used are those of Greenberg.[1] The ordinates represent numbers of cars above the maximum that can be served without the reversible lane.

of oversaturation. Although $\gamma_1 > \gamma_2$, we must start the rush period by assigning the reversible lane to Eastbound traffic because it cannot be utilized fully westbound. According to the preceding section, the policy which exhausts both queues as soon as possible, and minimizes the total delay, is given by the service curves $O_1A_1B_1$, $O_2A_2B_2$, $OAA'B$, and involves one lane reversal. We first compute the expressions for $Q_i$ near the end of the rush period, namely,

$$Q_1 + 12t = 1907.5, \qquad t \geq 90$$
$$Q_2 + 12t = 2190 \;\;, \qquad t \geq 105 \tag{8}$$

where $t$ is taken in minutes, measured from 4:15 p.m. Using Eqs. 4 we then find that the earliest end of the rush period and the time of lane reversal are given by

$$T = 4\!:\!15 + 116.2 \text{ min} \approx 6\!:\!11$$
$$\tau_{21} = 4\!:\!15 + 84.2 \text{ min} \approx 5\!:\!39. \tag{9}$$

Another possible consideration in tunnel lane management is the prevention of excessive spillback of the waiting queue into the streets of Manhattan.[1] The adaptation of the solution is similar to that given in a previous paper[4] for the case of limiting spillback from an exit ramp of an expressway. Let us assume that we want to limit the size of the westbound queue to a value lower than $Q_1{}^*$, Fig. 2. The appropriate policy is found as follows: the cumulative demand curve 1 is displaced downwards by $Q_1{}^*$. The service curve of 1 must then be above this displaced curve. Drawing the tangents to this curve, as shown in Fig. 2, we find a policy given by the service curves $O_1C_1D_1F_1$, $O_2C_2D_2F_2$, and $OCC'DD'F$. The price of limiting the westbound queue is given by the area of the polygon $CAA'BFD'DC'C$. In Fig. 2 we have taken $Q_1{}^* = 350$ cars and found that two lane reversals are required, starting at about 4:51 and 5:27.

It is interesting to observe that the detailed behavior of the demand is not required in order to obtain the optimal solution. It is sufficient to have a dependable estimate of the total number of cars that would have demanded service at the two entrances of the tunnels on or before, say, 6:00 p.m., plus the residual rate of demand after that time. If, however, the constraint on the size of the westbound queue is to be taken into account, the exact shape of $Q_1$ is required.

## 4. Effect of Fluctuations

The preceding solution is a deterministic one, but may be used as a starting point for an adaptive control system sensitive to fluctuations. Let us assume that we have a dependable and timely estimate of fluctuations of the demand about an expected reference function such as that of Fig. 2. An on-line computer may then periodically revise the extrapolated estimate of the terminal expressions for $Q_i(t)$, and hence the switchover time $\tau_{21}$. The lane reversal may then be effected on the basis of this updated value of $\tau_{21}$. It is seen from Eqs. 4 that this adjustment is particularly easy to compute if we assume that $b_i$ remain constant and only the $c_i$ vary. This is so because the switchover time is a linear function of the $c_i$. After the lane reversal the monitoring of the demand will continue. If the terminal expressions for $Q_i(t)$ change appreciably, an additional lane reversal may be in order. The test of the necessity of this additional lane reversal may be obtained using the considerations of this paper. Roughly speaking, new fluctuations necessitate an additional lane reversal if they displace the terminal straight lines, $Q_i(t)$, with respect to each other so that queueing is prolonged for the stream which does not use the reversible lane near the end of the rush period. The relative displacement of the $Q$-lines must be at least equal to $E$ before the additional lane reversal can be considered. In view of the fact that this reversal is a relatively complex · operation, it is very likely that it will not be executed unless large fluctuations are observed.

As an example, let us consider the effect of a breakdown of a car inside the tunnel, one of the most frequent fluctuations. Such a breakdown reduces the throughput in the corresponding direction until the disabled vehicle is cleared. The effect of reducing the throughput is exactly the same as the effect of increasing the input by an equal amount. For the purpose of computing the switchover time we can assume that the constant $c_i$ entering Eq. 1, corresponding to the direction along which the breakdown occurs, has been suddenly changed by an amount $c_i^+$. The latter can be estimated fairly accurately in such an emergency. Let us then evaluate the changes, over the lane control $OA_1B_1$ and $OA_2B_2$ of Fig. 2, which will be required when a breakdown occurs at time $t_b$, along one or the other direction. We distinguish two cases, depending on whether $t_b$ is greater or smaller than $\tau_2$ given in Eq. 4.

I. $t_b \leq \tau_{21}$:

A new switchover time is computed, $\langle \tau_{21} \rangle$, given by

$$\langle \tau_{21} \rangle = \max \{t_b, \tau_{21} + (\tau_{21}^+)_i\} \tag{10}$$

where $i$ denotes the direction along which the breakdown occurs, and the $(\tau_{21}^+)_i$ are given by

$$\begin{aligned} (\tau_{21}^+)_1 &= -b_2 c_1^+/d \\ (\tau_{21}^+)_2 &= b_1 c_2^+/d. \end{aligned} \tag{11}$$

II. $t_b > \tau_{21}$:

The switchover has taken place and the expected operating conditions of the tunnel near the end of the rush period are shown in Fig. 3. The breakdown raises the appropriate cumulative demand curve by an amount $c_i^+$.

If the breakdown is Westbound, i.e., along the direction 1, nothing can be done. The best policy is to continue the Westbound assignment of the reversible lane. If, however, the breakdown occurs Eastbound, Fig. 3, it has

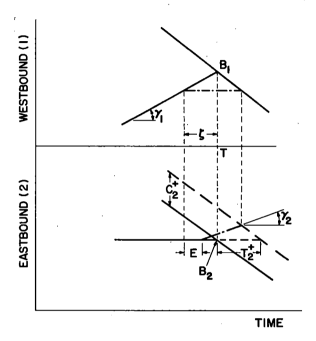

**TIME**

FIGURE 3.   Adaptive change of optimal policy near the end of the rush period, to account for an effective increase of the total Eastbound demand by $c_2^+$. The dash-dot lines show the revised policy.

the effect of lengthening the rush period eastbound by an amount

$$T_2^+ = c_2^+/b_2 \tag{12}$$

where $b_2$ is the constant entering Eq. 1. If $T_2^+ > (1 + \epsilon)E$, an additional lane reversal is required. The constant $\epsilon > 0$ is introduced to account for the relative inconvenience of a lane reversal. If we wish to exhaust both queues simultaneously, we must reverse the lane a time $\zeta$ before the time $T$ given in Eqs. 4, where

$$\zeta = b_1(E\gamma_2 + c_2^+)/d. \tag{13}$$

In a similar manner we can take into account more breakdowns, the effects of which may partially or totally cancel out if they occur in opposing directions.

## Acknowledgment

The author wishes to thank Leslie C. Edie of the Port of New York Authority who first brought this problem to his attention. In addition, he wishes to thank R. S. Foote and I. Greenberg of the same organization for supplying Reference 1.

## References

1. I. Greenberg, Preliminary Analysis of the Lincoln Tunnel Changeover Problem, Report of The Port of New York Authority, Tunnels and Bridges Department, April 1963.
2. D. C. Gazis and R. B. Potts, The Oversaturated Intersection, *Proc., Second Intern. Symp.* on Road Traffic Theory, J. Almond, Ed., O.E.C.D., Paris, (1965).
3. D. C. Gazis, Optimum Control of a System of Oversaturated Intersections, *Operations Res.* **12,** 815–831 (1964).
4. D. C. Gazis, "Spillback From an Exit Ramp of an Expressway, Highway Research Record, No. 89, 39–46 (1965).

# Methods for Describing
# Time-Dependent Waits
# at Traffic Merges

DONALD P. GAVER, Jr.

Carnegie Institute of Technology
Pittsburgh, Pennsylvania

Under simplified conditions the problem of crossing or merging with main road traffic from a side street may be viewed as a single-server queueing problem, with the queue developing on the side street being of interest. Here we are concerned with the expected waiting times of side street drivers who arrive at some finite time after some initial instant; the initial instant chosen is of interest because it marks a change in traffic conditions such as may occur at the beginning of a day or at afternoon rush hour.

The basic model treated is the following: individual cars arrive from the side road at the intersection according to a stationary Poisson process of rate $\lambda$; each side road driver requires a minimum or critical gap in main road traffic in order to merge; if main road traffic is stationary Poisson with negligible block durations then opportunities for entry from the side road occur at independently and identically distributed time intervals, generically denoted by $C$ (actually, the independence may be guaranteed only if merging drivers essentially utilize most of their critical gap). The Laplace-Stieltjes transform associated with $C$ may be derived by conditional expectations in a manner entirely the same as is used to characterize completion times in preemptive-repeat priority queues. Assuming that there are two classes of side road drivers, each of which selects a new critical gap independently from its appropriate distribution at the appearance of a new main road gap (Weiss-Maradudin behaviour within each class), then

$$u(s) = E[e^{-sC}] = p_1 \frac{(s + \nu)\varphi_1(s + \nu)}{s + \nu\varphi_1(s + \nu)} + p_2 \frac{(s + \nu)\varphi_2(s + \nu)}{s + \nu\mu_2(s + \nu)} \; ;$$

$$\varphi_i(t) = E[e^{-zL_i}], i = 1, 2$$

$C$ may then be utilized in place of the service time in the conventional queueing formulas. It is used in the time-dependent results discussed here.

The following situations are considered:

1. Initially $i$ $(i = 0, 1, 2, \ldots)$ cars are present in the side road queue, the first

having just occupied the entry position. The situation is *non-stationary*, i.e., traffic intensity $\rho = \lambda E[C] > 1$.

2. Initially a random number of cars are present, the distribution thereof being determined by the stationary distribution presumed to exist at the end of the former (non-rush-hour) regime. After the initial instant the situation is non-stationary because of increase in $\lambda$ or $C$, the latter being due to increase in main road traffic.

For both cases 1 and 2 an asymptotic formula is given that estimates expected wait at time $t$ after the initial constant:

1:
$$E[W(t)] \sim (\rho - 1)t + E[C]\left\{i + \frac{x_1^{i}}{1 - x_1}\right\}$$

where $x_1$ is the smallest positive root of $x = u[\lambda(1 - x)]$.

2:
$$E[W(t)] \sim (\rho - 1)t + E[C]\left\{E_1(i) + \frac{1}{1 - x_1} E_1(x_1^{i})\right\}$$

where $E_1(\cdot)$ refers to expectation with respect to the stationary distribution assumed to prevail at the initial instant.

Asymptotic formulas for 1 and 2 are compared to the result of a new method of numerical inversion of the Laplace transform, applied to the transform of $E[W(t)]$.

Also examined numerically is the expected waiting time for the following situation:

3. Initially $i$ cars are present at the side street queue. The situation is stationary thereafter. But we are concerned with average waits a *finite* time after the initial instant, so "steady state" queueing formulas are of doubtful accuracy.

# Limit Theorems for the Output of Certain Types of Traffic Queues

MARCEL F. NEUTS

Purdue University, Lafayette, Indiana

The following queueing model may be of interest in the study of certain traffic problems. It was brought to mind by the consideration of an unscheduled car-ferry, but it is of such generality that it may have wider applications.

Consider a single server and customers arriving according to a Poisson process. After a departure, if less than $L$ customers are waiting, the server must wait until there are $L$ customers present before he starts service. If there are $L$ or more customers present, but less than $K(K \geq L)$ then all customers are served at once. If there are more than $K$ customers present, then exactly $K$ customers enter service together and the others must wait for the next service epoch. We assume that the service times are stochastically independent, given the bulk sizes, but the service times may depend on the bulk sizes.

The analysis of the queue is based on the fact that the queue length immediately after departures, together with the interdeparture times, form a semi-Markov process with transition probabilities $Q_{ij}(x)$ $(i, j, = 0, 1, \ldots)$.[1,2]

In this communication we are interested mainly in the limiting properties of the number $N(t)$ of customers served in an interval $[0, t]$,

Let $\zeta_n$ denote the number of customers leaving the queue at the end of the $n$th service. Then if $\xi_n$ is the queue length immediately after the $n$th departure, we have $\zeta_n = f(\xi_{n-1})$ given by:

$$\zeta_n = L \quad \text{for} \quad \xi_{n-1} \leq L$$
$$= \xi_{n-1} \quad \text{for} \quad L \leq \xi_{n-1} \leq K$$
$$= K \quad \text{for} \quad \xi_{n-1} \geq K$$

We may apply the general limit theorems of Pyke and Schaufele[3] for functions defined on a semi-Markov process.

*Theorem 1*

As $t \to \infty$ we have:

$$\frac{N(t)}{t} \xrightarrow{\text{a.s.}} A = \frac{L \sum_{\nu=0}^{L-1} \pi_\nu + \sum_{\nu=L}^{K-1} \nu\pi_\nu + K\left[1 - \sum_{\nu=0}^{K-1} \pi_\nu\right]}{\sum_{\nu=0}^{L-1} \pi_\nu[\alpha_L + (L-\nu)\lambda^{-1}] + \sum_{\nu=L}^{K-1} \pi_\nu\alpha_\nu + \alpha_K\left[1 - \sum_{\nu=0}^{K-1} \pi_\nu\right]}$$

*193*

in which $(\pi_0, \pi_1, \ldots)$ are the stationary probabilities for the imbedded Markov chain, when the queue is ergodic. The quantities $\alpha_L, \alpha_{L+1}, \ldots, \alpha_K$ are the mean service times for batches of size $L, L + 1, \ldots, K$, respectively.

*Theorem 2*

Let $A$ be the constant found in Theorem 1, then if the service time distributions have a finite second moment and if the queue is ergodic, the random variable:

$$t^{-1/2}[N(t) - tA] \tag{2}$$

converges in law to a normal random variable with zero mean and variance $\sigma^2$ given by

$$\sigma^2 = \left( \sum_{i=0}^{\infty} \eta_i \pi_i \right)^{-1} \left\{ \sum_{i=0}^{\infty} \pi_i \zeta_i^{(2)} + 2 \sum_{i=0}^{\infty} \sum_{k \neq j} \sum_{r \neq j} (\xi_{ik} \zeta_r \pi_i)_j M_{kr}(\infty) \right\} \tag{3}$$

in which

$$\sum_{i=0}^{\infty} \eta_i \pi_i = \sum_{i=0}^{L-1} \pi_i [\alpha_i - (L - i)\lambda^{-1}] + \sum_{i=L}^{K-1} \pi_i \alpha_i + \alpha_K \left[ 1 - \sum_{v=0}^{K-1} \pi_v \right] \tag{4}$$

and

$$\zeta_i^{(2)} = f^2(i) - A \sum_{k=0}^{\infty} \int_0^{\infty} x^2 \, dQ_{ik}(x) \tag{5}$$

$$\xi_{ik} = f(i) Q_{ik}(\infty) - A \int_0^{\infty} x \, dQ_{ik}(x) \tag{6}$$

$$\zeta_r = f(r) - A \sum_{k=0}^{\infty} \int_0^{\infty} x \, dQ_{rk}(x) \tag{7}$$

$$_j M_{kr}(\infty) = \frac{\mu_{kj} + \mu_{jr} - \mu_{kr}}{\mu_{rr}} \tag{8}$$

in which the $\mu_{kj}$ are the first moments of the first passage times from state $k$ to state $j$ in the semi-Markov process described above.

## References

1. Marcel F. Neuts, On a General Bulk Queue, Forthcoming in the Mimeo Series, Dept. of Statistics, Purdue University, 1965.
2. Marcel F. Neuts, Semi-Markov Analysis of a Bulk Queue, Mimeo Series No. 37, Dept. of Statistics, Purdue University, 1965.
3. Pyke, Ronald and Schaufele, Ronald, Limit Theorems for Markov Renewal Process, *Ann. Math. Stat.* **35**, 1746–1764 (1964).

# The Estimation of Origin-Destination Trips Using a Transition Matrix Method

*EIJI KOMETANI*

Kyoto University, Kyoto, Japan

## Abstract

Origin-Destination patterns are analyzed for zoned cities using a transition matrix, each element of which gives the transition probability for the movement of vehicle from one zone to another. The analysis is developed so that estimates can be made of current and future traffic patterns. Several examples are given comparing these predicted volumes with actual traffic.

## I. Introduction

IF WE EXAMINE the movement of taxicabs in order to investigate the operating properties of vehicles in general, we find that this operation is similar to a random process. A taxi goes out of the garage to pick up passengers, brings them to their destination at their request, and then returns to move about again looking for passengers. For this driver, the decisions regarding origin and destination are entirely random. These "stochastic trips" are repeated throughout the work day and each day of operation is over when the tour of duty is expired.

If we consider all taxicab movements in a given city, we may cite an additional property, i.e., all taxicabs can be considered to operate with a common transition probability. This assumption can also be established in cases other than that of taxicabs. However, different types of vehicles or modes of transportation will have a particular transition matrix associated with it. For example, a scheduled bus run has a fixed operating route, and all entries will consist of 0 and 1.

We must point out one particular exception in the case of taxicabs. There are some vehicles which carry passengers from the garage to a passenger's destination and then return to the garage to wait for future passengers. In these cases, the stochastic assumption for the operation of vehicles during the work hours is not valid. Frequent returns to the garage cannot be considered a stochastic process and, therefore, must be considered differently.

We divide vehicles into two operating groups so that vehicles in each group have nearly the same work hours or number of trips per day, and a common transition matrix.

In this paper we define these classified sets as a particular "group of cars." However, when it comes to the difficult task of making real estimates, due to insufficient data about operating conditions, we make the usual classification of vehicles, i.e., autos, taxicabs, trucks, buses, etc.

Since we assume interzonal traffic volume in the area is generated through the dispersion of garages and a transition matrix, we do not consider the microscopic details of individual trajectories.

## 2. The Idealized Model

To examine whether computed values fit the actual origin-destination ($OD$) traffic volume, we tentatively assume the operating pattern in each "group of cars" as follows:

1. All cars are parked in garages before their work day.
2. At the beginning of the work day they go to the zone assigned according to a given transition probability.
3. When they arrive at the zone they park for a given period of time (this time also can be given through a probability matrix).
4. After spending the assigned period of time parked, cars select the next zone according to the transition probability and proceed to the next zone.
5. They park there for the given period of time.
6. The operations are repeated. If the last driving operation would extend into overtime, the cars cancel this final trip and return to their garages. In this manner the entire daily operation of the vehicle is described.

The $OD$ traffic volume, using the above method, can easily be simulated on an electronic computer. Taking the nine wards ($Ku$) of Kyoto as zones to be considered, we numbered each, as follows:

1: Kita-Ku 2: Kamigyo-Ku 3: Sakyo-Ku 4: Nakagyo-Ku 5: Higashiyama-Ku
6: Shimogyo-Ku 7: Minami-Ku 8: Ukyo-Ku 9: Fushimi-Ku

Because of insufficient data relating to the transition probabilities, we classified vehicles into two groups—passenger cars and commercial vehicles.

Furthermore, since it is difficult to check the number of vehicles belonging to each zone by investigating the sites of garages, we assigned to a given zone this number by using registrations. In the first trip, the number of vehicles registered in a given zone start from that zone. Table I lists the number of

TABLE I.    Number of Registered Vehicles
in Kyoto City (1962)

| Zone number | Passenger cars | Commercial vehicles |
|---|---|---|
| 1 | 1337 | 788 |
| 2 | 1945 | 1286 |
| 3 | 1519 | 730 |
| 4 | 2754 | 3048 |
| 5 | 1974 | 1746 |
| 6 | 2459 | 3135 |
| 7 | 1808 | 2065 |
| 8 | 2947 | 2351 |
| 9 | 1600 | 1926 |

registered vehicles for each zone for Kyoto. Transition probabilities were calculated with $OD$ traffic volume observed in 1962 (given in Table II) using the equation

$$P_{ij} = \frac{a_{ij}}{\sum_{k=1}^{r} a_{ik}}$$

(1)

where $a_{ij}$ = traffic volume from zone $i$ to zone $j$, and
$r$ = number of zones.

Table III gives the elements of the transition matrix computed by this method. The necessary parking times for this computation is shown in Table IV, and the interzonal traveling times are given in Table V. These values are common to both the passenger cars and the commercial vehicles.

The work day is the total time from the beginning to the end of the daily operation. In this mathematical model each vehicle makes as many trips as possible during the work day. Since the work day controls the number of trips

TABLE II(1).   OD Table of Kyoto City in 1962 (passenger cars)

| O \ D | 1 | 2 | 3 | 4 | 5 | 6 | 7 | 8 | 9 |
|---|---|---|---|---|---|---|---|---|---|
| 1 | 2119 | 2113 | 1429 | 2813 | 309 | 1772 | 439 | 810 | 80 |
| 2 | 1887 | 4708 | 2770 | 4441 | 1220 | 3931 | 375 | 827 | 207 |
| 3 | 1334 | 2435 | 6975 | 3967 | 3051 | 3423 | 110 | 212 | 22 |
| 4 | 2807 | 4936 | 3935 | 11822 | 4446 | 10864 | 1473 | 1374 | 768 |
| 5 | 450 | 1257 | 2709 | 4601 | 8230 | 4987 | 809 | 395 | 568 |
| 6 | 1724 | 3653 | 2937 | 10259 | 5441 | 16480 | 3224 | 1754 | 945 |
| 7 | 307 | 294 | 310 | 1379 | 681 | 3499 | 2930 | 227 | 870 |
| 8 | 905 | 736 | 330 | 1955 | 169 | 1391 | 411 | 2173 | 22 |
| 9 | 118 | 297 | 222 | 542 | 616 | 922 | 780 | 73 | 2234 |

| 1: | Kita-Ku | 2: | Kamigyo-Ku | 3: | Sakyo-Ku |
|---|---|---|---|---|---|
| 4: | Nakagyo-Ku | 5: | Higashiyama-Ku | 6: | Shimogyo-Ku |
| 7: | Minami-Ku | 8: | Ukyo-Ku | 9: | Fushimi-Ku |

TABLE II(2).   OD Table of Kyoto City in 1962 (commercial vehicles)

| O \ D | 1 | 2 | 3 | 4 | 5 | 6 | 7 | 8 | 9 |
|---|---|---|---|---|---|---|---|---|---|
| 1 | 1557 | 1748 | 561 | 1077 | 239 | 773 | 269 | 506 | 124 |
| 2 | 1754 | 6011 | 1341 | 3200 | 650 | 1873 | 340 | 868 | 305 |
| 3 | 406 | 943 | 4030 | 1893 | 900 | 1249 | 308 | 429 | 141 |
| 4 | 1282 | 3028 | 1847 | 11101 | 1543 | 6969 | 1227 | 2670 | 803 |
| 5 | 233 | 775 | 931 | 1460 | 1798 | 1955 | 523 | 322 | 462 |
| 6 | 764 | 2073 | 1262 | 6786 | 1840 | 10278 | 2071 | 1933 | 1313 |
| 7 | 404 | 404 | 321 | 1414 | 502 | 1930 | 3395 | 592 | 742 |
| 8 | 584 | 828 | 430 | 2587 | 450 | 2094 | 584 | 2704 | 213 |
| 9 | 118 | 316 | 89 | 723 | 508 | 1330 | 720 | 317 | 4438 |

TABLE III(I).   Transition Probability (passenger cars)

| D \ O | 1 | 2 | 3 | 4 | 5 | 6 | 7 | 8 | 9 |
|---|---|---|---|---|---|---|---|---|---|
| 1 | 0.178 | 0.178 | 0.120 | 0.237 | 0.026 | 0.149 | 0.037 | 0.068 | 0.007 |
| 2 | 0.093 | 0.231 | 0.136 | 0.218 | 0.060 | 0.193 | 0.018 | 0.041 | 0.010 |
| 3 | 0.062 | 0.113 | 0.324 | 0.184 | 0.142 | 0.159 | 0.005 | 0.010 | 0.001 |
| 4 | 0.066 | 0.116 | 0.093 | 0.279 | 0.105 | 0.256 | 0.035 | 0.032 | 0.018 |
| 5 | 0.019 | 0.052 | 0.113 | 0.192 | 0.343 | 0.208 | 0.034 | 0.016 | 0.024 |
| 6 | 0.037 | 0.079 | 0.063 | 0.221 | 0.117 | 0.355 | 0.069 | 0.038 | 0.021 |
| 7 | 0.029 | 0.028 | 0.030 | 0.131 | 0.065 | 0.333 | 0.279 | 0.022 | 0.083 |
| 8 | 0.112 | 0.091 | 0.041 | 0.242 | 0.021 | 0.172 | 0.051 | 0.267 | 0.003 |
| 9 | 0.020 | 0.051 | 0.038 | 0.093 | 0.106 | 0.159 | 0.134 | 0.013 | 0.386 |

TABLE III(2).   Transition Probability (commercial vehicles)

| D \ O | 1 | 2 | 3 | 4 | 5 | 6 | 7 | 8 | 9 |
|---|---|---|---|---|---|---|---|---|---|
| 1 | 0.227 | 0.225 | 0.082 | 0.157 | 0.035 | 0.113 | 0.039 | 0.074 | 0.018 |
| 2 | 0.107 | 0.367 | 0.082 | 0.196 | 0.040 | 0.115 | 0.021 | 0.053 | 0.019 |
| 3 | 0.039 | 0.092 | 0.391 | 0.184 | 0.087 | 0.121 | 0.030 | 0.042 | 0.014 |
| 4 | 0.042 | 0.099 | 0.061 | 0.364 | 0.051 | 0.229 | 0.040 | 0.088 | 0.026 |
| 5 | 0.025 | 0.082 | 0.098 | 0.154 | 0.296 | 0.207 | 0.055 | 0.034 | 0.049 |
| 6 | 0.027 | 0.073 | 0.045 | 0.240 | 0.065 | 0.363 | 0.073 | 0.068 | 0.046 |
| 7 | 0.042 | 0.042 | 0.033 | 0.146 | 0.052 | 0.199 | 0.350 | 0.061 | 0.076 |
| 8 | 0.056 | 0.079 | 0.041 | 0.247 | 0.043 | 0.200 | 0.056 | 0.258 | 0.020 |
| 9 | 0.014 | 0.037 | 0.010 | 0.084 | 0.059 | 0.155 | 0.084 | 0.037 | 0.520 |

TABLE IV.  Parking Time (minutes)

| Zone number | Parking time |
|:-----------:|:------------:|
| 1 | 23 |
| 2 | 25 |
| 3 | 11 |
| 4 | 6 |
| 5 | 13 |
| 6 | 3 |
| 7 | 56 |
| 8 | 99 |
| 9 | 95 |

TABLE V.  Interzonal Traveling Time in Kyoto City (minutes)

| O \ D | 1 | 2 | 3 | 4 | 5 | 6 | 7 | 8 | 9 |
|:-----:|:--:|:--:|:--:|:--:|:--:|:--:|:--:|:--:|:--:|
| 1 | 10 | 10 | 15 | 15 | 35 | 20 | 30 | 20 | 40 |
| 2 |    | 8  | 10 | 10 | 15 | 12 | 20 | 15 | 30 |
| 3 |    |    | 8  | 12 | 12 | 15 | 24 | 20 | 25 |
| 4 |    |    |    | 10 | 18 | 12 | 20 | 12 | 25 |
| 5 |    |    |    |    | 8  | 12 | 18 | 20 | 20 |
| 6 |    |    |    |    |    | 7  | 12 | 15 | 20 |
| 7 |    |    |    |    |    |    | 5  | 15 | 12 |
| 8 |    |    |    |    |    |    |    | 10 | 30 |
| 9 |    |    |    |    |    |    |    |    | 12 |

in a day, we used $5\frac{1}{2}$ hours as a reasonable period of time after many trial examinations in the range from 3–8 hours, and compared these results with $OD$ patterns. Table VI shows the traffic volume for a $5\frac{1}{2}$ hour work day. Here we can see that in most cases the computed results compare favorably with the actual $OD$ pattern. In those cases where there is a large discrepancy, the calculated values are larger than actual values. They are also related to the outlying parts of the city in common, especially Ukyo-Ku and Fushimi-Ku, the newly developed areas.

We can identify some factors influencing the $OD$ values in each district; differences in parking time or driving time, and the inconsistencies between the sites of car registrations and garage locations. We, therefore, extended parking time in the Ukyo-Ku and Fushimi-Ku. However, we could not derive any differences in these patterns except by decreasing the total number of trips. Since errors in driving time have an influence on all $OD$ trips, we believe that it has approximately the same effect as the change in the number of hours in a work day and, therefore, did not take this into consideration. Having incomplete data on garage locations, we cannot be absolutely sure of the differences in the registration sites and the garage locations. We will discuss this problem later.

Finally, to expedite the calculations, we used one vehicle as a substitute for a group of registered vehicles in each zone, and it's trips are assumed to be equivalent to the trips of the other cars in the same zone. After calculating $OD$ traffic volume for a 10 day period, the average value of a work day was taken as shown in Table VI.

These simplified methods of computation may produce an error in the $OD$ pattern. Therefore, to minimize this error, we simulated 10 days of operation of a single car as a substitute for 100 registered cars. (We could, of course, simulate all cars one after another, if an unlimited amount of computer time were available.)

However, we found almost no differences in the computed $OD$ pattern. We believe additional errors were being generated 'by random numbers used in this simulation. We therefore used several sets of random numbers and found that each $OD$ traffic volume varied only by 20% for the same calculation.

After taking into account all of the factors discussed above, we find that the computed values related with Fushimi-Ku and Ukyo-Ku are still larger than the real values. It is of interest, therefore, to examine this problem on a theoretical basis.

In the simulation the operation of a vehicle ends after a fixed number of hours. From another point of view we may say that each car's operation finishes when it completes an average number of trips for a day. Here all direct relation to the total period of operating time disappears. Traffic generation becomes possible without direct relation to operating time and parking time. Since it is unnatural to believe that the actual number of hours

TABLE VI.   Calculated Values of OD Traffic by Simulation (hours of operation—5.5 hours)

(passenger cars)

| D⟍O | 1 | 2 | 3 | 4 | 5 | 6 | 7 | 8 | 9 |
|---|---|---|---|---|---|---|---|---|---|
| 1 | 2441 | 2405 | 1322 | 2376 | 403 | 1577 | 656 | 686 | 107 |
| 2 | 1686 | 4405 | 2579 | 4528 | 1257 | 3997 | 494 | 970 | 400 |
| 3 | 1314 | 2251 | 6510 | 3458 | 2919 | 3634 | 243 | 425 | 213 |
| 4 | 2329 | 4506 | 3814 | 12547 | 4116 | 10126 | 1425 | 1009 | 848 |
| 5 | 426 | 1197 | 2774 | 4483 | 7363 | 5597 | 891 | 675 | 598 |
| 6 | 1948 | 3698 | 3028 | 9648 | 5593 | 16147 | 3186 | 1825 | 802 |
| 7 | 414 | 463 | 499 | 1498 | 715 | 4444 | 2881 | 351 | 662 |
| 8 | 1075 | 909 | 407 | 2324 | 432 | 1493 | 658 | 2321 | 432 |
| 9 | 227 | 336 | 194 | 846 | 658 | 791 | 875 | 323 | 3066 |

(commercial vehicles)

| D⟍O | 1 | 2 | 3 | 4 | 5 | 6 | 7 | 8 | 9 |
|---|---|---|---|---|---|---|---|---|---|
| 1 | 1983 | 2245 | 430 | 1293 | 266 | 650 | 233 | 484 | 118 |
| 2 | 1867 | 5789 | 1215 | 3379 | 499 | 1834 | 300 | 717 | 478 |
| 3 | 379 | 877 | 4883 | 2066 | 882 | 1333 | 427 | 378 | 162 |
| 4 | 1175 | 3185 | 1877 | 9573 | 1440 | 6116 | 1655 | 2475 | 1007 |
| 5 | 204 | 947 | 852 | 1248 | 2109 | 1758 | 537 | 544 | 615 |
| 6 | 802 | 1842 | 1511 | 5746 | 1565 | 8212 | 2075 | 1662 | 1225 |
| 7 | 379 | 496 | 504 | 1372 | 582 | 1672 | 2392 | 935 | 693 |
| 8 | 649 | 780 | 450 | 2906 | 506 | 2129 | 686 | 2369 | 454 |
| 9 | 320 | 463 | 226 | 763 | 481 | 1253 | 857 | 621 | 4082 |

is always fixed, we will be able to achieve the same goal in deciding the movement of cars more realistically through the assignment of trip number. However, in this case the last trip of the day is not assigned via the transition
probability matrix. The last trip returns the vehicle to the place of its origin.
This is the only difference from the simulation model.

## III. The Markov Process

We assume that the garage sites correspond to the registration sites. We
denote the number of vehicles in each zone in the district as $T_1, T_2, T_3 \ldots T_r$,
where $r$ is the number of zones and $T$ is the total number of registered vehicles
i.e.,

$$T = \sum_{i=1}^{r} T_i \tag{2}$$

We then construct $\mathbf{P}$, the transition matrix, between each zone,

$$\mathbf{P} = \begin{pmatrix} P_{11}, & P_{12}, & P_{13}, & \ldots, & P_{1r} \\ P_{21}, & P_{22}, & P_{23}, & \ldots, & P_{2r} \\ \ldots & \cdot & & & \\ \ldots & \cdot & & & \\ P_{r1}, & P_{r2}, & \ldots & \ldots, & P_{rr} \end{pmatrix} \tag{3}$$

This is a matrix where the sum of the elements in each row is unity.

Initially each vehicle starts from the zone where the garages are located and
completes its first trip, the number of vehicles $T_i^{(2)}$ belonging to the zone $i$
that actually exists in each zone is given by the row vector,

$$(T_1^{(2)}, T_2^{(2)}, \ldots, T_r^{(2)}) = (T_1, T_2, \ldots, T_r)\mathbf{P} \tag{4}$$

This is written more briefly as,

$$\mathbf{T}^{(2)} = \mathbf{TP} \tag{4'}$$

where $\mathbf{T}$ is a row vector.

We can obtain $OD$ tables in the form of the matrix,

$$\begin{pmatrix} T_1 P_{11}, & T_1 P_{12}, & \ldots, & T_1 P_{1r} \\ T_2 P_{21}, & T_2 P_{21}, & \ldots, & T_2 P_{2r} \\ \cdot & & & \\ \cdot & & & \\ \cdot & & & \\ T_r P_{r1}, & T_r P_{r2}, & \ldots, & T_r P_{rr} \end{pmatrix} \tag{5}$$

or as the product of the diagonal matrix,

$$
\begin{pmatrix}
T_1 & & & & & 0 \\
 & T_2 & & & & \\
 & & T_3 & & & \\
 & & & \cdot & & \\
 & & & & \cdot & \\
0 & & & & & T_r
\end{pmatrix}
\tag{5'}
$$

and the transition matrix $\mathbf{P}$. Similarly, the state vector $\mathbf{T}^{(N)}$ before the $N$th trip is given as,

$$\mathbf{T}^{(N)} = \mathbf{T}^{N-1}\mathbf{P}$$

or

$$= \mathbf{T}\mathbf{P}^{N-1} \tag{6}$$

In particular the $OD$ table of the $N$th trip is shown as

$$
\begin{pmatrix}
T_1^{(N)} & & & & 0 \\
 & T_2^{(N)} & & & \\
 & & \cdot & & \\
 & & & \cdot & \\
0 & & & & T_r^{N}
\end{pmatrix}\mathbf{P}
\tag{7}
$$

Here the total $OD$ table for the day is required and not the $OD$ table for every hour of travel. If we make the average number of trips in a day $N$, the generated traffic volume in each zone, denoted by the row vector, $A^{(N)}$ is,

$$\mathbf{A}^{(N)} = \mathbf{T} + \mathbf{T}^{(2)} + \mathbf{T}^{(3)} + \ldots \mathbf{T}^{N}$$
$$= \mathbf{T}(\mathbf{I} + \mathbf{P} + \mathbf{P}^2 + \mathbf{P}^3 \ldots \mathbf{P}^{N-1}) \tag{8}$$

$N$ is the "total number added until the $N$th trip". Here

$$\mathbf{A}^{(N)} = (A_1^{(N)}, A_2^{(N)}, \ldots A_r^{(N)})$$

where $\mathbf{I}$ is the identity matrix. Therefore, the $OD$ table consisting of the total trips of $N$ travel times are shown as

$$
\begin{pmatrix}
A_1^{(N)} & & & & 0 \\
 & A_2^{(N)} & & & \\
 & & \cdot & & \\
 & & & \cdot & \\
0 & & & & A_r^{(N)}
\end{pmatrix}\mathbf{P} =
\begin{pmatrix}
A_1^{(N)}P_{11}, & A_2^{(N)}P_{12}, & \ldots, & A_1^{(N)}P_{1r} \\
A_2^{(N)}P_{21}, & A_2^{(N)}P_{22}, & \ldots, & A_2^{(N)}P_{2r} \\
\cdot & & & \\
\cdot & & & \\
\cdot & & & \\
A_r^{(N)}P_{r1}, & A_r^{(N)}P_{r2}, & \ldots, & A_r^{(N)}P_{rr}
\end{pmatrix}
\tag{9}
$$

In the model used in the simulation, the vehicles return to the place where each vehicle originated. We must therefore add a trip which returns the vehicle to its origin after the $(N-1)$th trip. The probability that a vehicle which belongs to zone $i$ exists in zone $j$ at the beginning of the $N$th trip is given by the $ij$th entry of the matrix $\mathbf{P}^{N-1}$ (denoted by $P_{ij}^{(N-1)}$), and this is multiplied by $T_i$

to obtain the number of cars which return from $j$ to $i$. Accordingly, we may multiply $T_1, T_2, \ldots, T_r$ to each column in $\mathbf{P}^{N-1}$. Thus the $OD$ traffic volume for the last trip is shown in matrix form

$$
\begin{pmatrix}
T_1 P_{11}^{(N-1)}, & T_2 P_{21}^{(N-1)} & \cdots, & T_r P_{r1}^{N-1} \\
T_1 P_{12}^{(N-1)}, & T_2 P_{22}^{(N-1)} & \cdots, & T_r P_{r2}^{(N-1)} \\
& & \cdots, & \\
& & \cdots, & \\
T_1 P_{1r}^{(N-1)}, & T_2 P_{2r}^{(N-1)} & \cdots, & T_r P_{rr}^{(N-1)}
\end{pmatrix}
\tag{10}
$$

and the $ij$ entry of the following matrix shows the total number of cars which move from zone $i$ to $j$.

$$
\begin{pmatrix}
A_1^{(N-1)} P_{11} + T_1 P_{11}^{(N-1)}, & A_1^{(N-1)} P_{12} + T_2 P_{21}^{(N-1)}, & \cdots & A_1^{(N-1)} P_{1r} + T_r P_{r1}^{(N-1)} \\
A_2^{(N-1)} P_{21} + T_1 P_{12}^{(N-1)}, & A_2^{(N-1)} P_{22} + T_2 P_{22}^{(N-1)}, & \cdots & A_2^{(N-1)} P_{2r} + T_r P_{r2}^{(N-1)} \\
A_r^{(N-1)} P_{r1} + T_1 P_{1r}^{(N-1)}, & A_r^{(N-1)} P_{r2} + T_2 P_{2r}^{(N-1)}, & \cdots & A_r^{(N-1)} P_{rr} + T_r P_{rr}^{(N-1)}
\end{pmatrix}
\tag{11}
$$

Using a property of the Markov process, if $\mathbf{P}$ is regular, $\mathbf{P}^N$ becomes the limiting matrix $\langle \mathbf{W} \rangle$ as $N$ goes to infinity, i.e.,

$$
\lim_{N \to \infty} \mathbf{P}^N = \langle \mathbf{W} \rangle
\tag{12}
$$

Where,

$$
\langle \mathbf{W} \rangle =
\begin{pmatrix}
\omega_1, & \omega_2, & \cdots & \omega_r \\
\omega_1, & \omega_2, & \cdots & \omega_r \\
& & \cdots & \cdots \\
& & \cdots & \cdots \\
\omega_1, & \omega_2, & \cdots & \omega_r
\end{pmatrix}
\tag{13}
$$

Each row of the matrix $\langle \mathbf{W} \rangle$ is equal. Therefore, we define the following row vector

$$
\omega = (\omega_1, \omega_2, \omega_3, \ldots, \omega_r), \text{ and}
\tag{14}
$$

since every row of $\langle \mathbf{W} \rangle$ is $\omega$, we can obtain $\omega$ by solving the equation

$$
\omega \mathbf{P} = \omega
$$

subject to the condition that

$$
\omega_1 + \omega_2 + \ldots + \omega_r = 1
\tag{15}
$$

Entries for the transition matrix $\mathbf{P}$ for Kyoto used to solve Eq. 15 are given in Table III (1). The corresponding solution to Eq. 15 is:

$$\omega_1 = 0.0604, \quad \omega_2 = 0.1065, \quad \omega_3 = 0.1132$$

$$\omega_4 = 0.2185, \quad \omega_5 = 0.1273, \quad \omega_6 = 0.2482$$

$$\omega_7 = 0.0554, \quad \omega_8 = 0.0405, \quad \omega_9 = 0.0300$$

The transition matrix **P** given in Table III (1) is approximately equal to ⟨**W**⟩ when $N = 6$, and we may consider them equivalent in the steady state. The value of **P**⁶ is shown in Table VII. The main reason why it reaches a steady state quickly is because there is only a small difference between **P** and ⟨**W**⟩ initially. It would appear that this matrix also converges considerably rapidly for other cities. In most cities of Japan the average number of trips is usually greater than seven, so that **P**⁶ reaches a steady state just before the end of the daily operation.

TABLE VII.   P⁶ Values (passenger cars)

| D\O | 1 | 2 | 3 | 4 | 5 | 6 | 7 | 8 | 9 |
|---|---|---|---|---|---|---|---|---|---|
| 1 | 0.061 | 0.107 | 0.114 | 0.219 | 0.127 | 0.248 | 0.055 | 0.040 | 0.029 |
| 2 | 0.061 | 0.107 | 0.114 | 0.219 | 0.127 | 0.248 | 0.055 | 0.040 | 0.029 |
| 3 | 0.061 | 0.107 | 0.114 | 0.219 | 0.127 | 0.248 | 0.055 | 0.040 | 0.029 |
| 4 | 0.061 | 0.107 | 0.113 | 0.219 | 0.127 | 0.248 | 0.055 | 0.041 | 0.029 |
| 5 | 0.060 | 0.106 | 0.114 | 0.219 | 0.128 | 0.249 | 0.055 | 0.040 | 0.030 |
| 6 | 0.060 | 0.106 | 0.113 | 0.218 | 0.127 | 0.249 | 0.056 | 0.041 | 0.030 |
| 7 | 0.060 | 0.106 | 0.112 | 0.218 | 0.127 | 0.249 | 0.057 | 0.040 | 0.030 |
| 8 | 0.061 | 0.107 | 0.113 | 0.219 | 0.126 | 0.248 | 0.055 | 0.041 | 0.030 |
| 9 | 0.059 | 0.105 | 0.111 | 0.217 | 0.128 | 0.249 | 0.058 | 0.040 | 0.033 |

The calculated average number of trips per day in Kyoto, for example, is 10.4 for passenger cars, and 7.6 for commercial vehicles. The early assumption where the trip number for each vehicle is assumed to be constant is, of course, unreasonable. However, we cannot as yet take this variable into account in this particular model. Presently, we interpret the fact that the average number of trips is 10.4 means that there are days when the trip number is 10, and days when the trip number is 11, with ratio of 6 to 4. Then, by calculating the $OD$ trip using Eq. 15, we can observe, as in Table VIII, that the calculated results approximate those of the simulation results.

From the above investigation, we find that the simulation results by using a given work period is very nearly equal to the Markov chain result using an average number of trips per day. Trips relating to the two zones, Ukyo-Ku and Fushimi-Ku, however, still have calculated values larger than those found in practice. We believe the main reason for this is due to the inconsistencies in garage and registration sites.

In the Markov process for the steady state the equation

$$(T_1^{(\infty)}, T_2^{(\infty)}, \ldots, T_r^{(\infty)}) = \lim_{N \to \infty} (T_1^{(N)}, T_2^{(N)}, \ldots, T_r^{(N)})$$

$$= (T_1, T_2, \ldots, T_r)\langle \mathbf{W} \rangle$$

$$= (\omega_1, \omega_2, \ldots, \omega_r)T$$

or

$$\mathbf{T}^{(\infty)} = \omega T, \qquad (16)$$

TABLE VIII. Calculated OD Traffic by Markov Process under Transient State (passenger cars)

| O \ D | 1 | 2 | 3 | 4 | 5 | 6 | 7 | 8 | 9 |
|---|---|---|---|---|---|---|---|---|---|
| 1 | 2073 | 2073 | 1401 | 2957 | 302 | 1730 | 513 | 799 | 82 |
| 2 | 1830 | 4580 | 2693 | 4316 | 1184 | 3824 | 348 | 813 | 197 |
| 3 | 1239 | 2275 | 6529 | 3763 | 2860 | 3202 | 96 | 198 | 120 |
| 4 | 2587 | 4558 | 3698 | 10959 | 4120 | 10054 | 1370 | 1260 | 633 |
| 5 | 441 | 1203 | 2617 | 4443 | 7975 | 4820 | 783 | 369 | 536 |
| 6 | 1628 | 3442 | 2771 | 9738 | 5145 | 15641 | 3085 | 1674 | 927 |
| 7 | 337 | 325 | 354 | 1532 | 758 | 3889 | 3273 | 256 | 958 |
| 8 | 1173 | 951 | 427 | 2539 | 454 | 1852 | 534 | 2799 | 231 |
| 9 | 152 | 386 | 286 | 696 | 793 | 1198 | 1004 | 201 | 2892 |

exists. Therefore, the traffic generating power of the arbitrary zone $i$ is equal to a concentrated traffic volume, and also equal to the value of the total number of registered vehicles $T$ multiplied by the fixed rate $\omega_i$. In other words, in a steady state the traffic has a fixed volume which bears no relation with the initial distribution of cars. This equation demonstrates that in the zone where $T_i$ is large the registered number of vehicles is large; in a zone where $\omega_i$ is large a traffic generating power is high. As we mentioned before, the transition matrix converges rapidly and since registration sites do not coincide with garage sites, we use instead $T\omega_i$ as the number of cars belonging to the zone $i$. Then using Eq. 6 we can now write

$$\mathbf{T} = \omega T \qquad (17)$$

thus
$$T^{(2)} = TP = T\omega P = T\omega$$
In like manner, we have
$$T = T^{(2)} = T^3 = \ldots T^N = \omega T \tag{18}$$

This states that the number of vehicles in each zone is constant even after an arbitrary trip. The $OD$ traffic volumes for every trip is given by

$$\begin{pmatrix} T\omega_1 P_{11}, & T\omega_1 P_{12}, & \ldots, & T\omega_1 P_{1r} \\ T\omega_2 P_{21}, & T\omega_2 P_{22}, & \ldots, & T\omega_2 P_{2r} \\ & & \ldots, & \\ & & \ldots, & \\ T\omega_r P_{r1}, & T\omega_r P_{r2}, & \ldots, & T\omega_r P_{rr} \end{pmatrix}. \tag{19}$$

The $OD$ traffic volume total up to the $N$th trip is given by,

$$TNP_\omega, \tag{20}$$

where

$$P_\omega = \begin{pmatrix} \omega_1 P_{11}, & \omega_1 P_{12}, & \ldots, & \omega_1 P_{1r} \\ \omega_2 P_{21}, & \omega_2 P_{22}, & \ldots, & \omega_2 P_{2r} \\ \omega_r P_{r1}, & \omega_r P_{r2}, & \ldots, & \omega_r P_{rr} \end{pmatrix}. \tag{21}$$

$P_\omega$ is a matrix which could rightly be termed the trip probability matrix. The $i, j$ entry of this matrix expresses the probability that an arbitrary trip

TABLE IX.   Calculated $OD$ Traffic by $TNP_\omega$ Method in Steady State (passenger cars)

| O \ D | 1 | 2 | 3 | 4 | 5 | 6 | 7 | 8 | 9 |
|---|---|---|---|---|---|---|---|---|---|
| 1 | 2063 | 2063 | 1375 | 2731 | 306 | 1719 | 420 | 783 | 78 |
| 2 | 1891 | 4699 | 2770 | 4431 | 1222 | 3935 | 363 | 840 | 210 |
| 3 | 1337 | 2445 | 701 | 3973 | 3075 | 3438 | 115 | 210 | 21 |
| 4 | 2751 | 4833 | 3878 | 11652 | 4374 | 10677 | 1452 | 1337 | 745 |
| 5 | 458 | 1261 | 2751 | 4661 | 8347 | 5062 | 821 | 382 | 592 |
| 6 | 1757 | 3763 | 2999 | 10506 | 5558 | 16847 | 3285 | 1814 | 993 |
| 7 | 306 | 306 | 325 | 1344 | 688 | 3515 | 2961 | 229 | 879 |
| 8 | 890 | 707 | 325 | 1872 | 172 | 1337 | 401 | 2063 | 21 |
| 9 | 105 | 287 | 210 | 535 | 611 | 917 | 780 | 78 | 2216 |

selected belongs to an $OD$ trip between $i$ and $j$. The traffic volume from zones $i$ to $j$, arising from vehicles returning to their garages, may be regarded as being in a steady state, and therefore this contribution is given by the term, $T_j\omega_i$. The traffic volume between $i$ and $j$ after the end of all trips is given as

$$T(N-1)\omega_i P_{ij} + T\omega_j\omega_i$$
$$= TN\omega_i P_{ij} + T\omega_i(\omega_j - P_{ij}).$$

Since we can assume that $N$ is greater than seven, and since the value of $(\omega_j - p_{ij})$ is relatively small, we may disregard the second term in comparison with the first term. Therefore, we may estimate the $OD$ traffic volume by using Eq. 20.

Table IX shows the traffic volume calculated using Eq. 20 for the movement of passenger cars in Kyoto. This result is more nearly equivalent to the actual $OD$ pattern than any of the other techniques used above. Equation 20, which we term the "$TNP_\omega$" method is convenient for computation and is most useful in practice.

## IV. Estimating Future OD Traffic

Since the "$TNP_\omega$" method has proved to be useful in calculating current volumes, we now suggest how it can be used in calculating future traffic. The variables which need to be estimated are $T$, the total number of registrations in the area concerned, $N$ the average number of trips, and $\mathbf{P}$ the transition matrix.

An estimation procedure performed in the city of Amagasaki is as follows:

    a. Investigate the operation of vehicles registered in the city with a sampling rate of 1/10. (As a result, we adopted the four groups of vehicles: passenger cars, trucks, special vehicles, and minicars.)

    b. The average number of trips $N$ calculated were 7.6, 7.8, 7.6, and 6.7, respectively, for the above mentioned four groups of vehicles.

    c. From investigations on vehicle operations, we calculated the transition probability of each vehicle group (the area was divided in six zones). From this transition probability $\mathbf{P}$ we calculated $\omega$, and then calculated the trip probability matrix $\mathbf{P}_\omega$ using Eq. 21. Using the total number of registrations, $T$, we calculated $OD$ traffic volume using Eq. 20, i.e.,

$$TNP_\omega$$

and confirmed that the result agreed with the present $OD$ Table.

    d. As an economic index having the closest relation with the transition probability, we took such factors as number of establishments, number of shops, persons engaged by industry group, proceeds of sales, floor space, etc., and obtained correlation coefficients between transition probabilities and a combined economic indexer for both zones of origin and destination.

A product form was chosen because a simple sum always indicated a lower correlation than in the case of product form. Assuming the equation

$$P_{ij} = K(A_iA_j)^\alpha(B_iB_j)^\beta R_{ij}^\delta \tag{23}$$

where the constants $K$, $\alpha$, $\beta$, and $\delta$ were estimated by the method of "least squares." Here $A_i$ and $A_j$ are the number of incorporated shops in zones $i$ and $j$, and $B_i$ and $B_j$ are the sales per year in zones $i$ and $j$. $R_{ij}$ is the travel time between zones $i$ and $j$. We changed the value of $K$ calculated in this manner so that $K$ could have a directional property, and determined $K_{ij}$ so that the equation,

$$P_{ij} = K_{ij}(A_iA_j)^\alpha(B_iB_j)^\beta R_{ij}^\delta \tag{24}$$

was always consistent.

  e. Assuming that the constants of Eq. 24 will not change in the future, we estimated the future transition matrix $\mathbf{P}$ by substituting the future economic indices $A$ and $B$ in each zone and new travel times, $R_{ij}$, shortened (hopefully) by road improvements, into Eq. 24. From this we calculated a new limiting vector, $\boldsymbol{\omega}$.

  f. Assuming the functional form for the relationship between economic indices and changes in the number of registered vehicles in the city, we derived the values for the parameters by the method of *least squares*. We then estimated the number of registered vehicles in each class of cars in the future target year.

  g. The calculated $OD$ traffic volume was then made using Eq. 20.


## V. Conclusion

Assuming that cars have the same transition probability and the same number of trips, we can calculate the $OD$ traffic volume using the property of Markov chains. As a way of estimation, the method of "$TNP_\omega$" of Eq. 20 appears to be the most useful. In estimating future traffic volume the estimation of the future transition probability is most difficult. By this method we can calculate theoretically the $OD$ traffic volume for the cars which belong to the area concerned, but cannot do so in those cases where cars, foreign to the area, come in or pass through the area concerned. Though the most accurate method to ascertain the transition probability is at present to investigate vehicle operation directly, we can see from Eq. 1 that we can obtain an approximation to this matrix from the present $OD$ table. We suggest that this method can also be extended to the case where cars are assigned different trip numbers, and also where cars can return directly to their garage during the work day, and in like manner make repeated trips.

# A Theoretical Model of Commuter Traffic in Towns

*R. J. SMEED\**

Road Research Laboratory, Ministry of Transport
Middlesex, England

A theoretical model of commuter traffic in the central areas of towns has previously been developed by the writer[1,2] and used to calculate the area required for roads in idealised towns. The present paper[3] extends this model and avoids an earlier approximation. As before, data on the capacity of roads, the density of workplaces, and the fraction of the ground area devoted to roads in actual towns are used.

It is assumed that the central area of the town is circular, that people live outside this area but work inside it, and that workplaces are distributed uniformly in those parts of the central area not devoted to roads. (In previous work it was assumed that workplaces were distributed over the whole of the central area, without reference to the requirements for road space.) Three different routing systems for the journey to work within the central area are considered, as follows:

*Ring routing.* From the outskirts of the central area along an external ring road to the point nearest the destination, and then along a radial road.

*Radial-arc routing.* From the outskirts of the central area along a radial as far as the circular road on which the destination lies, and then along the circular road.

*Radial routing.* From the outskirts along a radial to a central core within which the route transfers to the radial on which the destination lies. The whole of this central core is devoted to roads.

Two alternative assumptions are made about the radial roads:

a. they are "one-way" (but reversible) i.e., that the same roads are used inwards during the morning peak period and outwards during the evening peak period;

b. they are "two-way" (but effectively divided) so that half the carriageway is available only for inward traffic and half only for outward traffic.

Calculations are made of the distance traveled per unit area at different distances from the centre, of the average distance traveled, and of the radius of the central area when provision is made for all traffic demands. There are quite large differences in the radius of the central area for a given number of workers, according to the type of routing adopted. For large populations the required radius can vary by a factor of two, according to the routing system.

* Present address: University College London, London, England.

*211*

The maximum number of people who can travel to work within the central area when a fixed proportion of it is devoted to roads is calculated. Taking values of road capacity, car occupancy (1.5), and proportion of ground space devoted to roads (12%) appropriate for Central London, and assuming a 2-hour peak period, the maximum members of commuters who could travel by car for different routing systems are as follows:

|  | Number of car commuters (thousands) | |
|---|---|---|
|  | One-way roads (reversible) | Two-way roads (divided) |
| Ring routing (excluding area of ring road from calculation) | 2500 | 620 |
| Ring routing (including area of ring road in calculation) | 90 | 60 |
| Radial-arc routing | 160 | 100 |
| Radial routing | — | 70 |

It is shown that in most practical cases the earlier approximation produced a relatively small error.

The relation between the average journey time within the central area and the number of commuters in a given town is calculated for the case of radial-arc routing.

## References

1. The Traffic Problems in Towns, *Manchester Statistical Soc.* (1961).
2. The Effect of Some Kinds of Routing Systems on the Amount of Traffic in the Central Areas of Towns, *J. Inst. Highway Eng.*, **10**, Part 1 (1963).
3. A Theoretical Model of Commuter Traffic in Towns, *J. Inst. Maths. Applics.*, **1**, 208 (1965).

# Traffic Assignment—The Atcode Model

*B. ROY and H. LE BOULANGER*

Metra-International
Society of Economics and Applied Mathematics
Paris, France

This model is intended primarily to give an approximate reconstitution of routes taken by motorists so as to deduce the total vehicle traffic which each road section in the network will have to support over a given period. Nevertheless, it has been elaborated in such a way that it can be used for other purposes, such as the study of the load on a mass transportation network.

The traffic assignment procedure used is based on Dantzig's algorithm for finding the shortest routes in a network. In the graph representing the network an explicit distinction is made between *intersections* and *nodes*. The latter are the entry (or exit) points of roads at intersections. This distinction makes it simple to take account of all the particular features of the network as regards travel direction regulations.

The model was programmed in three stages on a *CDC* 3600.

The first, starting from inter- and intra-zone trip flows given by generation models, uses simple hypotheses to compute trip flows between intersections in the network under study.

The second constructs the "trees" of minimum paths (time, distance, or cost) from one intersection to all other intersections in the network.

The third makes an "all-or-nothing" assignment of the inter-intersection flows given in the first part to the various links that make up the routes constructed in the second part. The distinction between intersections and nodes results in separating inter-intersection links (whose extremities are nodes which do not belong to the same intersection) and links within intersections.

For the inter-intersection link the program provides automatically its total traffic assignment and its breakdown in trip flows.

One can obtain, if required, the same information for links within intersections.

A first experimental program has been written, of which the current limitations are the number of intersections in the network ≤150, the number of nodes ≤1700, and the number of links ≤7800.

For an urban street system divided into about 20 zones and comprising 150 intersections, of which 20 were complex, giving a total of 290 nodes and about 650 links of which 400 were inter-intersection links, the whole program was computed in under 4 minutes.

Advanced programming in machine language on *CDC* 3600 is in progress and the definitive program will have the following capacities:

    number of zones, 128
    number of intersections, 512
    number of nodes, 4096
    number of arcs, 16,000

and will be operational in September.

The mathematical properties of this model suggest useful prospects for economic study of traffic flow and its control.

# Testing a Traffic Assignment Algorithm

KNUD R. OVERGAARD

The Technical University of Denmark
Copenhagen, Denmark

## Abstract

A modified algorithm for the so-called Wayne arterial assignment method is presented. Different test runs are described. These indicated that the Wayne method can be considered an iterative procedure for solving the traffic assignment problem in accordance with the principle of equal travel times. Outlined is an extension of the algorithm to work on expressions for travel resistance, other than time.

## Introduction

THE FIRST method used for assigning traffic to a street network was very subjective, as the traffic engineer simply pointed out which route would accommodate each particular zone-to-zone movement.

Later, the diversion curve, which splits traffic between two routes, was invented. Because of the special conditions under which such curves are derived they cannot, however, be of general use.

The so-called all-or-nothing methods assign all the traffic between two zones to the optimal route (usually the criterion considered is time). Due to the time-flow relationship associated with every street the fastest route, however, is not uniquely determined; it depends on traffic volumes throughout the network. Therefore a system solution is needed.

In 1952 Wardrop[1] set forth two different principles for assigning traffic to a street network on a system basis.

1. The principle of equal travel times states that travel times are identical on all routes used between two zones and less than (or equal to) the travel time on all unused routes.
2. The principle of minimizing average travel time (or total travel time).

The principle of equal travel times seems logical as no driver is able to reduce his travel time by using another route in this situation. On the other hand, the principle of minimizing total travel time does not apply to traffic in general, but may be useful in connection with certain types of traffic control.

According to Jorgensen[2] the principle of equal travel times is equivalent to the minimization problem

$$\min \sum_{ij} \int_0^{f_{ij}} t_{ij} \, df_{ij}$$

subject to

$$Af^{(k)} = G^{(k)}$$

$$f_{ij}^{(k)} \geq 0 \qquad \text{all } ij \text{ and } k$$

where $t_{ij}$ = travel time over arc $ij$

$f_{ij}$ = total flow over arc $ij \left( = \sum_k f_{ij}^{(k)} \right)$

$f_{ij}^{(k)}$ = flow over arc $ij$ originating at node $k$

$f^{(k)}$ = flow vector for flow originating at node $k$

$A$ = node-arc incidence matrix

$G^{(k)}$ = supply vector for traffic originating at node $k$.

If travel times were independent of flows this minimization problem would be a problem in linear programming for which standard methods are available.

No standard methods are available for solving the problem when travel times are flow-dependent. In this case, however, the problem can be transformed to an enlarged linear program if each travel time function is replaced by a step function.

For the networks occurring in practice the resulting linear program may be of a size which exceeds the capabilities of existing computers even when a decompositon algorithm is used.

At present work is going on at the University of California, Berkeley, to find a new algorithm adjusted to this special type of a linear program.

As the results obtained by solving the assignment problem as a linear program are only approximate (because of the step function used for the time-flow relationship), it is worthwhile to look for other ways of obtaining approximate solutions to the problem.

## Description of an Algorithm

Investigating the different methods available for traffic assignment, it was discovered that an algorithm proposed by Smock[3] probably tends to distribute traffic in accordance with the principle of equal travel times. To check this a program has been written for an IBM 7074 computer and test runs have been carried out at I/S Datacentralen, Copenhagen.

The algorithm developed works as follows:

1. Using travel times corresponding to zero flow the fastest route between every pair of zones is found.

2. Traffic between every pair of zones is assigned to the route found and traffic is summed for every arc.

3. Travel time for every arc is revised according to a formula of the type

$$t^{(i)} = a^{(q^{(i)}/C)^b} t_0 L$$

where $t^{(i)} =$ travel time in the $i$th iteration (min)

$q^{(i)} =$ flow in the $i$th iteration (vph)

$C =$ practical capacity (vph)

$t_0 =$ travel time per mile at zero flow (min/mi)

$L =$ length of arc (mi)

$a$ and $b =$ parameters.

Eight sets of values for $C$, $t_0$, $a$, and $b$, corresponding to different types of streets, have been developed from time-flow relationships proposed by Irwin and von Cube.[4]

$a$ expresses the ratio between travel time at practical capacity and travel time at zero flow. Values used range from 1.0 (travel time independent of flow—used for artificial arcs) to 1.7. This represents the main departure from Smock's so-called Wayne method, which has a ratio of $e$ (2.718) between travel time at capacity and travel time at zero flow for all types of streets. The value of the ratio used by Smock is high and, furthermore, the ratio is known not to have the same value for all street types, so it was felt that the method would be improved by introducing a more realistic time-flow relationship into the algorithm.

4. Using the new travel times the fastest route between every pair of zones is found.

5. Traffic between every pair of zones is split equally between the two routes found so far, and traffic is summed for every arc.

6. Travel time for every arc is revised and a third set of fastest routes is determined. This time traffic is split in thirds, each part being assigned to one of the three routes found until now (if the same route is found more than once, it receives a corresponding number of shares of the traffic).

7. The process is repeated until changes in flows and travel times from one iteration to another are sufficiently small.

## Test Runs

The network used for the test runs was a proposed future street plan for the city of Kolding (35,000 inhabitants). It was made up of 52 nodes, 35 of which were zone centroids, and 130 directed arcs. The number of trips assigned totaled about 100,000.

In the first test run 20 iterations were carried out to see if the process converges so that equal travel times over routes used result for each pair of zones, and to get information about the rate of convergence.

Figure 1 shows the network and the flows after the first and after the twentieth iteration.

The heaviest loaded arc was assigned more than 30,000 trips in the first iteration, but because of the time-flow relationship this number dropped to less than 22,000 in the twentieth iteration.

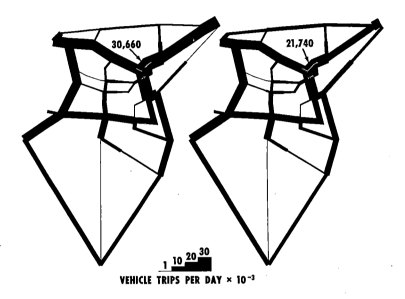

FIGURE I.   Vehicle trips per day after I (left) and after 20 iterations.

To find out if travel times on routes carrying traffic between two zones were equal, 66 pairs of zones, between which more routes seemed likely to be used, were selected for further study. Because of the small size of the network, only 3 pairs of zones used three routes, 45 used two, and 18 used only one.

For each of the 3 pairs of zones using three routes the travel times on the different routes were in fact the same (e.g., 4.25–4.26–4.25 min).

In 26 cases out of the 45 using two routes, travel times were not identical. Closer examination showed that of the two routes found in each case, one was found in only 1 iteration (usually in the second), while the other was found in 19 iterations. This means that one-twentieth of the traffic between the zones used one route, while rest of the traffic used the other route.

In the case of an infinite number of iterations the limiting distribution is zero traffic on one route and all the traffic on the other route. This implies that the principle of equal travel times does in fact apply here also as the "extra" route may be considered an unused route.

The principle of equal travel times determines the flows on arcs uniquely, but not the flows on routes. However, the important thing in practice is the total number of trips on the arcs, and not on the routes, many of which may contribute traffic to the flow on a particular arc.

Table I shows how the arc flows converge. 77 out of the total number of 130 arc (corresponding to 59 %) were assigned traffic volumes in the first iteration, which deviate less than 10 % from the volumes assigned to the same arcs in the twentieth iteration. Twenty two arcs have deviations between 10 and 20 %, etc. Instead of comparing the arc flows for each iteration against the flows found in the last iteration it would, of course, have been better to use the limiting flow values, had they been known.

To see how the relative loading of the network affects the rate of convergence, another test run (8 iterations) was carried out, the capacity of every arc being less than in the first test.

Table II, made up in the same way as Table I, summarizes how flows on the 130 arcs in each of the five first iterations deviate from the flows found after 8 iterations.

It is felt that the capacities used for the second test run balance better with the travel demand than did the capacities in the first run.


## Concluding Remarks

The test runs have given a practical indication that the modified Wayne method used (and certainly also the original Wayne method) can be considered an iterative procedure for solving the traffic assignment problem in accordance with the principle of equal travel times. A theoretical proof of the convergence would be welcomed.

The number of iterations to be carried out depends on the network, the travel demand, the degree of convergence wanted, and the money or the computer time available.

From the test runs it was concluded that 5 iterations would be appropriate. In this particular case, however, the actual computer cost for one more iteration was about only $3.

It is felt that even if 5 iterations are needed the Wayne method constitutes the best method available at the moment for solving the assignment problem in accordance with the principle of equal travel times. As time passes, however, it is possible that some mathematical programming technique will prove to be more effective.

At this point the following question naturally arises: "Do actual traffic flows correspond to the principle of equal travel times?" As the test runs described here assigned future traffic to a future network, this study cannot answer the question for lack of observed flows. Until now no investigation of

TABLE I. Absolute and Relative Distribution of the Per Cent Deviations Between Arc Flows in Each of the Five First Iterations and the 20th iteration

| Derivation from 20th iteration | Iteration | | | | | | | | | |
|---|---|---|---|---|---|---|---|---|---|---|
| | *1* | | *2* | | *3* | | *4* | | *5* | |
| 0–10% | 77 | 59% | 90 | 69% | 110 | 85% | 111 | 85% | 116 | 89% |
| 10–20% | 22 | 17% | 25 | 19% | 8 | 6% | 9 | 7% | 8 | 6% |
| 20–30% | 11 | 8% | 5 | 4% | 5 | 4% | 5 | 4% | 4 | 3% |
| 30–40% | 5 | 4% | 3 | 2% | 1 | 1% | 4 | 3% | 2 | 2% |
| 40–50% | 7 | 5% | 3 | 2% | 2 | 2% | 1 | 1% | | |
| 50–60% | 4 | 3% | | | 3 | 2% | | | | |
| 60–70% | 2 | 2% | 1 | 1% | 1 | 1% | | | | |
| 70–80% | 1 | 1% | 2 | 2% | | | | | | |
| 80–90% | 1 | 1% | | | | | | | | |
| 90–100% | | | 1 | 1% | | | | | | |
| | 130 | 100% | 130 | 100% | 130 | 101% | 130 | 100% | 130 | 100% |

TABLE II. Absolute and Relative Distribution of the Per Cent Deviations between Arc Flows in Each of the Five First Iterations and the 8th Iteration (Test run With Other Arc Capacities Than Those Used for Table I)

| Derivation from 8th iteration | Iteration | | | | | | | | | |
|---|---|---|---|---|---|---|---|---|---|---|
| | *1* | | *2* | | *3* | | *4* | | *5* | |
| 0–10% | 36 | 28% | 56 | 43% | 95 | 73% | 110 | 85% | 118 | 91% |
| 10–20% | 20 | 15% | 32 | 25% | 22 | 17% | 13 | 10% | 10 | 8% |
| 20–30% | 27 | 21% | 24 | 18% | 7 | 5% | 5 | 4% | 2 | 2% |
| 30–40% | 17 | 13% | 4 | 3% | 3 | 2% | 1 | 1% | | |
| 40–50% | 11 | 8% | 2 | 2% | 1 | 1% | 1 | 1% | | |
| 50–60% | 10 | 8% | | | | | | | | |
| 60–70% | 9 | 7% | 5 | 4% | 1 | 1% | | | | |
| 70–80% | | | 3 | 2% | 1 | 1% | | | | |
| 80–90% | | | 1 | 1% | | | | | | |
| 90–100% | | | | | | | | | | |
| 100–150% | | | 1 | 1% | | | | | | |
| 150–200% | | | 2 | 2% | | | | | | |
| | 130 | 100% | 130 | 101% | 130 | 100% | 130 | 101% | 130 | 101% |

the problem seems to have been carried out. If the principle does not apply, it is possible that some other principle of equilibrium holds, as for example, that of equal travel costs.

The algorithm described here will work with that principle also without any major changes. In fact, the program has already been used for assigning traffic to the network in the test city using $c^{(i)} = t^{(i)} + 3.2L$ instead of $t^{(i)}$. With this cost expression 1 mile corresponds to 3.2 minutes. It is possible that more sophisticated expressions for travel resistance than $t^{(i)}$ and $c^{(i)}$ can be developed.

We may conclude that the traffic assignment problem still offers great opportunities for mathematical thinking as well as for engineering experimentation.

## Acknowledgement

The author wishes to thank the department of the city engineer of Copenhagen and the Technical University of Denmark, who sponsored this study. Thanks also to Mr. H. Beck of I/S Datacentralen, who wrote the computer program, and to Mr. A. Nyvig, who supplied the data for Kolding.

## References

1. J. G. Wardrop, Some Theoretical Aspects of Road Traffic Research, *Proc. Inst. Civil Eng.* 325–378 (1952).
2. 2. N. O. Jorgensen, Some Aspects of the Urban Traffic Assignment Problem, Graduate Report, ITTE, Berkeley, 1963.
3. R. B. Smock, A Comparative Description of a Capacity-Restrained Traffic Assignment, HRB, *Highway Research Record*, 6, 12–40 (1953).
4. N. A. Irwin, and H. G. von Cube, Capacity Restraint in Multi-Travel Mode Assignment Programs HRB Bulletin 347, 258–289 (1962).

# Traffic Assignment with Flow-Dependent Journey Times

Road Research Laboratory
Ministry of Transport
Harmondsworth, Middlesex, England

## Abstract

An important stage of most traffic surveys is generally known as assignment. This is the process by which journeys, the origins and destinations of which are known, are assigned to a proposed new network. A common assumption is that traffic travels by the quickest route. Recently attention has been given to methods of assigning traffic to a network in which the journey time along each link of the network increases as the flow on the link increases.

This paper is concerned with a solution to this problem in which no driver can improve his journey time by changing to a different route. It is thought that this situation tends to occur in practice, particularly with commuter traffic in towns.

In the case of two alternative roads between an origin destination pair, with the journey time on each link a function of the total flow in both directions, it is shown that, in general, the solution has the feature that traffic in at least one direction travels on only one route.

An efficient iterative process is given for finding the distribution of traffic on alternative one-way routes between a single origin and destination to a given degree of accuracy. An alternative iteration process, in which a weighted mean of each assignment and the previous iteration is produced, has been used to obtain a solution for practical networks. The weighting factors for each iteration were chosen on the basis of the behavior of the successive estimates of flows on a selection of streets. It is suggested that a standard procedure of this type should not be applied without such manual checking.

## Introduction

AN IMPORTANT stage of most traffic surveys is generally known as *assignment*. This is the process by which journeys, the origins and destinations of which are assumed to be known, are assigned to the proposed new road network. It has been found that, of the many factors affecting a driver's choice of route, journey time is the most important and a large number of assignments have been carried out on this basis. The simplest assumption is that every driver travels to his destination by the quickest available route, based on fixed journey times on sections.

This method does not, however, take account of the effect of the traffic on the journey time. As the traffic on a given road increases, the speed tends to fall and, hence, the journey time of vehicles using the road increases. Neglect of this fact could lead to errors in an assignment. For example, in the case of a proposed fast bypass relieving a congested high street, for the bypass to prove effective the journey time by it must be shorter than through the high street. Consequently, an assignment by quickest route using existing journey times will result in most of the traffic traveling by the bypass. In practice, however, the traffic on the high street might be reduced sufficiently for the speed on it to increase substantially so that some of the traffic would be attracted *back* on this street from the bypass. The final distribution of traffic could be rather different from the answer given by the "all or nothing" method with fixed journey times.

A number of organizations have carried out assignments in which allowance has been made for the decrease in journey speed with increasing flow. All the methods that have been used so far, some of which have been summarized by Mosher,[1] require repeated assignments to be made. Since the aim in some of the earlier work was to avoid overloading particular links, such assignments have become known as *capacity-restrained* assignments. The methods used probably lead to approximately the right solution, but there seems to have been no attempt to justify the methods of iteration used. This paper attempts to throw a little more light on the problems involved.

## The Required Solution

The solution aimed at by the Road Research Laboratory is one in which the driver travels by the quickest route, taking into account the effect of the amount of traffic on the road. With this solution, no driver can improve his journey time by changing to a different route. It follows that all routes actually used by drivers traveling between any given origin and destination will have the same journey time, and all other possible routes between the same origin and destination will take longer. It is thought that something approaching this situation tends to occur in practice, particularly with commuter traffic in towns. Although some drivers, particularly those who do not make the journey regularly, will not make any effort to find the quickest route, it is probable that they will travel on one of the routes given by the solution. The correct balance of flow to give approximately equal journey times on the alternative routes will be maintained by regular drivers who are willing to change their routes in order to make their journeys in the quickest possible time. As evidence of this balancing effect, observation has shown that when severe congestion is caused by road works it tends to disperse after a few days, suggesting that an appreciable proportion of regular drivers soon transfer to alternative routes when they become quicker. Another related solution that has been considered[2] is the one in which the total time spent traveling on the road network is minimized. In general, the two solutions will be different. Minimization of total journey time seems unlikely to be achieved in practice, however, except by enforcement and automatic diversion signs. This solution also has the disadvantage that it may result in a few drivers being very seriously delayed. The only solution considered in this paper is the one in which each driver travels by his quickest route.

It is not immediately obvious that there is a unique solution. In an attempt to throw some light on the problem, some simple examples are considered.

It is assumed throughout the paper that the journey time on a road section is an increasing function of flow.

## Two-Way Sections

It is reasonable to assume that, on some roads at least, to a first approximation, journey time is a function only of the total flow, not of the flows in each direction separately. Let us consider, therefore, the effect of this assumption on the problem. Consider a very simple example, as shown in Fig. 1, where

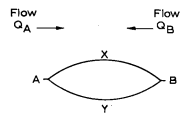

FIGURE I.    Two alternative roads between A and B.

traffic traveling between $A$ and $B$ has the choice of two roads $X$ and $Y$, and suppose there is a flow $Q_A$ wanting to travel from $A$ to $B$ and $Q_B$ wanting to travel from $B$ to $A$. In general, when the journey time is a function only of the total flow on each route, it can be shown that there is no solution in which the traffic in each direction distributes itself on both roads, because drivers in one direction at least will always be able to improve their journey time by changing to another route. If the journey time is a function of the individual flows in the two directions, a solution with all non-negative flows may or may not exist. This is demonstrated in Figs. 2–4.

In this type of diagram the distribution of flow is represented by a point within a rectangle whose sides represent the total flow from $A$ to $B$ and $B$ to $A$, respectively (see Fig. 2). The distance of the point from the four sides of the

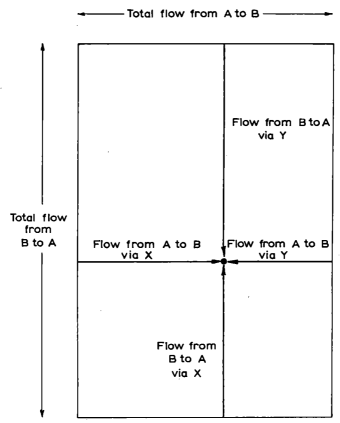

FIGURE 2.   Diagrammatic representation of traffic on network shown in Fig. 1.

rectangle represents the four different flows. The locus of points that correspond to flows giving equal journey time via $X$ and $Y$ from $A$ to $B$ can be shown on such a diagram. The locus of equal journey times from $B$ to $A$ can be shown similarly. Starting from an arbitrary distribution of traffic, drivers from $A$ to $B$ seeking the quickest route will shift the point representing the distribution of traffic horizontally towards the $A$ to $B$ locus. Drivers in the reverse direction will move the point vertically towards the $B$ to $A$ locus. If the two loci intersect within the rectangle, the effect of both sets of drivers

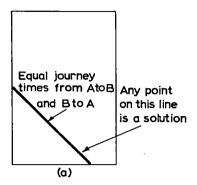

(a)

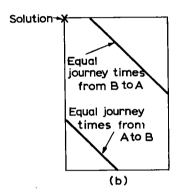

(b)

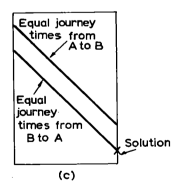

(c)

FIGURE 3.    Diagrammatic representation of traffic on network shown in Fig. 1. Journey time a function of total flow on the road.

will be to produce a distribution of traffic corresponding to the point of intersection. If the loci do not intersect within the rectangle then a distribution will be produced in which traffic in at least one direction travels by only one road.

If the journey-time/flow relation depends on flow in the direction of travel only, the locus of equal journey time from *A* to *B* on the diagram will be a vertical line; that for *B* to *A* will be a horizontal line, and the two loci will always intersect within the rectangle. If the journey time depends on the total

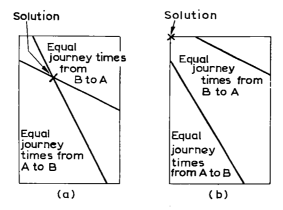

(a)                    (b)

FIGURE 4.   Diagrammatic representation of traffic on network shown in Fig. 1. Journey time a function of the individual flows in the two directions.

flow, the curves of equal journey time will be straight lines at 45° to the sides of the rectangle. If the lines coincide, any point on the line is a solution (see Fig. 3a). If they do not coincide then the traffic in at least one direction travels by one road only (Figs. 3b and 3c). Figures 4a and 4b show two examples where the journey time is a linear function of the individual flow in each direction.

The rest of the paper is devoted to considering assignments where the journey time on a section is dependent on the flow in the direction of travel only. Any result will be true in the symmetrical case where the journey-time/flow relation and the flow are the same in both directions.

## Two Alternative Roads

Let us now consider the simplest possible case of two alternative one-way roads $X$ and $Y$, with journey-time/flow relations, between $A$ and $B$ and flow $Q$ wishing to travel from $A$ to $B$. We shall try to solve it with as few iterations as possible by a method of successive assignments. Let $Q_n$ represent the $n$th estimate of flows and $q_n$ the flows obtained by an all or nothing assignment using the journey times calculated from $Q_{n-1}$. An all or nothing assignment will always assign all the traffic to either $X$ or $Y$. In the general case, assuming nothing about the roads, the best initial estimate of flow $Q_0$ is that half the traffic travels on each road. If this estimate allocates too much traffic to one road, say $X$, the journey time based on this flow will be higher than on $Y$ and the first assignment, which will be based on these journey times, will put

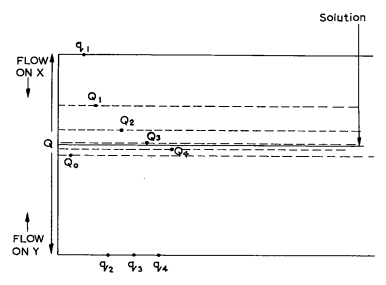

FIGURE 5.    Iteration process for two alternative one-way routes.

all the traffic on $Y$. It is evident from this result that the final solution lies above $Q_0$ in the upper half of the diagram in Fig. 5, and that the "best" estimate of $Q_1$ is midway between the first estimate and the first assignment, as shown. If this estimate results in all the traffic being assigned to $X$, the solution must lie below $Q_1$ in the diagram and, therefore, because of the limitation imposed by the first assignment, it also lies between $Q_0$ and $Q_1$. The best estimate will be midway between $Q_0$ and $Q_1$. If the third estimate $Q_2$ results in all the traffic again being assigned to $X$ then, because of the limitation imposed by the previous estimates, $Q_3$ must lie midway between $Q_2$ and $Q_0$. The process can be continued as shown in Fig. 5.

This process is equivalent to

$$Q_n = Q_{n-1} + \tfrac{1}{2}(\tfrac{1}{2})^{n-1}q_n - \tfrac{1}{2}(\tfrac{1}{2})^{n-1}Q_0, \qquad n = 1, 2, \ldots \qquad (1)$$

The difference between $Q_n$ and the true solution will not exceed $(\tfrac{1}{2})^n Q_0$.

## Three or More Alternative Roads

The method can be extended to three parallel roads $X$, $Y$, and $Z$ between $A$ and $B$, and this is shown diagrammatically in Fig. 6. The height of the large triangle gives the total traffic from $A$ to $B$, and the distance of any point within

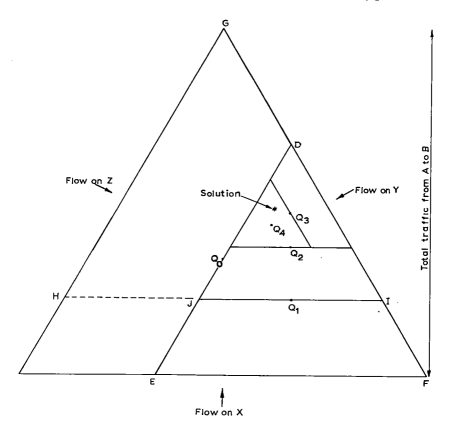

FIGURE 6.   Iteration process for three alternative one-way routes.

it from the three sides of the triangle represents the distribution of traffic on the three roads. The initial estimate is again assumed to be the one in which the traffic is distributed equally on all the roads, and this will be represented by the centroid of the triangle. The first assignment will assign all traffic to the road that has the least travel time with the assumed distribution of traffic. The initial estimate must therefore underestimate the amount of traffic on that road. It follows that if the road to which traffic is assigned is, say, $Z$ then the solution must lie within triangle $DEF$ and the best estimate $Q_1$ is obtained by taking the centroid of this triangle. If this second estimate results in traffic being assigned to X, the solution must lie within triangle $GHI$ and, therefore, because of the limitation imposed by the first assignment, within triangle $DJI$. The process can be continued as shown in Fig. 6.

This is equivalent to

$$Q_n = Q_{n-1} + \tfrac{1}{3}(\tfrac{2}{3})^{n-1}q_n - \tfrac{1}{3}(\tfrac{2}{3})^{n-1}Q_0, \qquad n = 1, 2, \ldots \tag{2}$$

The difference between $Q_n$ and the true solution will not exceed $2 \times (\tfrac{2}{3})^n Q_0$.

This process can be extended to $r$ alternative roads between $A$ and $B$, when the best $n$th estimate of the solution is given by

$$Q_n = Q_{n-1} + \frac{1}{r}\left(\frac{r-1}{r}\right)^{n-1} q_n - \frac{1}{r}\left(\frac{r-1}{r}\right)^{n-1} Q_0, \qquad n = 1, 2, \ldots \tag{3}$$

where the initial estimate $Q_0$ is a flow of $Q/r$ on each road. The difference between $Q_n$ and the true solution will not exceed $(r-1)\left(\frac{r-1}{r}\right)^n Q_0$.

These formulae throw some light on the processes involved, but they do not have direct application to a network of streets in a town. In practice it is very likely that some of the alternative routes have parts in common and, in any case, the problem is complicated by the presence of traffic making other movements.

## Method of Solution for a Network

The procedure adopted in assignments to a network carried out at the Laboratory is an iterative one based on the way traffic is believed to behave in practice. The method was also considered by Beckman, McGuire, and Winsten.[3] A journey-time/flow relation is obtained or assumed for each link, and at each stage traffic is assigned to the quickest route then available. A first estimate of the flows is obtained by assigning all the traffic to the network using measured or estimated journey times. The journey times on each link are then recalculated from the journey-time/flow relation using the set of estimated flows. The $n$th estimate of flow on a road $Q_n$ is given by

$$Q_n = \alpha_n q_n + \beta_n Q_{n-1} \tag{4}$$

where $q_n$ is the flow obtained by an "all or nothing" assignment using journey times corresponding to the $(n-1)$th estimate of flows and $\alpha_n$, $\beta_n$ are weighting factors. This process is equivalent to re-assigning a proportion of all movements at each stage. In general, $\alpha_n + \beta_n = 1$, but an alternative method is to take $\alpha_n + \beta_n = \gamma_n < 1$ for the initial iterations, increasing $\gamma_n$ by stages to unity. Each iteration is then equivalent to some new traffic entering the network and a proportion of the original traffic redistributing itself. The speed of convergence of the process to the correct answer depends on the choice of $\alpha_n$ and $\beta_n$.

The process has been applied to some simple examples below.

## Three Alternative Roads

The effect of an iteration of the form given by Eq. 4, taking $\alpha_n = \frac{1}{5}$ for all $n$, to three alternative roads is shown in Fig. 7. For simplicity, linear journey-

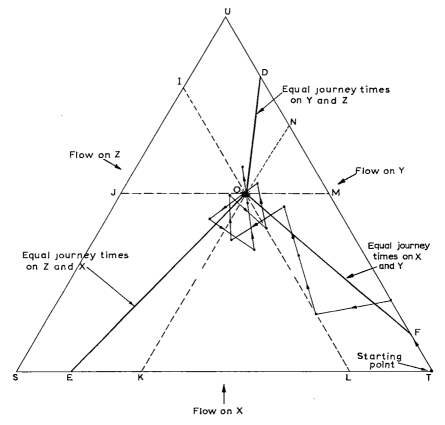

FIGURE 7.    Example of an iteration process of the form $Q_n = 0.2q_n + 0.8Q_{n-1}$ for three alternative one-way routes.

time/flow relations were assumed and the lines of equal journey time are $OD$, $OE$, and $OF$, where $O$ is the solution. These lines must lie in regions $NOI$, $JOK$, $LOM$, respectively. It is evident that if, for example, an estimate lies in the region $OETF$ then an assignment using journey times given by this estimate will put all the traffic on $X$. Successive iterations approach the true solution

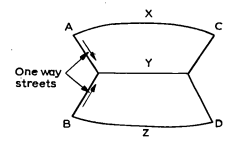

The only traffic movements are from A to C and from B to D.
Traffic from A to C can travel by X or Y
Traffic from B to D can travel by Y or Z

FIGURE 8.   Simple network with more than one origin and destination.

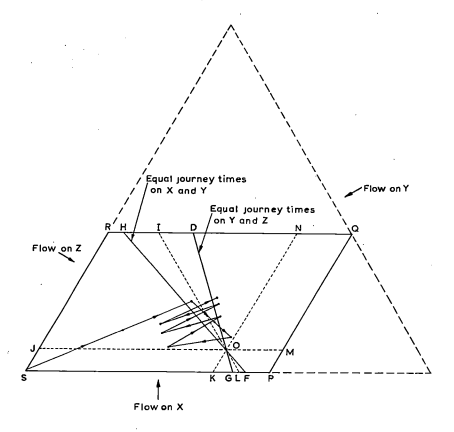

FIGURE 9.   Diagrammatic representation of traffic on network of type shown in Fig. 8.

and then oscillate about it. Consideration of simple examples shows that after a large number of iterations the maximum error in the flow on any road will be $2\alpha_n$ times the total amount of traffic and, in general, will be very much less. In the general case of $r$ alternative roads the maximum error will be $(r - 1)\alpha_n$ times the total traffic. By successively reducing the value of $\alpha_n$ it is possible to obtain flow estimates which converge to the correct solution.

## More than one Origin and Destination

A number of assignments were carried out on the very simple network shown in Fig. 8, using an electronic computer. For simplicity $\alpha$ was taken as a constant and $\beta$ as $1 - \alpha$. It was found that if $\alpha$ was 0.5, the process oscillated widely. By taking $\alpha$ small enough (0.05), a good approximation to the solution was eventually obtained after a large number of iterations. These results suggest that an iteration process where $\alpha_n$ decreases as $n$ increases would converge to the solution.

The traffic on such a network can be represented as lying in a triangle truncated to a parallelogram, as shown in Fig. 9. Linear journey-time/flow relations were assumed, and in the figure $HF$ represents the line where journey times on $X$ and $Y$ are equal and $DG$ represents the line where journey times on $T$ and $Z$ are equal. An assignment using journey times given by an estimate lying in the regions indicated will assign the traffic as shown below.

Estimate in region $OHSG$ traffic to $Z$ and $X$, i.e., to point $Q$
Estimate in region $OGF$   traffic to $X$ and $Y$, i.e., to point $R$
Estimate in region $OFQD$ traffic to $Y$,      i.e., to point $S$
Estimate in region $ODH$   traffic to $Y$ and $Z$, i.e., to point $P$

The angle $DOH$ can be quite small. And the figure shows that unless a weighted average with $\alpha_n$ small is taken, it is possible for an iteration process to oscillate indefinitely from regions $OHSG$ to $OFQD$ across one of the other regions (triangle $ODH$ in the figure.)

## Practical Examples

A number of assignments using speed/flow relations have been made to an actual town network using the method given by Eq. 4. Graphs of the successive estimates of the flows on the principal streets of the network were plotted and these were used to choose $\alpha_n$ and $\beta_n$, and to decide when convergence had been reached. It was found that a lightly loaded network converged satisfactorily after about 5 iterations even with $\alpha_n = \beta_n = 0.5$. With these weighting factors, however, a more heavily loaded network oscillated and showed no tendency to converge. Convergence has been reached in loaded networks using the following weighting factors.

Method 1. $\alpha_n = 0.5$ $\beta_n = 0.5,$ $n = 1$ to 4
$\alpha_n = 0.25$ $\beta_n = 0.75,$ $n = 5$ to 10
$\alpha_n = 0.15$ $\beta_n = 0.85,$ $n = 11$ to 16
$\alpha_n = 0.1$ $\beta_n = 0.9,$ $n = 17$ to 20

Method 2. $\alpha_0 = \frac{1}{2}$ $\beta_0 = 0$
$\alpha_1 = \frac{1}{4}$ $\beta_1 = \frac{3}{8}$
$\alpha_2 = \frac{1}{4}$ $\beta_2 = \frac{1}{2}$
$\alpha_3 = \frac{1}{4}$ $\beta_3 = \frac{5}{8}$
$\alpha_4 = \frac{1}{4}$ $\beta_4 = \frac{3}{4}$
$\alpha_n = \frac{1}{8}$ $\beta_n = \frac{7}{8},$ $n = 5$ to 8
$\alpha_n = \frac{1}{16}$ $\beta_n = \frac{15}{16},$ $n = 9$ to 11

On the limited amount of work carried out, it would seem that Method 2, in which the traffic is loaded gradually on to the network, requires fewer iterations to reach convergence. However, it appears that as many as 10 to 15 iterations may be required.

It is suggested that in using these methods the values of $\alpha_n$ and $\beta_n$ given above should be used as a general guide for the initial iterations only, and that the values used in subsequent iterations should be determined from the behaviour of the successive estimates of flows on some typical streets. If the traffic on some roads continues to increase or decrease the correct solution has not been reached. If oscillations in flow occur their magnitude can be reduced by decreasing the proportion of the traffic reassigned at each stage.

## Acknowledgements

The author is indebted to her colleagues at the Laboratory for their help in the preparation of this paper and particularly to Mr. P. D. Whiting. The paper is contributed by permission of the Director of Road Research. Crown copyright, reproduced by permission of the Controller of Her Britannic Majesty's Stationery Office.

## References

1. W. W. Mosher, A Capacity Restraint Algorithm for Assigning Flow to a Transport Network, *Highw. Res. Rec.,* **6,** 41–70 (1963).
2. J. G. Wardrop, Some Theoretical Aspects of Road Traffic Research, *Proc. Instn. Civ. Engrs,* Part III, 1, **2,** 325–62 (1952).
3. M. Beckmann, C. B. McGuire and C. B. Winsten, "Studies in the Economics of Transportation." New Haven, Yale University Press, 1956.

# Investment in a Network to Reduce the Length of the Shortest Route

*TONY M. RIDLEY*

Department of Civil Engineering
University of California, Berkeley, California

An important but neglected problem in the analysis of transportation systems is that of the allocation of funds to improve the network. Assume that for a transportation network, traffic distribution data (fixed units of interzonal transfers) are given. Associated with each arc in the network are unit travel costs, times or distances, and capacities. Traffic assignment procedures may be used to find the minimum total travel cost to distribute the traffic.

The problem of investment may be separately formulated as that of either increasing arc capacity or decreasing unit travel cost. Consider the latter. Assume that there is a given saving in unit travel cost on an arc for each unit of investment in that arc. The problem is how to allocate the budget to produce the greatest reduction in minimum total travel cost.

The initial assignment of traffic suggests which arcs should receive investment. However, as the investment proceeds, the assignment of traffic changes. With a large network the number of assignment and investment possibilities produces a complex combinatorial problem.

A special case of the above is the *shortest route problem*. This is equivalent to the traffic assignment problem for one unit of flow between a single pair of nodes in a network below capacity.

The algorithm proposed for investment to reduce the shortest route is an extension of a shortest route algorithm and uses a concept suggested by Wollmer.[1]

Consider the building of an early tree in a network for each of $X$ units of budget available for investment ($X = 0, 1, 2, \ldots$). Assume that the shortest routes have been found from the origin, 0, to a set of nodes $S$, for $X$ units of investment. Label these nodes $u_i(X)$, $i \, \varepsilon \, S$.

The set $S^*$ consists of all remaining unlabeled nodes. Also assume that the early trees have been obtained; i.e., all nodes labeled, for all units of investment $0, 1, 2, \ldots$ $(X - 1)$. Define

$$x = \text{number of units of investment in an arc}$$

$$t_{ij}(x) = \text{length of arc } ij \text{ after } x \text{ units of investment in that arc}$$

then a new node $j$ may be added to the set $S$ by defining

$$u_j(X) = \min_{i \varepsilon S} \left[ u_i(X - x) + \min_{j \varepsilon S^*} t_{ij}(x) \right]$$

$$0 \le x \le X$$

$$u_0(X) = 0 \qquad \text{for all } X$$

Starting with $X = 0$ the labeling algorithm is used until a shortest path tree is completed. This is repeated for $X = 1, 2, \ldots$ until $X$ reaches its maximum value, the total budget available.

## Reference

1. R. Wollmer, Removing Arcs from a Network, *Operations Res.*, **12**, No. 6, 934 (1964).

# Sky Count Measurement of Urban Congestion and Demand

THOMAS D. JORDAN

The Port of New York Authority, New York

During the past four years The Port of New York Authority has been actively engaged in the development and application of aerial photographic techniques for the analysis of transportation problems[1]. These techniques have recently been applied to the problem of measuring and evaluating simultaneous traffic operations throughout large urban areas, in accordance with the principle that total traffic measurement is a prerequisite for the scientific management of extensive urban street networks.

The study herein described has for its principal objective the measurement of current traffic demands imposed on a critical street network during a peak traffic period. The study area grid segment extends from the Battery, at the southern tip of Manhattan Island, 6000 feet north, and 4800 feet east. In addition to vehicular population counts, congestion counts are obtained and the inter-relationship of these two variables is determined based on average cell characteristics. For this study the traffic demand level, $D$, in a given cell is defined as the average number of active vehicles observed. The congestion level, $C$, is defined as the average number of active vehicles found in queues.

Flight operations are conducted at an altitude of 7000 ft using a vertical reconnaissance camera with a lens of 6-in. focal length and an image size of $9 \times 9$ in. Five observations of the study area are obtained at 15-minute intervals during the 0800–0900 peak traffic period. A grid segment of 180 cells is superimposed on the developed negatives and the number of queued and total active vehicles is counted in each cell. These data are recorded on punch cards to facilitate processing and presentation by an electronic computer programmed for this purpose.

Implicit to this form of analysis is the criterion that a change in signalization, street directional patterns or other aspects of traffic management which reduce average congestion levels throughout the range of demand values would constitute an overall improvement. Conversely, a signalization change which results in elevation of the general $C/D$ relationship may be considered as detrimental to total traffic operations in the network.

The basic criteria of traffic congestion and demand employed in the strategic Sky Count technique do not involve consideration of traffic speeds, travel times, and flow rates. Measurement of these and similar parameters may be undertaken by means of tactical photographic studies carried out subsequent to the determination of general traffic characteristics.

To date a total of 28 grid segment surveys of the type described in this paper have been completed. On the basis of these initial studies, it appears that a large body of comprehensive traffic data will soon be available for the mathematical evaluation of metropolitan traffic operations.

## Reference

1. T. D. Jordan, *Traffic Eng. and Control*, **7** (5) (1965).

# Optimal Policies for the Control of an Undersaturated Intersection*

R. B. GRAFTON and G. F. NEWELL†

Brown University

Providence, Rhode Island

## Abstract

The methods of dynamic programming are used to determine optimal policies for control of an intersection of two traffic streams. An optimal policy is defined as one which minimizes the total delay from time 0 to $+\infty$, discounted with an exponential weight factor. Traffic is treated as a continuous fluid with constant arrival rates and constant departure rates during the green time of the traffic light. Optimal policies are found as functions of arbitrary queue lengths and light phase at time 0. A control algorithm proposed by Dunne and Potts, switch the light as soon as a queue vanishes, is shown to be optimal in the above sense for some initial states. However, if the initial queues are very large, and the departure rates unequal for the two traffic streams, the optimal policy will involve one or more policy modifications in which the light is switched to the lane of higher flow before the queue in the other lane vanishes. If, on the other hand, the initial queues are very small, the optimal policy may include one or more modifications in which the light is kept green for a certain length of time after a queue has vanished.

## I. Introduction

THERE IS A tremendous variety of problems associated with the optimal control of traffic intersections, but so far only a few special cases have been treated in the traffic literature. Wardrop[1], Webster[2], and Miller[3] have determined settings for a fixed-cycle light which minimize the average delay per

* The results presented in this paper were obtained in the course of research sponsored by the National Science Foundation under Grant NSF-GP1 and NSF-GP4011 to Brown University.

† Present adress: Institute of Transportation and Traffic Engineering, University of California, Berkeley.

239

car when the arrival rates are constant. Gazis and Potts[4] obtained conditions for the optimal control of an intersection which becomes oversaturated for some finite length of time. Gazis[5] has also extended this to two intersections. Dunne and Potts[6] proposed some control algorithms for an undersaturated intersection with constant arrivals which guarantee that, for any initial state, the system will eventually achieve a limit cycle for which the average equilibrium delay per car is a minimum. A few attempts have also been made to study systems of intersections.

Here we shall illustrate how the methods of dynamic programming can be used to obtain optimal policies. We will apply these methods to the model proposed by Dunne and Potts, and obtain optimal transient policies as a function of the initial queue lengths.

The objective of an optimal policy is to minimize some quantity such as the average wait per car or the total delay of all cars entering the system. Here we choose to minimize the total discounted delay at an intersection of only two competing traffic streams, which is defined as

$$D_\mu(x_0, t_0; P) = \int_0^\infty [x(t; P) + y(t; P)]e^{-\alpha t}\, dt \tag{1}$$

The quantities $x(t; P)$ and $y(t; P)$ are the queue lengths for the two traffic streams at time $t$, which depend upon the policy $P$ for control of the light. The quantity $e^{-\alpha t}$ is a discount factor introduced primarily to ensure that the integral is finite. The use of a discount factor can be justified if we agree that time saved now is worth more than time saved in the future. In the analysis of Eq. 1, however, we shall choose $\alpha$ arbitrarily small and evaluate Eq. 1 as a power series in $\alpha$ keeping only terms of order $\alpha^{-1}$ and $\alpha^0$. If time or money is valued at about 5% per year, then $\alpha = 0.95$ $(\mathrm{yr})^{-1} \sim 10^{-7}$ $(\mathrm{min})^{-1}$.

The total discounted delay is a function of the initial state of the system as well as the policy $P$ (which may itself depend upon the initial state). We specify the initial state by three quantities: the initial queue lengths $x_0$ and $y_0$ in lanes one and two, and the direction of the light $\mu$. We take $\mu = 1$ or 2 if the light is initially green on lane one or lane two. It is assumed that the light is green for some direction at time zero, and not yellow.

Regardless of what specific model we treat (which determines how $x(t; P)$ and $y(t; P)$ depend upon $P$), the problem of finding a policy which minimizes Eq. 1 has the structure of a dynamic programming process as described by Bellman[7]. Our physical system is characterized at any time $t$ by state variables $[\mu, x(t; P), y(t; P)]$ and at any time (except when the light is yellow) the controller has but two choices—to switch the light or not.

According to Bellman's principle of optimality, an optimal policy has the property that whatever the initial state of the system and the initial decisions until time $\tau$, the remaining decisions after time $\tau$ must constitute an optimal policy with respect to the state resulting from the first decisions. This principle applied to Eq. 1 gives the functional equation

$$D_\mu(x_0, y_0; P_m) = \min_P \left\{ \int_0^\tau [x(t; P) + y(t; P)]e^{-\alpha t}\, dt + e^{-\tau\alpha}D_{\mu'}(x_0'; y_0'; P_m') \right\} \quad (2)$$

where $P_m$ and $P_m'$ are optimal policies from the states $(\mu, x_0, y_0)$ and $(\mu', x_0', y_0')$, respectively, and $(\mu', x_0', y_0')$ is the state which results at time $\tau$ from the policy $P$.

It is known[8] that $D_\mu(x_0, y_0; P_\mu)$ has a unique minimum, however the optimal policy $P_m$ may not be unique.

The traffic flow model to which we apply this principle is the one studied by Dunne and Potts[6]. In this model, traffic is treated as if it were a continuous fluid. Arrival rates are assumed to be constant for all time and given by

$q_1, q_2$ = arrival rates in lanes one and two.

The departure rates are constant during the green time for each lane (flows start and stop instantaneously). Let

$s_1, s_2$ = saturation (departure) rates in lanes one and two

$d_1, d_2 = s_1 - q_1,\ s_2 - q_2$ = queue discharge rates.

These flow rates are chosen so that the intersection is undersaturated. If

$$a = (q_1 q_2)/(d_1 d_2)$$

then this condition implies that $0 \leq a < 1$ (this is equivalent to the condition $0 < q_1/s_1 + q_2/s_2 < 1$ given by Dunne and Potts[6]). The lengths of the green and red times will depend on the policy $P$, but there is a fixed lost time or yellow time $L$ between each green-red switch of the light.

## 2. The Basis Policy

Dunne and Potts[6] show that the best policy for the equilibrium cycle (for most flows) is to switch the light when a queue becomes zero. It seems plausible that this policy may also be optimal for some transient cases. We shall, therefore, first evaluate the discounted delay for this policy, which we label the basis policy $P_0$. We will then compare this with various other policies to determine under what conditions it is optimal.

Figure 1 shows the evolution of the two queues under the policy $P_0$ starting from some arbitrary initial state $(x_0, y_0)$ with $\mu = 1$. If $x_j$ and $y_j$ represent the maximum queue lengths in lanes one and two, respectively, during the $j$th cycle, then $x_j, y_j$ satisfy the difference equations

$$\begin{aligned} x_{j+1} &= ax_j + 2q_1 s_2 L/d_2 \\ y_{j+1} &= ay_j + 2q_2 s_1 L/d_1 \end{aligned} \qquad j \geq 1$$

For $0 \leq a < 1$, the solution of these equations[6], can be written as the sum of an equilibrium part and a transient:

$$x_j = x_\infty + (x_1 - x_\infty)a^{j-1}$$
$$y_j = y_\infty + (y_1 - y_\infty)a^{j-1} \qquad j \geq 1 \tag{3}$$

where

$$x_1 = (q_1/d_2)y_0 + ax_0 + q_1(d_2 + s_2)L/d_2$$
$$y_1 = y_0 + (q_2/d_1)x_0 + q_2L \tag{4}$$

and

$$x_\infty = \frac{2Lq_1s_2}{d_2(1-a)}, \qquad y_\infty = \frac{2Lq_2s_1}{d_1(1-a)}$$

are the equilibrium values of $x_j$ and $y_j$.

To evaluate $D_\mu(x_0, y_0, P_0)$ from Eq. 1, we write

$$D_\mu(x_0, y_0; P) = D_{\mu x}(x_0, y_0) + D_{\mu y}(x_0, y_0) \tag{5}$$

as the sum of the contributions from the $x$ and $y$ queues. We need only compute $D_{\mu x}(x_0, y_0)$, however, since $D_{\mu y}(x_0, y_0)$ can be inferred from it by interchange of notation for lanes one and two. The value of $D_{\mu x}(x_0, y_0)$ can in turn be written as the discounted delay until the time $\tau$ when $x(\tau; P_0)$ vanishes for the first time, plus a discount factor, $e^{-\alpha\tau}$, times the discounted delay from this time on. The evaluation of $D_\mu(x_0, y_0; P_0)$ is thus reduced to the evaluation of $D_{1x}(0, y_0)$, the discounted delay in lane one, starting from an empty queue in lane one.

The quantity $D_{1x}(0, y_0)$ is the discounted area under the graph of $x(t; P_0)$ in Fig. 1, with $x_0 = 0$, and can be written as the sum of integrals over successive triangles of height $x_j$, Eq. 3. Thus

$$D_{1x}(0, y_0) = \sum_{j=1}^{\infty} \int_{t_{j-1}}^{t_j} x(t; P_0)e^{-\alpha t} \, dt$$
$$= \sum_{j=1}^{\infty} \exp(-\alpha t_{j-1}) \int_0^{c_j} x(t_{j-1} + t; P_0)e^{-\alpha t} \, dt \tag{6}$$

where $c_j$ is the duration of the $j$th cycle with equilibrium value $c$, and

$$t_j = \sum_{k=1}^{j} c_k = jc + (x_1 - x_\infty)s_1(1 - a^j)[(1 - a)q_1d_1]^{-1}$$

To evaluate Eq. 6 as a power series in $\alpha$, we expand each term in powers of $\alpha$, except for the factor $\exp(-\alpha jc)$, so as to obtain an expression of the form

$$\sum_{j=1}^{\infty} e^{-(j-1)\alpha c}\{A_1 + A_2a^j + A_3a^{2j} + \alpha B_j + \alpha^2 C_j(\alpha)\}$$

in which $A_1$, $A_2$, and $A_3$ are independent of both $\alpha$ and $j$, $B$, is independent of $\alpha$, and both $B_j$ and $C_j(\alpha)$ are bounded uniformly in $j$ for finite $\alpha$. Evaluation of the terms $A_1$, $A_2$, etc., and summation of the series gives the result:

$$D_{1x}(0, y_0) = \frac{x_\infty}{2\alpha} + \frac{x_\infty^2}{12}\left(\frac{1}{d_1} - \frac{1}{q_1}\right) + \frac{(x_1 - x_\infty)s_1(x_1 + ax_\infty)}{2(1 - a^2)q_1d_1} + O(\alpha)$$

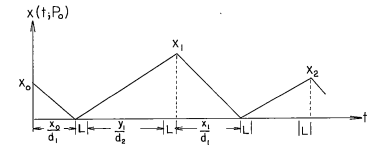

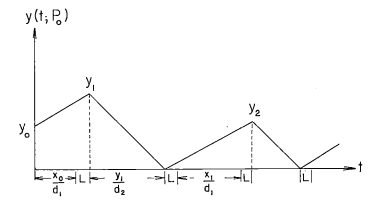

FIGURE I.    Queue evolution for basis policy.

From this we finally obtain for arbitrary $x_0$, $y_0$,

$$D_{1x}(x_0, y_0) = \frac{x_\infty}{2\alpha} + \frac{x_\infty^2}{12}\left(\frac{1}{d_1} - \frac{1}{q_1}\right) + \frac{x_0(x_0 - x_\infty)}{2d_1}$$

$$+ \frac{s_1(y_1 - y_\infty)[q_1(y_1 - y_\infty) + d_2(1 + a)x_\infty]}{2(1 - a^2)\,d_1^2 d_2^2} + O(\alpha) \qquad (7)$$

$$D_{1y}(x_0, y_0) = \frac{y_\infty}{2\alpha} + \frac{y_\infty^2}{12}\left(\frac{1}{d_2} - \frac{1}{q_2}\right) + \frac{y_1(y_1 - y_\infty)}{2d_2}$$

$$+ \frac{(y_0 + y_1 - y_\infty)(x_0 + d_1L)}{2d_1} + \frac{q_1 s_2(y_1 - y_\infty)(ay_1 + y_\infty)}{2(1 - a^2)\,d_1 d_2^2} + O(\alpha)$$

in which $y_1$ is given by Eq. 4. Expressions for $D_{2x}(x_0, y_0)$ and $D_{2y}(x_0, y_0)$ are obtained from Eq. 7 by interchange of notation for the two lanes.

The important terms for our subsequent analysis are the coefficients of $\alpha^0$ which are quadratic functions of the initial queue lengths $x_0$ and $y_0$.

## 3. Comparison Policies

There are only two types of variation one can make in the basis policy—switch before a queue is empty, or switch at some non-zero time after it empties. Any policy can be considered as the basis policy modified by application of these variations at appropriate time points. We, therefore, consider next the two policies:

*Policy $P_\mu'$*: Switch immediately at time $t = 0$ from the state $(\mu, x_0, y_0)$ and pursue the basis policy thereafter.

*Policy $P_\mu''$*: Allow the queue which is discharging from state $(\mu, x_0, y_0)$ at time $t = 0$ to become empty and remain empty for a time $\theta_\mu$, then switch and pursue the basis policy.

The total discounted delays for $P_\mu'$, and $P_\mu''$ can be evaluated by the same methods as used for $P_0$ and they have a form similar to Eq. 7. The coefficients of $\alpha^{-1}$ are the same for all these policies and the coefficients of $\alpha^0$ are quadratic forms in $x_0$ and $y_0$. We shall be mainly interested, however, in the delay differences between $P_\mu'$ or $P_\mu''$ and $P_0$. If these differences are denoted by

$$\delta_\mu'(x_0, y_0) = D_\mu^{*}(x_0, y_0; P_\mu') - D_\mu(x_0, y_0; P_0)$$
$$\delta_\mu''(x_0, y_0, \theta_\mu) = D_\mu(x_0, y_0; P_\mu'') - D_\mu(x_0, y_0; P_0)$$

then we find (after some algebra), that to order $\alpha$,

$$\delta_1'(x_0, y_0) = x_0[k_1 - (s_2 - s_1)y_0][(1 + a) d_1 d_2]^{-1}$$
$$\delta_1'(x_0, y_0) = y_0[k_1^* + (s_2 - s_1)x_0][(1 + a) d_1 d_2]^{-1} \tag{8}$$

where

$$k_1 = (y_\infty - q_2 L)(s_1 + s_2) + 2s_1 d_2 L$$

and

$$\delta_1''(x_0, y_0, \theta_1) = \theta_1 k_2[\tfrac{1}{2} q_2 \theta_1 - z_0]$$
$$\delta_2''(x_0, y_0, \theta_2) = \theta_2 k_2^*[\tfrac{1}{2} q_1 \theta_2 - z_0^*] \tag{9}$$

where

$$z_0 = k_3 - y_0 - x_0 q_2 / d_1$$
$$k_3 = q_1 L(q_2 + d_2 \beta) / s_1$$
$$\beta = (s_1 + s_2 a)(s_2 + s_1 a)^{-1}$$
$$k_2 = (s_2 + s_1 a)[d_2(1 - a^2)]^{-1}$$

The starred variables are obtained from the corresponding unstarred ones by interchange of notation for lanes 1 and 2.

Since $P_1'$ and $P_0$ represent the same policies if the initial state is $(1, 0, y_0)$, it follows that $\delta_1'(0, y_0)$ must be zero for all $y_0$. This, plus the fact that $\delta_1'(x_0, y_0)$ must (to order $\alpha$) be a quadratic in $(x_0, y_0)$, implies that it is the product of $x_0$ and a linear function of $x_0, y_0$, as is indeed true of Eq. 8. That $P_\mu''$ and $P_0$ coincide if $\theta_\mu = 0$ implies that $\delta_\mu'(x_0, y_0, 0) = 0$ for all $x_0, y_0$, as in Eq. 9.

It is convenient now to introduce a state space consisting of two separate two-dimensional spaces of points $(x_0, y_0)$, one for $\mu = 1$, the other for $\mu = 2$. From any point in this state space where one of the $\delta$'s is negative, the basis policy $P_0$ is certainly not optimal because either $P_\mu'$ or $P_\mu''$ would give a smaller delay than $P_0$. Since the $\delta$'s in Eqs. 8 and 9 are either linear or products of linear expressions in $(x_0, y_0)$, the regions of the state space where a $\delta$ is negative are bounded by straight lines.

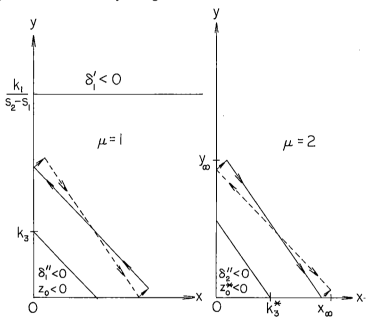

FIGURE 2.   State space separated into regions where $\delta$'s are positive and negative, with equilibrium cycle.

For policy $P_2'$, we see from Eq. 8 that if $s_2 > s_1$, then $\delta_2'(x_0, y_0) > 0$ for all $x_0, y_0 > 0$. Thus, it never pays to apply the policy $P_2'$ if it represents a switch from the lane of higher departure rate, $s_2$, to that of a lower departure rate, $s_1$, while there is still a queue to serve ($y_0 > 0$). On the other hand, with $s_2 > s_1$, $\delta_1'(x_0, y_0)$ is negative for $y_0 > k_1/(s_2 - s_1)$. If at time 0, the light is green for lane one (with the lower departure rate, $s_1$) and the queue in lane two is larger than $k_1/(s_2 - s_1)$, then it is advantageous to switch the light immediately (independent of the queue $x_0$ in lane one). It pays to accept the penalty of the lost time $L$ in switching the light to gain the advantage of the higher flow. If $s_2 < s_1$, the same conclusions follow except for an interchange of the lanes. If $s_1 = s_2$ then both $\delta_1'(x_0, y_0)$ and $\delta_2'(x_0, y_0)$ are positive; policy $P_\mu'$ is never advantageous for any $q_1, q_2$.

Figure 2 shows the region where $\delta_1'(x_0, y_0)$ is negative for $s_2 > s_1$. It is bounded by the horizontal line $y_0 = k_1/(s_2 - s_1)$.

For policy $P_1''$, $\delta_1''(x_0, y_0, \theta_1)$ is negative for some $\theta_1 > 0$ if, and only if, $z_0 < 0$. Since $k_3 > 0$, the boundary, $z_0 = 0$, is a straight line in the $(x_0, y_0)$ plane with positive intercepts and the region $z_0 < 0$, $x_0 > 0$, $y_0 > 0$ where $\delta_1''(x_0, y_0, \theta_1) < 0$ forms a triangle as shown in Fig. 2. There is also a triangle in the space $\mu = 2$ where $\delta_2''(x_0, y_0, \theta_2) < 0$. If $x_0$, $y_0$ are so small as to lie in one of these triangles, it is then advantageous not to switch the light immediately when a queue empties. If one did switch it would soon be necessary to switch back again and suffer a second lost time penalty. It is better to delay the switch until the queue in the other lane has grown large enough that serving it justifies paying the price for switching.

It is perhaps more natural to think of the policy $P_1''$ applied from state $(1, x_0, y_0)$ at time 0, as a modification that is made at time $t = x_0/d_1$ when the $x$-queue vanishes and the state is $(1, 0, y_0 + q_2 x_0/d_1)$, because, until this time there is no difference between the policies $P_1''$ and $P_0$. To investigate the implications of this and of application of either $P_\mu'$ or $P_\mu''$ at other times $t > 0$, it is desirable to determine the locus of all future state points ($\mu$, $x(t; P), y(t; P)$) for these policies.

## Trajectories

For $\mu = 1$ and $x_0 > 0$, queue one decreases at the rate $d_1$ and queue two increases at the rate $q_2$. The locus of future states in the $(1, x, y)$ plane therefore generates a straight line segment of slope $(-q_2/d_1)$. Similarly if $\mu = 2$, the locus is a straight line of slope $(-d_2/q_1)$. While the light is yellow, both queues increase at rates $q_1$ and $q_2$, and the point $(x(t; P), y(t; P))$ traces a line segment of slope $q_2/q_1$ for a time $L$.

Dunne and Potts[6] drew trajectories in a single state space $(x, y)$ for both $\mu = 1$ and $\mu = 2$. The complete trajectory then forms a continuous path of connected line segments which are traversed in a directed sense as time increases. Here it may be convenient to retain the two separate spaces but to draw as dashed lines those parts of the trajectory which do not belong to the value of $\mu$ in question, as in Fig. 2. While the light is yellow, the state does not belong to either $\mu = 1$ or $\mu = 2$, but we can draw the trajectory segment for this transition in either space. We will not admit the possibility that during the lost time we will change our mind and switch the light back.

For the basis policy $P_0$, the trajectory starting at $(1, x_0, y_0)$ follows the straight line of slope $(-q_2/d_1)$ through $(1, x_0, y_0)$ until it hits the boundary at $x = 0$. Then the trajectory joins a line segment of slope $+q_2/q_1$ for a time $L$ and jumps to the space $\mu = 2$. Here it follows a trajectory of slope $(-d_2/q_1)$ until $y = 0$, then connects with another line segment of slope $+q_2/q_1$ for a time $L$ and jumps back to the space $\mu = 1$, etc.

For the policy $P_\mu'$, the light turns yellow from a state with non-zero queues.

Thus the trajectory contains a line segment of slope $+q_2/q_1$ starting from a point other than a boundary point ($x = 0$ or $y = 0$). For policy $P_\mu''$, the light stays green even though a queue is empty. If $\theta_1 > 0$, the trajectory moves upward along the boundary $x = 0$, with $y$ increasing at a rate $q_2$, then connects with a line segment for the switch. If $\theta_2 > 0$, the trajectory moves to the right along the boundary $y = 0$. Figures 3, 4, and 5 show possible trajectory paths with $P_\mu'$ and $P_\mu''$ type modifications.

Any point along the trajectory for some policy $P$ can be considered as the "initial state" for the subsequent developments. The results of the last section, therefore, determine the gains or losses from application of a modification $P_\mu'$ or $P_\mu''$ at any point along the trajectory of the basis policy $P_0$. We can conclude from this that the basis policy is not optimal if its trajectory at any time passes through a region of the state space where one of the $\delta$'s is negative, because the policy $P_\mu'$ or $P_\mu''$ applied at such time would give less delay.

Equation 3 showed that if $0 < a < 1$, the basis policy will always converge to an equilibrium cycle. If however, the flows $q_1$ and/or $q_2$ are sufficiently small it is possible that the equilibrium cycle will cross the triangular regions where $\delta_\mu'' < 0$, in which case the optimal equilibrium cycle will involve a repeated application of a $P_\mu''$ policy. These cases were not treated by Dunne and Potts, and they will not be considered here either. When they do arise, the cycle times are so short that the continuum approximation is not very accurate anyway. We will assume that the equilibrium cycle always lies above or to the right of the triangles where $\delta_1''$ or $\delta_2'' < 0$ as shown in Fig. 2.

It is not necessary to make similar assumptions regarding the policy $P_\mu'$. One can easily show that the equilibrium cycle can not enter the region where $\delta_\mu' < 0$. We will be concerned here only with various policies for transient control in which the transient may originate or enter a region where a $\delta$ is negative, but the policy leads to an equilibrium cycle in which the basis policy is known to be the optimal equilibrium strategy.

Returning to the policies $P_\mu'$ and $P_\mu''$, we can now ask: if the basis policy crosses a region where a $\delta$ is negative, what is the best policy among those involving just one modification $P_\mu'$ or $P_\mu''$?

For the basis policy, the trajectory converges monotonically to the equilibrium cycle. Since the equilibrium cycle lies between the regions where $\delta_\mu' < 0$ and $\delta_\mu'' < 0$, a single trajectory from any initial state can not, with policy $P_0$, cross both a region $\delta_\mu' < 0$ and a region $\delta_\mu'' < 0$, but it could cross one or the other more than once. If the basis policy trajectory crosses $\delta_\mu' < 0$ during more than one cycle, the largest gain is obtained by application of $P_\mu'$ during the first crossing, when the state is furthest from equilibrium. Similarly if the trajectory crosses one of the triangles where $\delta_\mu'' < 0$, the maximum gain is achieved by application of a $P_\mu''$ policy during the first cycle. We must still determine, however, in the former case, at what point along the trajectory segment of the first cycle one should apply $P_\mu'$ and, in the latter case, the optimal choice of $\theta_\mu$.

From Eq. 8 we see that the curves of constant $\delta_1'(x_0, y_0)$ are hyperbolas with asymptotes $x = 0$, and $y = k_1/(s_2 - s_1)$. If a basis policy trajectory enters the region $\delta_1' < 0$ at the boundary $y = k_1/(s_2 - s_1)$, it crosses to the boundary $x = 0$ along a line of slope $(-q_2/d_1)$. Along this path $\delta_1'(x, y)$ goes from zero to a minimum and back to zero. The optimal policy $P_1'$ is to switch where $\delta_1'(x, y)$ is least. If we take the derivative of Eq. 8 with $dy/dx = -q_2/d_1$ the minimum is found to lie on the line

$$y = (q_2/d_1)x + k_1/(s_2 - s_1) \tag{10}$$

which passes through the corner of the region $\delta_1' < 0$ at $x = 0$, $y = k_1/(s_2 - s_1)$ with slope $+q_2/d_1$. The optimal switch point for policy $P_1'$ is the point where the trajectory first crosses this line.

For policy $P_\mu''$ we see from Eq. 9 that for given $\theta_\mu$, the lines of constant $\delta_1''$ are straight lines which are along trajectory paths. That these must be trajectory paths is obvious from the nature of the policy $P_\mu''$. If one is at a state with $x_0, y_0 > 0$, the future gain from $P_\mu''$ remains constant until the modification in policy is actually applied, namely when a queue vanishes.

The parameter $z_0$ is the difference between the $y$ queue length when $x$ reaches zero and the corresponding queue length at the boundary where $x = 0$ and $\delta_1'' = 0$, $y = k_3$. If we write Eq. 9 in the form

$$\delta_1''(x_0, y_0, \theta_\mu) = [-z_0^2 + (q_2\theta_1 - z_0)^2]k_2/(2q_2) \tag{11}$$

it is clear that the minimum value of $\delta_1''$ occurs when $q_2\theta_1 = z_0$. This value of $\theta_1$ is the time it takes for the trajectory point to move from the point where it first hits the boundary $x = 0$ to the corner of the triangle where $x = 0$ and $\delta_1'' = 0$. The interpretation of this is that when the trajectory reaches the boundary $x = 0$, the optimal $P_1''$ policy is to remain on this boundary until the state reaches a point such that if this point were the initial state, it would not pay to stay on the boundary any longer.

As yet we have not proved for any policy that it is optimal among all policies, but we do now have the formulas from which we can evaluate the discounted delay for an arbitrary policy. The total discounted delay for a policy $P$ which starts at the state $(\mu, x_0, y_0)$, makes the variations $P_\mu'$ when the trajectory reaches states $S_1', S_2', \ldots, S_n'$, and the variations $P_\mu''$ when the trajectory reaches the states $S_1'', S_2'', \ldots, S_m''$ (in any order), and then follows the basis policy (as must any policy which approaches the equilibrium policy) is

$$D_\mu(x_0, y_0; P_0) + \sum_{k=1}^{n} \delta'(S_k') + \sum_{k=1}^{m} \delta''(S_k'') \tag{12}$$

where the $\delta$'s are evaluated at the states $S_k'$ or $S_k''$.

The only formulas we shall need now to determine the optimal policies are the formulas for the $\delta$'s and the trajectory paths. Despite the fact that the $\delta$'s have a simple functional dependence upon $x_0$, $y_0$, that could probably have been inferred without detailed calculation, the values of the coefficients $k_1$, $k_2$, etc., in these formulas were more difficult to evaluate because a modification in policy changes the whole future course of the trajectory.

In the next two sections we shall determine the optimal policies from an arbitrary initial state, but we will consider separately two classes of initial states. Let the line segments of the equilibrium cycle trajectory, Fig. 2, be extended in each space, $\mu = 1$ and $\mu = 2$, so as to intersect both boundaries $x = 0$ and $y = 0$; thus, each space is divided into two regions. In Section 5 we consider the case in which the initial state $(\mu, x_0, y_0)$ lies in the region of the space $\mu$ above the equilibrium cycle, and in Section 6 the case in which it is below. In the former it will turn out that the optimal policy involves only $P_\mu{}'$ type modifications; in the latter only $P_\mu{}''$ type modifications, but in each case they may occur more than once.

## 5. Optimal Policy, Case I

We number the lanes so that the lane with the higher saturation rate is called lane 2, thus $s_2 > s_1$, and assume that the initial state $(\mu, x_0, y_0)$ lies above the equilibrium cycle of the space $\mu$.

Let $S$ be the piecewise linear curve $S_1$, $S_2$, ... shown in Fig. 3 joining the points $(\xi_j, \eta_j)$, $j = 0, 1, \ldots$, in the space $\mu = 1$, where:

$$\xi_j = j(q_2/d_1)Y + j(j-1)(1-a)d_1 Y/2q_2$$
$$\eta_j = k_1/(s_2 - s_1) + jY, \qquad Y = 2Ls_1s_2/(s_2 - s_1) \tag{13}$$

The first segment $S_1$ lies on the line of Eq. 10.

We will prove here that the following policies are optimal.

*Theorem 1*

*a.* If the trajectory for the basis policy $P_0$ does not enter the region $\delta_1{}' < 0$, then it is optimal.

*b.* If the initial state lies in the space $\mu = 2$ or below curve $S$ in the space $\mu = 1$, but the basis policy trajectory crosses the region $\delta_1{}' < 0$, then the optimal policy is to apply the modification $P_1{}'$ each time the trajectory meets the curve $S$.

*c.* If the initial state lies above $S$ in the space $\mu = 1$, the optimal policy is to apply $P_1{}'$ at time zero and thereafter pursue the policy described in *a* or *b*, whichever is applicable.

A trajectory for the optimal policy in Case (*b*) is shown in Fig. 3.

This theorem is derived from the following properties of optimal policies for states above the equilibrium cycle.

**Property 1.**   For the optimal policy, the last deviation (if there is any) from $P_0$ must be a $P_1'$ type modification which occurs either on the line given by Eq. 10 or above it, within the triangle formed by: $S_1$, the $\mu = 2$ trajectory through $(\xi_1, \eta_1)$, and the boundary $x = 0$.

*Proof:*  By the principle of optimality, Eq. 2, the future policy starting from the point of the last deviation from $P_0$ must be optimal. Equation 12 then

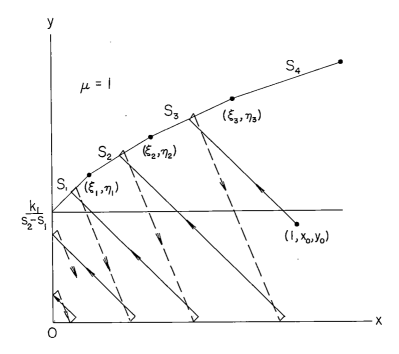

FIGURE 3.   Optimal policy trajectory of Theorem 1.

implies that the $\delta$ for this last modification must be non-positive, otherwise $P_0$ would give less (or the same) delay from this point. It is easy to see, how-ever, that no trajectory starting from points above the equilibrium cycle can ever enter the region below and, in particular, the regions where $\delta_{\mu}'' < 0$. Consequently, the last modification must be $P_1'$ and occur where $\delta_1' < 0$. But it cannot occur at a point below the line given by Eq. 10 because from such a point it is possible to follow the optimal $P_1'$ policy described in Section 4 for which the switch is postponed until the state reaches the line given by Eq. 10. Neither can it occur outside the triangle described above because then the basis policy trajectory after the last switch will reenter the region $\delta_1' < 0$. Hence, it would be advantageous to apply $P_1'$ again after the last modifica-tion. The coordinates of the point $(\xi_1, \eta_1)$ are evaluated so as to satisfy the conditions that this point lie on the line given by Eq. 10 and the $P_1'$ trajectory from this point passes through the point $(0, k_1/(s_2 - s_1))$.

**Property 2.**    For the optimal policy, the last deviation from $P_0$ other than $P_1'$-type modifications is not a $P_2'$.

*Proof:* Suppose there is a last $P_2'$ modification at some arbitrary state, point 1 of Fig. 4a with $y < 0$; then, the subsequent trajectory, 1, 2, 3, 4, 5 contains no

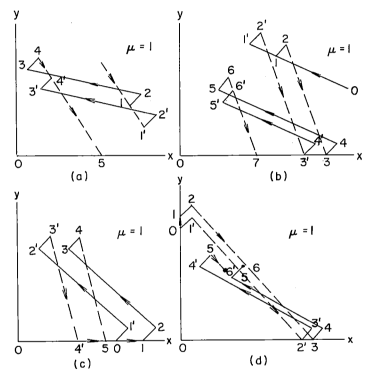

FIGURE 4.    Diagrams used in proving Theorem I.

deviations from $P_0$ except possibly at point 3. Point 3 may be on the boundary $x = 0$ or not. Consider also the alternative trajectory for which the last $P_2'$ modification at point 1 is postponed until the trajectory reaches state 1', and then follows 2', 3', 4', 5 with the segment 2'–3' of the same length as 2–3. Both trajectories arrive at state 5 simultaneously, but a simple calculation shows that the latter trajectory always has less delay. Consequently, the former policy is not optimal and the last $P_2'$ type modification must be on the boundary $y = 0$; thus there is no modification from $P_0$ here.

**Property 3.**    If no $P_\mu''$-type modifications occur, then the optimal policy is as described in theorem 1.

*Proof:* From properties 1 and 2 we conclude that if there are any modifications from $P_0$ other than $P_\mu''$ type, they must all be $P_1'$. If the optimal policy is not $P_0$, then either the last $P_1'$ modification occurs on $S_1$ or it occurs at time zero. For example suppose the last $P_1'$ modification occurs above $S$ at $t > 0$. Then it must have reached that state by previously passing through other states from which a switch would have given a more negative $\delta_1'$. Property 3 is therefore true if the optimal policy contains one or zero modifications $P_1'$. Now, suppose it contains two or more.

Consider the section of trajectory shown in Fig. 4b, starting at point 0 and ending at 7, with path $1, 2, \ldots, 6$, and compare it with other possible trajectories having paths such as $1', 2', \ldots, 6'$, all of which reach point 7 at the same time. For each choice of point $1'$, point $5'$ is chosen so that $6'$ lies on the line 6–7. Let points $2, 2', 6,$ and $6'$ have heights $y_{n-1}, y_{n-1}', y_n,$ and $y_n'$, respectively. If among this family of paths from 0 to 7 there is one for which

$$y_{n-1} - y_n = Y \tag{14}$$

we will label it as the trajectory $1, 2, \ldots, 6$. Then, an evaluation of the delays for these paths shows that the delay for $1', 2', \ldots, 6'$ is larger than for $1, 2, \ldots, 6$ by a positive multiple of $(y_{n-1}' - y_{n-1})^2$. Thus $1, 2, \ldots, 6$ is the optimal path from 0 to 7. If there is no admissible trajectory (with non-negative queues) which satisfies Eq. 14, then the optimal path is the one for which $|y_{n-1} - y_n - Y|$ is least among the allowed paths.

If the optimal policy contains two or more modifications $P_1'$, its trajectory will contain a section like one of those shown in Fig. 4b with the last $P_1'$ modification represented by point 5 or $5'$ which must lie on the line segment $S_1$. The second segment $S_2$ of Eq. 13 is defined as the locus of all points represented by point 1 of Fig. 4b which satisfy Eq. 14 with point 5 on $S_1$. The only circumstances under which the next to the last modification $P_1'$ could fail to occur on $S_2$ is that point 0 of Fig. 4b is the initial state and it lies above $S_2$ so that the trajectory path along the segment 0, 1, 1' does not contain the optimal switch point 1. If such is the case, however, the optimal path from 0 to 7 is the one for which the switch from the line 0, 1, 1' occurs as close to point 1 as possible, that is, at the initial point. Thus Property 3 is true if there are two $P_1'$ modifications.

The extension of the argument to 3 and more $P_1'$ modifications follows the same pattern. The coordinates of the end points of $S_j$ are solutions of difference equations which relate $(\xi_j, \eta_j)$ to $(\xi_{j-1}, \eta_{j-1})$, and are obtained through the conditions that the segment $S_j$ is the locus of all points 1 of Fig. 4b which satisfy Eq. 14 with point 5 on segment $S_{j-1}$. The only circumstances under which a $P_1'$ modification could fail to lie on $S$ is that it occur at time 0.

**Property 4.** The optimal policy contains no $P_\mu''$ type modifications. This with Property 3 then proves Theorem 1.

*Proof:* If there were a $P_\mu''$ modification there would be a last one, and thereafter the policy would have Property 3. By property 1, the last $P_\mu''$ must be followed by at least one $P_1'$ and it must be in accord with Property 3. In Fig. 4c the trajectory 0, 1, ..., 5 is a trajectory with a $P_2''$ modification, 0–1, followed by a $P_1'$ at point 3. The trajectory 0, 1', ..., 5' is the same except that the $P_2''$ modification is applied at point 4' insteady of 0. Both paths reach point 5 simultaneously, but the latter obviously has shorter average queue lengths. Therefore, 0, 1, ..., 5 cannot be optimal. The $P_2''$ modification cannot exist anywhere in the optimal policy.

In Fig. 4d the trajectory 0, 1, ..., 6 contains a $P_1''$ modification at 0 followed by a $P_1'$ at point 5. For some non-zero length of the segment 0–1, a trajectory 0, 1', ..., 6' can be constructed in such a way that the two paths simultaneously reach points 6 and 6', which have the same value of $y$, but with point 6 to the right of 6'. The total discounted future delay from point 6 is larger than from point 6' because at some future time one must serve the excess $x$-queue that exists at point 6. Also, the delay along the path 0, 1, ..., 6 is larger than along 0, 1', ..., 6'. The path 0, 1, ..., 6, is therefore not optimal and, consequently, the optimal policy could not have a $P_1''$ type modification either.

## 6. Optimal Policy, Case 2

We consider now the case in which the initial state $(\mu, x_0, y_0)$ lies below the equilibrium cycle. For this it is convenient to number the lanes so that the initial state is $(1, x_0, y_0)$ with $\mu = 1$.

The following policies are optimal.

*Theorem 2*

   *a.* If the trajectory for the policy $P_0$ from $(1, x_0, y_0)$ does not pass through states where $\delta_1'' < 0$ or $\delta_2'' < 0$, then $P_0$ is the optimal policy.

   *b.* If the initial state is in the region $\delta_1'' < 0$ and the trajectory for the optimal $P_1''$ policy (Section 4) does not enter the region $\delta_2'' < 0$, then this policy is optimal. The trajectory goes from the initial state to the boundary $x = 0$, and remains there until $y = k_3$. After that the basis policy is followed. The necessary and sufficient conditions that this trajectory not enter the region $\delta_2'' < 0$ is that the trajectory from $(1, 0, k_3)$ does not switch immediately into this region, i.e.,

$$k_3 + s_2 L \geq k_3^* d_2/q_1 \tag{15}$$

a condition which depends (in a rather complicated way) on the flows $q_1, s_1$, etc., but does not depend upon the initial state.

   *c.* Suppose neither *a* nor *b* apply and the initial state parameter $z_0$, Eq. 9, satisfies

$$z_0 \leq [k_3^* d_2/q_1 - k_3 - s_2 L] a\beta/(1 - a\beta) \equiv k_3 - k_4 \tag{16}$$

Equation 16 states that the initial state $(1, x_0, y_0)$ lies above a line

$$y = -q_2 x/d_1 + k_4 \qquad (17)$$

which has a $y$ intercept $k_4$ defined by Eq. 16. It may be negative. Then, the optimal policy trajectory goes from the initial state to the boundary $x = 0$ above $k_4$ where a switch is made (with $\theta_1 = 0$). It next proceeds to a point on the boundary $y = 0$ in the region $\delta_2'' < 0$ (otherwise Case $a$ would apply), and stays on this boundary until $x = k_3^*$. After that, policy $P_0$ is followed.

$d$. If none of the above cases apply, then $k_4 > 0$ (otherwise Case $c$ would apply) and the initial state lies below the line given by Eq. 17, which is located, within the region $\delta_1'' < 0$. The optimal policy trajectory goes from the initial state to a state on the boundary $x = 0$ below $k_4$ and remains there until $y = k_4$. At the state $(1, 0, k_4)$ Case $c$ applies and the remainder of the optimal policy is as described in $c$.

Trajectories for Cases $c$ and $d$ are illustrated in Fig. 5a, starting from points 0 and 1, respectively.

These four cases include all possibilities. Only case $d$, which involves application of both $P_1''$ and $P_2''$, has more than one deviation from the basis policy.

Before proving Theorem 2, we will derive a few properties of optimal policies for states below the equilibrium cycle.

**Property 1.** For the optimal policy, the last deviation from $P_0$ (if there is one) must be either $P_1''$ or $P_2''$ for which, respectively, the trajectory stays on the boundary $x = 0$ or $y = 0$ from a point $y < k_3$ or $x < k_3^*$ until $y = k_3$ or $x = k_3^*$ is reached. If Eq. 15 is false, the last deviation must be $P_2''$.

Part $a$ of Theorem 2 follows directly from this because no trajectory from $(1, x_0, y_0)$ will enter the region $\delta_1'' < 0$ or $\delta_2'' < 0$ if the basis policy trajectory doesn't. Consequently, there can be no last deviation $P_1''$ or $P_2''$ satisfying Property 1.

*Proof:* The last deviation from $P_0$ must be one with a negative $\delta$. It cannot be a $P_\mu'$, however, because to reach the region where $\delta_\mu' < 0$, the trajectory must cross the equilibrium cycle and pass through states from which the optimal policy is known by Theorem 1, to be $P_0$. The last deviation must, therefore, be a $\delta_\mu''$; it must also be one with the optimal $\theta_\mu$ as in Section 4. The trajectory after the last $P_\mu''$ must not again enter a region where $\delta_\mu'' < 0$. Thus, if Eq. 15 is false the last deviation from $P_0$ must be a $P_2''$.

**Property 2.** The optimal policy contains no $P_\mu'$ modifications.

*Proof:* Suppose there were $P_\mu'$ modifications, the last of which was a $P_1'$. Let point 0 of Fig. 5b represent the point of the last $P_1'$ and 0, 1, . . . , 5 the subsequent path. According to Property 1, either point 2 and/or 5 must be in a region where $\delta_\mu'' < 0$ in order that it be possible to apply the final $P_1''$ or $P_2''$

policy. In the former case we consider the alternative path 0, 1′, 2′, 3′, 2, 3, . . . with a non-zero $\theta_2$ from 3′ to 2. Formula 12 for $D_\mu(x_0, y_0; P)$ differs for the two policies in that the alternative policy has a negative $\delta_2''$ from the segment 3′–2 where the original policy has a positive $\delta_1'$ for the step 0–1. The

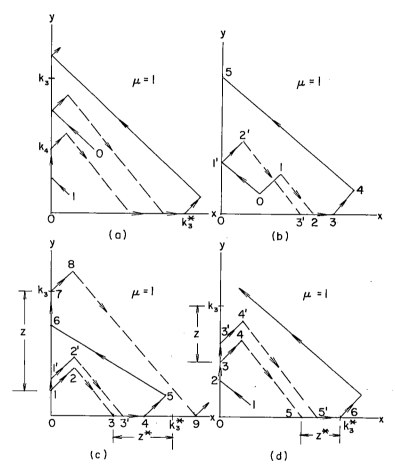

FIGURE 5.  Diagrams used in proving Theorem 2 and (5a) optimal policy trajectories of Theorem 2.

alternative policy, therefore, has a smaller discounted delay. If point 2 is not in the region $\delta_2'' < 0$, then 5 must be in the region $\delta_1'' < 0$, and similar considerations for the trajectory 0, 1′, 5, . . . with a non-zero $\theta_1$ from 1′ to 5 shows that the original policy is not optimal in this case either. If the last of the $P_\mu'$ modifications is $P_2'$ insteady of $P_1'$, the same arguments apply after an interchange of lanes 1 and 2.

**Property 3.**    If Eq. 15 is true, the optimal policy from $(1, x_0, y_0)$ contains no $P_2''$ modifications.

*Proof:* If there were a $P_2''$ modification, the trajectory would include a section $3, 4, 5, \ldots$ as in Fig. 5c, with the $P_2''$ occurring at point 3. Since the initial state is $\mu = 1$ and there are no $P_\mu'$ modifications, the trajectory must reach point 3 from 1. Point 1 must lie below $k_3$ because of property 1 and Eq. 15.

We now compare the trajectory $1, 2, 3, \ldots$ with the trajectory $1, 1', 2', 3', 4, \ldots$ in which a $P_1''$ modification of duration $\theta_1$ is applied at point 1 giving also a reduction $q_2\theta_1/d_2$, in the value of $\theta_2$ at point 3. The net reduction in total discounted delay, $\rho$, to first order in $\theta_1$, is found from Eq. 7 to be

$$\rho = k_2\theta_1(z - z^*a\beta \, d_2/q_1) \tag{18}$$

in which $z$ and $z^*$ are the distances shown in Fig. 5c and

$$a\beta = (s_2a^2 + s_1a)/(s_2 + s_1a) < 1$$

Equation 15, however, implies that $k_3^*$ lies inside the trajectory segment $7, 8, 9$ from $k_3$, which in turn implies that

$$z > z^*d^2/q_1 > z^*a\beta \, d_2/q_1 \tag{19}$$

Therefore, the expression given by the right-hand side of Eq. 18 is positive and the policy $1, 2, 3, \ldots$ can be improved.

We can now prove part $b$ of Theorem 2. Since Eq. 15 holds and no $P_\mu'$ or $P_2''$ modifications are allowed (Properties 2, 3), the optimal policy may have only $P_1''$ type modifications with the last one ending at the point $(k_3, 0)$ as illustrated by the segment 6–7 of Fig. 5c. We can, however, gain an additional negative $\delta_1''$ if the trajectory stays on the boundary $x = 0$ from point 1 to 6 instead of going around the cycle $2, 3, 4, 5$. The trajectory for the optimal policy, therefore, does not leave the boundary $x = 0$ anywhere below $y = k_3$. The optimal policy is as described in Theorem 2, part $b$.

Finally to prove parts $c$ and $d$ of Theorem 2, we note that if Eq. 15 is false, then the last modification from $P_0$ must, by Property 1, be $P_2''$. By the same arguments as in Property 3, but with the lane numbers interchanged, we conclude that after the trajectory first reaches the boundary $y = 0$ with $\mu = 2$, it has no subsequent $P_1''$ modifications. Furthermore, it stays on this boundary until $x = k_3^*$. This follows from Theorem 2, part $b$ but with the lane numbers interchanged. We are justified in applying these results with interchange of lane numbers because the condition that Eq. 15 be false (the trajectory from $(1, 0, k_3)$ meets $y = 0$ at $x < k_3^*$), plus the condition that the regions $\delta_1'' < 0$ and $\delta_2'' < 0$ are below the equilibrium cycle, imply that the trajectory from $(2, k_3^*, 0)$ meets the boundary $x = 0$ above $k_3$. Thus the condition obtained from Eq. 15 by interchange of lanes is satisfied.

The only remaining question is whether or not a $P_1''$ modification is to be made when the trajectory from the state $(1, x_0, y_0)$ first meets the boundary

$x = 0$. As in the proof of Property 3 we consider the net difference in total discounted delay between trajectories $1, 2, 3, \ldots, 6, \ldots$ and $1, 2, 3', 4',$ $5', 6, \ldots$ of Fig. 5d. Equation 18 is still valid for a small $\theta_1$ applied at point 3; but the first part of Eq. 19 is reversed (because Eq. 15 is), so it is possible that the right hand side of Eq. 18 may have either sign (or be zero) depending upon the flow parameters and initial state. If Eq. 16 is true, then the right hand side of Eq. 18 is negative when points 2 and 3 coincide ($z = z_0$), so that any positive $\theta_1$ increases the delay. Consequently, the optimal policy is to choose $\theta_1 = 0$ at point 2. This proves part $c$ of Theorem 2.

If $k_4 > 0$ and the initial state is below the line given by Eq. 17, then a positive $\theta_1$ at point 2 decreases the delay. As long as Eq. 18 remains positive while point 3 moves upward, it is advantageous to move it still higher. If, however, the right-hand side of Eq. 18 becomes negative, the trajectory has gone too far along the boundary. The optimal policy is to switch where Eq. 18 is zero. This is the point $(0, k_4)$, which proves part $d$ of Theorem 2.

## References

1. J. G. Wardrop, Some Theoretical Aspects of Road Traffic Research, *Proc. Instn. Civ. Engrs.*, II, 1 325–378 (1952).
2. F. V. Webster, Traffic Signal Settings, Road Research Technical Paper No. 39, Her Majesty's Stationry Office, London (1958).
3. A. J. Miller, Settings for Fixed-Cycle Traffic Signals, *Operational Res. Q.*, **14**, 373–386 (1963); Proc. 2nd. Conference, Australian Road Res. Bd. (1964).
4. D. C. Gazis and R. B. Potts, The Oversaturated Intersection, *Proc. Second Intern. Symp. on Theory of Road Traffic Flow*, J. Almond, Ed., O.E.C.D., Paris (1965).
5. D. C. Gazis, Optimum Control of a System of Oversaturated Intersections, *Operations, Res.* **12**, 815–831 (1964).
6. M. C. Dunne and R. B. Potts, Algorithm for Traffic Control, *Operations, Res.*, **12**, 870–881 (1964).
7. R. E. Bellman, "Dynamic Programming," Princeton Univ. Press, Princeton, New Jersey, 1957.
8. R. E. Bellman, ibid, pp. 121.

# Analysis of a Computer Control
# of an Isolated Intersection

*MICHAEL C. DUNNE and RENFREY B. POTTS*

Mathematics Department
University of Adelaide
South Australia

## Abstract

An exact mathematical analysis is given of the operational characteristics of a signalized intersection for which the control strategy is to switch the lights when the favored queue empties. The vehicle arrivals are assumed to be generated by a binomial process, and the departure rates are assumed constant. The model simulates a possible mode of computer control of an intersection.

## Introduction

AUTOMATIC DEVICES for controlling a traffic intersection have developed rapidly from the simple fixed-cycle traffic light to the flexible vehicle-actuated and volume-density lights, and more recently to lights controlled by a central computer. Much has been written on the theory of the operation of a fixed-cycle light. That most relevant to the present work is the book by Beckman, McGuire, and Winsten,[1] in which vehicle arrivals are assumed generated by a binomial process, and the paper by Uematu,[2] in which a random walk model is used. The theory of vehicle-actuated lights has been developed by Tanner[3] and by Darroch, Newell, and Morris.[4] The latter have given a very complete analysis based on the broad assumptions of random lost time at each switch of the lights and arbitrary distribution of departure headways, but with the specific assumption of arrival headways being exponentially distributed random variables. As pointed out by these authors, this assumption of Poisson arrivals, allowing relatively high probabilities for small headways, leads to the unrealistic possibility of a flow during the extension of the green phase which is higher than the saturation flow through the intersection when the queue discharges.

With the advent of central computer control of traffic lights, the spectrum of possible strategies for switching the lights has become unlimited, but it is far from obvious which strategies are likely to be most efficient. To date it appears that little more has been done beyond simulating the familiar vehicle-actuated and volume-density controllers. In an attempt to analyze possible algorithms for adaptive control by a computer, the authors have previously considered[5] a simple algorithm and derived its operational characteristics on the assumption of constant arrival and departure rates. In this paper it is also assumed that the departure rates are constant but the arrivals are assumed to be generated by a binomial process. The control strategy analyzed is one for which the light is switched immediately, the queue being favored is emptied, a strategy which is a special case of the algorithm considered in the earlier paper. The operational characteristics of this type of control are obtained by deriving exact probability distributions for the phase and cycle times, and for the queue lengths when the lights are switched.

In the Toronto pilot study,[6] the arriving traffic is recorded in the central computer as a series of 0's and 1's from a periodical scanning (say every $\tau$ sec) of single-lane presence detectors. Each detector registers a pulse if a vehicle crosses it during a $\tau$-sec interval, and this interval is chosen sufficiently small so that two cars, because of their finite length and limited speed, cannot cross a detector during the same interval. The assumption of binomial arrivals is equivalent to assuming that the 0's and 1's are uncorrelated, which is unrealistic for heavy or pulsed traffic.

The strategy of switching the lights when the favored queue empties would be interpreted differently for different systems depending on the type of detectors used and their placement. It is intended to extend the analysis to the case when the lights are switched when a certain gap (represented by a string of 0's) is detected in the favored traffic stream. This strategy would be more analogous to vehicle-actuated control. The authors optimistically hope that they may have the opportunity to experiment with computer-like control of an intersection in order to test the assumptions of the various theories and to compare the operational characteristics for different control algorithms.

## Mathematical Model

Consider a simple intersection controlled by a two-phased traffic light. For simplicity, attention will be confined to only two of the four traffic arms, and it will be assumed that each approach is one lane and that right and left turns are neglected. This simple model is similar to one used in the Toronto system and is realistic for a properly designed two-phase intersection because two lanes usually predominate in determining the light settings, especially under tidal flow conditions at peak periods. Left-turning vehicles either filter through the oncoming traffic or make their turn during the amber period, while right turners can turn fairly freely provided that the pedestrian traffic is light.

Each green phase is supposed to consist of a lost time $l\tau$ sec, during which no vehicles cross the intersection, followed by an effective green time, during which the traffic discharges at a constant rate. This rate, the so-called saturation flow, is taken to be the same for each arm. The vehicle arrivals, assumed to be generated by a binomial process, are described by letting $q_i$ be the probability of one arrival in arm $i = 1, 2$ in each of the intervals $(k\tau, k\tau + \tau)$, $k = 0, 1, 2, \ldots$, and by denoting the probability of no arrival by $p_i = 1 - q_i$. For convenience, the time interval $\tau$ is taken equal to the time interval between vehicle departures, although the analysis could be extended to cover other choices. As a numerical example, suppose that $\tau = 2$ sec, and $q_1 = 0.4$, $q_2 = 0.3$; the saturation flow is then 1800 vph, and the arriving traffic flows on arms 1 and 2 are 720 vph and 540 vph, respectively.

During the lost time at the beginning of each green phase, no vehicles cross the intersection. Hence, if the number of vehicles queued in arm $i$ at time $t = k\tau$ is denoted by $n_i(k\tau)$, then

> (a) $n_i(k\tau + \tau) = n_i(k\tau) + 1$     with probability $q_i$
>
> (b) $n_i(k\tau + \tau) = n_i(k\tau)$        with probability $p_i$

If the subsequent effective green favors arm 1 so that vehicles arrive at arms 1 and 2 but discharge only from arm 1, then

> (c) $n_1(k\tau + \tau) = n_1(k\tau)$        with probability $q_1$
>
> (d) $n_1(k\tau + \tau) = n_1(k\tau) - 1$     with probability $p_1$
>
> (e) $n_2(k\tau + \tau) = n_2(k\tau) + 1$     with probability $q_2$
>
> (f) $n_2(k\tau + \tau) = n_2(k\tau)$        with probability $p_2$

Equations (a) through (f), together with four additional ones governing the case when arm 2 is favored, characterize a two-dimensional walk, the analysis of which yields the operational characteristics of the control of the intersection.

## Random Walk Analysis

The manner in which the queue lengths vary may be illustrated by a graph in which $n_2(t)$ is plotted against $n_1(t)$. As vehicles arrive at or depart from the intersection, the representative point or particle traces out a two-dimensional random walk from lattice point to lattice point. Since the control strategy requires the lights to be switched when queues are emptied, lattice points on the $n_1 = 0$ and $n_2 = 0$ axes act as reflecting points, and the axes themselves as reflecting barriers. An analysis of this random walk enables an exact evaluation of the probability distributions describing one phase, one cycle, or any number of cycles of the traffic light.

## One Phase

Define $R_i(r, s; l)$ to be the conditional probability that if arm $i$ has the green light and if there were $r$ vehicles in arm $i$ at the beginning of the green phase, then there are $s$ vehicles in the opposing arm at the end of the phase. Denote the corresponding generating function by

$$\phi_i(r, z; l) = \sum_{s=0}^{\infty} R_i(r, s; l)z^s \tag{1}$$

The effect of the lost time is to imply that

$$R_i(r, s; l) = R_i(r + l, s; 0) \tag{2}$$

and hence

$$\phi_i(r, z; l) = \phi_i(r + l, z; 0) \tag{3}$$

To evaluate $\phi_1$, for example, assume that arm 1 has the green light and that there were $r + l$ vehicles in this arm at $t = 0$, the beginning of effective green phase. The generating function for the probability that this queue emptied at time $t = k\tau$ is the negative binomial (see Reference 7, p. 253)

$$\xi_1(z) = \left[\frac{p_1 z}{1 - q_1 z}\right]^{r+l} \tag{4}$$

If $X_j$ is the number of arrivals at arm 2 in the interval $(j\tau - \tau, j\tau)$, the probability generating function of $X_j$ is

$$\zeta_2(z) = p_2 + q_2 z \tag{5}$$

The probability generating function of $s = n_2(k\tau) = X_1 + X_2 + \cdots + X_k$ is therefore

$$\phi_1(r + l, z; 0) = \xi_1[\zeta_2(z)]$$

so that

$$\phi_1(r, z; l) = \left[\frac{p_1(p_2 + q_2 z)}{1 - q_1(p_2 + q_2 z)}\right]^{r+l} \tag{6}$$

A similar expression for $\phi_2(r, z, l)$ is obtained from Eq. 6 by interchanging the subscripts on the $p$'s and $q$'s.

## One Cycle

Define $\theta_i^{(1)}(r, z)$ to be the generating function for the conditional probability that there are $r'$ vehicles in arm $i$ at the end of a cycle, given that there were $r$ vehicles in arm $i$ at the beginning of the cycle. Then, for example,

$$\theta_1^{(1)}(r, z) = \sum_{s=0}^{\infty} R_1(r, s; l)\phi_2(s, z; l)$$

$$= \phi_2(l, z; 0)\phi_1[r, \phi_2(1, z; 0); l]$$

or

$$\theta_1^{(1)}(r, z) = [\alpha(z)\beta(z)]^l[\beta(z)]^r \tag{7}$$

where

$$\alpha(z) = \phi_2(1, z; 0) = \frac{p_2(p_1 + q_1 z)}{1 - q_2(p_1 + q_1 z)} \tag{8}$$

and

$$\beta(z) = \phi_1[1, \phi_2(1, z; 0); 0] = \frac{p}{1 - qz} \tag{9}$$

with

$$p = \frac{p_1 p_2}{p_1 p_2 + q_1 q_2} \tag{10}$$

and

$$q = 1 - p = \frac{q_1 q_2}{p_1 p_2 + q_1 q_2} \tag{11}$$

## n Cycles

If $\theta_1^{(n)}(r, z)$ is the generating function for $n$ cycles defined in a similar way as the definition for $\theta_1^{(1)}(r, z)$, it then satisfies the recurrence relation

$$\theta_1^{(n)}(r, z) = [\alpha(z)\beta(z)]^l\theta_1^{(n-1)}[r, \beta(z)] \tag{12}$$

Since there were $r$ vehicles in arm 1 at the beginning of the first cycle,

$$\theta^{(0)}(r, z) = z^r \tag{13}$$

and, hence, the solution of the recurrence relation (Eq. 12) is

$$\theta_1^{(n)}(r, z) = [(\alpha)(\beta)(\alpha\beta)(\beta^{(2)}) \ldots (\alpha\beta^{(n-1)})(\beta^{(n)})]^l[\beta^{(n)}]^r \tag{14}$$

In this expression,

$$\beta^{(n)} = \beta(\beta(\ldots \beta(z) \ldots)) \tag{15}$$

is the $n$th iteration of $\beta(z)$ and $\alpha(z)$, $\beta(z)$, $\alpha[\beta^{(n)}]$ have been abbreviated to $\alpha$, $\beta$, $\alpha\beta^{(n)}$, respectively.

## Evaluation of $\theta_1^{(n)}(r, z)$

The form of expression (Eq. 14) is familiar in the theory of Markov processes and it is of interest that for this binomial model its explicit evaluation is possible. It is clear from Eq. 9 that $\beta^{(n)}$ will be a bilinear function of $z$ which, since it must be equal to 1 when $z = 1$, can be assumed to be of the form

$$\beta^{(n)} = \frac{p - qz - qa_n(1 - z)}{p - qz - qb_n(1 - z)} \tag{16}$$

without loss of generality. The functional equation $\beta^{(n)} = \beta^{(n-1)}(\beta(z))$ implies that

$$\frac{p - qz - qa_n(1 - z)}{p - qz - qb_n(1 - z)} = \frac{p - qp(1 - qz)^{-1} - q^2 a_{n-1}(1 - qz)^{-1}(1 - z)}{p - qp(1 - qz)^{-1} - q^2 b_{n-1}(1 - qz)^{-1}(1 - z)}$$

$$= \frac{p - qz - q(q/p)a_{n-1}(1 - z)}{p - qz - q(q/p)b_{n-1}(1 - z)}$$

so that $a_n$ and $b_n$ satisfy the same recurrence relation

$$a_n = (q/p)a_{n-1} \qquad b_n = (q/p)b_{n-1} \tag{17}$$

Since

$$a_1 = 1 \quad \text{and} \quad b_1 = q/p, \qquad a_n = b_{n-1} = (q/p)^{n-1} \tag{18}$$

giving

$$\beta^{(n)} = \frac{p - qz - q(q/p)^{n-1}(1 - z)}{p - qz - q(q/p)^n(1 - z)} \tag{19}$$

This result, together with Eq. 8, yields

$$(\alpha)(\beta)(\alpha\beta)(\beta^{(2)}) \ldots (\alpha\beta^{(n-1)})(\beta^{(n)})$$

$$= \frac{(p - q)^2(p_1 + q_1 z)}{\left[p - qz - q\left(\dfrac{q}{p}\right)^n (1 - z)\right]\left[p - qz - \dfrac{p_1 q_1}{p_1 p_2 + q_1 q_2}\left(\dfrac{q}{p}\right)^n (1 - z)\right]} \tag{20}$$

which, on substitution in Eq. 14, gives an explicit expression for $\theta_1^{(n)}(r, z)$. The similar result for $\theta_2^{(n)}(r, z)$ is obtained by changing subscripts in Eq. 20.

## Steady State

A steady state or state of statistical equilibrium is achieved when the intersection is undersaturated. The condition for this is $q_1 q_2 < p_1 p_2$ or $q < p$, and if this inequality holds $\beta^{(n)} \to 1$ as $n \to \infty$ and, hence,

$$\lim_{n \to \infty} \theta_1^{(n)}(r, z),$$

the generating function of the steady-state probabilities, is independent of $r$, the initial number of vehicles. From Eq. 20 the explicit result for this generating function is

$$\theta_1(z) = \lim_{n \to \infty} \theta_1^{(n)}(r, z) = \left[\frac{(p - q)^2(p_1 + q_1 z)}{(p - qz)^2}\right]^l \tag{21}$$

It is easy to verify that this expression satisfies the functional equation

$$\theta_1(z) = [\alpha(z)\beta(z)]^l \theta_1[\beta(z)] \tag{22}$$

which is the limiting form of the recurrence relation (Eq. 12). Similar results hold for $\theta_2(z)$.

The steady-state probabilities $p_i(m)$, for the number of vehicles in the arm of the intersection with the red phase when the light is switched, are the coefficients in the expansion of $\theta_i(z)$ about the origin

$$\theta_i(z) = \sum_{m=0}^{\infty} p_i(m)z^m \tag{23}$$

## Operational Characteristics

An exact description of the operational characteristics of the traffic-light control follows from the solution of the random walk problem. Provided the intersection is undersaturated, the operation approaches statistical equilibrium and the steady-state probabilities give the probabilities of the queue lengths when the light is switched and give the phase durations.

For example, the mean queue lengths are given by

$$\langle n_1 \rangle = E(n_1) = \left[ \frac{d}{dz} \ln \theta_1(z) \right]_{z=1} = \frac{lq_1(p_1 + q_2)}{p_1p_2 - q_1q_2} \tag{24}$$

and similarly

$$\langle n_2 \rangle = \frac{lq_2(p_2 + q_1)}{p_1p_2 - q_1q_2} \tag{25}$$

A slightly more complicated calculation gives the variances as

$$\mathrm{var}\,(n_1) = E[(n_1 - \langle n_1 \rangle)^2] = lq_1p_1 \left[ 1 + \frac{2q_2p_2}{(p_1p_2 - q_1q_2)^2} \right] \tag{26}$$

with a similar result for var $(n_2)$.

The probability distributions for the green phase durations in the steady state can be obtained from their generating functions which may be shown to be

$$\Theta_i(z) = \left[ \frac{p_iz}{1 - q_iz} \right]^l \theta_i\left( \frac{p_iz}{1 - q_iz} \right) \tag{27}$$

The mean and variances of the green phase durations for arm 1 are

$$\langle g_1 \rangle = E(g_1) = \frac{l\tau(p_2 + q_1)}{p_1p_2 - q_1q_2} \; \sec \tag{28}$$

and

$$\mathrm{var}\,(g_1) = \frac{2l\tau^2 q_1p_2}{(p_2 - q_1)^2} \; (\sec)^2 \tag{29}$$

with similar expressions for $\langle g_2 \rangle$ and var $(g_2)$.

It is interesting to note that, as might have been expected, the values of $\langle n_i \rangle$ and $\langle g_i \rangle$ are precisely those obtained in the previous paper[5] in which the vehicles were assumed to arrive at a constant rate. For that model, of course, the variances and higher moments are all zero. The setting of a fixed cycle light with phases $\langle g_1 \rangle$, $\langle g_2 \rangle$ gives, in general, maximum efficiency for constant arrival rates but infinite delay when fluctuations are present.[8] The classic Webster formula[9] minimizes the average delay by approximately doubling the phase durations. The consequent loss of efficiency would be avoided with the adaptive computer control considered in this paper as the phase durations shorten or lengthen about their average values as the traffic demand fluctuates.

## Numerical Example

To illustrate the analytical results obtained above, suppose that $\tau = 2$ sec, $q_1 = q_2 = 0.4$, $l = 3$, so that the saturation flow is 1800 vph, the traffic flows on each arm are 720 vph, and the lost time is 6 sec. Then (dropping the subscripts 1, 2 since the arms are identical)

$$\theta(z) = \left[ \left( \frac{5}{9 - 4z} \right)^2 \left( \frac{3 + 2z}{5} \right) \right]^3 \qquad (30)$$

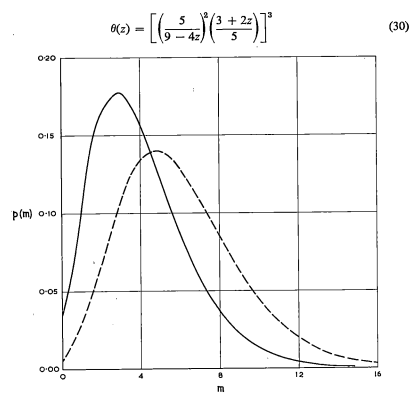

FIGURE I.   Plot of the probability $p(m)$ that in the steady state there are $m$ vehicles in the arm of the intersection with the red phase when the light is switched. The saturation flow is 1800 vph; the traffic flow on each arm is 720 vph; and the lost time is 4 sec for the solid curve and 6 sec for the dashed curve. The probabilities are defined only for integral values of $m$, but the curves have been drawn joining the points to facilitate the comparison.

from direct substitution into Eq. 21. Expansion of $\theta(z)$ as a power series gives numerical values for the stationary probabilities for the queue lengths when the light is switched:

$$p(0) = 0.00635\ldots, \qquad p(1) = 0.02964\ldots, \qquad p(2) = 0.06868\ldots, \qquad (31)$$

which are plotted in Fig. 1. The mean and variance are obtained from Eqs. 24 and 26:

$$\langle n \rangle = 6, \qquad \text{var}(n) = 9.36 \tag{32}$$

It is evident from Fig. 1 that the mean exceeds the mode. For comparison, a second set of results using $l = 2$ has been illustrated in Fig. 1; the lost time is now 4 sec, other traffic conditions being kept the same.

For the mean and variance of the phase durations in the steady state, the following results have been obtained from Eq. 28 and 29:

$$\langle g \rangle = 30 \text{ sec}, \qquad \text{var}(g) = 144 \text{ (sec)} \tag{33}$$

## Acknowledgment

The authors acknowledge the support of General Motors-Holden's Pty. Ltd., which has enabled this research project to be carried out. One of the authors (M. C. D.) has held a special G.M.H. post graduate scholarship. The authors have greatly benefited from discussions with Dr. J. N. Darroch, University of Michigan, whose suggestions have enabled an early draft of this paper to be considerably shortened and improved. The authors have also had helpful discussions with Dr. G. F. Newell, Brown University, and Mr. R. W. J. Morris, South Australian Highways Department.

## References

1. M. Beckman, C. B. McGuire, and C. B. Winsten, "*Studies in the Economics of Transportation.*" Yale University Press, New Haven, Connecticut, 1956.
2. T. Uematu, On Traffic Control at an Intersection Controlled by the Repeated Fixed-Cycle Traffic Light," *Ann. Instit. Stat. Math.* **9,** 87–107 (1958).
3. J. C. Tanner, A Problem of Interference Beween Two Queues, *Biometrika,* **40,** 58–69 (1953).
4. J. N. Darroch, G. F. Newell, and R. W. J. Morris, Queues for a Vehicle-Actuated Traffic Light, *Operations Res.,* **12,** 882–895 (1964).
5. M. C. Dunne and R. B. Potts, Algorithm for Traffic Control, *Operations Res.,* **12,** 870–881 (1964).
6. J. T. Hewton, Toronto Installs All-Purpose Electronic Computer for Traffic Signal Control, *Traff. Eng. Cont.,* **5,** 589–594 (1964).
7. W. Feller, "*An Introduction to Probability Theory and its Applications,*" Vol. 1 (2nd Ed.), Wiley, New York, 1957.
8. J. G. Wardrop, Some Theoretical Aspects of Road Traffic Research, *Proc. Instit. Civil Eng.* Part II, **1, 2,** 325–362 (1952).
9. F. V. Webster, Traffic Signal Settings, *Road Research Technical Paper,* No. 39, Road Research Laboratory, H.M.S.O., England, 1958.

# The Delay Problem for Crossing an $n$ Lane Highway

*DENOS C. GAZIS*

IBM Watson Research Center
Yorktown Heights, New York

*GORDON F. NEWELL\**

Division of Applied Mathematics
Brown University
Providence, Rhode Island

*PETER WARREN†*

IBM World Trade
Stockholm, Sweden

*GEORGE H. WEISS*

National Institutes of Health
Bethesda, Maryland

## Abstract

We consider the problem of calculating the statistics of delay at a stop sign on a minor road due to $n$ lanes of independent, Poisson streams of traffic on an intersecting major road. It is assumed that the gap acceptance function has the form $\alpha(G_1, G_2, \ldots, G_n) = \alpha_1(G_1)\alpha_2(G_2) \ldots \alpha_n(G_n)$ where the subscripts refer to the lanes.

\* Present address: Institute for Transportation and Traffic Engineering, University of California, Berkeley.
† Present address: Department of Mathematics, University of Wisconsin, Madison Wisconsin.

We calculate the first and second moments of the waiting time for the special case of step functions for the $\alpha_i(G)$. A simulation study shows that the waiting time density can be approximated by Pearson Type III distributions. An approximate formula for the moments of waiting time is also given, which represents the $n$ lane highway by an equivalent single lane highway for which simpler formulae are available.

## I. Introduction

THERE HAS BEEN considerable interest in the problem of delay at a stop sign.[1-5] Essentially, the delay problem as it has been treated, is the following: a car arrives at a stop sign on a minor road at time $t = 0$, and the driver sees a single lane of traffic on the major road. The cars on the major road pass the stop sign at times $t_1, t_2, t_3, \ldots$, where the headways $t_2 - t_1, t_3 - t_2, \ldots$ are assumed to be identically distributed independent random variables. The waiting driver has some criterion for selecting a suitable gap in the traffic for his merging or crossing maneuver. One is then interested in calculating the probability density of the wait for the first acceptable gap.

It is evident that the model outlined in the last paragraph is appropriate for the case of a single car merging into a stream of traffic on a highway, rather than as a description of highway crossing. For the latter problem, a more realistic calculation should take into account the fact that there are several, rather than a single, lanes of traffic on the major highway. Very few results have appeared on the $n$ lane crossing problem because it is an order of magnitude more difficult than the single lane merging problem. Tanner calculated the delay when the gap acceptance function depends on the minimum gap in the $n$ lanes, and is the same unit step function for each.[2] Weiss and Maradudin gave an expression for the composite gap distribution function for $n$ lanes, but they failed to note that successive gaps are correlated when the headway densities in the individual lanes are not negative exponential.[5] Hence, their results can be used only to calculate the delay when each lane has a negative exponential headway distribution and when the gap acceptance function depends only on the minimum gap in the $n$ lanes.

The most general form of the gap acceptance function for an $n$ lane highway can be written as $\alpha(G_1, G_2, \ldots, G_n)$, where $G_j$ is the gap in lane $j$, i.e., the time to the arrival of the next car in lane $j$ at the intersection, and $\alpha$ is the probability of accepting the gap configuration $G_1, G_2, \ldots, G_n$. It appears to be quite difficult to calculate delay distributions or moments of these distributions for this most general gap acceptance function. However, it is possible to derive information about delays when $\alpha(G_1, \ldots, G_n)$ is assumed to be of the special form

$$\alpha(G_1, \ldots, G_n) = \alpha_1(G_1)\alpha_2(G_2) \ldots \alpha_n(G_n) \tag{1}$$

that is, when a decision must be made independently on the acceptability of the gap in each lane.

Equation 1 does not entirely specify the model,* as it does in the single lane case, since it is possible to have different amounts of information available when a given set of gaps is rejected. In the present paper we consider a model in which a given set of gaps, $\{G_j\}$, is first ordered so that $G_{j_1} \leq G_{j_2} \leq \cdots \leq G_{j_n}$. Then $G_{j_1}$ is examined for acceptability. If it is acceptable, $G_{j_2}$ is examined, and so forth. The probability of rejecting all $n$ gaps is $1 - \alpha(G_1, \ldots, G_n)$, where $\alpha$ is given in Eq. 1. If $G_{j_r}$ is the shortest unacceptable gap, the time to the next regeneration point of a renewal process is chosen equal to $G_{j_r}$ and no knowledge of $G_{j_{r+1}}, G_{j_{r+2}}, \ldots$ is assumed. It may appear that another plausible model is one in which all the gaps are examined for acceptability, and the end of the largest unacceptable gap is chosen as the regeneration point. However, this definition of the regeneration points is improper as seen from the following example. Consider the simple case of crossing two streams with a gap acceptance probability function

$$\alpha(G_1, G_2) = H(G_1 - T)H(G_2 - T) \tag{1a}$$

where $H(x)$ is the unit step function. If at time $t = 0$ we observe both gaps, $G_i^0$, and find $G_1^0$ unacceptable but $G_2^0$ acceptable, then the largest unacceptable gap is $G_1^0$. However, the time $t = G_1^0$ is not a proper regeneration point because at this time we shall have the information that the residual gap in lane 2 is at least as large as $(T - G_1^0)$.

While there are field measurements of the gap acceptance function for a single lane[4], there is virtually no information on the detailed form of this function for $n$ lanes. Hence, we assume Eq. 1 for mathematical convenience, although this assumption has some plausibility as well. Furthermore, we conjecture that our results will be robust with regard to the detailed structure of $\alpha(G_1, \ldots, G_n)$. A second assumption required for the present calculations is that the headway distribution in each lane is negative exponential, assuring the Markovian property for the system to be described. We have not succeeded in extending our calculations to the case of non-Poisson headway distributions, but it is known both experimentally and theoretically[6-8] that the negative exponential headway distribution is suitable for the description of light traffic. These limitations in our results should be borne in mind by the reader.

## 2. Analysis

The probability density for the headways in lane $j$ will be denoted by

$$\varphi_j(G) = \sigma_j e^{-\sigma_j G} \tag{2}$$

where $\sigma_i$ is the reciprocal of mean headway between cars in lane $j$. It can also

* The authors wish to thank Dr. Jan Gustavsson, Royal Institute of Technology, Sweden, and Dr. Betty Flehinger, IBM Research, for discussions on this matter.

be interpreted as the mean density of cars in lane $j$. We shall calculate an expression for the moment generating function

$$\Omega^*(s) = E(e^{-st}) = \int_0^\infty e^{-st}\Omega(t)\,dt \tag{3}$$

where $\Omega(t)$ is the probability density for the delay $t$. The argument for obtaining $\Omega^*(s)$ is a simple one: either $t$ is equal to zero, with probability $\langle\alpha_1\rangle\langle\alpha_2\rangle\ldots\langle\alpha_n\rangle$, where $\langle\alpha_j\rangle$ is the probability that the gap in lane $j$ is acceptable, and is given by

$$\langle\alpha_j\rangle = \sigma_j \int_0^\infty e^{-\sigma_j x}\alpha_j(x)\,dx \tag{4}$$

or else the driver on the minor road waits for the duration of the smallest unacceptable gap. The end of this gap can be regarded as a regeneration point for the system. Let $\rho(t)$ be the probability density for the wait to the end of the first unacceptable gap, and let

$$\rho^*(s) = \int_0^\infty e^{-st}\rho(t)\,dt \tag{5}$$

The argument given above then suffices to establish the equation

$$\Omega^*(s) = \langle\alpha_1\rangle\langle\alpha_2\rangle\ldots\langle\alpha_n\rangle + \rho^*(s)\Omega^*(s) \tag{6}$$

or

$$\Omega^*(s) = \frac{\langle\alpha_1\rangle\ldots\langle\alpha_n\rangle}{1 - \rho^*(s)} \tag{7}$$

Now only the calculation of $\rho(t)$ is required. Let us suppose that the gap in lane $j$ is the smallest unacceptable one. This condition implies that the first car in any other lane either arrives after the one in lane $j$ (and the gap in this lane may or may not be acceptable), or else it arrives before the one in lane $j$, and the corresponding gap is acceptable. Hence, we can write

$$\rho(t) = \sum_{j=1}^n \sigma_j e^{-\sigma_j t}[1 - \alpha_j(t)]\prod_{\substack{k=1 \\ k \neq j}}^n \left\{e^{-\sigma_k t} + \sigma_k \int_0^t e^{-\sigma_k x}\alpha_k(x)\,dx\right\} \tag{8}$$

A tedious, and not too instructive, calculation confirms that $\rho^*(0) = 1 - \langle\alpha_1\rangle\langle\alpha_2\rangle\ldots\langle\alpha_n\rangle$ as it must, for the normalization $\Omega^*(0) = 1$.

One can derive formal expressions for the moments from Eqs. 7 and 8; but to derive any implications from these formulae we must specialize the $\alpha_j(G)$. In particular, let us assume that

$$\alpha_j(G) = H(G - T_j), \quad j = 1, 2, \ldots, n \tag{9}$$

where $H(x)$ is the unit step function defined by

$$H(x) = 0, x < 0; \quad H(x) = 1, x > 0 \tag{10}$$

It is possible to derive an expression for $\rho(t)$ directly from Eq. 8 in this case, but an alternative, and more direct approach, is instructive. Let us order the $T$'s so that* $T_1 < T_2 < \ldots < T_n$. The shortest unacceptable gap must occur in one of the time intervals $(0, T_1), (T_1, T_2), \ldots (T_{n-1}, T_n)$. Suppose that the first unacceptable gap $G$ satisfies $t < G < t + dt$, where $t$ lies in $(T_r, T_{r+1})$. This implies that the first car in lane 1 arrived after $T_1$, the first car in lane 2 arrived after $T_2$, and so on $\ldots$ , but the first car in one of the lanes $r + 1$, $r + 2, \ldots, n$ arrived at $G$. The probability density for this combination of events is

$$\rho_r(t) = e^{-(\sigma_1 T_1 + \sigma_2 T_2 + \ldots + \sigma_r T_r)} \sum_{j=r+1}^{n} \sigma_j e^{-(\sigma_{r+1} + \sigma_{r+2} + \ldots + \sigma_n)t}, \; T_r < t < T_{r+1}$$

$$= 0 \text{ otherwise} \tag{11}$$

and therefore

$$\rho(t) = \sum_{r=0}^{n-1} \rho_r(t). \tag{12}$$

Letting

$$\mu_j = \sigma_j + \sigma_{j+1} + \ldots + \sigma_n \tag{13}$$

we can calculate the Laplace transform $\rho^*(s)$ to be

$$\rho^*(s) = \frac{\mu_1}{\mu_1 + s} [1 - e^{-(\mu_1 + s)T_1}] + \frac{e^{-\sigma_1 T_1}\mu_2}{\mu_2 + s} [e^{-(\mu_2 + s)T_1} - e^{-(\mu_2 + s)T_2}]$$

$$+ e^{-(\sigma_1 T_1 + \sigma_2 T_2)} \frac{\mu_3}{\mu_3 + s} [e^{-(\mu_3 + s)T_2} - e^{-(\mu_3 + s)T_3}] \tag{14}$$

$$+ \ldots + e^{-(\sigma_1 T_1 + \sigma_2 T_2 + \ldots + \sigma_{n-1} T_{n-1})} \frac{\mu_n}{\mu_n + s} [e^{-(\mu_n + s)T_{n-1}} - e^{-(\mu_n + s)T_n}]$$

A direct calculation of $\rho(t)$, starting from Eq. 8 is given in Appendix A.

Moments of the delay distribution can be found from the formula

$$\langle t^r \rangle = (-1)^r \frac{d^r}{ds^r} \Omega^*(s) \big|_{s=0+} \tag{15}$$

In this way we find for the expected delay for $n$ lanes,

$$\langle t \rangle = e^{\sigma_1 T_1 + \sigma_2 T_2 + \ldots + \sigma_n T_n} \left\{ \frac{1}{\mu_1} + e^{-\mu_1 T_1}\left( \frac{1}{\mu_2} - \frac{1}{\mu_1} \right) \right.$$

$$+ e^{-\sigma_1 T_1 - \mu_2 T_2}\left( \frac{1}{\mu_3} - \frac{1}{\mu_2} \right) + e^{-\sigma_1 T_1 - \sigma_2 T_2 - \mu_3 T_3}\left( \frac{1}{\mu_4} - \frac{1}{\mu_3} \right) \tag{16}$$

$$\left. + \ldots - e^{-\sigma_1 T_1 - \sigma_2 T_2 - \ldots - \sigma_n T_n}\left( \frac{1}{\mu_n} + T_n \right) \right\}$$

* If any two $T$'s are equal we can add an infinitesimal increment $\Delta T$ to one of them. The results so obtained will differ from the actual results by a quantity $0(\Delta T)$. Hence the results to be derived are also valid when several of the $T$'s are equal.

The second moment is likewise calculated to be

$$\langle t^2 \rangle = 2\langle t \rangle^2 + 2e^{\sigma_1 T_1 + \sigma_2 T_2 + \ldots + \sigma_n T_n}\left\{ \frac{1}{\mu_1^2} + e^{-\mu_1 T_1}\left(\frac{1}{\mu_2} - \frac{1}{\mu_1}\right)\left(\frac{1}{\mu_2} + \frac{1}{\mu_1} + T_1\right) \right.$$

$$+ e^{-\sigma_1 T_1 - \mu_2 T_2}\left(\frac{1}{\mu_3} - \frac{1}{\mu_2}\right)\left(\frac{1}{\mu_2} + \frac{1}{\mu_3} + T_2\right) + \ldots \tag{17}$$

$$\left. - e^{-(\sigma_1 T_1 + \sigma_2 T_2 + \ldots + \sigma_n T_n)}\left(\frac{1}{\mu_n^2} + \frac{T_n}{\mu_n} + \frac{T_n^2}{2}\right)\right\}$$

When $T_1 = T_2 = \ldots = T_n = T$, i.e., when the gap acceptance function is

$$\alpha(G_1, G_2, \ldots, G_n) = H[\min(G_1, \ldots, G_n) - T] \tag{18}$$

the first two moments become

$$\langle t \rangle = \frac{e^{\mu_1 T_1} - 1 - \mu_1 T}{\mu_1}$$

$$\langle t^2 \rangle = 2\langle t \rangle^2 + \frac{2e^{\mu_1 T} - 2 - 2\mu_1 T + \mu_1^2 T^2}{\mu_1^2} \tag{19}$$

as can indeed be derived by using the results of reference 2.

In the special case $\sigma_1 = \sigma_2 = \ldots = \sigma_n = \sigma$ we find

$$\sigma\langle t \rangle = e^{\sigma(T_1 + T_2 + \ldots + T_n)}\left[\frac{1}{n} + \frac{e^{-n\sigma T_1}}{n(n-1)} + \frac{e^{-\sigma T_1 - (n-1)\sigma T_2}}{(n-1)(n-2)}\right.$$

$$\left. + \frac{e^{-\sigma(T_1 + T_2) - (n-2)\sigma T_3}}{(n-2)(n-3)} + \ldots - e^{-\sigma(T_1 + T_2 + \ldots + T_n)}(1 + \sigma T_n)\right]$$

$$\sigma^2\langle t \rangle^2 = 2\sigma^2\langle t \rangle^2 + 2e^{\sigma(T_1 + T_2 + \ldots + T_n)}\left[\frac{1}{n^2} + \frac{e^{-n\sigma T_1}}{n(n-1)}\left(\frac{1}{n} + \frac{1}{n-1} + \sigma T_1\right)\right. \tag{20}$$

$$+ \frac{e^{-\sigma T_1 - (n-1)\sigma T_2}}{(n-1)(n-2)}\left(\frac{1}{n-1} + \frac{1}{n-2} + \sigma T_2\right) + \ldots$$

$$\left. - e^{-\sigma(T_1 + T_2 + \ldots + T_n)}\left(1 + \sigma T_n + \frac{\sigma^2 T_n^2}{2}\right)\right]$$

For example when $n = 2$ we have

$$\sigma\langle t \rangle = \frac{e^{\sigma(T_1 + T_2)}}{2} + \frac{e^{\sigma(T_2 - T_1)}}{2} - (1 + \sigma T_2) \tag{21}$$

$$\sigma^2\langle t^2 \rangle = 2\sigma^2\langle t^2 \rangle + \frac{e^{\sigma(T_1 + T_2)}}{2} + e^{\sigma(T_2 - T_1)}\left(\frac{3}{2} + \sigma T_1\right) - \left(1 + \sigma T_2 + \frac{\sigma^2 T_2^2}{2}\right)$$

There seems little hope of inverting Eq. 7 and obtaining $\Omega(t)$, even in series form. We have run several simulation trials to determine the form of the waiting time density for representative values of the $\sigma_j$ and $T_j$. The simulation

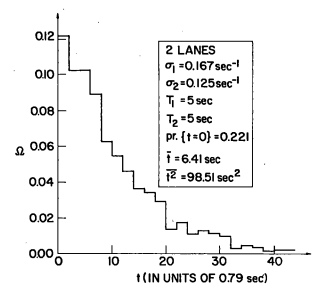

FIGURE I.   Histogram of the waiting time probability density, $\Omega(t)$, vs. waiting time, $t$, obtained from 2000 simulation experiments of crossing two lanes.

program executed a crossing experiment a large number of times and evaluated the histogram of the waiting time density. Negative exponential streams were generated along the major highway by random number techniques, and step functions were used for gap acceptance. The simulation program can, of course, be adapted easily to handle other traffic inputs and gap acceptance functions.

Results of some of these simulations are presented in Figs. 1–4. A comparison between theoretical and simulation values of the first and second moment is shown in Table I for a few cases. We have fit the simulation histograms to

TABLE I.   Comparison of Theoretical and Simulation Results for the Crossing of Two Lanes

| | | | | Theoretical | | Simulation | |
|---|---|---|---|---|---|---|---|
| $\sigma_1$ (sec$^{-1}$) | $\sigma_2$ (sec$^{-1}$) | $T_1$ (sec) | $T_2$ (sec) | $\langle t \rangle$ (sec) | $\langle t^2 \rangle$ (sec$^2$) | $\langle t \rangle$ (sec) | $\langle t^2 \rangle$ (sec$^2$) |
| 0.125 | 0.083 | 5 | 7 | 5.57 | 82.30 | 5.32 | 71.41 |
| 0.125 | 0.125 | 5 | 9 | 12.61 | 373.56 | 12.36 | 364.14 |
| 0.167 | 0.167 | 5 | 7 | 13.35 | 401.89 | 13.17 | 383.31 |
| 0.250 | 0.167 | 5 | 9 | 29.55 | 1854.02 | 29.27 | 1833.38 |
| 0.250 | 0.250 | 5 | 7. | 32.47 | 2204.64 | 33.01 | 2274.37 |

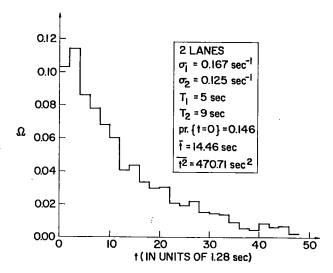

FIGURE 2.   Histogram of the waiting time probability density, $\Omega(t)$, vs. waiting time, $t$, obtained from 2000 simulation experiments of crossing two lanes.

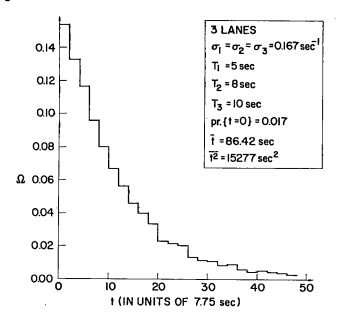

FIGURE 3.   Histogram of the waiting time probability density, $\Omega(t)$, vs. waiting time, $t$, obtained from 2000 simulation experiments of crossing three lanes.

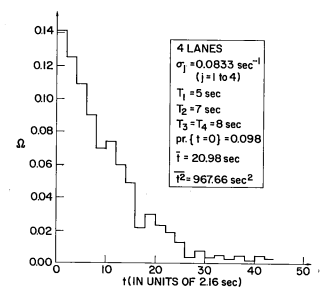

FIGURE 4.  Histogram of the waiting time probability density, $\Omega(t)$, vs. waiting time, $t$, obtained from 2000 simulation experiments of crossing four lanes.

Pearson curves[9], and have found that the type III curve (gamma distribution) satisfactorily represents most of the experimental curves.

## 3. The "Flying Start"

The theory just outlined is easily extended to take into account the flying start, i.e., the situation in which a driver on the side road has a different gap acceptance function at $t = 0$ than he does if he waits a non-zero amount of time. Specifically we assume that the gap acceptance function at $t = 0$ is

$$\alpha_0(t_1, t_2, \ldots, t_n) = \alpha_{10}(t_1) \ldots \alpha_{n0}(t_n) \tag{22}$$

in which the $\alpha_{j0}(t)$ may differ from the $\alpha_j(t)$ which are used for subsequent gaps. Let $\Omega_1{}^*(s)$ be the Laplace transform of the probability density for the delay following the first unacceptable gap. We will also use the notation

$$\langle\alpha\rangle = \langle\alpha_1\rangle\langle\alpha_2\rangle \ldots \langle\alpha_n\rangle, \quad \langle\alpha_0\rangle = \langle\alpha_{10}\rangle\langle\alpha_{20}\rangle \ldots \langle\alpha_{n0}\rangle \tag{23}$$

Further, we let $\rho_0(t)$ be the probability density for the wait to the end of the first unacceptable gap, where $\rho_0(t)$ is given by the expression in Eq. 8 with the $\alpha_j(t)$ replaced by $\alpha_{j0}(t)$. Then, $\Omega_{(s)}^*$ and $\Omega_{1(s)}^*$ satisfy the relationships

$$\Omega^*(s) = \langle\alpha_0\rangle + \rho_0{}^*(s)\Omega_1{}^*(s)$$

$$\Omega_1{}^*(s) = \langle\alpha\rangle + \rho^*(s)\Omega_1{}^*(s) \tag{24}$$

which yield the solution

$$\Omega^*(s) = \langle \alpha_0 \rangle + \frac{\langle \alpha \rangle \rho_0{}^*(s)}{1 - \rho^*(s)} \tag{25}$$

Equation 25 reduces to Eq. 7 when $\alpha_j(t) = \alpha_{j0}(t)$. When the gap acceptance functions are step functions, i.e., when

$$\alpha_j(t) = H(t - T_j), \quad \alpha_{j0}(t) = H(t - T_{j0}), \quad j = 1, 2, \ldots, n \tag{26}$$

expressions for the first two moments can be derived from those given in Eqs. 16 and 17. Moments of the delay time for the present case can be obtained by differentiating Eq. 25 and setting $s = 0$. Hence formal expressions for the moments appear in terms of derivatives of $\rho_0{}^*(s)$ and $\rho^*(s)$ evaluated at $s = 0$. These, in turn, can be related to the detailed expressions given in Eqs. 16 and 17. For example, Eq. 7 implies that

$$\left. \frac{d\rho^*}{ds} \right|_{s=0} = \langle \alpha \rangle \langle t \rangle = e^{-(\sigma_1 T_1 + \ldots + \sigma_n T_n)} \langle t \rangle \tag{27}$$

where $\langle t \rangle$ is the first moment whose form appears in Eq. 16. From this it follows that in the case of the flying start the average delay time can be expressed as

$$\langle t \rangle = \langle \alpha_0 \rangle \langle t_0 \rangle + (1 - \langle a_0 \rangle) \langle t_1 \rangle \tag{28}$$

where $\langle t_0 \rangle$ is given by Eq. 16 with the $T_j$ replaced by $T_{j0}$, and $\langle t_1 \rangle$ is given by Eq. 16 without modification. In similar fashion we find for the second moment

$$\langle t^2 \rangle = \langle \alpha_0 \rangle (\langle t_0{}^2 \rangle + 2 \langle t_0 \rangle \langle t_1 \rangle - 2 \langle t_0 \rangle^2) + (1 - \langle \alpha_0 \rangle) \langle t_1{}^2 \rangle \tag{29}$$

where $\langle t_0{}^2 \rangle$ and $\langle t_1{}^2 \rangle$ have an obvious interpretation.

## 4. Approximate Formulae

It is well known that a multiple Poisson stream with parameters $\sigma_1, \sigma_2, \ldots,$ $\sigma_n$ can be replaced by a single stream with parameter $\sigma = \sigma_1 + \sigma_2 + \ldots \sigma_n$. One may ask whether it is possible to replace the step gap acceptance function given in Eqs. 1 and 9 by a gap acceptance function for the composite single stream. A natural guess would be to take step function

$$\alpha(t) = H(t - \langle T \rangle) \tag{30}$$

where

$$\langle T \rangle = (\sum_j \sigma_j T_j)/(\sum_j \sigma_j) \tag{31}$$

This approximation appears to work well for all cases of interest. For example, some detailed results for the first and second moment of the waiting time, for the two and three lane case, are presented in Table II.

The good fit in the two lane case is seen by computing the relative error of the approximation for the mean waiting time. If we denote the approximate

TABLE II.    Comparison of Theoretical and Approximate Results for the Crossing of Two, Three, and Four Lanes. The Approximate Results were Obtained Using Weighted Average $T$ and the Equivalent Single Poisson Stream

| No. of lanes | $\sigma_j$ (sec$^{-1}$) | $T_j$ (sec) | Theoretical | | Approximate | |
|---|---|---|---|---|---|---|
| | | | $\langle t \rangle$ (sec) | $\langle t^2 \rangle$ (sec$^2$) | $\langle t \rangle$ (sec) | $\langle t^2 \rangle$ (sec$^2$) |
| 2 | $\sigma_1 = 0.125$ $\sigma_2 = 0.125$ | $T_1 = 5$ $T_2 = 7$ | 12.61 | 373.6 | 12.01 | 336.0 |
| 2 | $\sigma_1 = 0.250$ $\sigma_2 = 0.167$ | $T_1 = 5$ $T_2 = 9$ | 29.55 | 1854 | 28.54 | 1723 |
| 3 | $\sigma_1 = 0.083$ $\sigma_2 = 0.125$ $\sigma_3 = 0.125$ | $T_1 = 5$ $T_2 = 7$ $T_3 = 8$ | 20.08 | 881.1 | 19.80 | 855.6 |
| 3 | $\sigma_1 = 0.125$ $\sigma_2 = 0.167$ $\sigma_3 = 0.167$ | $T_1 = 5$ $T_2 = 7$ $T_3 = 8$ | 41.08 | 3512 | 40.66 | 3437 |
| 4 | $\sigma_1 = 0.083$ $\sigma_2 = 0.125$ $\sigma_3 = 0.125$ $\sigma_4 = 0.125$ | $T_1 = 5$ $T_2 = 7$ $T_3 = 8$ $T_4 = 8$ | 49.69 | 5108 | 49.30 | 5025 |
| 4 | $\sigma_1 = 0.125$ $\sigma_2 = 0.167$ $\sigma_3 = 0.167$ $\sigma_4 = 0.167$ | $T_1 = 5$ $T_2 = 7$ $T_3 = 8$ $T_4 = 8$ | 130.06 | 34205 | 129.4 | 33861 |

value by $\langle t_a \rangle$, then a measure of the relative error is

$$\epsilon_1 = \frac{\langle t \rangle - \langle t_a \rangle}{\langle t_a \rangle} = \frac{\sigma_1}{\sigma_2} \frac{e^{\sigma_2(T_2 - T_1)} - [\sigma_2(T_2 - T_1) + 1]}{e^{\sigma_1 T_1 + \sigma_2 T_2} - (1 + \sigma_1 T_1 + \sigma_2 T_2)} \tag{32}$$

The relative error is

$$\epsilon = \frac{\langle t \rangle - \langle t_a \rangle}{\langle t \rangle} = \frac{\epsilon_1}{1 + \epsilon_1} \tag{33}$$

Both $\epsilon$ and $\epsilon_1$ are small for the cases of moderately heavy traffic, as indicated by the results of Table II. For very light traffic the parameter $\epsilon_1$ has the approximate form

$$\epsilon_1 \sim \frac{\sigma_1 \sigma_2 (T_2 - T_1)^2}{(\sigma_1 T_1 + \sigma_2 T_2)^2} \tag{34}$$

which is obtained by expanding each exponential exp $(\sigma_i T_j)$ as

$$1 + \sigma_j T_j + \frac{\sigma_j^2 T_i^2}{2}$$

Equation 24 appears to give a maximum value. For heavy traffic Eq. 32 is approximated by

$$\epsilon_1 \sim \frac{\sigma_1}{\sigma_2} e^{-(\sigma_1 + \sigma_2) T_1} \tag{25}$$

which is close to zero. In view of the inherent limitations of the theory, it appears that the above approximations will suffice for practical purposes.

## References

1. M. S. Raff, *J. Am. Stat. Soc.*, **46**, 114 (1951).
2. J. C. Tanner, *Biometrika*, **38**, 383 (1951).
3. A. J. Mayne, *Biometrika*, **41**, 375 (1954).
4. R. Herman, and G. H. Weiss, *J. Operations Res.*, **9**, 828 (1961).
5. G. H. Weiss, and A. A. Maradudin, *J. Operations Res.*, **10**, 74 (1962).
6. W. F. Adams, *J. Inst. Civil Eng.*, **4**, 121 (1936).
7. G. H. Weiss, and R. Herman, *Quart. Appl. Math.*, **22**, 121 (1962).
8. L. Breiman, *Ann. Math. Stat.*, **34**, 308 (1963).
9. M. G. Kendall, and A. Stuart, "The Advanced Theory of Statistics," second edition. Hafner, New York, 1963.

## Appendix A

Equation 8, for this special case, can be written as

$$\rho(t) = \sum_{j=1}^{n} \sigma_j e^{-\sigma_j t} [1 - H(t - T_j)] \prod_{\substack{k=1 \\ k \neq j}}^{n} \{ e^{-\sigma_k T_k} H(t - T_k)$$
$$+ e^{-\sigma_k t} [1 - H(t - T_k)] \} \tag{A.1}$$

When the product is multiplied out it is seen that each term of the resulting sum has a multiplicative factor of the form

$$U_1(t - T_{j_1}) U_2(t - T_{j_2}) \ldots U_n(t - T_{j_n})$$

where each $U_j(x)$ can be either $H(t - T_j)$ or $1 - H(t - T_j)$. Let us order the $T$'s so that $T_1 \leq T_2 \leq \ldots \leq T_n$. We can remark that $[1 - H(t - T_j)]$ $H(t - T_k) = 0$ for $k > j$ except for perhaps a single point. Hence, in the product Eq. A1 the only nonzero contributions will come from terms of the form

$$H(t - T_1) H(t - T_2) \ldots H(t - T_j)[1 - H(t - T_{j+1})]$$
$$\times [1 - H(t - T_{j+2})] \ldots [1 - H(t - T_n)] = H(t - T_j)[1 - H(t - T_{j+1})] \tag{A.2}$$

and

$$\prod_{j=1}^{n} [1 - H(t - T_j)] = 1 - H(t - T_1) \qquad \text{(A.3)}$$

Hence, taking all these remarks into account, we find that $\rho(t)$ can be written

$$\rho(t) = \mu_1 e^{-\mu_1 t}[1 - H(t - T_1)] + e^{-\sigma_1 T_1}\mu_2 e^{-\mu_2 t}H(t - T_1)[1 - H(t - T_2)]$$

$$+ \ldots + e^{-(\sigma_1 T_1 + \sigma_2 T_2 + \ldots + \sigma_{n-1}T_{n-1})}\mu_n e^{-\mu_n t}H(t - T_{n-1})[1 - H(t - T_n)] \quad \text{(A.4)}$$

whose Laplace transform is Eq. 14.

# Pedestrian Queueing at an
# $n$ Lane Intersection

## GEORGE H. WEISS

National Cancer Institute
National Institutes of Health
Bethesda, Maryland

## Abstract

The statistics of the size of a pedestrian queue at an $n$-lane intersection are calculated. It is shown that the approximations that are valid for the step gap acceptance function for traffic delay are also valid for the study of queue size.

IN THE PREVIOUS[1] paper we have examined the problem of the waiting time of a single car at an intersection with $n$ lanes of traffic where the gap acceptance function is given in Eq. 1 and the headway density of Eq. 2. In this paper we shall calculate the statistics of the pedestrian queue. It will be assumed that pedestrians arrive at the intersection as a Poisson process with rate parameter $\lambda$ and remain waiting in queue until a suitable gap presents itself, at which time the pedestrians cross as a group. The gap acceptance functions for each pedestrian will be assumed to be the same step function, and are given by Eq. 9 of the previous paper. The present analysis can be considered an extension of the work of Tanner,[2] who assumed that the gap acceptance function was

$$\alpha(G_1, G_2, \ldots G_n) = H(\min_i G_i - T) \tag{1}$$

thus reducing the problem to the single lane case. It was shown[1] that the first two moments of the waiting time for the case $\alpha_i(G) = H(G - T_i)$ could be adequately approximated by those for the single lane case with $\alpha(G) = H(G - \langle T \rangle)$ where the lumped traffic flow rate $\sigma$ and $\langle T \rangle$ are given by

$$\sigma = \sum_{i=1}^{n} \sigma_i, \qquad \sigma \langle T \rangle = \sum_{i=1}^{n} \sigma_i T_i \tag{2}$$

It is not surprising that the same conclusion also follows for the statistics of the pedestrian queue.

We discuss the present problem in terms of the embedded Markov chain, a technique originally applied to this problem in reference 3. To define the regeneration points we introduce the notion of a cycle, i.e., the time between two successive regeneration points. Since regeneration points will be taken at instants when a car on the highway passes the waiting queue, we may distinguish two types of cycle—those in which the queue crosses initially, and those in which the initial queue remains. Let us call these 0- or 1-cycles, respectively. If a regeneration point occurs at $t = 0$ and the following cycle is a 0-cycle, we choose as the next regeneration point the time of arrival of the earliest car (first in its lane) which causes an unacceptable gap. If the following cycle is a 1-cycle, we choose as the next regeneration point the time of arrival of the car which causes the earliest unacceptable gap.

It was shown[1] that the probability density for the duration of a 0-cycle is

$$\rho_0(t) = \sum_{i=1}^{n} \sigma_i e^{-\sigma_i t}[1 - H(t - T_i)] \prod_{\substack{k=1 \\ k \neq i}}^{n} \{H(t - T_k) + e^{-\sigma_k t}[1 - H(t - T_k)]\} \quad (3)$$

To calculate the probability density for the duration of a 1-cycle we order the $T$'s so that $T_1 \leq T_2 \leq \ldots \leq T_n$. Suppose that the car in lane 1 arrives at $t$ $(> T_1)$ and causes the earliest delay time. Then the car in lane $j$ $(>1)$ must arrive at some time greater than $t + T_j - T_1$ so that it not cause an earlier delay time. The probability density for this event is

$$\sigma_1 \exp\left[-\sigma_1 t - \sigma_2(t + T_2 - T_1) - \sigma_3(t + T_3 - T_1) - \ldots\right]H(t - T_1)$$
$$= \sigma_1 \exp\left(-\sigma\langle T\rangle\right) \exp\left(-\sigma(t - T_1)\right)H(t - T_1) \quad (4)$$

In a similar fashion one can account for all other possibilities, and we find for the probability density of a 1-cycle,

$$\rho_1(t) = \sum_{i=1}^{n} \sigma_i e^{-\sigma\langle T\rangle} e^{-\sigma(t - T_i)} H(t - T_i) \quad (5)$$

In what follows we will require the expected duration of a random cycle. This quantity will be denoted by $v$ and is

$$v = \int_0^\infty t[\rho_0(t) + \rho_1(t)] \, dt = \frac{e^{-\sigma\langle T\rangle}}{\sigma} \sum_{i=1}^{n} \left(\frac{\sigma_i}{\sigma} + \sigma_i T_i\right) + \int_0^\infty t\rho_0(t) \, dt$$
$$= \frac{e^{-\sigma\langle T\rangle}}{\sigma} [1 + \sigma(\langle t\rangle + \langle T\rangle)] \quad (6)$$

where $\langle t\rangle$ is the expected waiting time of a single pedestrian (cf. Eq. 7)[1].

We define $\theta_j$ to be the equilibrium probability for there being $j$ pedestrians in queue, and the transition probabilities $p_{rm}$, for the number of pedestrians in queue to go from $r$ to $m$ on successive regeneration points. If

$$\theta = (\theta_0, \theta_1, \theta_2, \ldots) \quad ; \quad \mathbf{P} = (p_{rm}) \quad (7)$$

then $\theta = \theta P$. We shall begin by calculating the $p_{rm}$. During a 0-cycle the transition in pedestrian numbers, $r \to m$, can go only to values of $m$ greater than or equal to $r$, whereas in the case of a 1-cycle $m$ is unrestricted since the $r$ pedestrians cross immediately. It is now possible to write explicit expressions for the transition probabilities by noting that all pedestrians will cross during an unblocked portion of a cycle, and no pedestrians cross during a blocked portion. This implies that for a completely blocked cycle we have

$$p_{rm}^{(0)} = 0, \quad m < r$$

$$= \int_0^\infty p_0(t) e^{-\lambda t} \frac{(\lambda t)^{m-r}}{(m-r)!} \, dt, \quad m \geq r \tag{8}$$

For a partially blocked cycle we have

$$p_{rm}^{(1)} = \frac{e^{-\sigma \langle T \rangle}}{\sigma} \sum_{i=1}^n \sigma_i e^{-\lambda T_i} \frac{(\lambda T_i)^m}{m!} \tag{9}$$

since pedestrians queue only during the blocked part of the interval. This last expression is independent of $r$ since by assumption all of $r$ pedestrians initially in queue cross, leaving none in queue. Finally, we can write

$$p_{rm} = p_{rm}^{(0)} + p_{rm}^{(1)} \tag{10}$$

so that the transition matrix $P$ takes the form

$$\mathbf{P} = \begin{bmatrix} \Delta_0 + \epsilon_0 & \Delta_1 + \epsilon_1 & \Delta_2 + \epsilon_2 & \cdots \\ \epsilon_0 & \Delta_0 + \epsilon_1 & \Delta_1 + \epsilon_2 & \cdots \\ \epsilon_0 & \epsilon_1 & \Delta_0 + \epsilon_2 & \cdots \\ \epsilon_0 & \epsilon_1 & \epsilon_2 & \cdots \\ \cdot & \cdot & \cdot & \\ \cdot & \cdot & \cdot & \\ \cdot & \cdot & \cdot & \end{bmatrix} \tag{11}$$

where $\Delta_j$ and $\epsilon_j$ are defined by

$$\Delta_j = \frac{1}{j!} \int_0^\infty p_0(t)(\lambda t)^j e^{-\lambda t} \, dt$$

$$\epsilon_j = \frac{e^{-\sigma \langle T \rangle}}{j! \, \sigma} \sum_{i=1}^n \sigma_i e^{-\lambda T_i}(\lambda T_j)^j \tag{12}$$

These results imply that the $\theta_j$ satisfy

$$\theta_j = \epsilon_j + \sum_{r=0}^j \theta_r \Delta_{j-r}$$

which may be solved by introducing the generating functions

$$\theta(s) = \sum_{n=0}^{\infty} \theta_n s^n$$

$$\epsilon(s) = \sum_{n=0}^{\infty} \epsilon_n s^n = \frac{e^{-\sigma\langle T\rangle}}{\sigma} \sum_{r=1}^{n} \sigma_r e^{-\lambda T_r (1-s)} \tag{14}$$

$$\Delta(s) = \sum_{n=0}^{\infty} \Delta_n s^n = \int_0^{\infty} p_0(t) e^{-\lambda t(1-s)}\, dt$$

From Eqs. 13 and 14 we find

$$\theta(s) = \frac{\epsilon(s)}{1 - \Delta(s)} \tag{15}$$

The most useful application of this formula is as a moment-generating function. For example, we calculate the expected number in the queue to be

$$\langle m \rangle = \sum_{m=0}^{\infty} m \theta_m = \frac{\Delta'(1) + \epsilon'(1)}{1 - \Delta(1)} \tag{16}$$

But

$$1 - \Delta(1) = 1 - \int_0^{\infty} p_0(t)\, dt = e^{-\sigma\langle T\rangle} \tag{17}$$

and

$$\Delta'(1) + \epsilon'(1) = \lambda(\langle t\rangle + \langle T\rangle) e^{-\sigma\langle T\rangle} \tag{18}$$

where $t$ is the expected waiting time of a single pedestrian. Hence, combining Eqs. 16 through 18 we find, for the expected number of pedestrians in queue at a regeneration point

$$m = \lambda(\langle T\rangle + \langle t\rangle) \tag{19}$$

An exact expression for $\langle t\rangle$ is given,[1] but as a more important point it is shown that a good approximation to $\langle t\rangle$ is

$$\langle t\rangle \sim \frac{1}{\sigma}(e^{\sigma\langle T\rangle} - 1 - \sigma\langle T\rangle) \tag{20}$$

In this approximation

$$\langle m\rangle = \frac{\lambda}{\sigma}(e^{\sigma\langle T\rangle} - 1) \tag{21}$$

which is just the same as Tanner's expression for crossing a single lane with gap acceptance function $\alpha(t) = H(t - \langle T\rangle)$. In similar fashion we can show that the variance of the number is also approximated well by that calculated for the crossing of a single lane with $\alpha(t) = H(t - \langle T\rangle)$.

We now consider the problem of calculating the generating function for the number of pedestrians in queue at a random time. For this purpose we follow the analysis of Weiss,[3] making the necessary modifications to take into account the effect of $n$ lanes. The first step is to calculate transition probabilities $\beta_{rm}$, where $\beta_{rm}$ is defined to be the probability that there are $m$ pedestrians in queue at a random time conditional on there being $r$ in queue at the preceding regeneration point. Let $\eta_m$ be the probability that there are $m$ pedestrians in queue at a random time. The $\eta_m$ can be expressed as

$$\eta_m = \sum_{r=0}^{\infty} \theta_r \beta_{rm} \tag{22}$$

so that we need only calculate the $\beta_{rm}$ since we know the $\theta_r$, at least formally from their generating function given in Eq. 15. The $\beta_{rm}$ will be expressed in terms of auxiliary functions $\delta_{mr}^{(j)}(y, t)$ which are conditional transition probabilities: $\delta_{rm}^{(j)}(y, t)$ is defined to be the probability that there are $m$ pedestrians in queue at a random time in a $j$-cycle given that there were $r$ in the queue at the preceding regeneration point, that the sum of the forward and backward delays is $t$, and that the forward delay is $y$. For cycles of type 0 we must have $m \geq r$ since the cycle is entirely blocked. For this case we have

$$\delta_{rm}^{(0)}(y, t) = \frac{[\lambda(t - y)]^{m-r}}{(m - r)!} e^{-\lambda(t-y)}, \quad m \geq r \tag{23}$$

$$= 0 \qquad\qquad , \quad m < 0$$

Since all pedestrians cross at the first regeneration point for cycles of type 1, new additions to the queue can be made only during the blocked time. Hence, if the blocked time occurs because of a car in lane $j$ there is a contribution to $\delta_{rm}^{(1)}(y, t)$:

$$\frac{[\lambda(T_j - y)]^m}{m!} e^{-\lambda(T_j-y)}[1 - H(T_j - y)] + \delta_{m0} H(T_j - y)$$

valid for all $m$. The probability of picking a random time with a forward delay in $(y + dy)$ is $dy/t$ (where $t$ is the cycle time), and the probability density for $t$, which is the sum of forward and backward delay time, is $t\rho_0(t)/v$ for a cycle of type 0 and $\sigma_j t \exp(-\sigma T) \exp[-\sigma(t - T_j)]H(t - T_j)/v$ when the blocking car is in lane $j$. Some idea of the proof of these formulae can be obtained from the reasoning following Eq. 2.36 of Weiss.[3] Hence, $\beta_{rm}$ can be expressed as

$$\beta_{rm} = \frac{1}{\sigma}\left\{ \int_0^{\infty} \rho_0(t)\, dt \int_0^t \frac{(\lambda y)^{m-r}}{(m - r)!} e^{-\lambda y}\, dy \right.$$
$$\left. + e^{-\sigma\langle T \rangle} \sum_{i=1}^{n} \sigma_i \int_{T_i}^{\infty} e^{-\sigma(t-T_i)}\, dt \left[ \int_0^{T_i} \frac{(\lambda y)^m}{m!} e^{-\lambda y}\, dy + (t - T_i)\delta_{m0} \right] \right\} \tag{24}$$

where the first term is defined to be zero for $r > m$, and where we have made minor changes in the variables of integration. It can be seen that $\lambda_{rm}$ has the decomposition

$$\beta_{rm} = A_{m-r} + B_m \tag{25}$$

where $A_j = 0$ for $j < 0$ and the $A_j$ and $B_j$ have generating functions

$$A(s) = \frac{1}{v} \int_0^\infty p_0(t) \, dt \int_0^t e^{-\lambda y(1-s)} \, dy$$

$$B(s) = \frac{1}{v} \sum_{i=1}^n \sigma_i \int_{T_i}^\infty e^{-\sigma(t-T_i)} \, dt \left[ \int_0^{T_i} e^{-\lambda y(1-s)} \, dy + (t - T_i) \right] \tag{26}$$

The substitution of Eq. 25 into Eq. 22 leads to

$$\eta_m = B_m + \sum_{r=0}^m \theta_r A_{m-r} \tag{27}$$

hence the generating functions satisfy

$$\eta(s) = B(s) + A(s)\theta(s) \tag{28}$$

from which moments can be obtained by differentiation. The first moment, for example, has the expression

$$\eta'(1) = \frac{1}{v} \left\{ \frac{\lambda}{2} \int_0^\infty t^2 p_0(t) \, dt + \frac{\lambda}{2\sigma} e^{-\sigma\langle T \rangle} \sum_{i=1}^n \sigma_i T_i^2 + \langle m \rangle \int_0^\infty t \, p_0(t) \, dt \right\}$$

We might first remark that according to Eq. 6 and the result of Eq. 20 we can make the approximation

$$v \sim 1/\sigma \tag{30}$$

Secondly, the term $\int_0^\infty t^2 p_0(t) \, dt$ is expressible in terms of $\langle t \rangle$ as in Eq. 6, and we can also write

$$\int_0^\infty t^2 p_0(t) \, dt = (\langle t^2 \rangle - 2\langle t \rangle^2) e^{-\sigma\langle T \rangle} \tag{31}$$

Both $\langle t \rangle$ and $\langle t^2 \rangle$ are adequately approximated by equivalent terms derived from the single lane case with $\alpha(t) = H(t - \langle T \rangle)$. Hence, the integrals in Eq. 29 can also be approximated in like fashion. Finally, if we make the replacement

$$\sum_{i=1}^n \sigma_i T_i^2 \rightarrow \sigma \langle T \rangle^2 \tag{32}$$

then the expected number of pedestrians in queue can be written

$$\eta'(1) \sim \frac{\lambda}{\sigma} (e^{\sigma\langle T \rangle} - 1 - \sigma\langle T \rangle) \tag{33}$$

i.e., in the same form as for the single lane case. We have shown[1] that $\langle t \rangle$ and $\langle t^2 \rangle$ are adequately approximated by the like parameters derived from the single lane case with the parameters of Eq. 2. In similar fashion Eq. 32

is also good in the range of parameters of interest. For example, when

$$\sigma_1 = \sigma_2 = \sigma_3 = \sigma_4 = 0.167 \text{ sec}^{-1}$$

$$T_1 = 5 \text{ sec} \qquad T_2 = 7 \text{ sec} \qquad T_3 = 8 \text{ sec} \qquad T_4 = 9 \text{ sec}$$

$$\sum \sigma_j T_j^2 = 36.57 \text{ sec}$$

$$\sigma \langle T \rangle^2 = 35.11 \text{ sec}$$

Similar results for other parameter values indicate that the expected number values agree to within experimental error, as do values of the second moments.

Thus, the results of the previous paper, as well as those of the present note, indicate that most results of interest for the $n$ lane delay problem with a gap acceptance function of the form of Eq. 1[1] can be approximated by corresponding results for the single lane case with $\alpha(t) = H(t - T)$. One might conjecture that like approximations are valid for the more general gap acceptance function of Eq. 1,[1] but no investigations have been undertaken on this question. In fact, it is not clear what form one should choose for the equivalent single lane gap acceptance function. One guess might be

$$\alpha(t) = \frac{1}{\sigma} \sum_{i=1}^{n} \sigma_i \alpha_i(t) \tag{34}$$

but this choice has not been examined even for the particular case $\alpha_j(t) = H(t - T_j)$.

## References

1. D. C. Gazis, G. F. Newell, P. Warren and G. H. Weiss. These Proceedings.
2. J. C. Tanner, *Biometrika*, **38**, 383 (1951).
3. G. H. Weiss, *J. Res. Bur. Stds.* **67B**, 229 (1963).

# On the Theory of Deterministic Cyclic Traffic Flows in Networks

*W. R. BLUNDEN and R. L. PRETTY*

School of Traffic Engineering
University of New South Wales
Sydney, Australia

## Abstract

In this paper input and output flows at traffic signals are represented by Fourier series. A general formula for average delay, embracing both the steady-state queueing effects and the relative frequency and phase relationships of the input and output waves for an input wave of arbitrary form, has been developed:

$$\langle d \rangle = \frac{1}{2\lambda s} \int_0^{ab/c} q(t)\left(1 - \frac{2bt}{ac}\right)dt + \frac{1}{2}(1 - \lambda)c$$

where $\langle d \rangle$ is the average delay per vehicle
 $a/b$ is the relative frequency of input to output cycle
 $\lambda$ is the effective green time of the appropriate phase of cycle of length, $c$
 $s$ is the saturation flow
 $q(t)$ is the input flow at time $t$.

The general result is applied to a number of examples, viz.

(a) Input flow having the same period as signal cycle but different form and phase relationship.
(b) Input and output flow having different periods.
(c) The "oversaturated" intersection.

An attempt is made to describe how the theory may be applied to the problem of flow in networks.

## Introduction

IN RECENT YEARS a good deal of work has been done on the delay/flow characteristics[1,2,3] and the timing of isolated fixed-time signals. Generally, the output flow has been taken as uniform during the green period, and the input as stochastic, usually simply stochastic. However, when signals are in close proximity, particularly when they form part of an interconnected system, the input has a well-defined cyclic character. Further, under conditions of high traffic intensity the instantaneous flow during the cycle tends to be uniform and, as a result, the familiar queueing effects resulting from randomness may be of less significance than the cycle time and phase relationship of one intersection to another.

While effects of the latter kind have been conveniently studied by graphical methods, the authors feel that with the wider implications of network flow in mind, an analytical approach to the problem may be of value. As a result, the following study sets out to represent the cyclic output and input flows as continuous variables by means of Fourier series.

## Theoretical Analysis

In the following theory, an arm of a signalized intersection with a given cycle or period of length $c$ is studied. It is assumed that there is a finite number

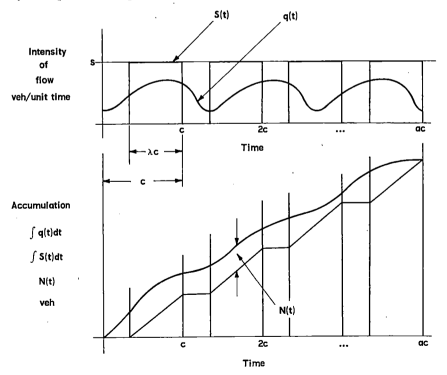

FIGURE I.    Input and output waveforms and vehicle accumulation.

of consecutive traffic light cycles over which there is saturated flow through the arm of the intersection over all effective green times. It is also assumed that there are no vehicles waiting at the beginning of the first of these cycles.

To satisfy these assumptions, if $\lambda s$ is the mean arrival flow during this study interval with $s$ the saturation flow, then $\lambda c$ must also be the effective green time. Without these conditions, the simple analysis which follows does not apply.

The arrival flow $q(t)$ is known at all instants over the study interval and, in general, has period $(ac/b)$, where $a$ and $b$ are integers having no common factor.

The departure flow $S(t)$ has period $c$, so the number of vehicles waiting at the lights, $N(t)$, has period $ac$. $q(t)$, $S(t)$, and $N(t)$ are illustrated in Fig. 1. Over $a$ cycles

$$S(t) = s, \qquad (m - \lambda)c < t < mc, \qquad m = 1, 2 \ldots a$$

$$= 0, \qquad \text{elsewhere}$$

For each cycle $S(t)$ may be represented by the Fourier series:

$$S(t) = s + \sum \alpha_n \cos \frac{2n\pi t}{c} + \sum \beta_n \sin \frac{2n\pi t}{c}$$

with the notation that the summations are from $n = 1$ to $\infty$. Thus

$$S(t) = \lambda s - \frac{s}{\pi} \sum \frac{1}{n} \sin 2n\pi(1 - \lambda) \cos \frac{2n\pi t}{c}$$

$$- \frac{s}{\pi} \sum \frac{1}{n} \{(1 - \cos 2n\pi(1 - \lambda))\} \sin \frac{2n\pi t}{c} \tag{1}$$

$q(t)$ may also be represented by a Fourier series over the period $ac/b$.

$$q(t) = \lambda s + \sum A_n \cos \frac{2n\pi bt}{ac} + \sum B_n \sin \frac{2n\pi bt}{ac} \tag{2}$$

where

$$A_n = \frac{2b}{ac} \int_0^{ac/b} q(t) \cos \frac{2n\pi bt}{ac} \, dt$$

and

$$B_n = \frac{2b}{ac} \int_0^{ac/b} q(t) \sin \frac{2n\pi bt}{ac} \, dt$$

The net flow through the intersection $= q(t) - S(t)$. Then

$$N(t) = \int_0^t \{q(t') - S(t')\} \, dt'$$

Substituting from Eqs. 1 and 2

$$N(t) = \frac{ac}{2\pi b} \sum \frac{1}{n} A_n \sin \frac{2n\pi bt}{ac} + \frac{ac}{2\pi b} \sum \frac{1}{n} B_n \left(1 - \cos \frac{2n\pi bt}{ac}\right)$$

$$+ \frac{sc}{2\pi^2} \sum \frac{1}{n^2} \sin 2n\pi(1 - \lambda) \sin \frac{2n\pi t}{c}$$

$$+ \frac{sc}{2\pi^2} \sum \frac{1}{n^2} \{1 - \cos 2n\pi(1 - \lambda)\}\left(1 - \cos \frac{2n\pi t}{c}\right)$$

With $N(t)$ having a period of $a$ cycles, $\lambda sac$ vehicles arrive during this time. The average delay per vehicle, $\langle d \rangle$, is given by

$$\langle d \rangle = \int_0^{ac} \frac{N(t)dt}{\lambda sac}$$

$$= \frac{ac}{2\pi \lambda ab} \sum \frac{1}{n} B_n + \frac{c}{2\pi^2 \lambda} \sum \frac{1}{n^2} \{1 - \cos 2n\pi(1 - \lambda)\}$$

With the convenient relation that

$$\sum \frac{1}{n^2}(1 - \cos nx) = \frac{x}{4}(2\pi - x) \tag{3}$$

$$\langle d \rangle = \left[\frac{a}{2\pi \lambda sb} \sum \frac{1}{n} B_n + \frac{1}{2}(1 - \lambda)\right]c \tag{4}$$

With the Fourier sine series identity

$$1 - \frac{2bt}{ac} = \sum \frac{2}{n\pi} \sin \frac{2n\pi bt}{ac}$$

$$\sum \frac{1}{n} B_n = \frac{\pi b}{ac} \int_0^{ac/b} q(t) \left(1 - \frac{2bt}{ac}\right) dt$$

So that finally

$$\langle d \rangle = \frac{1}{2\lambda s} \int_0^{ac/b} q(t) \left(1 - \frac{2bt}{ac}\right) dt + \frac{1}{2}(1 - \lambda)c \tag{4a}$$

This is a surprisingly simple result to express the combined effect of the Clayton queueing delay[4] for regular arrivals, and the delay resulting from a cyclic input flow with arbitrary form, period, and phase relationship to the cycle of operation of the output. The linear combination of the two components is of interest. It suggests that if random fluctuations were added to the time varying flow it may be necessary only to replace the second term by an appropriate expression for the stochastic queueing delay and leave the first term to take account of the cycle and phase relationship between signals. The authors are currently investigating this. The following examples illustrate some applications of this general result.

## Application to Some Particular Problems

*Case I.*   Input Flow Having Same Period as Signal Cycle.
For comparison purposes a sine wave and a constant input is compared with a square wave of identical form to the output wave. Figure 2 indicates the form (and phase relationship) of these inputs. The phase displacement $x$ is

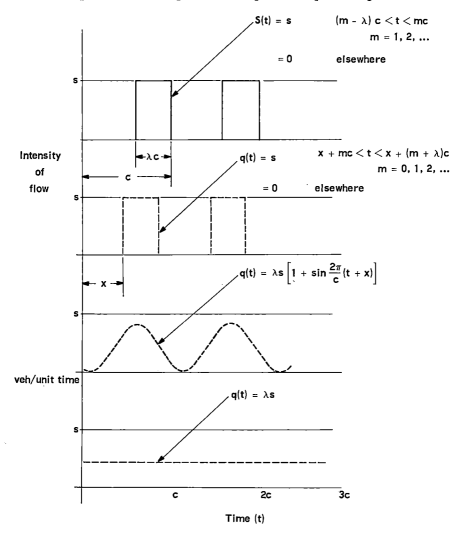

FIGURE 2. Waveforms for pulsed, sinusoidal, and "constant" input to signal with pulsed output of same frequency.

defined as the time interval between the start of the red phase and the point
on the arriving wavefront which has a flow intensity equal to $\lambda s$. In the case
of a square wave, this is synonymous with the arrival of the first vehicle of a
new batch.

(a) *For the square wave input:*

$$q(t) = s, \qquad (x + mc) < t < x + (m + \lambda)c, \qquad m = 0, 1 \ldots$$

$$0 < x < (1 - \lambda)c$$

and $q(t) = 0$ elsewhere.

Further

$$a = 1, \qquad b = 1$$

and from Eq. 4a

$$\langle d \rangle = (1 - \lambda)c - x \tag{5}$$

(b) *For the sine wave:*

$$q(t) = \lambda s \left\{ 1 + \sin \frac{2\pi}{c}(t + x) \right\} \qquad 0 < x < c$$

Again with $a = b = 1$ and using Eq. 2

$$B_i = s \cos \frac{2\pi x}{c}$$

$$B_i = 0 \qquad i > 1$$

Hence the average delay from Eq. 4 is

$$\langle d \rangle = \left\{ \frac{1}{2\pi} \cos \frac{2\pi x}{c} + \frac{1}{2}(1 - \lambda) \right\} c \tag{6}$$

(c) *For constant input:* $s, B_n = 0$

and the average delay is constant and equal to

$$\langle d \rangle = \tfrac{1}{2}(1 - \lambda)c \tag{7}$$

Figure 3 shows the number of arrivals, and the number in the system (i.e.,
number queueing) at various points in the cycle. Figure 4 indicates how the
delay varies with the phase displacement, i.e., Eqs. 5, 6, 7.

*Case II.*    Input and Output Waves with Different Period.

This case has direct application to a system of coordinated signals where a
variety of boundary conditions (cross flows, pedestrian phases, tolerances in
adjustment) may result in differences in the cycle times of successive signals.
For the purposes of this example we can take a square wave input of period
$ac/b$ and initial phase displacement $x$, measured between the start of the red
discharge wave and the arrival of the first vehicle from the previous signal, as
shown in Fig. 5.

Then, with

$$q(t) = s, \qquad x + m\frac{a}{b}c < t < x + (m + \lambda)\frac{a}{b}c, \qquad m = 0, 1 \ldots a$$

$$= 0, \qquad \text{elsewhere}$$

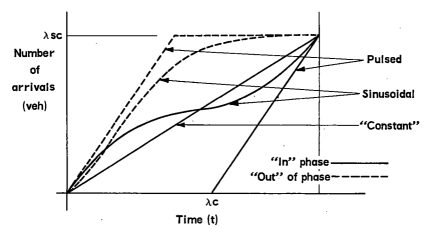

FIGURE 3.   Vehicle accumulation curves for inputs in Fig. 2.

After substitution in Eq. 4a and simplifying

$$\langle d \rangle = \frac{1}{2}\left\{\frac{a}{b} + 1\right\}(1 - \lambda)c - x$$

If $z$ is the time of arrival of the first vehicle of the platoon before the first green time of the $a$ cycles of the second light, then

$$z = (1 - \lambda)c - x$$

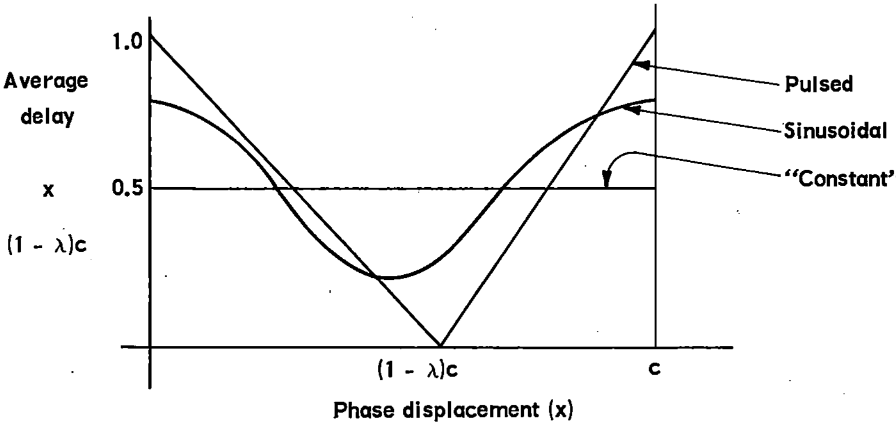

FIGURE 4.   Average delay as function of phase displacement between input and output.

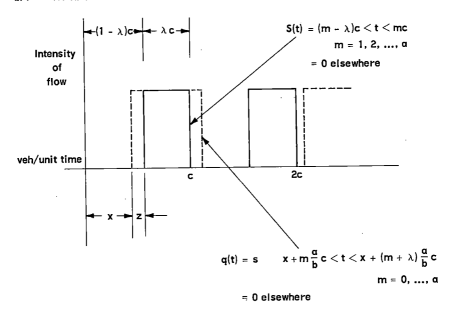

FIGURE 5. Cycle and phase relationships for input and output waveforms of different period.

and

$$\langle d \rangle = \frac{1}{2}(1 - \lambda)\left(\frac{a}{b} - 1\right)c + z$$

If the upstream signal has cycle time $c'$, then more simply

$$\langle d \rangle = \tfrac{1}{2}(1 - \lambda)(c' - c) + z \qquad\qquad (8)$$

with

$$z < (1 - \lambda)c$$

$z$ also has a lower limit, $z_{\min}$, with $z_{\min} \geq 0$, because there would otherwise be a period of unsaturation during the $a$ cycles  If $z$ were set less than $z_{\min}$, after unsaturation the system would degenerate to $z > z_{\min}$ for subsequent cycles. For minimum delay $z$ should be set equal to $z_{\min}$ if possible. There is a simple relationship for $z_{\min}$ according to whether $c' < c$ or $c' > c$.

If $c' < c$, inspection of the diagrams (Fig. 6a) representing arrival and departure flows and the number of queued vehicles at any time, shows that for minimum delay there should be no vehicles left in the queue at the end of the green time of the first cycle. Then

$$z_{\min} = (1 - \lambda)(n - 1)c'$$

and

$$\langle d \rangle = \tfrac{1}{2}(1 - \lambda)[(2n - 1)c' - c]$$

where $n$ is the smallest integer such that $nc' \geq c$.

If $c' > c$, a similar inspection (Fig. 6b) shows that minimum delay is achieved if there are no vehicles in the queue at the start of the red time of the $(a - n' + 2)$th cycle. Then

$$z_{\min} = \tfrac{1}{2}(1 - \lambda)(n'c - c')$$

and

$$\langle d \rangle = \tfrac{1}{2}(1 - \lambda)[(2n' - 1)c - c'] \qquad (10)$$

where $n'$ is the smallest integer such that $n'c \geq c'$.

Equations 9 and 10 show that the delay is independent of the direction of

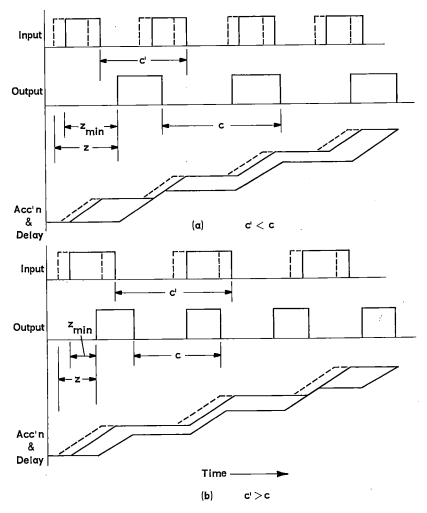

FIGURE 6.   Phase relationships for minimum delay.

flow. The general result is:

$$\langle d \rangle = \tfrac{1}{2}(1 - \lambda)[(2n - 1)c - c'] \qquad (11)$$

where $c'$ is the greater cycle time and $c$ is the lesser cycle time.

*Case III.* The "Oversaturated" Intersection.

As a final example, there is the case of peak period traffic.[6] The input flow, $q(t)$, is shown in Fig. 7. The saturated state of the intersection is allowed to

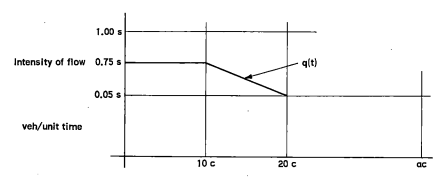

FIGURE 7. Input waveform for the "oversaturated" intersection.

continue for a time after the end of the peak period to permit the queue to disperse. During the "$a$" cycles, $\lambda$ is required to be $[(3.75/a) + 0.5]$ instead of the off-peak value of 0.5. The arrival flow is

$$q(t) = \tfrac{3}{4}s, \qquad\qquad 0 < t < 10c$$

$$= \left(1 - \frac{t}{40c}\right)s, \qquad 10c < t < 20c$$

$$= \tfrac{1}{2}s, \qquad\qquad 20c < t < ac$$

Hence, with $b = 1$, we obtain from Eq. 4a, after simplification,

$$\langle d \rangle = \left[\frac{5}{24\lambda}\left(9 - \frac{140}{a}\right) + \frac{1}{2}(1 - \lambda)\right]c, \qquad \text{with} \quad a \geq 20$$

and

$$\lambda = \frac{3.75}{a} + 0.5$$

It is clear that the highest value of $\lambda$ (from the smallest value of $a$) will give the least average delay per vehicle. However, it is supposed that requirements of cross traffic and pedestrians at the intersection restricts $\lambda$ to a maximum of 0.625.

Then, $a = 30$ to give $\lambda = 0.625$, and $\langle d \rangle = 1.63c$.

*Case IV.*   Other Examples.

It is not difficult to imagine other examples to which the general formula may be applied. The following represent situations of practical interest:

a. A square or sine wave representing a high traffic intensity pulse from the green phase of the previous intersection, followed by a low intensity pulse for turning traffic from its red phase

b. Short pulses of traffic intensity greater than the saturation flow rate arising from constriction at the intersection caused by turning vehicles

c. Gaussian input pulses. (See Reference 6.)

## Application to Networks

In a network there is clearly a problem of optimization. Except for the case of alternate one-way streets with a simple rectangular pattern and carrying equal flows on all streets on each of the grid axes, optimization is quite difficult to achieve.

An initial calculation for a network is the minimum cycle time for each intersection. For two-phase signals with mean approach flows $\lambda_1 s$ and $\lambda_2 s$, and saturation as described above, the minimum cycle time $c$ is given by

$$c = \frac{L}{1 - (\lambda_1 + \lambda_2)} \tag{12}$$

where $L$ is the minimum lost time per cycle. If saturation is maintained, then $c$ may be increased only if $L$ is artificially increased by an all-red time.

The simplest case to consider is the linear "network." If the flow is unidirectional and the cycle times at each intersection are the same, then Eq. 5 shows that the progression delay, in fact the total delay, can be made zero. If, however, the cross flows are all different, the setting of equal cycle times will introduce additional delay to the cross traffic flows.

The authors are currently working on the analytical solution to this problem, but at the time of writing have not completed the investigation. In the meantime a numerical example will suffice to indicate the nature of the problem.

The following set of numerical examples shows the difference in average delay per vehicle for a simple network of two intersections. The average delay for flow between the intersections is minimized by proper choice of the $z$ values according to Eq. 11.

The lost time per cycle is taken as a minimum of 12 sec, implying a minimum of 6 sec between phases. The saturation flow is 1800 vph. The approach flows shown in Fig. 8 are in vph and are assumed uniform in time. The travel time between intersections is 12 sec in either direction. The cycle times are $c_1$ and $c_2$ sec. Using Eq. 12, the minimum values of $c_1$ and $c_2$ are 60 sec and 30 sec, respectively.

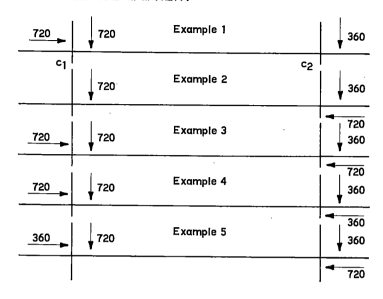

FIGURE 8.   Flow patterns for simple linear "network."

Two cases are considered:

and
$$(a)\ c_1 = 60, \qquad c_2 = 60$$
$$(b)\ c_1 = 60, \qquad c_2 = 30$$

Table I sets out the average delay per vehicle in seconds for all vehicles using the system.

The examples show that it is not always desirable to use a uniform cycle time for a network. It is not possible from this to formulate a general set of rules for the setting of cycle times for any network. It is probably necessary to resort to the use of Eq. 11, and trial and error with promising cases.

Equation 11 applies to the particular case of a square wave input with no turning traffic from the adjacent intersection. However, the general result given by Eq. 4a has the important implication that the first term is a "link"

TABLE I

| Example No. | Case | |
| --- | --- | --- |
| | (a) | (b) |
| 1 | 19.2 | 20.4 |
| 2 | 19.2 | 16.8 |
| 3 | 22.3 | 24.9 |
| 4 | 20.0 | 22.0 |
| 5 | 20.0 | 19.0 |

term which permits the inputs to the $(m, n)$th intersection to be related to the outputs from the $(m - 1, n)$, $(m + 1, n)$, $(m, n - 1)$ and $(m, n + 1)$ adjacent intersections.

## References

1. F. V. Webster, Traffic Signal Settings, R. R. L. Techn. Paper 39 (London, 1958).
2. A. J. Miller, Settings for Fixed-Cycle Traffic Signals, *Proc. Second Conf. A.R.R.B.*, Paper No. 131 (1964).
3. G. F. Newell, Approximation Methods for Queues With Application to the Fixed-Cycle Traffic Light, (unpublished) 1964.
4. A. J. H. Clayton, Road Traffic Calculations, *J. Inst. Civ. Engrs.*, 16: **7**, 247 (1940).
5. D. C. Gazis, and R. B. Potts, The Oversaturated Intersection, *Proc. Second Intern. Symp. on Theory of Road Traffic Flow*, J. Almond, Ed., O.E.C.D. Paris (1965).
6. M. J. Grace, and R. B. Potts, Diffusion of Traffic Platoons, *Proc. First Conf. A.R.R.B.*, 1: **1**, 260 (1962).

# Intersection Control
# by Vehicle-Actuated Signals

R. W. J. MORRIS and P. G. PAK-POY

Traffic Engineering Branch
Highway and Local Government Department
South Australia

This paper describes the results to date of a research project designed to investigate the operational characteristics of vehicle-actuated traffic signal controllers. The author's approach to the problem has been to postulate models of sufficient simplicity to obtain their exact solution, both theoretically and by computer simulation, yet sufficiently representative of their practical counterpart to provide results of practical importance.

The paper concentrates on the behavior of a simple vehicle-actuated signal, and in so doing sheds light on the problems of more sophisticated control.

The simple vehicle-actuated controller described allocates a preset guaranteed minimum green time. This is extended to a preset maximum time provided vehicles arrive at a "detector" located in each approach road with headways less than a preset value $\beta$ seconds, referred to as the "vehicle interval" or "unit extension." On a particular green phase, if a headway greater than $\beta$ occurs, the green light changes to amber during which no vehicles can enter the intersection. Then it changes to red at which time the red light on the other phase changes to green. Vehicles are assumed to discharge at a constant rate.

Using this model as a basis, the authors were able to make the following conclusions regarding the behavior of an isolated two-phase, simple, vehicle-actuated signal:

1. There exists a value of $\beta$ which minimizes the average delay per vehicle using the intersection, referred to as the "optimum vehicle interval."

2. The optimum vehicle interval for most practical cases is independent of the intersection geometry and is the same for both phases irrespective of the ratio of the traffic flows per phase.

3. Values of the optimum vehicle interval (sec) $vs.$ the total hourly traffic flow (veh/hr) entering the intersection from all four approaches are given in Table I:

4. The average delay per vehicle using the intersection is typically one half that for an equivalent fixed-cycle signal.

5. The design capacity and stability of operation is greater than that for an equivalent fixed-cycle signal.

## TABLE I.

| Optimum vehicle Interval (sec) | Total hourly traffic flow entering intersection (veh/hr) |
|:---:|:---:|
| 2 | $\geq 3000$ |
| 3 | 1800–3000 |
| 4 | 1400–1800 |
| 5 | 1000–1400 |
| 6 | 600–1000 |
| 8 | $\leq 600$ |

6. The effect of using a value of the vehicle interval greater than optimal is to reduce the percentage of cars stopped by the signals, to increase the average cycle time, and to increase the average delay per vehicle.

Although the above results apply to an idealized state of affairs, it is logical to believe that they apply to many practical situations.

With regard to the development of an efficient controller the results of the project to date indicate that for many practical situations, including multiphase control a controller making maximum use of the technique of counting in the delayed vehicles and switching phases as soon as the last delayed vehicle has cleared, will be quite satisfactory. This aspect together with balancing the unit extension against the number of delayed vehicles on the red phase has formed the basis for the development of a controller that can be utilized in coordinated signal systems.

# A Mixed-Integer Linear Program for Synchronizing Traffic Signals for Maximal Bandwidth

*JOHN D. C. LITTLE*

Sloan School of Management
Massachusetts Institute of Technology
Cambridge, Massachusetts

Traffic signals can be synchronized so that a car, starting at one end of a main artery and traveling at preassigned speeds, can go to the other end without stopping for a red light. The portion of a signal cycle for which this is possible is called the *bandwidth* for that direction. Ordinarily the bandwidth in each direction is single, i.e., is not split into two or more intervals within a cycle. For this case we formulate the arterial problem as a mixed-integer linear program:

*Given:*
 1. an arbitrary number of signals,
 2. the fraction of the cycle that is red at each signal,
 3. upper and lower limits on signal period,
 4. upper and lower limits on speed each way between adjacent signals,
 5. limits on change in speed, and
 6. a constant of proportionality between the two bandwidths.

*Find:*
 1. a common signal period,
 2. speeds between signals, and
 3. the relative phasing of the signals so as to maximize the sum of the bandwidths.

Several variants of the problem are also formulated.

A branch and bound algorithm is developed for solving the given mixed-integer linear program by solving a sequence of ordinary linear programs. A ten signal example is worked out.

The problem of synchronizing a network of signals is also formulated. The resulting program consists of the arterial programs for the individual streets plus a set of further constraints that arise because the streets connect together to form closed loops. The objective function used for the network program is a weighted sum of the bandwidths in each direction on each artery. A seven signal example is worked out by branch and bound methods.

For further details, see Reference 1.

## Reference

1. J. D. C. Little, The Synchronization of Traffic Signals by Mixed-Integer Linear Programming, *Oper. Res.* **14,** 568 (1966).

# Mean Waiting Time at an Intersection

*P. H. FARGIER*

Ministere des Travaux Publics et des Transports
Arcueil, Seine, France

The purpose of the paper is to derive and use a relationship between the mean waiting time $E(w)$ of a vehicle at an intersection and the mean number $E(q)$ of waiting vehicles at the beginning of a red phase.

First, two relationships between $E(w)$, $E(q)$, and $E(n)$, which is the mean number of waiting vehicles, are obtained:

a. Each vehicle has to wait for the intersection clearance by every vehicle which has arrived before it.

b. On the average, the number of waiting vehicles is equal to the rate of arrivals multiplied by the waiting time of vehicles.

Through the elimination of $E(n)$, a formula between $E(w)$ and $E(q)$ is obtained. This formula is similar to one given by Beckmann, McGuire, and Winsten,[1] but it is valid in much more general conditions, such as variable red and green phase, and variable clearing time of vehicles.

Expressions of $E(w)$ can be derived whenever $E(q)$ can be computed, and particularly in the following cases:

a. A secondary road crosses a priority road.

The duration of the fictitious "green phases" may be assumed to have an exponential distribution. $E(q)$ is equal to the mean number of waiting vehicles during the green phases. A formula equivalent to that given by Tanner is found.[2]

b. Signals getting red only when there is no waiting vehicle.

In this case $E(q) = 0$. Red phases of a stream depend on the "busy period" brought by the red phases of the crossed stream, i.e., periods elapsing between the end of a red phase and the instant when the corresponding queue vanishes. An appendix gives formulae of the mean and the variance of these "busy periods" as a function of those of the red phases.

c. Fixed cycle-times.

If we know the probability generating function of the number of vehicles present at a given time during a green phase, we can derive that of the number of vehicles present after a duration equal to the clearing-time of a vehicle, which we assume to be fixed. It is also possible to compute the probability generating function at the end of a red phase if we know the probability generating function of that red phase beginning. If we are in the stationary case, we can write that, after a cycle, the generating function is identical to the initial one which is still unknown. This relationship enables us to compute $E(q)$. Yet its expression is quite complicated and includes the zeros of a function of the complex variable. Graphs are under computation for a more convenient use. The computations we made in a particular case gave results close to that derived from Webster formula.

Besides the above cases where a mathematical solution has been obtained, the general relation between $E(w)$ and $E(q)$ presents some interest and, more particularly, can help in the choice of experimental studies and simulation processes.

## References

1. M. J. Beckman, C. B. McGuire and C. B. Winsten, Studies in the Economics of Transportation, Yale University Press, 1956.
2. J. C. Tanner, *Biometrika*, **38**, 383 (1951).

# Numerical Results for Queueing for Gaps in a Traffic Stream

*J. W. COHEN and S. J. deLANGE*

Mathematical Institute
Delft, Netherlands

The paper presents numerical results for the model studied in an earlier paper "Queueing for gaps in a traffic stream."[1]

In a single-lane highway traffic stream the headways are supposed to be independent stochastic variables, identically distributed with distribution $C(t)$, average $\mu$. Traffic on the minor road is Poissonian with parameter $\lambda$. A driver on the minor road, arriving at the intersection and finding no waiting vehicles, stops and decides to cross or to wait for the next gap according to the gap-acceptance probability $A(t)$, where $t$ is the time until the passing of the next vehicle of the highway-stream. If he waits for the next gap, then this gap of length $\tau$ is accepted for crossing with probability $A(t)$, and so on. A driver not at the head of the queue waits until the car in front of him crosses the highway; he decides to follow this car or to wait for the next gap according to the follow probability. If the driver waits then at the beginning of the next gap, he is at the head of the queue and accepts this gap with probability $A(t)$. It is assumed that no time is lost either by taking a decision or by crossing the highway. The two models described differ only in the choice of the follow probability. In the $Ak$-model the follow probability is a constant $k$, $0 \leq k \leq 1$. In the $AA$-model the follow probability is equal to the gap-acceptance probability $A(t)$. The results given in Reference 1 refer to the steady state, which is ultimately reached for the $Ak$-model if

$$\rho = \lambda\mu(1 - k)\bigg/\int_0^\infty A(t)\,dC(t) < 1 \tag{1}$$

whereas for the $AA$-model the steady state is always reached because we have taken here

$$A(t) = 1, \quad \text{for} \quad t > \tau \quad \text{and} \quad C(\tau) < 1$$

i.e., gaps always occur here in which the whole queue is emptied. In the $AA$-model $A(t)$ as given by Eq. 1 has been approximated by step-functions in the numerical calculations.

$$
\begin{aligned}
A(t) &= 0, & t &< 1 \\
&= 1 - \exp\{-(t - 1)/0.667\}, & 1 &\leq t \leq 2.67 \\
&= 1, & t &> 2.67
\end{aligned}
\tag{2}
$$

Calculations for the $Ak$-model were also performed for $A(t)$ as given by Eq. 1. The differences between results obtained for the $Ak$-model using Eq. 1, and two different step-functions approximating Eq. 1, are small. In all the calculations $C(t)$ has been taken to be

$$C(t) = 0, \qquad\qquad\qquad\qquad\qquad\qquad\qquad t < 0.267$$

$$C(t) = 1 - \exp\{-(t - 0.267)/(\mu - 0.267)\}, \qquad t \geq 0.267$$

The following properties are given for the $Ak$-model.

*a.* The mean waiting time as a function of $\lambda\mu \bigg/ \displaystyle\int_0^\infty A(t)\, dC(t)$, for different values of $k$ and $\mu$, respectively, and as a function of $\rho$ for different values of $k$.

*b.* The probability of arriving in an empty system and the probability of crossing without delay, for different values of $\mu$ and $k$ as a function of $\lambda$, and also as a function of $\rho$.

For the $AA$-model the graphs are given for both the approximating step-functions. They are the mean waiting time:

*a.* as a function of $\lambda$ for different values of $\mu$,

*b.* as a function of $\mu$ for different values of $\lambda$,

*c.* as a function of $\lambda\mu \bigg/ \displaystyle\int_0^\infty A(t)\, dC(t)$ for different values of $\lambda$ and $\mu$.

As the results were obtained recently, no comparison with the actual situation or with other works in this field could be made.

## Reference

1. J. W. Cohen and A. J. Stam, Queueing for Gaps in a Traffic Stream, Report T. H., Mathematical Institute, Delft, 1963.

# The Optimum Bus Service: A Theoretical Model for a Large Uniform Urban Area

*E. M. HOLROYD*

Road Research Laboratory
Ministry of Transport
Harmondsworth, Middlesex, England

## Abstract

The problem of finding the optimum positions of bus routes and the optimum frequency of buses on each route in an urban area is considered, the criterion of optimality being that the sum of the time-costs of the journeys and the cost of providing the bus service should be a minimum. This problem is studied theoretically by examining a model of a bus system operating in a large uniform area, with the routes forming a square grid, buses running right across the area, and the same frequency of buses on each route. Assuming that passengers choose the quickest available routes, and making certain other assumptions, formulae are derived giving the average times on a journey spent walking, waiting for buses, and riding on buses, in terms of the parameters of the model. The cost of providing the bus service is also found in terms of these parameters. By adding the time-costs of the journeys the total cost of travel is obtained. The values of the route-spacing and the service-interval which minimize this total cost are found in terms of the other parameters, namely the value of time, the cost of operating a bus, the regularity of the buses, the density of journeys, the walking speed, and the bus speed. An alternative method of selecting routes is indicated, which leads to similar formulae by a simpler argument. Some suggestions are made for further work.

## Introduction

IN A NUMBER of recent papers (see, for example, Creighton *et al.*,[1] and Beckmann[2]) consideration has been given to the optimum location of a road network in an area in which the origins and destinations of journeys are distributed in some simple way, independently of the position of the network.

It has been assumed that travel can take place at a higher speed (or lower cost) on the network than in the rest of the area, and the optimum network is that which minimizes the combined cost of road construction and travel. In this paper a similar approach is used in the determination of an optimum bus service, the quantity to be minimized being the cost of providing the service plus the time-costs of travel. In addition to the positions of the routes the frequencies of service have to be determined; these affect the times that passengers will spend waiting for buses. In this paper a simple theoretical model of a bus service is analyzed; a description of the application of similar principles to the operation of a real bus undertaking has been given by Harding.[3]

## Model of a Bus System

The following assumptions are made. (A complete summary of the notation is given in the Appendix.)

1. The bus system operates in a uniform area, large enough for the edge-effects to be neglected. The routes form a square grid with spacing $s$, the buses run right across the area with speed $v$ (including stops), and the service-interval (i.e., the average time-interval between successive buses on a route) has the same value, $i$, on all routes. (This is the simplest type of system that can be considered, and not necessarily the optimum type; more general systems should also be investigated.)

2. Travelers can walk anywhere in the area with speed $u$ ($< v$), but only in the two directions parallel to the bus-routes; they can get on or off a bus at any point of its route. (The effect of the spacing of bus stops is a subject which deserves examination, but which will not be considered here.)

3. The average waiting time for a bus, $w$, is proportional to the service-interval $i$: $w = hi$, say, where $h$ is a constant. (This is a severe restriction. It implies firstly that the buses always have vacant seats, i.e., off-peak conditions; if $i$ increases to the point where the buses begin to be full, some passengers will have to wait for two or more buses, and $w$ will increase sharply. Secondly, the assumption implies that the times at which passengers arrive at the bus stops are not related to the arrival times of the buses; this will be approximately true in practice if the bus service is either frequent or irregular. If passengers arrive at random and get on the first bus that comes, it can be shown[4] that $w = \frac{1}{2}(1 + c_i{}^2)i$, where $c_i$ is the coefficient of variation of the intervals between the arrivals of successive buses; the assumption that $h$ is constant therefore implies, thirdly, that $c_i$ is independent of $i$. For regular bus arrivals $c_i = 0$ and $h = \frac{1}{2}$, while for random bus arrivals $c_i = 1$ and $h = 1$.)

4. A passenger cannot predict the time he will have to wait for a bus; he knows only its expected or average value, $w$. (This would be true if the buses arrived randomly with a known frequency, or if the timetable specified the frequency but not the times of arrival of the buses.)

5. Each passenger selects the route from his origin to his destination which has the lowest expected total journey time (walking, waiting, and riding on buses). (It would be more rational to select the route with the lowest expected total cost, i.e., fares plus time-costs, but to use this assumption we should have to introduce a specific fare-structure. Certain types of fare-structure, however, can be dealt with under the "quickest route" assumption. If the fare is proportional to the distance, the effect on choice of route is equivalent to a reduction in bus speed; if there is a fixed fare to pay on each bus, this is equivalent to an increase in average waiting time; and if there is a fixed fare for the complete journey, the quickest route will also be the cheapest, provided that the possibility of walking the whole distance is eliminated.)

6. The analysis will be limited to those journeys which require at least one bus in each of the two perpendicular directions. (If the journeys are long compared with the route-spacing, the majority of journeys will be of this type, but further work is needed to allow for the possibilities of using only one bus and of walking the whole distance.)

7. Origins of journeys are uniformly distributed over the area, and so are destinations. They are linked so that the positions of the origin and the destination of a particular journey within their respective cells of the route network are independent. (This assumption will be satisfied exactly for all route-spacings only if origins and destinations are linked completely at random, which is unrealistic for a large area. The assumption will be a good approximation, however, if the mean and standard deviation of journey length are large compared with the route-spacing.)

8. The time-costs of the journeys are proportional to the total journey time, and the cost of the bus service is proportional to the number of buses operating.

On the basis of these assumptions, the average time for a journey and the cost of the bus service, and hence the total cost of transport, will be determined in terms of the parameters of the model. The values of the route-spacing and the service-interval which minimize the total cost of transport will then be determined in terms of the other parameters, which are regarded as fixed.

### Selection of the Quickest Route

Let $t$ be the expected total time for a particular journey, and let the expected times spent walking, waiting, and riding on buses be $t_p$, $t_w$, and $t_r$. Let the total distances walked and traveled on buses be $p$ and $r$, and the number of buses used be $n$. Then

$$t = t_p + t_w + t_r = p/u + nw + r/v$$

We wish to find $E(t)$, the average of $t$ over all journeys. Since

$$E(t) = E(p)/u + E(n)w + E(r)/v$$

we have to determine $E(p)$, $E(n)$, and $E(r)$. The first step is to find a rule for selecting the quickest route between two given points.

Let $P_1$ be the origin of a journey and let $P_2$ be its destination. Let $Q_1$ be the point at which the passenger gets on the first bus of the journey, and let $Q_2$ be the point where he gets off the last one. If $Q_1$ and $Q_2$ are on perpendicular routes (Fig. 1a), $n = 2$; if they are on parallel routes (Fig. 1b), $n = 3$. Let $O_1$ be the corner of the cell containing $P_1$ which is nearest to $P_2$, and let $O_2$ be the corner of the cell containing $P_2$ which is nearest to $P_1$ (see Fig. 1). (Since we are considering only journeys which require at least two buses, we may assume that the cells containing $P_1$ and $P_2$ do not lie in the same or adjoining "rows" or "columns" of the route network.)

It is obvious that the first bus on which the passenger travels must run along one of the four sides of the cell containing $P_1$, and that he will walk to this side by the quickest route. Thus $Q_1$ must be the foot of the perpendicular from $P_1$ on to one of the sides of the cell containing $P_1$ (see Fig. 1). Similarly, $Q_2$ will be the foot of the perpendicular from $P_2$ to one of the sides of the cell containing $P_2$. Now if $Q_1$ and $Q_2$ lie on perpendicular bus routes, as in Fig. 1a, they determine the route of the journey completely. If they lie on parallel bus routes, as in Fig. 1b, they still determine its length, the only indeterminate factor being the choice of the link between the two parallel routes. In both cases the route from $Q_1$ to $Q_2$ is the shortest possible in distance. Thus the selection of the quickest route from $P_1$ to $P_2$ reduces to the choice of $Q_1$ and $Q_2$ from four possible positions each, giving a choice of sixteen possible combinations.

It will now be shown that, given that $P_2$ lies, for example, "south" and "west" of $P_1$, as in Fig. 1, i.e., given the positions of $O_1$ and $O_2$ in their respective cells, the choice of $Q_1$ and $Q_2$ depends only on the positions of $P_1$ and $P_2$ within their respective cells, and not on the actual cells in which the points lie. Let $\langle LM \rangle$ denote the "rectangular" distance from a point $L$ to a point $M$, i.e., the length of the shortest path from $L$ to $M$ running in the directions parallel to the bus routes. Then, because of the definitions of $O_1$ and $O_2$, it is clear (see Fig. 1) that

$$\langle Q_1 Q_2 \rangle = \langle Q_1 O_1 \rangle + \langle O_1 O_2 \rangle + \langle O_2 Q_2 \rangle$$

Now the expected time for the whole journey from $P_1$ to $P_2$ is

$$\frac{P_1 Q_1}{u} + \frac{\langle Q_1 Q_2 \rangle}{v} + \frac{Q_2 P_2}{u} + n(Q_1, Q_2)w$$

where

$$n(Q_1, Q_2) = \begin{cases} 2 \text{ if } Q_1, Q_2 \text{ are on perpendicular bus routes} \\ 3 \text{ if } Q_1, Q_2 \text{ are on parallel bus routes} \end{cases}$$

and this equals

$$\frac{P_1 Q_1}{u} + \frac{\langle O_1 O_1 \rangle}{v} + \frac{\langle O_1 O_2 \rangle}{v} + \frac{\langle O_2 Q_2 \rangle}{v} + \frac{Q_2 P_2}{u} + n(Q_1, Q_2)w$$

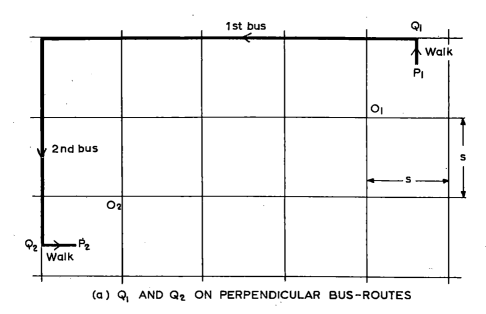

(a) $Q_1$ AND $Q_2$ ON PERPENDICULAR BUS-ROUTES

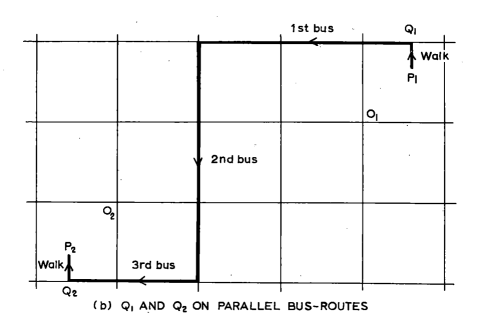

(b) $Q_1$ AND $Q_2$ ON PARALLEL BUS-ROUTES

FIGURE I.    The route of a journey.

Now $(P_1Q_1/u + \langle Q_1O_1 \rangle/v)$ is the time taken to get from $P_1$ to $O_1$ via $Q_1$ (ignoring waiting time), $(\langle O_2Q_2 \rangle/v + Q_2P_2/u)$ is the time taken to get from $O_2$ to $P_2$ via $Q_2$ (ignoring waiting time), and $\langle O_1O_2 \rangle/v$ is a constant. Thus, to minimize the expected time from $P_1$ to $P_2$, $Q_1$ and $Q_2$ should be chosen so as to minimize the sum of the three quantities:

    *a.* time for journey $P_1Q_1O_1$ (ignoring waiting time)
    *b.* time for journey $O_2Q_2P_2$ (ignoring waiting time)
    *c.* expected waiting time $n(Q_1, Q_2)w$

This does not, of course, imply that the route necessarily passes through $O_1$ and $O_2$; it may in fact pass through either, neither, or both of these points.

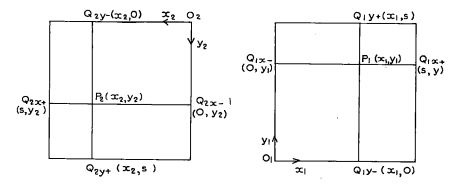

FIGURE 2.   The possible positions of $Q_1$ and $Q_2$.

We shall take $O_1$ as the origin of a coordinate system for the cell containing $P_1$, with its positive axes lying along the sides of the cell. Let the coordinates of $P_1$ be $(x_1, y_1)$. Let $Q_{1x-}$, $Q_{1x+}$, $Q_{1y-}$, $Q_{1y+}$, be the points with coordinates $(O, y_1)$, $(s, y_1)$, $(x_1, O)$, and $(x_1, s)$, respectively (see Fig. 2); these are the four possible positions of $Q_1$. Let $t_{1x-}$ be the time taken to walk from $P_1$ to $Q_{1x-}$ and travel by bus from $Q_{1x-}$ to $O_1$ (excluding waiting time), and let $t_{1x+}$, $t_{1y-}$, and $t_{1y+}$ be defined similarly. Thus

$$t_{1x-} = \frac{x_1}{u} + \frac{y_1}{v}$$

$$t_{1x+} = \frac{s - x_1}{u} + \frac{s + y_1}{v}$$

$$t_{1y-} = \frac{y_1}{u} + \frac{x_1}{v}$$

$$t_{1y+} = \frac{s - y_1}{u} + \frac{s + x_1}{v}$$

We take $O_2$ to be the origin of a similar coordinate system for the cell containing $P_2$ (see Fig. 2), and define precisely similar quantities with the subscript 2 in place of 1. (Note that $x_2$ and $y_2$ increase in the opposite directions from $x_1$ and $y_1$.)

The problem is to select one of the four quantities $t_{1x-}, t_{1x+}, t_{1y-}, t_{1y+}$, and one of the four quantities $t_{2x-}, t_{2x+}, t_{2y-}, t_{2y+}$, so that the sum of these two quantities and the waiting time $nw$ is a minimum, where $n = 2$ if the selected quantities have one $x$ suffix and one $y$ suffix, and $n = 3$ otherwise. Since the choice between $t_{ix-}$ and $t_{ix+}$ ($i = 1, 2$) does not affect the value of $n$, we can eliminate the larger of the two quantities from consideration. Now

$$t_{ix-} < t_{ix+}$$

if

$$\frac{x_i}{u} + \frac{y_i}{v} < \frac{s - x_i}{u} + \frac{s + y_i}{v}$$

i.e., if

$$x_i < \frac{v + u}{2v} s$$

Thus if we define

$$t_{ix} = \min (t_{ix-}, t_{ix+})$$

we have

$$t_{ix} = \begin{cases} \dfrac{x_i}{u} + \dfrac{y_i}{v}, & x_i < \dfrac{v + u}{2v} s \\ \dfrac{s - x_i}{u} + \dfrac{s + y_i}{v}, & x_i > \dfrac{v + u}{2v} s \end{cases} \tag{1}$$

Similarly, if we define

$$t_{iy} = \min (t_{iy-}, t_{iy+})$$

we find that

$$t_{iy} = \begin{cases} \dfrac{y_i}{u} + \dfrac{x_i}{v}, & y_i < \dfrac{v + u}{2v} s \\ \dfrac{s - y_i}{u} + \dfrac{s + x_i}{v}, & y_i > \dfrac{v + u}{2v} s \end{cases} \tag{2}$$

The problem has now been reduced so that instead of having to find the minimum of 16 quantities we need consider only 4, namely

$$t_{xx} = t_{1x} + t_{2x} + 3w$$
$$t_{yy} = t_{1y} + t_{2y} + 3w$$
$$t_{xy} = t_{1x} + t_{2y} + 2w$$
$$t_{yx} = t_{1y} + t_{2x} + 2w$$

Let

$$t_m = \min (t_{xx}, t_{yy}, t_{xy}, t_{yx})$$

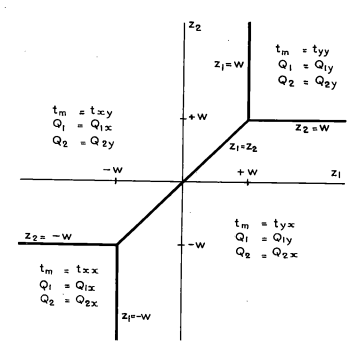

FIGURE 3.   The conditions determining the value of $t_m$ and the positions of $Q_1$ and $Q_2$.

If we now define

$$z_1 = t_{1x} - t_{1y}$$
$$z_2 = t_{2x} - t_{2y}$$

(3)

it may easily be verified that the necessary and sufficient conditions for each of the above four quantities to be the smallest are as follows:

$$
\begin{array}{llll}
z_1 < -w, & z_2 < -w, & t_m = t_{xx} \\
z_1 > w, & z_2 > w, & t_m = t_{yy} \\
z_1 < w, & z_2 > -w, z_1 < z_2, & t_m = t_{xy} \\
z_1 > -w, & z_2 < w, z_1 > z_2, & t_m = t_{yx}
\end{array}
$$

These conditions are illustrated in Fig. 3, in which the coordinate axes represent $z_1$ and $z_2$, and which makes it clear that the four sets of conditions account for all pairs of values of $z_1$ and $z_2$.

We shall also define a point $Q_{ix}$ ($i = 1, 2$) by

$$
Q_{ix} = \begin{cases} Q_{ix-}, & t_{ix} = t_{ix-} \\ Q_{ix+}, & t_{ix} = t_{ix+} \end{cases}
$$

so that

$$Q_{ix} = \begin{cases} (0, y_i), & x_i < \dfrac{v + u}{2v} s \\[2mm] (s, y_i), & x_i > \dfrac{v + u}{2v} s \end{cases}$$

The point $Q_{iy}$ is defined similarly with reference to $t_{iy}$. Then the conditions for $t_m$ may be rewritten in terms of $Q_1$ and $Q_2$, thus:

$$\begin{array}{llll} z_1 < -w, & z_2 < -w, & Q_1 = Q_{1x}, & Q_2 = Q_{2x} \\ z_1 > w, & z_2 > w, & Q_1 = Q_{1y}, & Q_2 = Q_{2y} \\ z_1 < w, & z_2 > -w, z_1 < z_2, & Q_1 = Q_{1x}, & Q_2 = Q_{2y} \\ z_1 > -w, & z_2 < w, z_1 > z_2, & Q_1 = Q_{1y}, & Q_2 = Q_{2x} \end{array}$$

These conditions may be expressed in a different form by putting

$$z_a = \min(z_1, z_2)$$
$$z_b = \max(z_1, z_2)$$

(so that either $a = 1$, $b = 2$, or $a = 2$, $b = 1$):

$$\begin{array}{lll} a. \ z_1 < -w, z_2 < -w, & Q_1 = Q_{1x}, & Q_2 = Q_{2x} \\ b. \ z_1 > w, z_2 > w, & Q_1 = Q_{1y}, & Q_2 = Q_{2y} \\ c. \ \text{neither } a \text{ nor } b, & Q_a = Q_{ax}, & Q_b = Q_{by} \end{array} \qquad (4)$$

## Determination of Mean Journey Time

The next step is to determine the value of $z_i$ $(i = 1, 2)$ at each point of the cell containing $P_i$. To do this we consider separately the four regions $A, B, C, D$, (see Fig. 4, in which $i = 1$) into which the cell is divided by the lines

$$x_i = \frac{v + u}{2v} s, \qquad y_i = \frac{v + u}{2v} s$$

Using Eqs. 3, 1, and 2, we find that in each of these regions $z_i$ varies from $-q$ to $+q$, where $q = (v^2 - u^2)/s2uv^2$, and that the contours of $z_i$ form a set of straight lines parallel to the diagonal of the region which passes through the corner of the cell, the distance between two contours being proportional to the difference between the corresponding values of $z_i$ (see Fig. 4). It follows that for a point selected at random from any of the regions $A, B, C, D$, and therefore from the whole cell, $z_i$ has a symmetrical triangular probability distribution between the limits $\pm q$, as shown in Fig. 5.

We can now find the average value of $n$, the number of buses used on a journey. The probability that $z < -w$ (assuming $w \leq q$) is given by the shaded area in Fig. 5:

$$P[z < -w] = \frac{(q - w)^2}{2q^2}$$

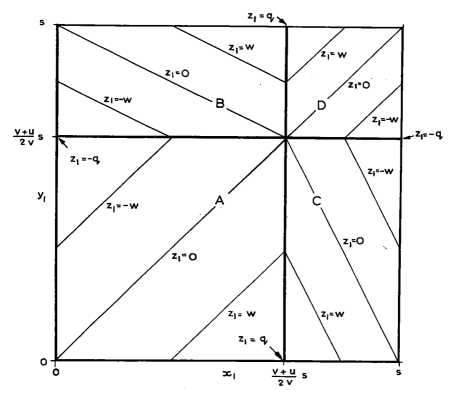

FIGURE 4.   Contours of $z_1$.

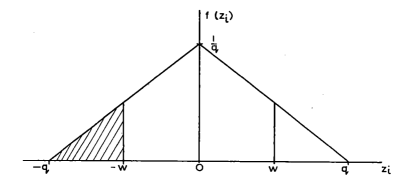

FIGURE 5.   Distribution of $z_i$.

Since $z_1$ and $z_2$ are distributed independently in the form shown in Fig. 5,

$$P[n = 3] = P[Q_1 = Q_{1x}, Q_2 = Q_{2x}] + P[Q_1 = Q_{1y}, Q_2 = Q_{2y}]$$

$$= P[z_1 < -w]P[z_2 < -w] + P[z_1 > w]P[z_2 > w]$$

$$= \frac{(q - w)^4}{2q^4} \quad (w \leq q)$$

Since $n$ must be either 2 or 3, it follows that

$$E(n) = 2 + \frac{(q - w)^4}{2q^4}, \quad (w \leq q)$$

If $w \geq q$, then $P[n = 3] = 0$, and $E(n) = 2$.

It remains to find the average distances walked and traveled on buses on a journey, $E(p)$ and $E(r)$.

Let $p_i$ = distance walked between $P_i$ and $Q_i$
$r_i$ = distance by bus between $Q_i$ and $O_i$
$p_{ix}$ = distance $P_iQ_{ix}$
$p_{iy}$ = distance $P_iQ_{iy}$
$r_{ix}$ = distance along bus routes between $Q_{ix}$ and $O_i$
$r_{iy}$ = distance along bus routes between $Q_{iy}$ and $O_i$

Thus, if $Q_i = Q_{ix}$, then $p_i = p_{ix}$ and $r_i = r_{ix}$ and if $Q_i = Q_{iy}$, then $p_i = p_{iy}$ and $r_i = r_{iy}$. Since the question whether $Q_i = Q_{ix}$ or $Q_{iy}$ is determined by the values of $z_1$ and $z_2$, we shall find the average values of $p_{ix}, p_{iy}, r_{ix}, r_{iy}$, for a given value of $z_i$.

By finding an expression for $E(p_{ix} \mid z_i)$ in each of the regions $A$, $B$, $C$, $D$, and weighting these by the areas of the regions, we obtain for the whole cell

$$E(p_{ix} \mid z_i) = \frac{v^2 + u^2}{4v^2} s\left(1 + \frac{z_i}{q}\right) \tag{5}$$

Similarly, we find

$$E(p_{iy} \mid z_i) = \frac{v^2 + u^2}{4v^2} s\left(1 - \frac{z_i}{q}\right) \tag{6}$$

$$E(r_{ix} \mid z_i) = \left\{1 - \frac{u}{2v}\left(1 + \frac{z_i}{q}\right)\right\} s \tag{7}$$

$$E(r_{iy} \mid z_i) = \left\{1 - \frac{u}{2v}\left(1 - \frac{z_i}{q}\right)\right\} s \tag{8}$$

Since $E(p_{ix} \mid z_i)$, $E(p_{iy} \mid z_i)$, $E(r_{ix} \mid z_i)$, $E(r_{iy} \mid z_i)$ are all linear functions of $z_i$, we can find the values of $E(p_{ix})$, etc., simply by substituting $E(z_i)$ for $z_i$. Now $z_1$ and $z_2$ are independently distributed in the form shown in Fig. 5, and it is a straightforward matter to show that

$$E(z_a) = E\{\min (z_1, z_2)\} = -7q/30$$
$$E(z_b) = E\{\max (z_1, z_2)\} = +7q/30$$

We consider first the case in which $w \geq q$, so that

$$-w \leq z_1 \leq w$$
$$-w \leq z_2 \leq w$$

Referring to the conditions of Eq. 4 for $Q_1$ and $Q_2$, we see that $a$ and $b$ are eliminated, and the rule for choosing $Q_1$ and $Q_2$ becomes simply

$$Q_a = Q_{ax}, \qquad Q_b = Q_{by}$$

Thus to find $E(p_a)$ we substitute $E(z_a)$ for $z_i$ in the Eq. 5 for $E(p_{ix} \mid z_i)$:

$$E(p_a) = \frac{23(v^2 - u^2)}{120v^2} s$$

Substitution of $E(z_b)$ for $z_i$ in $E(p_{iy} \mid z_i)$ gives the same value for $E(p_b)$. But

$$p = p_1 + p_2$$
$$= p_a + p_b$$

so that

$$E(p) = E(p_a) + E(p_b)$$
$$= \frac{23(v^2 + u^2)}{60v^2} s, \qquad w \geq q$$

In the same way, by substituting $E(z_a)$ for $z_i$ in $E(r_{ix} \mid z_i)$ and $E(z_b)$ for $z_i$ in $E(r_{iy} \mid z_i)$ we find that

$$E(r_a) = E(r_b) = \left(1 - \frac{23u}{60v}\right) s$$

Now the average rectangular distance from $P_i$ to $O_i$ is clearly $s$, and the distance traveled on buses is, therefore, less than the rectangular distance from origin to destination by an average amount $23us/60v$ at each end of the journey, that is by $23us/30v$ altogether. Thus if $d = $ rectangular distance from origin to destination, then

$$E(r) = E(d) - \frac{23u}{30v} s, \qquad w \geq q$$

We turn now to the case in which $w \leq q$. Referring to Eq. 4, we see that the only differences from the case $w \geq q$ occur

a. if $z_1 < -w$ and $z_2 < -w$, when $Q_b$ becomes $Q_{bx}$ instead of $Q_{by}$, and
b. if $z_1 > w$ and $z_2 > w$, when $Q_a$ becomes $Q_{ay}$ instead of $Q_{ax}$.

In case $b$ the expression for $E(p_i \mid z_i)$ changes from Eq. 5 to Eq. 6 (with "$i$" replaced by "$a$")—a reduction of $(v^2 + u^2)sz_a/2v^2q$, and the expression for $E(r_i \mid z_i)$ changes from Eq. 7 to Eq. 8 (with "$i$" replaced by "$a$")—an increase of $usz_a/vq$.

Now with $z_1$ and $z_2$ distributed independently as shown in Fig. 5, it can be shown that

$$E(z_a \mid z_1 > w, z_2 > w) = E\{\min(z_1, z_2) \mid z_1 > w, z_2 > w\}$$

$$= \frac{q + 4w}{5}$$

For those positions of $P_1$ and $P_2$ for which $z_1 > w$ and $z_2 > w$, therefore, the average reduction in $E(p)$ compared with the case in which $w \geq q$ is

$$\frac{(v^2 + u^2)s}{2v^2q} \cdot \frac{q + 4w}{5} \tag{9}$$

and the average increase in $E(r)$ is

$$\frac{us}{vq} \cdot \frac{q + 4w}{5}$$

Exactly the same average changes are found in $E(p)$ and $E(r)$ when $z_1 < -w$ and $z_2 < -w$.

The probability that $z_1 > w$ and $z_2 > w$ has been found to be $(q - w)^4/4q^4$. Thus the value of $E(p)$ when $w \leq q$ may be found by doubling this probability (to include the case $z_1 < -w$ and $z_2 < -w$), multiplying by the average reduction (Eq. 9), and subtracting the result from the expression for $E(p)$ when $w \geq q$. Thus

$$E(p) = \frac{23(v^2 + u^2)}{60v^2} s - \frac{(q - w)^4}{2q^4} \cdot \frac{(v^2 + u^2)s}{2v^2q} \cdot \frac{q + 4w}{5}$$

$$= \frac{23q^5 - 3(q - w)^4(q + 4w)}{60q^5} \cdot \frac{v^2 + u^2}{v^2} s, \qquad w \leq q$$

By a similar argument we find that

$$E(r) = E(d) - \frac{23u}{30v} s + \frac{(q - w)^4}{2q^4} \cdot \frac{us}{vq} \cdot \frac{q + 4w}{5}$$

$$= E(d) - \frac{23q^5 - 3(q - w)^4(q + 4w)}{30q^5} \cdot \frac{u}{v} s, \qquad w \leq q$$

Now we have seen that

$$E(t) = \frac{E(p)}{u} + \frac{E(r)}{v} + E(n)w$$

so that

$$E(t) = \frac{23q^5 - 3(q - w)^4(q + 4w)}{60q^5} \cdot \frac{v^2 + u^2}{uv^2} s$$

$$+ \frac{E(d)}{v} - \frac{23q^5 - 3(q - w)^4(q + 4w)}{30q^5} \cdot \frac{us}{v^2} + \left(2 + \frac{(q - w)^4}{2q^4}\right) w$$

$$= \frac{E(d)}{v} + \frac{23q^5 - 3(q - w)^5}{30q^5} q + 2w, \qquad w \leq q$$

and

$$E(t) = \frac{E(d)}{v} + \frac{23}{30}q + 2w, \qquad w \geq q$$

It will be convenient to partition the total journey time $t$ in a new way: we shall combine the amount by which $t_r$, the time spent on buses, differs from $d/v$, with $t_p$, the walking time, to give a quantity which will be called the effective walking time, and denoted by $t_p'$. Thus

$$t_p' = t_p + (t_r - d/v)$$

so that

$$t = t_p + t_r + t_w$$
$$= d/v + t_p' + t_w$$

Thus

$$E(t_p') = E(t_p) + E(t_r) - d/v$$

$$= \begin{cases} \dfrac{23q^5 - 3(q - w)^4(q + 4w)}{30q^5} q, & w \leq q \\[4mm] \dfrac{23}{30} q, & w \geq q \end{cases}$$

In either case

$$E(t_p') = \frac{v^2 - u^2}{v^2 + u^2} E(t_p)$$

It would have been possible to obtain $E(t_p')$ directly from Fig. 4, without first obtaining $E(p)$ and $E(r)$.

## Cost of the Bus Service

Having determined the times taken on the journeys, we must now obtain the other component of the cost of transport, namely the cost of providing the buses.

Let $b$ = cost of bus service per bus per unit time

$j$ = number of journeys originating per unit area per unit time.

A square of unit area with sides parallel to the bus routes will contain on average $1/s$ sections of bus route of unit length in each of two perpendicular directions, so that the length of route per unit area is $2/s$. The flow of buses along a route is $1/i$ in each direction, and the concentration of buses (i.e., buses per unit distance) on any route is, therefore, $2/iv$. The number of buses per unit area, say, $m$ is therefore given by

$$m = \frac{2}{s} \cdot \frac{2}{iv} = \frac{4}{siv}$$

and the average cost of the bus service per journey is

$$\frac{4b}{jsiv}$$

Since the average journey time has been found in terms of the quantities $q$ and $w$ rather than $s$ and $i$, it is convenient to express the cost of the bus service also in terms of $q$ and $w$, using the relations

$$q = \frac{v^2 - u^2}{2uv^2}\, s, \qquad w = hi$$

Thus, the average cost of the bus service per journey is

$$\frac{4b}{jsiv} = \frac{2bh(v^2 - u^2)}{juv^3qw} = \frac{a}{qw}$$

where

$$a = \frac{2bh(v^2 - u^2)}{juv^3}$$

## Minimization of Total Transport Cost

The criterion for finding the optimum bus system is that the total cost of all journeys should be a minimum, and since the number of journeys is fixed this is equivalent to minimizing the average total cost per journey.

Let $k$ = value of unit time to a passenger

$c$ = average total cost of travel per journey

$c_p'$ = average cost per journey of effective walking time

$c_w$ = average cost per journey of waiting time

$c_b$ = average cost per journey of bus service

We shall see later that we need only consider the case in which $w \le q$. Therefore,

$$c_p' = kE(t_p')$$

$$= k\frac{23q^5 - 3(q - w)^4(q + 4w)}{30q^5}\, q$$

$$c_w = kE(t_w)$$

$$= kE(n)w$$

$$= k\left(2 + \frac{(q - w)^4}{2q^4}\right)w$$

$$c_b = \frac{a}{qw}$$

Now

$$c = kE(t) + c_b$$
$$= k\{E(d)/v + E(t_p') + E(t_w)\} + c_b$$
$$= kE(d)/v + c_p' + c_w + c_b$$

and $c$ may also be expressed in terms of $q$ and $w$:

$$c = kE(t) + c_b$$
$$= k\left\{\frac{E(d)}{v} + \frac{23}{30}q + 2w - \frac{q}{10}\left(1 - \frac{w}{q}\right)^5\right\} + \frac{a}{qw}$$

We wish to find the values of $s$ and $i$ which make $c$ a minimum. Since $q$ and $w$ are constant multiples of $s$ and $i$, respectively, we may equally well minimize $c$ with respect to $q$ and $w$. We therefore differentiate $c$ partially with respect to $q$ and $w$ and equate the results to zero, obtaining

$$\frac{\partial c}{\partial q} = k\left\{\frac{23}{30} - \frac{1}{10}\left(1 - \frac{w}{q}\right)^5 - \frac{w}{2q}\left(1 - \frac{w}{q}\right)^4\right\} - \frac{a}{q^2 w} = 0$$

$$\frac{a}{qw} = k\left\{\frac{23}{30}q - \frac{q + 4w}{10}\left(1 - \frac{w}{q}\right)^4\right\}$$

i.e.,

$$c_b = c_p'$$

and

$$\frac{\partial c}{\partial w} = k\left\{2 + \frac{1}{2}\left(1 - \frac{w}{q}\right)^4\right\} - \frac{a}{qw^2} = 0$$

$$\frac{a}{qw} = k\left\{2 + \frac{1}{2}\left(1 - \frac{w}{q}\right)^4\right\}w$$

i.e.,

$$c_b = c_w$$

Thus, $c$ is a minimum when

$$c_p' = c_w = c_b$$

that is, when the three variable elements of the cost per journey are all equal. It is not intuitively obvious why this should be so, and it would be interesting to know whether the same result holds for route patterns other than the square grid. It is worth noting that when the bus service is paid for out of the fares collected and does not make a profit, $c_b$ is the average fare paid per journey.

Since $c_p' = c_w$ we get an equation connecting $w$ and $q$, namely

$$\frac{23q^5 - 3(q - w)^4(q + 4w)}{30q^5}q = 2w + \frac{(q - w)^4}{2q^4}w$$

If we put $f = w/q$ this reduces to

$$3(1 - f)^4(1 + 9f) + 60f - 23 = 0$$

which may be solved numerically, giving

$$f = 0.34565$$

i.e.

$$w = 0.34565q \tag{10}$$

This provides the justification for confining the calculation of the optimum service to the case $w \leq q$; if we had made similar calculations for the case $w \geq q$ we should have found that $c$ is a minimum when

$$w = 23q/60$$

which is outside the range of $w$ considered. There is, therefore, only one minimum $c$, given by Eq. 10.

We can now find the average number of buses per journey in the optimum situation:

$$E(n) = 2 + \tfrac{1}{2}(1 - f)^4$$
$$= 2.0917$$

Since $c_w = c_b$, we have

$$2.0917wk = \frac{a}{qw}$$

and substituting for $w$ from Eq. 10 gives

$$q = 1.5876 \sqrt[3]{\frac{a}{k}}$$

whence

$$w = 0.5488 \sqrt[3]{\frac{a}{k}}$$

Substituting for $q$, $w$, and $a$, gives finally

$$s = 4.0005 \sqrt[3]{\frac{bhu^2v^3}{jk(v^2 - u^2)^2}}$$

$$i = 0.6914 \sqrt[3]{\frac{b(v^2 - u^2)}{jkh^2uv^3}}$$

These two equations determine the optimum bus service of the type considered. We can also find the optimum number of buses per unit area, $m$:

$$m = \frac{4}{siv}$$
$$= 1.4462 \sqrt[3]{\frac{j^2k^2h(v^2 - u^2)}{b^2uv^3}}$$

and

$$c_b = \frac{bm}{j}$$
$$= 1.4462 \sqrt[3]{\frac{bk^2h(v^2 - u^2)}{juv^3}}$$

It follows that

$$c = kE(d)/v + c_v' + c_w + c_b$$

$$= kE(d)/v + 3c_b$$

$$= \frac{kE(d)}{v} + 4.3386 \sqrt[3]{\frac{bk^2h(v^2 - u^2)}{juv^3}}$$

By inspecting the equations for the optimum values of $s$, $i$, $m$, and $c$, the following qualitative conclusions may be drawn:

a. If the cost of the bus service per bus per unit time, $b$, increases, the routes should be spaced further apart and the frequency of buses reduced; the number of buses will therefore be reduced, but the total cost will still increase.

b. If the value of passengers' time, $k$, increases, the routes should be spaced closer together and the frequency of buses increased; the number of buses and the total cost will increase.

c. If the buses can be made to run more regularly (i.e., $h$ reduced) the routes should be spaced closer together and the frequency of buses reduced; the net effect will be a reduction in the number of buses and the total cost.

d. If the density of journey origins, $j$, is higher in one area than another, the routes should be more closely spaced and the frequency of buses higher. More buses will, therefore, be needed, but the total cost per journey will be lower.

e. If the speed of walking, $u$, could be increased, the routes should be spaced further apart and the bus frequency increased. The net effect would be to reduce the number of buses and the total cost.

The effect of the bus speed, $v$, is not obvious by inspecting the formulae. Differentiating, however, we find that as $v$ increases, $s$ decreases, and that $i$, $m$, and $c_b$ ($= c_v' = c_w$) all have a maximum when $v = u\sqrt{3}$; $c$, however, will always decrease as $v$ increases, since $E(d)$ has been assumed to be large. In practice, we may safely assume that $v > u\sqrt{3}$; we may, therefore, add the conclusion:

f. If the speed of the buses increases, the routes should be spaced closer together and the bus frequency increased. Because of the increased speed, however, this can be done with a reduced number of buses and a lower total cost.

## A Simpler Model for Choice of Route

The determination of the optimum bus service has been based on the assumption that passengers choose the routes which minimize their expected total journey times. There is an alternative assumption which is rather less realistic but which leads to a very much simpler analysis, namely, that a passenger walks in a straight line from his origin $P_1$ to the nearest point on a bus route, $Q_1$, travels by bus from $Q_1$ to $Q_2$, the nearest point on a bus route to his destination, and walks in a straight line from $Q_2$ to his destination $P_2$. The average distance walked and the average number of buses used will then be independent of $u$, $v$, and $w$. Moreover, it can be seen that, with an assumption about the adequate separation of $P_1$ and $P_2$ similar to that previously made, $E(r)$ will be independent of $s$ and $i$.

Then

$$c = c_r + c_p + c_w + c_b$$

where

$$c_r = kE(r)/v, \qquad c_p = kE(p)/u$$

Now

$$c_r = \text{constant (independent of } s \text{ and } i)$$

$$\bar{c}_p \propto \frac{ks}{u}$$

$$c_w \propto khi$$

$$c_b \propto \frac{b}{jsiv}$$

so that

$$c_p c_w c_b \propto \frac{bk^2h}{juv}$$

$$= \text{constant (independent of } s \text{ and } i)$$

Thus the problem of minimizing $c$ becomes that of minimizing the sum of the three quantities $c_p$, $c_w$, $c_b$, whose product is constant. This is achieved when the three quantities are all equal, i.e., when

$$c_p = c_w = c_b \propto \sqrt[3]{\frac{bk^2h}{juv}}$$

It follows that the optimum values of $s$, $i$, and $m$, are given by

$$s \propto \frac{uc_p}{k} \propto \sqrt[3]{\frac{bhu^2}{jkv}}$$

$$i \propto \frac{c_w}{kh} \propto \sqrt[3]{\frac{b}{jkh^2uv}}$$

$$m \propto \frac{1}{siv} \propto \sqrt[3]{\frac{j^2k^2h}{b^2uv}}$$

These relations correspond to the equations obtained under the "quickest route" assumption when $v$ is large compared with $u$. The argument used in this section is valid for types of route pattern other than the square grid; the route-spacing $s$ would, however, have to be defined more generally as some linear measure of the separation between adjacent routes.

## Further Work

A number of subjects requiring further research have emerged during the course of the analysis. The effect of short journeys and journeys approximately parallel to bus-routes should be investigated. A more realistic assumption about waiting times when the service is infrequent should be introduced. A similar analysis should be made for route patterns other than the square grid, not having the same frequency of buses on all routes. It would be of particular interest to know whether the relation $c_p' = c_w = c_b$ still holds for the optimum bus service. Work should be done on the effect of the spacing of bus stops along the routes, the effect of various fare-structures, and the effect of variation of journey density in space and time. Finally, the type of model used here should be examined in relation to a real bus system, to see how far the assumptions made approximate to reality, and to what extent the relations which have been developed can usefully be applied in a real situation.

## Acknowledgements

I am grateful to Mr. H. R. Kirby for checking the results of this paper, which is published by permission of the Director of Road Research.

## References

1. R. L. Creighton, I. Hoch, M. Schneider, and H. Joseph, Estimating Efficient Spacing for Arterials and Expressways, *Bull. Highw. Res. Bd*, Wash. (253), 1–43 (1960).
2. M. J. Beckmann, Some Principles in the Optimum Location of Highway Networks, Palermo Conference on Operational Research in Economics, 1963. (Unpublished.)
3. G. G. Harding, Something Old, Something New, Chelmsford, Essex (Municipal Passenger Transport Association), 1965.
4. P. I. Welding, Time Series Analysis as Applied to Traffic Flow, *Proc. Second Intern. Symp. on the Theory of Road Traffic Flow*, J. Almond, Ed., O.E.C.D. Paris (1965).

## APPENDIX

### Summary of Notation

$a$ $\quad = 2bh(v^2 - u^2)/juv^3$

$b$ $\quad =$ cost of bus service per bus per unit time

$c$ $\quad =$ average total cost of travel per journey

$c_b$ $\quad =$ average cost per journey of bus service

$c_p$ $\quad =$ average cost per journey of walking time

$c_p'$ $\quad =$ average cost per journey of effective walking time

$c_r$ $\quad =$ average cost per journey of time on buses

$c_w$     = average cost per journey of waiting time
$d$     = rectangular distance from origin to destination
$f$     = $w/q$
$h$     = a constant depending on the irregularity of the buses, defined by $w = hi$
$i$     = service-interval (i.e., the average time-interval between successive buses on a route)
$j$     = number of journeys originating per unit area per unit time
$k$     = value of unit time
$m$     = number of buses per unit area
$n$     = number of buses used on a particular journey
$p$     = distance walked on a particular journey
$p_i$     = distance walked between $P_i$ and $Q_i$
$p_{ix}$     = distance $P_i Q_{ix}$ ($p_{iy}$ similarly)
$q$     = $(v^2 - u^2)s/2uv^2$
$r$     = distance traveled on buses on a particular journey
$r_i$     = distance by bus between $Q_i$ and $O_i$
$r_{ix}$     = distance along bus routes between $Q_{ix}$ and $O_i$ ($r_{iy}$ similarly)
$s$     = route-spacing (i.e., the distance between adjacent parallel bus routes)
$t$     = expected total time for a particular journey
$t_{ix}$     = min $(t_{ix-}, t_{ix+})$ ($t_{iy}$ similarly)
$t_{ix-}$     = time between $P_i$ and $O_i$ via $Q_{ix-}$, excluding waiting time ($t_{ix+}, t_{iy-}, t_{iy+}$ similarly)
$t_p$     = walking time on a particular journey
$t_p'$     = effective walking time on a particular journey ($= t_p + t_r - d/v$)
$t_r$     = time on buses on a particular journey
$t_w$     = expected waiting time on a particular journey
$t_{xx}$     = $t_{1x} + t_{2x} + 3w$
$t_{xy}$     = $t_{1x} + t_{2y} + 2w$
$t_{yx}$     = $t_{1y} + t_{2x} + 2w$
$t_{yy}$     = $t_{1y} + t_{2y} + 3w$
$u$     = walking speed
$v$     = bus speed (including stops)
$w$     = average waiting time for a bus
$x_i$     = $x$-coordinate of $P_i$ relative to $O_i$ ($y_i$ similarly)
$z_a$     = min $(z_1, z_2)$
$z_b$     = max $(z_1, z_2)$
$z_i$     = $t_{ix} - t_{iy}$
$A$     = region of cell containing $P_i$ in which $x_i < (v + u)s/2v$, $y_i < (v + u)s/2v$. ($B, C, D$, are other regions of cell: see Fig. 4)
$O_1$     = corner of cell containing $P_1$ which is nearest to $P_2$
$O_2$     = corner of cell containing $P_2$ which is nearest to $P_1$
$P_1$     = origin of a journey
$P_2$     = destination of a journey
$Q_1$     = point of getting on first bus of journey
$Q_2$     = point of getting off last bus of journey
$Q_{ix}$     = $\begin{cases} Q_{ix-}(t_{ix} = t_{ix-}) \\ Q_{ix+}(t_{ix} = t_{ix+}) \end{cases}$ ($Q_{iy}$ similarly)
$Q_{ix-}$ = point with coordinates $(O, y_i)$
$Q_{ix+}$ = point with coordinates $(s, y_i)$
$Q_{iy-}$ = point with coordinates $(x_i, O)$
$Q_{iy+}$ = point with coordinates $(x_i, s)$

# A Traffic Simulator with Minimum Hardware

## F. G. HEATH

Manchester University

Manchester, England

This abstract covers the design and application of a traffic simulator constructed and operated in Manchester, England, over the last 5 years. Simulation on general-purpose computers has been known for several years, and certainly has the merit of quick application on easily available equipment.

A major disadvantage of this approach for serious traffic analysis is that the central processor of a computer is most wastefully used in generating random numbers, and is not particularly efficient in the counting and gating functions of queueing and control. Consequently, general-purpose computer simulation is far slower and more expensive than it need be, so that a subject as important as traffic flow can justify the design of a special-purpose simulator. Also, a computer cannot be easily employed as a teaching device for traffic engineers unless it has a special output indicator which can be designed as an integral part of any simulator.

The Manchester machine has a time quantum of $\frac{1}{3}$ sec, with 50 × speedup, slow, and stop facilities. Queue-length maximum was set at 64 (this would have been better at, say 256), and the maximum mean delivery rate in a single lane 1300 veh/hr (minimum increment 50 veh/hr). Queueing is simulated by counters, street by shift registers, and intersection logic by normal computer circuits as described by previous workers.

The random generator design is the feature which gives the machine its power. Chain code (shifting counter sequences or linear sequential codes) are used to provide economical random digits. $n$ stages of such equipment can provide $2^n - 1$ digits with only local nonrandomness. By combining two such code generators through half-adding circuits, unlimited sets of random digits can be generated, a new set for each machine clock pulse. Coarse and fine coincidence circuits generate the exponential arrival signals. A modern design of generator using 1mc logic circuits can give six independent random outputs with a maximum speed of 500 × real time for £1200 works cost.

Work up to date has been concerned with statistical proving of the generator, simulating simple intersections and roundabouts (including correlation with published results), and checking against more exact software simulations. The simulator is now connected over a data link to a process-control computer, and control experiments are about to start. Another very attractive possibility is to multiprogram the simulator. In the same way that a very fast computer can keep many independent programs going, so a fast simulator can service many inter-sections held in a core store, trading time for hardware.

The simulator has already proved that it can derive useful results and perform a valuable educational service. More important, the fact that more students want to work with it than we can get funds to support, shows that simulation can be a powerful recruiting agent for getting electronic engineers into traffic work.

# On Optimal Tolls for Highways, Tunnels, and Bridges

MARTIN J. BECKMANN

Department of Economics, Brown University
Providence, Rhode Island
and
Universität Bonn, Bonn, West Germany

## Abstract

This paper analyzes aspects of economic efficiency in the utilization of roads with and without tolls. Tolls are economically optimal if they induce an efficient use of the available road capacity. The long-run goal of financing additional roads through maximal toll revenues is compared with this short-run objective. Revenue maximizing tolls are shown to be higher. An optimal allocation of traffic among parallel roads is achieved without toll by equalization of travel time if, and only if, the road capacity functions differ only by a scale factor. A toll on only one of several roads is less efficient and should be smaller than in the case where tolls are charged on several or all parallel facilities.

## I. Introduction

FROM THE POINT of view of economic theory the relationship between traffic volume and travel time on a facility—its capacity curve—may be looked upon as a supply function. The volume of traffic attracted to the facility under alternative conditions—the desired number of trips over this facility—may be viewed as a demand function. The actual volume of traffic is that for which supply equals demand—the number of cars desiring to travel at existing travel times (say) is such as to generate the prevailing travel times. It has been repeatedly pointed out by economists[1,2,3] that the resulting volumes and travel times are larger than is economically efficient in the following sense. Reducing traffic flow by one car (per hour) would lead to a saving in total travel times expended which is larger than the travel time of that car. Among all users of that facility consider the one whose desire is the least. If there are enough road users this "marginal" user will be on the point of indifference between using this facility or an alternative road facility or, possibly, an alternative means of transportation. If he could be induced to switch, he would not be (appreciably) worse off and the other road users are better off. In other words, the delay which a user causes to all, including himself, is larger than the delay he suffers.

Pursuing this argument of a discrepancy between "private" and "social cost" measured in terms of travel time, one is led to the idea of correcting in some way the allocation of traffic among alternative facilities or of travel demand among alternative means of transportation from what it is when road users are free to make their choices. An idea appealing (at least) to economists is to minimize compulsion through the imposition of charges or tolls on the use of congested facilities at such levels that the gap between private and social cost is closed. This requires the measurement of:

1. the incremental delay to all traffic caused by an additional unit volume of traffic, and
2. the economic value or money equivalent of one hour of delay. A principal solution has been offered[1] and an econometric analysis giving some estimates has been made.[4,10,11] (See also References 2, 3, 5–9.)

Now on a number of high traffic facilities tolls are actually charged, although for reasons and on a basis different from the one advanced above.[7] Toll charges are set to pay off the capital invested in the facilities, and after that to pay for the construction of additional facilities.

Now with a perfectly functioning capital market it should be possible to raise funds in that market for whatever construction of transport facilities is economically desirable, and it would not be necessary to depend for financing on revenues from existing facilities. When the capital market functions properly any facility that can pay for itself from tolls and yield a return on the investment at least equal to the return that capital can earn elsewhere will be constructed. The desirability of anything beyond that is debatable and would have to be left to the discretion of taxpayers.

However, it is well known that the capital market does not function as perfectly as that. In addition, public bodies operating such facilities are subject to restrictions on their borrowing and financing. The upshot of these restrictions is that public facilities cannot be expanded to the point where their rate of return is in line with that of capital elsewhere: rather, in quite a few cases it remains above that. This is presumably the case with all those road facilities which experience high levels of congestion. Given this fact it is certainly economically defensible to resort to toll revenues as a means of financing additional facilities—after exhausting all possible uses of the capital market.

The question now arises as to what the optimal toll level should be for this purpose and how this long-run objective of speeding up the construction of additional facilities is to be reconciled with the short-term goal of rationing the use of the facilities at an efficient level.

## 2. Maximizing Toll Revenue

The object of financing is best served when toll revenue is maximized. Does this imply maximization of traffic volume? Does it lead to a greater or smaller volume of traffic than when a toll charge is levied that reflects the short-run objectives of making social cost of road use equal to private cost to road users?

Let $v$ denote traffic volume

$$v = f(t, m) \tag{1}$$

where $f$ is the demand for use of a facility. This demand $f$ is a function of travel time $t$ and of money cost $m$.

Given the characteristics of a facility, travel time is in turn a function of traffic volume

$$t = g(v) \tag{2}$$

Next, money cost of transportation is the sum of toll charges $q$ and of operating cost $c$. Operating cost of vehicles depends in turn on travel time

$$m = q + c(t)$$

or in view of Eq. 2

$$m = q + c(g(v)) \tag{3}$$

Substituting Eqs. 2 and 3 into Eq. 1 we obtain an implicit equation

$$v = f\{g(v), q + c[g(v)]\} \tag{4}$$

determining the demand for traffic as a function of toll charges $q$. Let this function be written

$$v = \varphi(q) \tag{5}$$

We are now ready to determine the toll charge $q$ which will maximize toll revenue $qv$. The condition is that the derivative of

$$qv \equiv q\varphi(q)$$

with respect to $q$ be zero.

$$\varphi(q) + q\varphi'(q) = 0 \tag{6}$$

Using the rules for the differentiation of implicit functions we have

$$\varphi'(q) = \frac{dv}{dq} = -\frac{\partial f/\partial q}{(\partial f/\partial v) - 1}$$

$$= -\frac{f_m}{f_t g_v + f_m c_t g_v - 1}$$

Substituting in Eq. 6

$$f - \frac{qf_m}{f_t g_v + f_m c_t g_v - 1} = 0$$

or

$$-qf_m/f = 1 - (f_t + f_m c_t)g_v \tag{7}$$

The left-hand expression is called the "elasticity of demand with respect to money cost"—a positive number since $f$ is a decreasing function of money cost $m$.

The right-hand side of Eq. 7 is unity minus the demand that is lost due to traffic conditions when flow is increased by one unit. Toll revenues are, therefore, maximized when the elasticity of demand with respect to money cost, plus the responsiveness of demand to an additional unit of traffic, add up to one.

When road users behave rationally, they should respond to a delay by 1 hour in the same way as to a toll of $\mu$ dollars where $\mu$ is the money value of 1 hour.

$$f_t = \mu f_m \tag{8}$$

Substituting Eq. 8 into Eq. 7 we have

$$-qf_m/f + (\mu f_m + c_t f_m)g_v = 1 \tag{9}$$

Now in the range of speeds that occur in tunnels or roads with high traffic volumes, the effect of speed on the money cost of operating a vehicle is small and will be neglected here. Then Eq. 9 simplifies to

$$q = \mu g_v f - \frac{f}{f_m} \tag{10}$$

For a discussion of this expression we turn to a consideration of what an efficient toll would be.

### 3. Efficient Road Use

It has been shown that the efficiency of road use requires that each traffic unit should be charged the money value of the delay which it causes to others.[1] If $q^*$ denotes this efficiency toll we have

$$q^* = \mu g_v f$$

Comparing with Eq. 10 we see that

$$q = q^* - \frac{f}{f_m} > q^*, \qquad \text{since } f_m < 0. \tag{11}$$

To maximize toll revenue a higher toll should thus be charged than is efficient for short-run optimal utilization. Equation 11 can be rewritten

$$q = a^* \left(1 - \frac{f}{q^* f_m}\right) \tag{12}$$

Here the expression $-(f/q^*f_m)$ represents the reciprocal of the elasticity of demand with respect to toll charges. Suppose, for instance, that demand has unit elasticity: a 1% increase of toll per vehicle leads to a 1% decrease of traffic. Then, the revenue maximizing toll would be twice the efficient toll and would cut traffic down to 50% of that which could efficiently use the facility.

It is quite likely—although this can be settled only by a careful econometric analysis—that the demand for the use of the tunnels and bridges in New York is inelastic—i.e., less elastic than unity. In that case the profit maximizing toll should of course be more than twice the efficient toll.

On the basis of a linear capacity function Walters[10] has estimated what the efficient toll charges per mile should be at various speeds in the Lincoln tunnel. Multiplying by the length of the tunnel—1.42 miles—and assuming a unit elasticity of demand, the following are the tolls for the tunnel:

| Speed (mi/hr) | Efficient toll ($) | Revenue max toll ($) |
|---|---|---|
| 20 | 1.35 | 2.70 |
| 25 | 0.40 | 0.80 |
| 30 | 0.25 | 0.50 |
| 35 | 0.125 | 0.25 |

If 30 mi/hr is a representative speed, and if the demand elasticity is near unity, The Port of New York Authority may not be far off from maximizing its toll income from the Lincoln tunnel. At high traffic volumes, however, when speed is 20 mi/hr or even less the toll would be too low to even allow an efficient use of the tunnel.

## Parallel Facilities: One Toll Road, One Free Road

The considerations of Sec. 2 and 3 concerning optimal tolls apply to a toll road also in the case when there exist parallel toll-free facilities. It is instructive, however, to analyze this case in some detail, to compare the distribution of traffic that then results with the distribution in a system of several toll roads and to evaluate the efficiency of both systems.

Assume first that the total demand for road travel in the system under consideration is fixed so that we need be concerned only with the optimal distribution of traffic. (This assumption, which will be dropped later, is made to avoid complications arising in formulating the proper economic objective when demand is variable. But it has no bearing on questions of efficiency at a given level of demand.) The demand for use of the toll road depends on the toll rate and on travel times on both facilities. Let $v_1$ denote flow on the toll road, $v_2$ flow on the free road, and $v$ the constant total.

$$v_1 = f(t_1, t_2, m)$$
$$v_2 = v - v_1 \tag{13}$$

Each road has a capacity function relating travel time to volume

$$t_i = g_i(v_i) \tag{14}$$

When the physical characteristics are comparable except for a scale factor— or "capacity" $c_i$—this function has the more specific form

$$t_i = g\left(\frac{v_i}{c_i}\right) \tag{15}$$

In view of Eqs. 13 and 14 the flow conditions may be summarized as follows

$$v_1 = f[g_1(v_1), g_2(v - v_1), m] \tag{16}$$

Now the efficient toll on road 1 will not be the toll that makes an efficient use of the entire system (see below) while the revenue maximizing toll on one road maximizes toll revenue for the system by assumption. The efficient toll on one road will be considered first. We shall then investigate in Sec. 5 what the efficient tolls are for a system of two toll roads and how they relate to revenue maximization.

Total delay is the sum of the products of travel times and traffic volumes

$$T = t_1 v_1 + t_2 v_2$$

Now the one road toll optimal for the system is that which minimizes $T$ subject to Eq. 16.

$$\min_m [g_1(v_1)v_1 + g_2(v - v_1)(v - v_1)]$$

subject to $v_1 = f_1[g(v_1), g_2(v - v_1), m]$. Total differentiation with respect to $m$ yields

$$[g_1'v_1 + g_1 - g_2'(v - v_1) - g_2]\frac{dv_1}{dm} = 0 \tag{17}$$

where

$$\frac{dv_1}{dm} = -\frac{f_m}{f_1 g_1' - f_2 g_2' - 1} \tag{18}$$

Assuming, as is reasonable, that the response of demand $v_1$ to tolls $m$ is negative for all $m$, the condition of optimality reduces to

$$v_1 g_1'(v_1) + g_1(v_1) = v_2 g_2'(v_2) + g_2(v_2) \tag{19}$$

Whatever the level of total traffic, i.e., even when total demand is dependent on tolls and times, this condition for the optimal allocation of traffic is applicable[1]. Interesting enough the toll $m$ does not occur in Eq. 19 explicitly—it is merely an instrument for bringing about the relative volumes $v_1$, $v_2$.

Equation 19 shows that when the two roads are of equal capacity, i.e., characterized by the same capacity function $f$, traffic should be divided equally between them. The toll is then zero.

If—without loss of generality—road 1 has the smaller capacity then, by definition

$$g_2(v) < g_1(v)$$
$$g_2'(v) < g_1'(v), \quad \text{for all } v.$$

Hence Eq. 19 requires that $v_1 < v_2$ i.e., the higher capacity road should accommodate more traffic, which is reasonable. The same happens in the absence of tolls since then

$$g_1(v_1) = g_2(v_2)$$

But this is equivalent to Eq. 19 only when equality of $g_i$ implies equality of $v_i g_i'$.

*Lemma.* Let $g_1(v)$, $g_2(v)$ be two monotone differentiable functions with the property that

$$v_1 g_1'(v_1) = v_2 g_2'(v_2)$$

whenever

$$g_1(v_1) = g_2(v_2)$$

Then there exists a function $g$ and a positive constant $c$ such that

$$g_1 = g(v)$$
$$g_2 = g(cv)$$

*Proof:*

Consider the inverse functions $v_i(g_i)$. Then,

$$\frac{v_1}{\dfrac{dv_1}{dg}} = \frac{v_2}{\dfrac{dv_2}{dg}} \quad \text{for all } g \text{ means that}$$

$$(\log v_1)' = (\log v_2)' \quad \text{or}$$
$$\log v_1(g) = \log v_2(g) + \log c$$
$$v_1(g) = c v_2(g)$$

Taking inverses again we have

$$g_1(v) = g(v)$$

say,

$$g_2(v) = g(cv)$$

which is what we set out to prove.

The meaning of the lemma is this: the optimal allocation of traffic among two parallel roads is achieved without toll by the equalization of travel times if, and only if, the two roads are similar except for a scale factor, i.e., if their capacity functions are identical in terms of suitable multiples of flow.

Except for this special case (which includes that of equal roads) the optimal allocation depends on tolls. Writing Eq. 19 in the form

$$g_1(v_1)\left(1 + \frac{v_1}{g_1}g_1'\right) = g_2(v_2)\left(1 + \frac{v_2}{g_2}g_2'\right) \tag{20}$$

An interpretation of the second terms in the parentheses may be given as follows. Consider the reciprocals

$$\frac{g_i}{v_i} \cdot \frac{1}{g_i'} \equiv \left(\frac{dv_i}{v_i}\right)\left(\frac{dg_i}{g_i}\right)^{-1}$$

They denote the relative increases in volume made possible by a unit increase in relative travel time, i.e., the percentage increase in flow that can be accommodated when travel time increases by 1 %. By analogy to the economic concept of the elasticity of supply this may be called the elasticity of the capacity function, or more briefly the elasticity of a road.

Suppose now that road 1 is less elastic than road 2. Equation 20 shows that to minimize total travel time, the more elastic road, for which at equal travel times the parenthesis in Eq. 20 has a smaller value, must attract the greater volume of traffic and, hence, generate a longer travel time $g_2$. Thus, the more elastic road should be used proportionately more heavily than the less elastic one.

The optimal allocation, i.e., the attempt to minimize total travel times or maximize average speed requires, therefore, that speeds on the two roads be different, the higher speed occurring on the less elastic—and presumable technically inferior road. To sustain this speed gap, tolls would have to be charged, or an equivalent rationing device be found. The toll level is determined by substituting in Eq. 16 the flow allocated to road 1, and solving for $m$.

No consideration has been given to differences in preferences for fast movement by different classes of drivers. The case for differentiating speeds on parallel facilities would be strengthened if such preferences were introduced into the analysis, and the result would be that the more capacious road is allocated to higher speed traffic. A theory of optimal speed differentiation to accommodate different classes of road users is a subject of interest in its own right, but one which cannot be pursued within the limits of this paper.

As long as total demand is given independently, the allocation discussed here optimizes the use of the entire system under the stated assumptions. (Because of the rigidity of total demand, the toll level in a system of two toll roads would be determinate only up to an additive constant which can be chosen to make the toll zero on one facility.) When total demand depends on tolls and times, this is no longer possible by charging just one toll, as we proceed to show.

## 5. Two Toll Roads

To bring out the relationship between efficient use of a parallel system of roads (in the general case of nonfixed total demand) and of toll revenue, a broader problem than the previous one must be considered, viz., where tolls may be charged on both roads. The demand functions are

$$f_i(g_1(v_1), g_2(v_2), m_1, m_2) = v_i, \qquad i = 1, 2 \tag{21}$$

No assumption about the sum $v_1 + v_2$ is implied. Toll revenue is

$$m_1 v_1 + m_2 v_2 \tag{22}$$

Maximization of Eq. 22 subject to Eq. 21 as constraints leads to

$$v_1 + \lambda_1 f_{1m_1} + \lambda_2 f_{2m_2} = 0 \tag{23.1}$$

$$v_2 + \lambda_1 f_{1m_2} + \lambda_2 f_{2m_2} = 0 \tag{23.2}$$

$$m_1 + \lambda_1 f_{11} g_1' + \lambda_2 f_{21} g_1' = -\lambda_1 \tag{23.3}$$

$$m_2 + \lambda_1 f_{12} g_2' + \lambda_2 f_{22} g_2' = -\lambda_2 \tag{23.4}$$

where $\lambda_1$ and $\lambda_2$ denote Lagrangian multipliers associated with the two constraints of Eq. 21

$$f_{ij} = \frac{\partial f_i}{\partial t_j} \qquad \text{and} \qquad f_{im_j} = \frac{\partial f_i}{\partial m_j}$$

Let $\mu$ again denote the money value of 1 hour. Rational road users should be just as sensitive to an increased delay of 1 hour as to an increased toll of $\mu$ dollars. Hence,

$$\mu f_{im_j} = f_{ij}, \qquad i, j = 1, 2$$

Substituting into Eqs. 23.1 and 23.2 we have

$$\mu v_1 + \lambda_1 f_{11} + \lambda_2 f_{21} = 0 \tag{24.1}$$

$$\mu v_2 + \lambda_1 f_{12} + \lambda_2 f_{22} = 0 \tag{24.2}$$

Now if the two roads are not similar in the sense of Sec. 4, the determinant

$$\begin{vmatrix} f_{11} & f_{12} \\ f_{21} & f_{22} \end{vmatrix} \neq 0$$

Multiplying Eq. 24.1 by $g_1'$ and Eq. 24.2 by $g_2'$, and subtracting from Eqs. 23.3 and 23.4, respectively, we have

$$m_1 - \mu g_1' v_2 = -\lambda_1$$

$$m_2 - \mu g_2' v_2 = -\lambda_2$$

Observing that $f_i < 0$ and $f_{ij} > 0$, $i \neq j$, it is easily shown that $\lambda_i < 0$. It follows that the revenue maximizing tolls are higher again than the tolls which achieve an efficient short-run allocation of road capacities.

The generalization to $m$ parallel facilities is immediate. To summarize: in a system of toll roads, maximization of toll revenue leads to higher tolls than is compatible with an efficient short-run utilization of the system.

The effect of a free road on the toll level and on total traffic may be estimated as follows. At any given level of total traffic the availability of a toll-free alternative facility reduces the demand for the use of the toll road—in the terminology of economics, the demand is then more elastic. This reduces the monopoly power of the owner of the toll road and makes the profit maximizing toll smaller than otherwise. The net effect is a greater flow on both roads and, hence, a smaller discrepancy on the toll road between revenue maximization and efficient utilization, while the free facility will always be over utilized. Whatever the level of total traffic is that emerges, a toll may still be found that maximizes economic efficiency or, rather, minimizes the loss inflicted by the system. But the outcome is less efficient than in the case where tolls may be charged on all roads. Of course, efficient tolls will be zero according to Eq. 21 whenever flows are small enough to make vehicles move independently of each other. But that is not a likely occurrence in situations where several parallel facilities have been constructed.

Finally, we may touch briefly on the question of whether it is better to have short-run efficiency in the utilization of traffic facilities or a speeding up of the construction of additional facilities through greater toll revenues. In the last analysis this requires a weighting of present versus future benefits and, therefore, a value judgment on which economics as a science cannot pass. It may be presumed, however, that many road users take a longer view than the economists' short run and would, therefore, not be opposed on general principle to having additional facilities at an earlier date even if that means paying higher tolls in the present.

## References

1. M. J. Beckmann, C. B. McGuire, and C. B. Winsten, "Studies in the Economics of Transportation." New Haven, Yale University Press, 1956.
2. James M. Buchanan, The Pricing of Highway Services, *Nat. Tax J.*, 5, 97–102, (1952).
3. H. Hotelling, The General Welfare in Relation to Problems of Taxation and of Railway and Utility Rates, *Econometrica*, 242–69 (July, 1938).
4. M. B. Johnson, On the Economics of Road Congestion, *Econometrica*, 32, 137–150 (1964).
5. Ministry of Transport, Road Pricing, The Economic and Technical Possibilities (Smeed Report). London, 1964, Her Majesty's Stationery Office.
6. H. Mohring and M. Horwitz, "Highway Benefits: An Analytical Framework." Northwestern University, 1962.
7. James C. Nelson, The Pricing of Highway, Waterway and Airway Facilities, *AER*, LII, 426–435 (May, 1962).

8. J. C. Tanner, Pricing the Use of Roads: A Mathematical and Numerical Study. *Proc. Second Intern. Symp. on the Theory of Road Traffic Flow*, J. Almond, Ed., O.E.C.D., Paris (1965).

9. W. Vickrey, Statement, U.S. Congress, Transportation Plan for the National Capital Region, Hearings before the Joint Committee on Washington Metropolitan Problems, p. 454–458, 563–571.

10. A. A. Walters, The Theory and Measurement of Private and Social Cost of Highway Congestion, *Econometrica*, **29**, 676–699 (1961).

11. J. G. Wardrop, Some Theoretical Aspects of Road Traffic Research, *Proc. Inst. Civ. Engin.*, Part II, **1** (2), 325–362 (1952).

# A Behavioral-Specific Component to System Construct for Traffic Flows

*J. B. ELLIS*

Department of Electrical Engineering
University of Waterloo
Waterloo, Canada

*and*

*D. N. MILSTEIN*

Department of Resource Development
Michigan State University
East Lansing, Michigan

Methods of systems analysis recently developed for the study of all types of discrete physical systems have been generalized to permit their application to the problems of traffic distribution and assignment on a road network. This method yields a model with the following properties:

1. The road network is modeled in terms of its *structure*. That is, the flow formula for each link is not a simple repetitive or canonical form, as in the gravity model, for example, but is built up from canonical component models by a rigorous construct procedure which reflects the particular network interconnection pattern.
2. Each *component*, i.e., origin, link or destination, is first modeled individually on a *behavioral* basis *specific* to the particular component type and trip purpose.
3. The network *interconnection* pattern is expressed mathematically in matrix form and governs the construct of flow formulae from the component models.

The paper discusses and solves a small-scale hypothetical example for extra-urban recreational traffic flows. The method so demonstrated has been applied by the Michigan Outdoor Recreation Demand Study in the Department of Resource Development, Michigan State University. It is soon to be applied to a study of recreational and other purpose flows on the highways of the Province of Ontario.

The example consists of a system containing two origin areas and three destination areas connected by six highway links. The origin areas are modeled as known flow sources,

$$F_i = \text{known}, \quad i = 1, 2$$

The destination areas are modeled as

$$F_j = A_j P_j, \quad j = 1, 2, 3$$

where $A_j$ is the purpose-specific attraction index of destination $j$, determined from a factor analysis of its facilities, $P_j$ is the propensity or pressure to travel, as measured across destination component $j$.

The variable $P_j$ is not as yet capable of being measured directly. Its significance is as follows: for a given demand pressure at the "gate" of a destination area, flow varies with attraction; for a given attraction, flow varies with demand pressure.

The highway links are modeled as

$$F_k = \frac{1}{R_k} P_k, \quad k = 1, 2, 3, 4, 5, 6$$

where $R_k$ is the purpose-specific travel friction of link $k$, given by

$$R_k = (T_k + m C_k)^e$$

where $T_k$ is the estimated driving time for link $k$, in hours, $C_k$ is the estimated direct cost (tolls and gasoline) for link $k$, in dollars, and $m$, $e$ are constants.

The system flow equations are constructed rigorously from these canonical component models by use of the interconnection matrix in a manner shown in detail in the paper. The results give link flows for alternative routes without the necessity for constructing diversion curves. In fact, diversion curves may be easily estimated by this method.

The results of the Michigan model, predicting seasonal flows of campers only at 55 state parks (from 77 origins over 208 links) were most encouraging. The flows predicted by the systems model and by a gravity model using the same attraction indices and links were compared with actual 1964 flows. The root-mean-square error of prediction by the systems model was 33.7%, as compared to 42.3% by the gravity model. As a rough indication of random or non-systematic fluctuations in such flows, the root-mean-square percentage change in actual destination flows from 1963 to 1964 was 33.4%.

# The Importance of Traffic Problems in the Economic Comparison of Two Urban Planning Alternatives

R. LOUE, M. GAUTIER, C. SCHERRER and M. NAIM

Department of Urban Planning and Transportation
Society of Economics and Applied Mathematics
Paris, France

An urban planning project in the different stages of its preparation poses problems of choice: these decisions become all the more difficult as the variables which figure in the project become more numerous, diverse in character, and closely interconnected. A tool is required to make it possible to estimate the whole of the consequences of a decision or set of decisions.

After various different approaches, we have developed an economic model for comparing two urban plans. This is a global model that takes account of the different facilities and sectors of activity of the urban area. It is based on the very broad criterion of social welfare function, a function of individual satisfactions that characterizes the economic value to the community of the urban planning project in question.

In practice, it is the difference in social welfare, which alone can be calculated, that permits alternatives to be compared.

Our paper consists of two parts: The first is devoted to describing the theoretical methods used to produce a workable expression of the difference in social welfare; the latter appears as the sum of the variations in the overall cost (including a value for time of person trips. Thus, six contributions are relative to individual transportation. They are:

1. Increase in receipts of mass transportation enterprises arising solely from variation in traffic.
2. Decrease, with constant traffic, in expenditure on person transportation by private means.
3. Decrease, with constant traffic, in the value of the time spent by persons making trips.
4. Decrease in expenditure on street services resulting from a change in the urban plan.

5. Decrease in expenditure by mass transportation enterprises as a result of a change in the urban plan.
6. The variation in income, with constant prices, of the enterprise that supplies parking spaces.

In the second part we describe the application of these methods to the actual case of the urban area of Saint-Etienne (France). After defining the solutions to be compared (increase in the density of the center or creation of a small satellite town) we discuss the values obtained for the principal terms which make up the variation in social welfare (housing, water, gas, electricity, sanitation, traffic, and parking) and we show the importance of these terms relative to person transportation.

The computation of these terms requires complete traffic studies employing traffic generation and assignment models.

# A Rostering Problem in Transportation

BRIAN T. BENNETT and RENFREY B. POTTS

Mathematics Department
University of Adelaide
South Australia

## Abstract

A detailed investigation is made of the problem of rostering operating crews for a city transportation system. If straight and broken shifts are used to give flexibility in coping with the morning and afternoon peak periods, it is shown that the problem of constructing the broken shifts can be formulated as an assignment problem with inadmissible squares. The solution is obtained using a variant of the Hungarian method. The analysis is illustrated by the construction of an optimal broken shift roster for bus drivers.

## Introduction

IN THE PLANNING of an effective and economical transportation system, two important problems often arise—the *timetable problem* and the *roster problem*.* In the first of these problems, a timetable has to be constructed so that the demand on the transportation system is adequately met to the satisfaction of the users. It might involve the construction of a timetable for the running of buses or flights of aircraft or, in a slightly broader sense, a timetable for the opening of toll booths or manning of railway stations. In the roster problem, personnel have to be rostered to operate the system in accord with the timetable. Although the two problems are not independent, it is convenient and customary to treat them separately. It is the second of these problems—the roster problem—which is the main subject of this paper.

A simple example of rostering attendants at a railway station has been solved by Vajda[1] using linear programming techniques. The number of

---

* The authors do not expect general acceptance of this terminology at an International Symposium as they have found it impossible to unravel the different and confusing usages of such terms as schedule, roster, rota, assignment, tour, and shift.

attendants required—8 between 1200 and 1600 hours, 14 between 1600 and 2000 hours, etc., as listed in Table I— constitutes the timetable. The *roster rules* are simply that the attendants work 8-hour shifts, beginning at 1200, 1600 hours, etc. The roster has to be constructed using the minimum number of attendants. The solution to the problem is illustrated by the Gantt type

TABLE I.   Attendants Roster Problem

*Time of day*

| | 1200 | 1600 | 2000 | 2400 | 0400 | 0800 | 1200 |
|---|---|---|---|---|---|---|---|
| *a.* | 8 | 14 | 5 | 3 | 8 | 10 | |

| | | | | | | |
|---|---|---|---|---|---|---|
| | 12 | | | | | |
| | | 2 | | | | |
| *b.* | | | 3 | | | |
| | | | | 10 | | |

| | 1200 | 1600 | 2000 | 2400 | 0400 | 0800 |
|---|---|---|---|---|---|---|
| *c.* | 12 | 14 | 5 | 3 | 10 | 10 |
| *d.* | 4 | 0 | 0 | 0 | 2 | 0 |

*a.* attendants required
*b.* optimal roster
*c.* attendants available
*d.* excess attendants

chart in Table I; 12 attendants sign on at 1200 hours and sign off at 2000 hours, 2 sign on at 1600 hours and sign off at 2400 hours, etc. In all, 27 attendants are required, although 4 are rostered but not needed for duty between 1200 and 1600 hours, and 2 between 0400 and 0800 hours, representing idle or slack time.

A more complicated problem arising in the rostering of air crews has been investigated by Feis.[2] The timetable consists of flight numbers and arrival and departure times for KLM aircraft operating between Amsterdam and the Near East, with stops at various intermediate points. The roster problem is to determine the assignment of air crews to the aircraft so that the total crew rest time at stopovers, involving hotel costs, is minimized. The roster rules give the minimum rest period for a crew at any stopover point, the period depending on how long the crew has been on duty. For each stopover point a cost matrix can be constructed giving the minimum rest periods for the crews arriving and departing on different flights. Feis gives a method for finding the optimum roster, but the details of the analysis depend heavily on the particular problem.

The most extensive work on roster problems seems to have been carried out by The Port of New York Authority in the scheduling and manning of the toll booths of the various bridges and tunnels under its jurisdiction.[3-6] As explained by Edie in his classic paper,[3] the number of toll booths required to be open at any time can be determined so that the forecasted traffic can be adequately handled. The manning of the toll booths in accord with this timetable then has to be scheduled as efficiently as possible within the severe and complicated restrictions of the allowed working tours or shifts. Typical of the roster rules are the following, as listed by Kunreuther:[5]

1. Each toll collector works an 8-hour shift.
2. Toll collectors must receive two 50-minute relief breaks during their 8-hour shifts.
3. All men must work both the first and last hours of their shifts.
4. No collector can work more than three straight hours.
5. All men must work at least one hour between two relief breaks.
6. Relief breaks cannot be split up between two men.
7. No man can either start or finish his tour between 2.00 a.m. and 6.00 a.m.

It is not surprising that Kunreuther commented "Due to these restrictions, it appears difficult if not impossible to depict this problem mathematically via techniques such as linear programming." Kunreuther had to resort to a graphical method, which did not guarantee an optimal roster.

These examples give some indication of the scope of roster problems and their difficulty. Little progress has been made in attempts to solve exactly the large roster problems which occur in many fields of transportation. Great effort, in particular, has been applied to the rostering of personnel for public transport systems, and it is the purpose of this paper to show that one, admittedly small, aspect of the problem of rostering bus drivers and conductors for a city bus system can be solved exactly by linear programming methods.

## Rostering Bus Crews

The timetable and roster problems associated with the operation of a bus system serving a city are immense. The trial and error methods commonly used for constructing bus timetables and duty rosters are ingenious but very time-consuming and do not guarantee that the buses and crews are being employed economically.

In a typical case, such as the bus system operated by the Municipal Tramways Trust in Adelaide, a city with a population of about 700,000, the bus system is separated into bus routes and the timetable constructed from the headways required to serve each route. These headways are determined from a forecast of the number of people wishing to travel on each route. In off peak periods the headways may have to be chosen as the maximum allowable (say 20 minutes) for a satisfactory service even though the buses may be lightly loaded. The actual times at which buses run on each route have to be chosen to ensure satisfactory dovetailing of buses where routes overlap. From the timetables for each route a master timetable is prepared which lists when buses leave and return to depots and when they pass relief points where crews can be replaced. From this master timetable the crew rosters have to be constructed, due allowance being made, for example, for the time taken for a driver to sign on and take a bus out of a depot or for a driver or conductor to travel to a relief point on a bus route. The roster rules governing the shifts men can work and the wages (including penalty rates) they must be paid are determined by award conditions and union agreements. To find a set of valid shifts which is compatible with the master timetable and is a minimum cost to the operating company is the essence of the roster problem.

To give some idea of the magnitude of the problem for a bus system, the M.T.T. employs about 500 drivers and 400 conductors to operate about 350 buses. The construction of a completely new timetable and roster would take some months' work by several expert and experienced clerks.

## Broken Shifts

It is characteristic of a city transportation system that commuters traveling to and from work create a heavy demand on the system in the early morning and late afternoon. There are, accordingly, two peaks in the number of buses required throughout a day. To man the buses by crews working *straight shifts* of about 8 to 9 hour duration is very uneconomical and it is common, at least in Australia and Europe, for the conditions of employment to allow the rostering of *broken shifts*, made up of a *morning tour* and an *afternoon tour*. The broken shifts, together with the straight shifts, give greater flexibility in constructing the roster to match the morning and afternoon peak periods. The usual procedure is first to form straight shifts, then morning and afternoon tours, and finally to pair up these tours to form broken shifts.

The problem solved in this paper is that of determining the most economical pairing of morning and afternoon tours. It will be shown that the problem can be formulated as an assignment problem for which optimum solutions can be computed. The technique will be illustrated by a detailed analysis of a specific example of constructing the 34 broken shifts for the drivers based at

TABLE II.    Diagonal Roster for Overtime Problem

| | Morning tour | | | | Afternoon tour | | | Broken shift |
|---|---|---|---|---|---|---|---|---|
| i | Sign on | Sign off | Duration (min) | j | Sign on | Sign off | Duration (min) | Duty (min) |
| 1 | 0751 | 1245 | 294 | 1 | 1530 | 1836 | 186 | 480 |
| 2 | 0806 | 1257 | 291 | 2 | 1617 | 1947 | 210 | 501 |
| 3 | 0613 | 1047 | 274 | 3 | 1410 | 1740 | 210 | 484 |
| 4 | 0620 | 1042 | 262 | 4 | 1405 | 1758 | 233 | 495 |
| 5 | 0717 | 1122 | 245 | 5 | 1515 | 1909 | 234 | 479 |
| 6 | 0625 | 1027 | 242 | 6 | 1445 | 1847 | 242 | 484 |
| 7 | 0725 | 1127 | 242 | 7 | 1340 | 1743 | 243 | 485 |
| 8 | 0613 | 1012 | 239 | 8 | 1417 | 1832 | 255 | 494 |
| 9 | 0553 | 0952 | 239 | 9 | 1525 | 1941 | 256 | 495 |
| 10 | 0734 | 1132 | 238 | 10 | 1430 | 1848 | 258 | 496 |
| 11 | 0750 | 1147 | 237 | 11 | 1345 | 1803 | 258 | 495 |
| 12 | 0733 | 1127 | 234 | 12 | 1355 | 1814 | 259 | 493 |
| 13 | 0614 | 1003 | 229 | 13 | 1420 | 1840 | 260 | 489 |
| 14 | 0647 | 1032 | 225 | 14 | 1405 | 1830 | 265 | 490 |
| 15 | 0741 | 1118 | 217 | 15 | 1355 | 1823 | 268 | 485 |
| 16 | 0641 | 1018 | 217 | 16 | 1511 | 1941 | 270 | 487 |
| 17 | 0637 | 1013 | 216 | 17 | 1457 | 1927 | 270 | 486 |
| 18 | 0704 | 1032 | 208 | 18 | 1435 | 1906 | 271 | 479 |
| 19 | 0612 | 0933 | 201 | 19 | 1350 | 1824 | 274 | 475 |
| 20 | 0757 | 1117 | 200 | 20 | 1340 | 1815 | 275 | 475 |
| 21 | 0735 | 1047 | 192 | 21 | 1405 | 1840 | 275 | 467 |
| 22 | 0634 | 0945 | 191 | 22 | 1410 | 1856 | 286 | 477 |
| 23 | 0735 | 1041 | 186 | 23 | 1450 | 1942 | 292 | 478 |
| 24 | 0741 | 1042 | 181 | 24 | 1450 | 1946 | 296 | 477 |
| 25 | 0604 | 0903 | 179 | 25 | 1440 | 1937 | 297 | 476 |
| 26 | 0621 | 0917 | 176 | 26 | 1305 | 1803 | 298 | 474 |
| 27 | 0648 | 0942 | 174 | 27 | 1305 | 1811 | 306 | 480 |
| 28 | 0756 | 1047 | 171 | 28 | 1315 | 1831 | 316 | 487 |
| 29 | 0615 | 0903 | 168 | 29 | 1229 | 1747 | 318 | 486 |
| 30 | 0654 | 0941 | 167 | 30 | 1300 | 1822 | 322 | 489 |
| 31 | 0742 | 1027 | 165 | 31 | 1345 | 1912 | 327 | 492 |
| 32 | 0745 | 1027 | 162 | 32 | 1241 | 1809 | 328 | 490 |
| 33 | 0738 | 1012 | 154 | 33 | 1410 | 2006 | 356 | 510 |
| 34 | 0808 | 1007 | 119 | 34 | 1255 | 1859 | 364 | 483 |

one of Adelaide's bus depots. As these drivers must sign on and off for both tours at this depot, the problem of pairing the tours for this depot is separate from the problem at other depots.

The roster rules for a broken shift, consisting of a morning tour paired with an afternoon tour, include the following:

1. Sign on for a morning tour shall not be earlier than 5:50 a.m.
2. Sign off for an afternoon tour shall not be later than 8:15 p.m.

3. Morning or afternoon tours exceeding 5 hours duration shall include a paid break of at least 20 minutes.

4. The *break* between morning and afternoon tours shall be at least $1\frac{1}{2}$ hours.

5. The *duty* (equal to the total time worked, i.e., the sum of the durations of the morning and afternoon tours) shall not exceed 9 hours.

6. The *spread* (equal to the time interval between morning sign on and afternoon sign off) shall not exceed 12 hours.

Morning and afternoon tours satisfying rules 1, 2, 3 will be called *valid tours*, and for the 34 drivers these are listed in Table II. Broken shifts obtained by pairing valid tours in accord with rules 4, 5, 6 will be called *valid broken shifts*. Optimization consists in forming valid broken shifts by pairing valid tours so that the total penalty payments are minimized. The *penalty payment*, in addition to the minimum wage, consists of two parts:

*a. Overtime penalty.*

Time and a half for duty exceeding $8\frac{1}{4}$ hours

*b. Excess spread penalty.*

Half time for spread exceeding $9\frac{3}{4}$ hours;
additional half time for spread exceeding $10\frac{3}{4}$ hours.

## Mathematical Formulation

The purpose of this section is to formulate the problem of constructing the 34 broken shifts as an assignment problem.

*Notation*

Let $a_{1i}, a_{2i}$ = sign on, off times of the $i$th morning tour

$$i = 1, 2, \ldots, 34$$

$b_{1j}, b_{2j}$ = sign on, off times of the $j$th afternoon tour

$$j = 1, 2, \ldots, 34$$

$d_{ij}$ = *duty* corresponding to the $(i, j)$ broken shift
      = total time worked in the broken shift formed by pairing the $i$th morning tour with the $j$th afternoon tour

$s_{ij}$ = *spread* of the $(i, j)$ broken shift

Then, if $a_{1i}, a_{2i}, b_{1j}$, and $b_{2j}$ are regarded as expressed in minutes,

$$d_{ij} = a_{2i} - a_{1i} + b_{2j} - b_{1j} \tag{1}$$

$$s_{ij} = b_{2j} - a_{1i} \tag{2}$$

and the *break* in the $(i, j)$ broken shift is equal to $b_{1j} - a_{2i} = s_{ij} - d_{ij}$.

According to roster rules 4, 5, 6 listed above, a broken shift formed by pairing valid tours is valid provided that

$$s_{ij} - d_{ij} \geq 90, \quad d_{ij} \leq 540, \quad s_{ij} \leq 720 \tag{3}$$

The *overtime* corresponding to the $(i, j)$ broken shift) is equal to:

duty exceeding 495 minutes ($8\frac{1}{4}$ hours)

$$= \begin{cases} 0 & \text{if} \quad d_{ij} \leq 495 \\ d_{ij} - 495 & \text{if} \quad d_{ij} \geq 495 \end{cases}$$

$$= \tfrac{1}{2} |d_{ij} - 495| + \tfrac{1}{2}(d_{ij} - 495) \tag{4}$$

The *excess spread* corresponding to the $(i, j)$ broken shift is equal to:

spread exceeding 585 minutes ($9\frac{3}{4}$ hours) $= \tfrac{1}{2} |s_{ij} - 585| + \tfrac{1}{2}(s_{ij} - 585)$. (5)

If $60r$ is the hourly wage rate the *penalty payment* for the $(i, j)$ broken shift is given by

$$p_{ij} = \tfrac{3}{2}r \times \text{overtime}$$
$$+ \tfrac{1}{2}r \times \text{spread exceeding } 9\tfrac{3}{4} \text{ hours}$$
$$+ \tfrac{1}{2}r \times \text{spread exceeding } 10\tfrac{3}{4} \text{ hours}$$

$$= \frac{r}{2} c_{ij}$$

where

$$c_{ij} = 3\{\tfrac{1}{2} |d_{ij} - 495| + \tfrac{1}{2}(d_{ij} - 495)\}$$
$$+ \{\tfrac{1}{2} |s_{ij} - 585| + \tfrac{1}{2}(s_{ij} - 585)\}$$
$$+ \{\tfrac{1}{2} |s_{ij} - 645| + \tfrac{1}{2}(s_{ij} - 645)\} \tag{6}$$

The values of $c_{ij}$, proportional to $p_{ij}$, will be referred to as the *cost* of the broken shift $(i, j)$ and this cost as a function of duty and spread is represented graphically in Fig. 1.

## Formulation as an assignment problem

A 1-1 pairing of the morning and afternoon tours can be represented by a *permutation P*; morning tour $i$ is paired with afternoon tour $P_i$, $i = 1, 2, \ldots,$ 34. Alternatively, the pairing can be represented by a $34 \times 34$ *permutation matrix* $X = [x_{ij}]$, i.e., a matrix $[x_{ij}]$ with

$$x_{ij} = 0, 1, \quad i, j = 1, 2, \ldots, 34 \tag{7}$$

$$\sum_{i=1}^{34} x_{ij} = \sum_{j=1}^{34} x_{ij} = 1, \quad i, j = 1, 2, \ldots, 34 \tag{8}$$

by interpreting $x_{ij}$ as

$$x_{ij} = \begin{cases} 1 & \text{if morning tour } i \text{ is paired with} \\ & \text{afternoon tour } j \\ 0 & \text{otherwise} \end{cases} \tag{9}$$

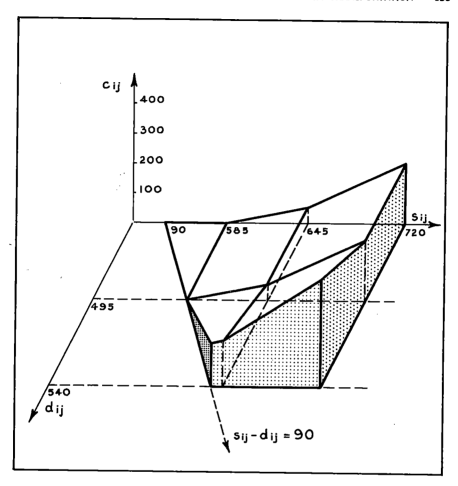

FIGURE 1.   The cost $c_{ij}$ of a broken shift $(i, j)$ as a function of the duty $d_{ij}$ and the spread $s_{ij}$. The cost, duty, and spread are measured in minutes (the diagram is not drawn to scale). Valid broken shifts correspond to the feasible region, defined by Eq. 3, which is subdivided into five fundamental regions, a typical one of which corresponds to the fundamental set defined by Eq. 54.

For $X$ to represent a set of valid broken shifts the inequalities of Eq. 3 have to be satisfied so that $X$ has to be a permutation matrix satisfying Eqs. 7, 8 and, in addition,

$$x_{ij} = 0, \qquad x_{ij} \notin V \tag{10}$$

where

$$V = \{x_{ij} \mid s_{ij} - d_{ij} \geq 90, d_{ij} \leq 540, s_{ij} \leq 720\} \tag{11}$$

The problem of forming valid broken shifts by pairing valid tours so that the total cost is minimized may now be formulated as the following *assignment problem with inadmissible squares*[7]:

find the permutation matrix      $X = [x_{ij}]$

which minimizes

$$\sum_{i,j=1}^{34} c_{ij}x_{ij} \tag{12}$$

$$\text{subject to } x_{ij} = 0, \qquad x_{ij} \notin V \tag{13}$$

where for the *cost matrix* $C = [c_{ij}]$, $c_{ij}$ is given by Eq. 6 and the *admissible set* $V$ is the set defined by Eq. 11.

With the usual terminology, a *feasible solution* of this assignment problem is a permutation matrix $X$ satisfying Eq. 13 and an *optimal solution* is a feasible solution which minimizes $\Sigma \, c_{ij}x_{ij}$. The corresponding broken shift rosters will also be called feasible and optimal.

The special structure of this assignment problem can be best illustrated by first considering the simpler *overtime problem* when only the duty is accounted for, break and spread conditions being ignored. A similar problem is obtained when only the spread is considered, and from these simpler problems the extension to the full broken shift problem can be easily made.

## Overtime Problem

### Intuitive Approach

If the excess spread penalties are ignored, the penalty payment is proportional to the overtime, and optimization consists in minimizing the *total overtime*. It is intuitively clear how this should be done—the longest morning tour should be paired with the shortest afternoon tour, the next to longest with the next to shortest, and so on. This *diagonal roster* (the significance of the name will be seen later) is easily obtained by listing the morning tours in order of decreasing duration and the afternoon tours in order of increasing duration. This is the ordering that has been used in Table II and the diagonal roster is obtained by pairing the first two tours, the next two, and so on. Other optimal rosters can be obtained from the diagonal one by exchanging afternoon tours between pairs of drivers in such a way that before and after the exchange *both* drivers (or *neither* driver) work overtime. Such an exchange will not alter the total overtime.

To give a rigorous justification of these intuitive results it is convenient to introduce the concept of undertime.

### Overtime and Undertime

The formulation of the overtime problem as an assignment problem is: find a permutation matrix

$$X = [x_{ij}]$$

which minimizes

$$\sum_{i,j=1}^{34} c_{ij} x_{ij} \qquad (14)$$

subject to

$$x_{ij} = 0 \quad \text{if} \quad x_{ij} \notin U \qquad (15)$$

where

$$c_{ij} = \tfrac{1}{2}|d_{ij} - 495| + \tfrac{1}{2}(d_{ij} - 495) \qquad (16)$$

and

$$U = \{x_{ij} \mid d_{ij} \leq 540\} \qquad (17)$$

The elements $c_{ij}$ of the cost matrix $C = [c_{ij}]$ represent the overtime involved in the $(i,j)$ broken shift. This cost matrix will be called the *overtime matrix* and, for the morning and afternoon tours ordered as in Table II, the matrix has the simple structure illustrated in Table III. The region above the heavy line contains the inadmissible squares for which $c_{ij} > 45$, implying that $d_{ij} > 540$. The inadmissible squares, and also the zeros, are grouped together because the special ordering of the rows and columns of the matrix means that

$$c_{ij} \geq c_{i+1j} \quad \text{and} \quad c_{ij} \leq c_{ij+1} \qquad (18)$$

which is easily verified from Table III. The derivation of this inequality follows from the inequalities

$$a_{2i} - a_{1i} \geq a_{2i+1} - a_{1i+1}, \qquad i = 1, 2, \ldots, 33 \qquad (19)$$

and

$$b_{2j} - b_{1j} \leq b_{2j+1} - b_{1j+1}, \qquad j = 1, 2, \ldots, 33 \qquad (20)$$

which are a consequence of the listing of the morning and afternoon tours in order of decreasing and increasing duration, respectively. The inequalities of Eqs. 19 and 20, together with Eq. 1, imply that

$$d_{ij} \geq d_{i+1j} \quad \text{and} \quad d_{ij} \leq d_{ij+1} \qquad (21)$$

from which the required inequality of Eq. 18 immediately follows.

The zeros in the overtime matrix correspond to a region of *undertime* which, for the $(i,j)$ shift, is defined by

$$c_{ij}' = \begin{cases} 495 - d_{ij} & \text{if} \quad d_{ij} \leq 495 \\ 0 & \text{if} \quad d_{ij} \geq 495 \end{cases}$$

$$= \tfrac{1}{2}|d_{ij} - 495| - \tfrac{1}{2}(d_{ij} - 495) \qquad (22)$$

Comparison with Eq. 4 for the overtime $c_{ij}$ shows that

$$c_{ij}' = c_{ij} - d_{ij} + 495$$

or

$$c_{ij}' = c_{ij} + a_{1i} - a_{2i} + b_{1j} - b_{2j} + 495 \qquad (23)$$

from Eq. 1. The transformation from $c_{ij}$ to $c_{ij'}$ is thus of the form

$$c_{ij}' = c_{ij} + \alpha_i - \beta_j + \gamma \qquad (24)$$

TABLE III.    Cost Matrix

| | | | | | | | | | | | | | | | | | |
|---|---|---|---|---|---|---|---|---|---|---|---|---|---|---|---|---|---|
| 0 | 9 | 9 | 32 | 33 | 41 | 42 | 54 | 55 | 57 | 57 | 58 | 59 | 64 | 67 | 69 | 69 | |
| 0 | 6 | 6 | 29 | 30 | 38 | 39 | 51 | 52 | 54 | 54 | 55 | 56 | 61 | 64 | 66 | 66 | |
| 0 | 0 | 0 | 12 | 13 | 21 | 22 | 34 | 35 | 37 | 37 | 38 | 39 | 44 | 47 | 49 | 49 | |
| 0 | 0 | 0 | 0 | 1 | 9 | 10 | 22 | 23 | 25 | 25 | 26 | 27 | 32 | 35 | 37 | 37 | |
| 0 | 0 | 0 | 0 | 0 | 0 | 0 | 5 | 6 | 8 | 8 | 9 | 10 | 15 | 18 | 20 | 20 | |
| 0 | 0 | 0 | 0 | 0 | 0 | 0 | 2 | 3 | 5 | 5 | 6 | 7 | 12 | 15 | 17 | 17 | |
| 0 | 0 | 0 | 0 | 0 | 0 | 0 | 2 | 3 | 5 | 5 | 6 | 7 | 12 | 15 | 17 | 17 | |
| 0 | 0 | 0 | 0 | 0 | 0 | 0 | 0 | 0 | 2 | 2 | 3 | 4 | 9 | 12 | 14 | 14 | |
| 0 | 0 | 0 | 0 | 0 | 0 | 0 | 0 | 0 | 2 | 2 | 3 | 4 | 9 | 12 | 14 | 14 | |
| 0 | 0 | 0 | 0 | 0 | 0 | 0 | 0 | 0 | 1 | 1 | 2 | 3 | 8 | 11 | 13 | 13 | |
| 0 | 0 | 0 | 0 | 0 | 0 | 0 | 0 | 0 | 0 | 0 | 1 | 2 | 7 | 10 | 12 | 12 | |
| 0 | 0 | 0 | 0 | 0 | 0 | 0 | 0 | 0 | 0 | 0 | 0 | 0 | 4 | 7 | 9 | 9 | |
| 0 | 0 | 0 | 0 | 0 | 0 | 0 | 0 | 0 | 0 | 0 | 0 | 0 | 0 | 2 | 4 | 4 | |
| 0 | 0 | 0 | 0 | 0 | 0 | 0 | 0 | 0 | 0 | 0 | 0 | 0 | 0 | 0 | 0 | 0 | |
| 0 | 0 | 0 | 0 | 0 | 0 | 0 | 0 | 0 | 0 | 0 | 0 | 0 | 0 | 0 | 0 | 0 | |
| 0 | 0 | 0 | 0 | 0 | 0 | 0 | 0 | 0 | 0 | 0 | 0 | 0 | 0 | 0 | 0 | 0 | |
| 0 | 0 | 0 | 0 | 0 | 0 | 0 | 0 | 0 | 0 | 0 | 0 | 0 | 0 | 0 | 0 | 0 | |
| 0 | 0 | 0 | 0 | 0 | 0 | 0 | 0 | 0 | 0 | 0 | 0 | 0 | 0 | 0 | 0 | 0 | |
| 0 | 0 | 0 | 0 | 0 | 0 | 0 | 0 | 0 | 0 | 0 | 0 | 0 | 0 | 0 | 0 | 0 | |
| 0 | 0 | 0 | 0 | 0 | 0 | 0 | 0 | 0 | 0 | 0 | 0 | 0 | 0 | 0 | 0 | 0 | |
| 0 | 0 | 0 | 0 | 0 | 0 | 0 | 0 | 0 | 0 | 0 | 0 | 0 | 0 | 0 | 0 | 0 | |
| 0 | 0 | 0 | 0 | 0 | 0 | 0 | 0 | 0 | 0 | 0 | 0 | 0 | 0 | 0 | 0 | 0 | |
| 0 | 0 | 0 | 0 | 0 | 0 | 0 | 0 | 0 | 0 | 0 | 0 | 0 | 0 | 0 | 0 | 0 | |
| 0 | 0 | 0 | 0 | 0 | 0 | 0 | 0 | 0 | 0 | 0 | 0 | 0 | 0 | 0 | 0 | 0 | |
| 0 | 0 | 0 | 0 | 0 | 0 | 0 | 0 | 0 | 0 | 0 | 0 | 0 | 0 | 0 | 0 | 0 | |
| 0 | 0 | 0 | 0 | 0 | 0 | 0 | 0 | 0 | 0 | 0 | 0 | 0 | 0 | 0 | 0 | 0 | |
| 0 | 0 | 0 | 0 | 0 | 0 | 0 | 0 | 0 | 0 | 0 | 0 | 0 | 0 | 0 | 0 | 0 | |
| 0 | 0 | 0 | 0 | 0 | 0 | 0 | 0 | 0 | 0 | 0 | 0 | 0 | 0 | 0 | 0 | 0 | |
| 0 | 0 | 0 | 0 | 0 | 0 | 0 | 0 | 0 | 0 | 0 | 0 | 0 | 0 | 0 | 0 | 0 | |
| 0 | 0 | 0 | 0 | 0 | 0 | 0 | 0 | 0 | 0 | 0 | 0 | 0 | 0 | 0 | 0 | 0 | |
| 0 | 0 | 0 | 0 | 0 | 0 | 0 | 0 | 0 | 0 | 0 | 0 | 0 | 0 | 0 | 0 | 0 | |
| 0 | 0 | 0 | 0 | 0 | 0 | 0 | 0 | 0 | 0 | 0 | 0 | 0 | 0 | 0 | 0 | 0 | |
| 0 | 0 | 0 | 0 | 0 | 0 | 0 | 0 | 0 | 0 | 0 | 0 | 0 | 0 | 0 | 0 | 0 | |

## for Overtime Problem

| 70 | 73 | 74 | 74 | 85 | 91 | 95 | 96 | 97 | 105 | 115 | 117 | 121 | 126 | 127 | 155 | 163 |
|---|---|---|---|---|---|---|---|---|---|---|---|---|---|---|---|---|
| 67 | 70 | 71 | 71 | 82 | 88 | 92 | 93 | 94 | 102 | 112 | 114 | 118 | 123 | 124 | 152 | 160 |
| 50 | 53 | 54 | 54 | 65 | 71 | 75 | 76 | 77 | 85 | 95 | 97 | 101 | 106 | 107 | 135 | 143 |
| 38 | 41 | 42 | 42 | 53 | 59 | 63 | 64 | 65 | 73 | 83 | 85 | 89 | 94 | 95 | 123 | 131 |
| 21 | 24 | 25 | 25 | 36 | 42 | 46 | 47 | 48 | 56 | 66 | 68 | 72 | 77 | 78 | 106 | 114 |
| 18 | 21 | 22 | 22 | 33 | 39 | 43 | 44 | 45 | 53 | 63 | 65 | 69 | 74 | 75 | 103 | 111 |
| 18 | 21 | 22 | 22 | 33 | 39 | 43 | 44 | 45 | 53 | 63 | 65 | 69 | 74 | 75 | 103 | 111 |
| 15 | 18 | 19 | 19 | 30 | 36 | 40 | 41 | 42 | 50 | 60 | 62 | 66 | 71 | 72 | 100 | 108 |
| 15 | 18 | 19 | 19 | 30 | 36 | 40 | 41 | 42 | 50 | 60 | 62 | 66 | 71 | 72 | 100 | 108 |
| 14 | 17 | 18 | 18 | 29 | 35 | 39 | 40 | 41 | 49 | 59 | 61 | 65 | 70 | 71 | 99 | 107 |
| 13 | 16 | 17 | 17 | 28 | 34 | 38 | 39 | 40 | 48 | 58 | 60 | 64 | 69 | 70 | 98 | 106 |
| 10 | 13 | 14 | 14 | 25 | 31 | 35 | 36 | 37 | 45 | 55 | 57 | 61 | 66 | 67 | 95 | 103 |
| 5 | 8 | 9 | 9 | 20 | 26 | 30 | 31 | 32 | 40 | 50 | 52 | 56 | 61 | 62 | 90 | 98 |
| 1 | 4 | 5 | 5 | 16 | 22 | 26 | 27 | 28 | 36 | 46 | 48 | 52 | 57 | 58 | 86 | 94 |
| 0 | 0 | 0 | 0 | 8 | 14 | 18 | 19 | 20 | 28 | 38 | 40 | 44 | 49 | 50 | 78 | 86 |
| 0 | 0 | 0 | 0 | 8 | 14 | 18 | 19 | 20 | 28 | 38 | 40 | 44 | 49 | 50 | 78 | 86 |
| 0 | 0 | 0 | 0 | 7 | 13 | 17 | 18 | 19 | 27 | 37 | 39 | 43 | 48 | 49 | 77 | 85 |
| 0 | 0 | 0 | 0 | 0 | 5 | 9 | 10 | 11 | 19 | 29 | 31 | 35 | 40 | 41 | 69 | 77 |
| 0 | 0 | 0 | 0 | 0 | 0 | 2 | 3 | 4 | 12 | 22 | 24 | 28 | 33 | 34 | 62 | 70 |
| 0 | 0 | 0 | 0 | 0 | 0 | 1 | 2 | 3 | 11 | 21 | 23 | 27 | 32 | 33 | 61 | 69 |
| 0 | 0 | 0 | 0 | 0 | 0 | 0 | 0 | 0 | 3 | 13 | 15 | 19 | 24 | 25 | 53 | 61 |
| 0 | 0 | 0 | 0 | 0 | 0 | 0 | 0 | 0 | 2 | 12 | 14 | 18 | 23 | 24 | 52 | 60 |
| 0 | 0 | 0 | 0 | 0 | 0 | 0 | 0 | 0 | 0 | 7 | 9 | 13 | 18 | 19 | 47 | 55 |
| 0 | 0 | 0 | 0 | 0 | 0 | 0 | 0 | 0 | 0 | 2 | 4 | 8 | 13 | 14 | 42 | 50 |
| 0 | 0 | 0 | 0 | 0 | 0 | 0 | 0 | 0 | 0 | 0 | 2 | 6 | 11 | 12 | 40 | 48 |
| 0 | 0 | 0 | 0 | 0 | 0 | 0 | 0 | 0 | 0 | 0 | 0 | 3 | 8 | 9 | 37 | 45 |
| 0 | 0 | 0 | 0 | 0 | 0 | 0 | 0 | 0 | 0 | 0 | 0 | 1 | 6 | 7 | 35 | 43 |
| 0 | 0 | 0 | 0 | 0 | 0 | 0 | 0 | 0 | 0 | 0 | 0 | 0 | 3 | 4 | 32 | 40 |
| 0 | 0 | 0 | 0 | 0 | 0 | 0 | 0 | 0 | 0 | 0 | 0 | 0 | 0 | 1 | 29 | 37 |
| 0 | 0 | 0 | 0 | 0 | 0 | 0 | 0 | 0 | 0 | 0 | 0 | 0 | 0 | 0 | 28 | 36 |
| 0 | 0 | 0 | 0 | 0 | 0 | 0 | 0 | 0 | 0 | 0 | 0 | 0 | 0 | 0 | 26 | 34 |
| 0 | 0 | 0 | 0 | 0 | 0 | 0 | 0 | 0 | 0 | 0 | 0 | 0 | 0 | 0 | 23 | 31 |
| 0 | 0 | 0 | 0 | 0 | 0 | 0 | 0 | 0 | 0 | 0 | 0 | 0 | 0 | 0 | 15 | 23 |
| 0 | 0 | 0 | 0 | 0 | 0 | 0 | 0 | 0 | 0 | 0 | 0 | 0 | 0 | 0 | 0 | 0 |

and such a transformation does not alter the optimal solutions of the assignment problem. For if $X = [x_{ij}]$ is a permutation matrix,

$$\sum_{i,j} c_{ij}' x_{ij} = \sum_{i,j} c_{ij} x_{ij} + \sum_{i,j} (\alpha_i x_{ij} - \beta_j x_{ij} + \gamma x_{ij})$$

$$= \sum_{i,j} c_{ij} x_{ij} + \sum_i \alpha_i - \sum_j \beta_j + \sum_i \gamma$$

i.e.,

$$\sum_{i,j} c_{ij}' x_{ij} = \sum_{i,j} c_{ij} x_{ij} + \text{constant}$$

For the transformation Eq. 23 this gives

$$\text{total undertime} = \text{total overtime} + \text{constant} \tag{25}$$

The problem of minimizing the total overtime is therefore equivalent to the problem of minimizing the total undertime. A roster for which no drivers work overtime (total overtime a minimum) is obviously optimal and the equivalence of the overtime and undertime problems proves what is not so obvious—that a roster for which all drivers work overtime (total undertime a minimum) is optimal.

More precisely, suppose that the undertime, overtime, and feasible regions are defined by the two *fundamental sets*

$$S = \{x_{ij} \mid d_{ij} \leq 495\} \tag{26}$$

$$T = \{x_{ij} \mid 495 \leq d_{ij} \leq 540\} \tag{27}$$

and the admissible set

$$U = S \cup T \tag{28}$$

Then $c_{ij} = 0$ if $x_{ij} \in S$ and $c_{ij}' = 0$ if $x_{ij} \in T$. If $X$ is a permutation matrix such that all $x_{ij} = 1$ are in $S$ or all $x_{ij} = 1$ are in $T$, then $X$ is an optimal solution.

## Exchange of Afternoon tours

Suppose that the driver working the broken shift $(p, q)$ exchanges afternoon tours with the driver working the broken shift $(r, s)$. If before and after the exchange neither driver works overtime, i.e., $x_{pq}, x_{rs}, x_{ps}, x_{rq} \in S$, the total overtime is unchanged. If before and after the exchange both drivers work overtime, i.e., $x_{pq}, x_{rs}, x_{ps}, x_{rq} \in T$, then the corresponding undertimes are all zero and again the total overtime is unchanged. Exchange of afternoon tours with either of these properties will therefore generate optimal solutions from a given optimal solution.

## Diagonal Solution

The diagonal solution is the solution corresponding to the diagonal roster. For the tours ordered as in Table II, this solution is the matrix with all elements on the principal diagonal equal to one, and all off-diagonal elements zero, i.e., the unit matrix $X = I$ with

$$x_{ij} = \begin{cases} 1, & i = j \\ 0, & i \neq j \end{cases} \tag{29}$$

The duties $d_{ii}$ for the broken shifts $(i, i)$ of the diagonal roster are listed in Table II and it can be easily verified that:

    1. the diagonal solution is feasible $(d_{ii} \leq 540)$.
    2. some broken shifts involve overtime $(d_{ii} \geq 495)$ and others undertime $(d_{ii} \leq 495)$.

The most useful properties of the diagonal solution are embodied in the following results:

*Lemma:* Any roster, feasible or not feasible, includes a broken shift with duty greater (less) than or equal to the maximum (minimum) duty of broken shifts in the diagonal roster.

*Theorem I:*
    If the diagonal solution is not feasible, there are no feasible solutions.
*Theorem II:*
    If the diagonal solution is feasible, it is an optimal solution.

In the present example, the lemma means that for any roster there must be a broken shift with a duty $\geq 510$ minutes and a broken shift with a duty $\leq 467$ minutes. From Theorem II it can be inferred that the diagonal roster is optimal.

*Proof of Lemma*

It has to be shown that for any permutation matrix $X$

$$\max_{x_{ij}=1} d_{ij} \geq \max_k d_{kk} \tag{30}$$

$$\min_{x_{ij}=1} d_{ij} \leq \min_k d_{kk}. \tag{31}$$

For any permutation matrix $X$,

$$\sum_{i=1}^{k} \sum_{j=k}^{34} x_{ij} \geq 1, \qquad k = 1, 2, \ldots, 34 \tag{32}$$

This is obvious for $k = 1$, and for $k = 2, \ldots, 34$ it follows by subtracting

$$\sum_{i=1}^{k} \sum_{j=1}^{k-1} x_{ij} = \sum_{j=1}^{k-1} \sum_{i=1}^{k} x_{ij} \leq k - 1 \tag{33}$$

from

$$\sum_{i=1}^{k} \sum_{j=1}^{34} x_{ij} = k \tag{34}$$

The inequality of Eq. 32 implies that for each $k = 1, 2, \ldots, 34$ there exists an $x_{ij} = 1$ with $i \leq k$ and $j \geq k$ and therefore, by Eq. 21 an $x_{ij} = 1$ with $d_{ij}$ such that $d_{ij} \geq d_{kk}$. The inequality Eq. 30 follows immediately. The derivation of Eq. 31 is similar.

*Proof of Theorem I*

This follows from Eq. 30. For if the diagonal solution is not feasible, the duty of at least one broken shift exceeds 540 minutes, and hence in any roster there is a broken shift with duty exceeding 540 minutes.

*Proof of Theorem II*

The proof of this theorem is more complicated. A transformation of the form of Eq. 24 will be exhibited which transforms the cost matrix to a non-negative matrix with zeros on the principal diagonal. A suitable transformation is

$$c_{ij}{}^* = c_{ij} + \alpha_i - \beta_j \tag{35}$$

with

$$\alpha_i = \begin{cases} 0, & i = 1 \\ \sum\limits_{r=1}^{i-1} (c_{rr} - c_{r+1r}), & i = 2, 3, \ldots, 34 \end{cases} \tag{36}$$

and

$$\beta_j = \begin{cases} c_{11}, & j = 1 \\ \sum\limits_{r=1}^{j-1} (c_{rr} - c_{r+1r}) + c_{jj}, & j = 2, 3, \ldots, 34 \end{cases} \tag{37}$$

It is easy to verify that

$$c_{ii}{}^* = 0, \quad i = 1, 2, \ldots, 34 \tag{38}$$

$$c_{j+1j}{}^* = 0, \quad j = 1, 2, \ldots, 33 \tag{39}$$

but more complicated to show that

$$c_{ij}{}^* \geq 0 \quad \text{if} \quad i < j \quad \text{or} \quad i > j + 1 \tag{40}$$

From the identities

$$c_{ij} = c_{jj} + \sum_{r=i}^{j-1} (c_{rj} - c_{r+1j}), \quad i < j \tag{41}$$

$$c_{ij} = c_{jj} - \sum_{r=j}^{i-1} (c_{rj} - c_{r+1j}), \quad i > j + 1 \tag{42}$$

it follows that

$$c_{ij}{}^* = \sum_{r=i}^{j-1} \{(c_{rj} - c_{r+1j}) - (c_{rr} - c_{r+1r})\}, \quad i < j \tag{43}$$

$$c_{ij}{}^* = \sum_{r=j+1}^{i-1} \{(c_{rr} - c_{r+1j}) - (c_{rj} - c_{r+1j})\}, \quad i > j + 1 \tag{44}$$

That these are non-negative is a consequence of the fact that $c_{rj} - c_{r+1j}$ is a non-decreasing function of $j$ for all $r$
i.e.,

$$\Delta^2{}_{rj}(c_{rj}) = c_{r+1j+1} - c_{rj+1} - c_{r+1j} + c_{rj}$$

$$= (c_{rj} - c_{r+1j}) - (c_{rj+1} - c_{r+1j+1}) \leq 0 \qquad (45)$$

$$r, j = 1, 2, \ldots, 33$$

where $\Delta_{rj}^2$ is the mixed second-order forward difference operator. The inequality of Eq. 45 can be easily checked by taking $2 \times 2$ submatrices from the overtime matrix in Table III. The proof* of Eq. 45 for $c_{ij}$ defined by Eq. 16 is obtained by listing the following six possible cases:

1. $d_{rj}, d_{r+1j}, d_{rj+1}, d_{r+1j+1} \leq 495$
$$\Delta_{rj}^2(c_{rj}) = 0$$
   by Eq. 4.

2. $d_{rj+1} > 495; d_{rj}, d_{r+1j}, d_{r+1j+1} \leq 495$
$$\Delta_{rj}^2(c_{rj}) = -(d_{rj+1} - 495) < 0$$

3. $d_{rj}, d_{rj+1} > 495; d_{r+1j}, d_{r+1j+1} \leq 495$
$$\Delta_{rj}^2(c_{rj}) = d_{rj} - d_{rj+1} \leq 0$$
   by Eq. 21.

4. $d_{rj+1}, d_{r+1j+1} > 495; d_{rj}, d_{r+1j} \leq 495$
$$\Delta_{rj}^2(c_{rj}) = d_{r+1j+1} - d_{rj+1} \leq 0$$

5. $d_{rj}, d_{rj+1}, d_{r+1j+1} > 495; d_{r+1j} \leq 495$
$$\Delta_{rj}^2(c_{rj}) = \Delta_{rj}^2(d_{rj}) + (d_{r+1j} - 495) \leq 0$$
   by Eq. 1.

6. $d_{rj}, d_{r+1j}, d_{rj+1}, d_{r+1j+1} > 495$
$$\Delta_{rj}^2(c_{rj}) = \Delta_{rj}^2(d_{rj}) = 0$$

## Spread Problem

The problem of minimizing the penalty payments due to excess spread, with the spread limited to 12 hours, is very similar to the overtime problem. The cost matrix $C = [c_{ij}]$ for this problem is given by

$$c_{ij} = \tfrac{1}{2} |s_{ij} - 585| + \tfrac{1}{2}(s_{ij} - 585)$$

$$+ \tfrac{1}{2} |s_{ij} - 645| + \tfrac{1}{2}(s_{ij} - 645) \qquad (46)$$

so that $C$ is the sum of two matrices each similar to the overtime matrix.

---

* The inequality of Eq. 45 holds for the similar, but simpler, cost matrix with elements $c_{ij} = |i - j|$, discussed by Parikh and Wets[8].

Corresponding to the sets $S$, $T$, $U$ defined by Eqs. 26–28 are the three fundamental sets

$$P = \{x_{ij} \mid s_{ij} \leq 585\} \tag{47}$$

$$Q = \{x_{ij} \mid 585 \leq s_{ij} \leq 645\} \tag{48}$$

$$R = \{x_{ij} \mid 645 \leq s_{ij} \leq 720\} \tag{49}$$

and the admissible set

$$W = P \cup Q \cup R \tag{50}$$

TABLE IV.  Diagonal Roster for Spread Problem

| | Morning tour | | | Afternoon tour | | Broken shifts |
| i | Sign on | Sign off | j | Sign on | Sign off | Spread (min) |
|---|---|---|---|---|---|---|
| 9 | 0553 | 0952 | 3 | 1410 | 1740 | 707 |
| 25 | 0604 | 0903 | 7 | 1340 | 1743 | 699 |
| 19 | 0612 | 0933 | 29 | 1229 | 1747 | 695 |
| 8 | 0613 | 1012 | 4 | 1405 | 1758 | 705 |
| 3 | 0613 | 1047 | 11 | 1345 | 1803 | 710 |
| 13 | 0614 | 1003 | 26 | 1305 | 1803 | 709 |
| 29 | 0615 | 0903 | 32 | 1241 | 1809 | 714 |
| 4 | 0620 | 1042 | 27 | 1305 | 1811 | 711 |
| 26 | 0621 | 0917 | 12 | 1355 | 1814 | 713 |
| 6 | 0625 | 1027 | 20 | 1340 | 1815 | 710 |
| 22 | 0634 | 0945 | 30 | 1300 | 1822 | 708 |
| 17 | 0637 | 1013 | 15 | 1355 | 1823 | 706 |
| 16 | 0641 | 1018 | 19 | 1350 | 1824 | 703 |
| 14 | 0647 | 1032 | 14 | 1405 | 1830 | 703 |
| 27 | 0648 | 0942 | 28 | 1315 | 1831 | 703 |
| 30 | 0654 | 0941 | 8 | 1417 | 1832 | 698 |
| 18 | 0704 | 1032 | 1 | 1530 | 1836 | 692 |
| 5 | 0717 | 1122 | 21 | 1405 | 1840 | 683 |
| 7 | 0725 | 1127 | 13 | 1420 | 1840 | 675 |
| 12 | 0733 | 1127 | 6 | 1445 | 1847 | 674 |
| 10 | 0734 | 1132 | 10 | 1430 | 1848 | 674 |
| 21 | 0735 | 1047 | 22 | 1410 | 1856 | 681 |
| 23 | 0735 | 1041 | 34 | 1255 | 1859 | 684 |
| 33 | 0738 | 1012 | 18 | 1435 | 1906 | 688 |
| 15 | 0741 | 1118 | 5 | 1515 | 1909 | 688 |
| 24 | 0741 | 1042 | 31 | 1345 | 1912 | 691 |
| 31 | 0742 | 1027 | 17 | 1457 | 1927 | 705 |
| 32 | 0745 | 1027 | 25 | 1440 | 1937 | 712 |
| 11 | 0750 | 1147 | 16 | 1511 | 1941 | 711 |
| 1 | 0751 | 1245 | 9 | 1525 | 1941 | 710 |
| 28 | 0756 | 1047 | 23 | 1450 | 1942 | 706 |
| 20 | 0757 | 1117 | 24 | 1450 | 1946 | 709 |
| 2 | 0806 | 1257 | 2 | 1617 | 1947 | 701 |
| 34 | 0808 | 1007 | 33 | 1410 | 2006 | 718 |

The cost matrix $C$ is a non-negative matrix with $c_{ij} = 0$ if $x_{ij} \in P$. For the set $Q$ one can define a non-negative matrix with elements

$$
\begin{aligned}
c_{ij}' &= c_{ij} + a_{1i} - b_{2j} + 585 \\
&= c_{ij} - (s_{ij} - 585) \\
&= \tfrac{1}{2} |s_{ij} - 585| - \tfrac{1}{2}(s_{ij} - 585) \\
&\quad + \tfrac{1}{2} |s_{ij} - 645| + \tfrac{1}{2}(s_{ij} - 645)
\end{aligned}
\tag{51}
$$

for which the optimal solutions are unchanged and $c_{ij}' = 0$ for $x_{ij} \in Q$. Similarly for the set $R$, one defines

$$
\begin{aligned}
c_{ij}'' &= \tfrac{1}{2} |s_{ij} - 585| - \tfrac{1}{2}(s_{ij} - 585) \\
&\quad + \tfrac{1}{2} |s_{ij} - 645| - \tfrac{1}{2}(s_{ij} - 645)
\end{aligned}
\tag{52}
$$

$c_{ij}'' \geq 0 \; i,j = 1, 2, \ldots, 34$ and $c_{ij}'' = 0$ for $x_{ij} \in R$

A useful ordering of the morning and afternoon tours is obtained by listing the morning tours in order of increasing sign-on times and the afternoon tours in order of increasing sign-off times. This listing is shown in Table IV. The diagonal roster for this problem is then obtained by pairing the first two tours, then the next two tours and so on. The largest spread for broken shifts in this roster is 718 minutes, and, therefore, by a lemma similar to that proved above, any roster will have a broken shift with spread greater than or equal to 718 minutes. As for the overtime problem, the diagonal roster determines whether or not the problem is feasible and, if feasible, it gives an optimal solution.

## Broken Shift Problem

The broken shift problem, as formulated in Eqs. 12 and 13 can now be analyzed by combining the results for the overtime problem and the spread problem. When rules 4, 5, 6 for break, duty, and spread are allowed for, five fundamental sets are obtained whose union is the admissible set $V$. The five corresponding regions in the $(d_{ij}, s_{ij})$ plane are evident in Fig. 1. It might have been expected that as the simpler problems had two and three fundamental sets, respectively, the full broken shift problem would have six fundamental sets. As is evident from Fig. 1, however, one of the sets degenerates because the corresponding region contracts to the point $d_{ij} = 495$, $s_{ij} = 585$. This occurs because the minimum break of 90 minutes happens to equal the difference between a spread of $9\frac{3}{4}$ hours and a duty of $8\frac{1}{4}$ hours.

To each of the fundamental sets there corresponds a non-negative matrix with elements of the form $c_{ij}' = c_{ij} + \alpha_i - \beta_j + \gamma$ and $c_{ij}' = 0$ for $x_{ij}$ in the set. For example, if

$$
\begin{aligned}
c_{ij}' &= c_{ij} + 2a_{1i} - 2b_{2j} + 1230 \\
&= 3\{\tfrac{1}{2} |d_{ij} - 495| + \tfrac{1}{2}(d_{ij} - 495)\} \\
&\quad + \tfrac{1}{2} |s_{ij} - 585| - \tfrac{1}{2}(s_{ij} - 585) \\
&\quad + \tfrac{1}{2} |s_{ij} - 645| - \tfrac{1}{2}(s_{ij} - 645)
\end{aligned}
\tag{53}
$$

TABLE V.    Cost Matrix

| 0 | 27 | 83 | 134 | 99 | 123 | 179 | 166 | 165 | 171 | 204 | 196 | 177 | 198 | 214 | 207 | 207 |
|---|----|----|-----|----|-----|-----|-----|-----|-----|-----|-----|-----|-----|-----|-----|-----|
| 15 | 18 | 100 | 140 | 90 | 118 | 193 | 172 | 156 | 165 | 210 | 202 | 179 | 204 | 220 | 198 | 198 |
| 0 | 0 | 0 | 36 | 39 | 63 | 66 | 102 | 105 | 111 | 111 | 114 | 117 | 132 | 141 | 147 | 147 |
| 0 | 0 | 0 | 0 | 3 | 27 | 30 | 66 | 69 | 75 | 75 | 78 | 81 | 96 | 105 | 111 | 111 |
| 0 | 0 | 22 | 4 | 0 | 0 | 19 | 15 | 18 | 24 | 24 | 27 | 30 | 45 | 54 | 60 | 60 |
| 0 | 0 | 0 | 0 | 0 | 0 | 0 | 6 | 9 | 15 | 15 | 18 | 21 | 36 | 45 | 51 | 51 |
| 0 | 0 | 30 | 12 | 0 | 0 | 27 | 6 | 9 | 15 | 22 | 18 | 21 | 36 | 45 | 51 | 51 |
| 0 | 0 | 0 | 0 | 0 | 0 | 0 | 0 | 0 | 6 | 6 | 9 | 12 | 27 | 36 | 42 | 42 |
| 0 | 0 | 0 | 0 | 0 | 0 | 0 | 0 | 0 | 6 | 6 | 9 | 12 | 27 | 36 | 42 | 42 |
| 0 | 0 | 39 | 21 | 0 | 0 | 36 | 0 | 0 | 3 | 19 | 11 | 9 | 24 | 33 | 39 | 39 |
| 0 | 0 | 55 | 37 | 0 | 0 | 52 | 3 | 0 | 0 | 32 | 24 | 6 | 26 | 42 | 36 | ·36 |
| 0 | 0 | 38 | 20 | 0 | 0 | 35 | 0 | 0 | 0 | 15 | 4 | 0 | 12 | 21 | 27 | 27 |
| 0 | 0 | 0 | 0 | 0 | 0 | 0 | 0 | 0 | 0 | 0 | 0 | 0 | 0 | 6 · | 12 | 12 |
| 0 | 0 | 0 | 0 | 0 | 0 | 0 | 0 | 0 | 0 | 0 | 0 | 0 | 0 | 0 | 0 | 0 |
| 0 | 0 | 46 | 28 | 0 | 0 | 43 | 0 | 0 | 0 | 23 | 12 | 0 | 0 | 3 | 0 | 0 |
| 0 | 0 | 0 | 0 | 0 | 0 | 0 | 0 | 0 | 0 | 0 | 0 | 0 | 0 | 0 | 0 | 0 |
| 0 | 0 | 0 | 0 | 0 | 0 | 0 | 0 | 0 | 0 | 0 | 0 | 0 | 0 | 0 | 0 | 0 |
| 0 | 0 | 9 | 0 | 0 | 0 | 6 | 0 | 0 | 0 | 0 | 0 | 0 | 0 | 0 | 0 | 0 |
| 0 | 0 | 0 | 0 | 0 | 0 | 0 | 0 | 0 | 0 | 0 | 0 | 0 | 0 | 0 | 0 | 0 |
| 6 | 0 | 64 | 44 | 0 | 0 | 59 | 10 | 0 | 0 | 39 | 28 | 2 | 12 | 19 | 0 | 0 |
| 0 | 0 | 40 | 22 | 0 | 0 | 37 | 0 | 0 | 0 | 17 | 6 | 0 | 0 | 0 | 0 | 0 |
| 0 | 0 | 0 | 0 | 0 | 0 | 0 | 0 | 0 | 0 | 0 | 0 | 0 | 0 | 0 | 0 | 0 |
| 0 | 0 | 40 | 22 | 0 | 0 | 37 | 0 | 0 | 0 | 17 | 6 | 0 | 0 | 0 | 0 | 0 |
| 0 | 0 | 46 | 28 | 0 | 0 | 43 | 0 | 0 | 0 | 23 | 12 | 0 | 0 | 3 | 0 | 0 |
| 0 | 0 | 0 | 0 | 0 | 0 | 0 | 0 | 0 | 0 | 0 | 0 | 0 | 0 | 0 | 0 | 0 |
| 0 | 0 | 0 | 0 | 0 | 0 | 0 | 0 | 0 | 0 | 0 | 0 | 0 | 0 | 0 | 0 | 0 |
| 0 | 0 | 0 | 0 | 0 | 0 | 0 | 0 | 0 | 0 | 0 | 0 | 0 | 0 | 0 | 0 | 0 |
| 5 | 0 | 62 | 43 | 0 | 0 | 58 | 9 | 0 | 0 | 38 | 27 | 1 | 11 | ·18 | 0 | 0 |
| 0 | 0 | 0 | 0 | 0 | 0 | 0 | 0 | 0 | 0 | 0 | 0 | 0 | 0 | 0 | 0 | 0 |
| 0 | 0 | 0 | 0 | 0 | 0 | 0 | 0 | 0 | 0 | 0 | 0 | 0 | 0 | 0 | 0 | 0 |
| 0 | 0 | 47 | 29 | 0 | 0 | 44 | 0 | 0 | 0 | 24 | 13 | 0 | 0 | 4 | 0 | 0 |
| 0 | 0 | 50 | 32 | 0 | 0 | 47 | 0 | 0 | 0 | 27 | 16 | 0 | 0 | 7 | 0 | 0 |
| 0 | 0 | 43 | 25 | 0 | 0 | 40 | 0 | 0 | 0 | 20 | 9 | 0 | 0 | 0 | 0 | 0 |
| 17 | 0 | 86 | 55 | 0 | 6 | 80 | 21 | 0 | 5 | 50 | 39 | 13 | 23 | 30 | 0 | 0 |

## for Broken Shift Problem

| | | | | | | | | | | | | | | | | |
|---|---|---|---|---|---|---|---|---|---|---|---|---|---|---|---|---|
| 210 | 231 | 243 | 222 | 255 | 273 | 285 | 288 | 324 | 340 | 350 | 400 | 377 | 378 | 408 | 465 | 489 |
| 201 | 237 | 249 | 224 | 246 | 264 | 276 | 279 | 330 | 346 | 356 | 410 | 383 | 369 | 414 | 456 | 480 |
| 150 | 159 | 162 | 162 | 195 | 213 | 225 | 228 | 231 | 255 | 285 | 291 | 303 | 318 | 321 | 405 | 429 |
| 114 | 123 | 126 | 126 | 159 | 177 | 189 | 192 | 195 | 219 | 249 | 255 | 267 | 282 | 285 | 369 | 393 |
| 63 | 72 | 75 | 75 | 108 | 126 | 138 | 141 | 144 | 168 | 198 | 204 | 216 | 231 | 234 | 318 | 342 |
| 54 | 63 | 66 | 66 | 99 | 117 | 129 | 132 | 135 | 159 | 189 | 195 | 207 | 222 | 225 | 309 | 333 |
| 54 | 63 | 66 | 66 | 99 | 117 | 129 | 132 | 142 | 159 | 189 | 218 | 207 | 222 | 226 | 309 | 333 |
| 45 | 54 | 57 | 57 | 90 | 108 | 120 | 123 | 126 | 150 | 180 | 186 | 198 | 213 | 216 | 300 | 324 |
| 45 | 54 | 57 | 57 | 90 | 108 | 120 | 123 | 126 | 150 | 180 | 186 | 198 | 213 | 216 | 300 | 324 |
| 42 | 51 | 58 | 54 | 87 | 105 | 117 | 120 | 139 | 155 | 177 | 215 | 195 | 210 | 223 | 297 | 321 |
| 39 | 59 | 71 | 51 | 84 | 102 | 114 | 117 | 152 | 168 | 178 | 228 | 205 | 207 | 236 | 294 | 318 |
| 30 | 39 | 45 | 42 | 75 | 93 | 105 | 108 | 126 | 142 | 165 | 202 | 183 | 198 | 210 | 285 | 309 |
| 15 | 24 | 27 | 27 | 60 | 78 | 90 | 93 | 96 | 120 | 150 | 156 | 168 | 183 | 186 | 270 | 294 |
| 3 | 12 | 15 | 15 | 48 | 66 | 78 | 81 | 84 | 108 | 138 | 144 | 156 | 171 | 174 | 258 | 282 |
| 0 | 2 | 11 | 0 | 24 | 42 | 54 | 57 | 83 | 99 | 114 | 159 | 136 | 147 | 167 | 234 | 258 |
| 0 | 0 | 0 | 0 | 24 | 42 | 54 | 57 | 60 | 84 | 114 | 120 | 132 | 147 | 150 | 234 | 258 |
| 0 | 0 | 0 | 0 | 21 | 39 | 51 | 54 | 57 | 81 | 111 | 117 | 129 | 144 | 147 | 231 | 255 |
| 0 | 0 | 0 | 0 | 0 | 15 | 27 | 30 | 33 | 57 | 87 | 95 | 105 | 120 | 123 | 207 | 231 |
| 0 | 0 | 0 | 0 | 0 | 0 | 6 | 9 | 12 | 36 | 66 | 72 | 84 | 99 | 102 | 186 | 210 |
| 0 | 18 | 27 | 2 | 0 | 0 | 3 | 6 | 48 | 64 | 74 | 124 | 101 | 96 | 132 | 183 | 207 |
| 0 | 0 | 5 | 0 | 0 | 0 | 0 | 0 | 17 | 18 | 39 | 78 | 57 | 72 | 86 | 159 | 183 |
| 0 | 0 | 0 | 0 | 0 | 0 | 0 | 0 | 0 | 6 | 36 | 42 | 54 | 69 | 72 | 156 | 180 |
| 0 | 0 | 5 | 0 | 0 | 0 | 0 | 0 | 17 | 9 | 21 | 60 | 39 | 54 | 68 | 141 | 165 |
| 0 | 2 | 11 | 0 | 0 | 0 | 0 | 0 | 23 | 15 | 6 | 51 | 28 | 39 | 59 | 126 | 150 |
| 0 | 0 | 0 | 0 | 0 | 0 | 0 | 0 | 0 | 0 | 0 | 6 | 18 | 33 | 36 | 120 | 144 |
| 0 | 0 | 0 | 0 | 0 | 0 | 0 | 0 | 0 | 0 | 0 | 0 | 9 | 24 | 27 | 111 | 135 |
| 0 | 0 | 0 | 0 | 0 | 0 | 0 | 0 | 0 | 0 | 0 | 0 | 3 | 18 | 21 | 105 | 129 |
| 0 | 17 | 26 | 1 | 0 | 0 | 0 | 0 | 38 | 30 | 10 | 54 | 19 | 9 | 44 | 96 | 120 |
| 0 | 0 | 0 | 0 | 0 | 0 | 0 | 0 | 0 | 0 | 0 | 0 | 0 | 0 | 3 | 87 | 111 |
| 0 | 0 | 0 | 0 | 0 | 0 | 0 | 0 | 0 | 0 | 0 | 0 | 0 | 0 | 0 | 84 | 108 |
| 0 | 3 | 12 | 0 | 0 | 0 | 0 | 0 | 24 | 16 | 0 | 40 | 5 | 0 | 18 | 78 | 102 |
| 0 | 6 | 15 | 0 | 0 | 0 | 0 | 0 | 27 | 19 | 0 | 43 | 8 | 0 | 21 | 69 | 93 |
| 0 | 0 | 8 | 0 | 0 | 0 | 0 | 0 | 20 | 12 | 0 | 36 | 1 | 0 | 14 | 45 | 69 |
| 0 | 29 | 38 | 13 | 0 | 0 | 0 | 0 | 50 | 42 | 22 | 72 | 31 | 0 | 44 | 0 | 0 |

TABLE VI.   Cost Matrix

| | | | | | | | | | | | | | | | | |
|---|---|---|---|---|---|---|---|---|---|---|---|---|---|---|---|---|
| 0 | 27 | xxx | xxx | 99 | 123 | xxx | xxx | xxx | xxx | xxx | xxx | xxx | xxx | xxx | xxx | xxx |
| 15 | 18 | xxx | xxx | 90 | 118 | xxx | xxx | xxx | xxx | xxx | xxx | xxx | xxx | xxx | xxx | xxx |
| xxx | xxx | 0 | 36 | xxx | xxx | 66 | xxx | xxx | xxx | 111 | xxx | xxx | xxx | xxx | xxx | xxx |
| xxx | xxx | 0 | 0 | xxx | xxx | 30 | xxx | xxx | xxx | 75 | 78 | xxx | xxx | xxx | xxx | xxx |
| 0 | xxx | 22 | 4 | 0 | 0 | 19 | 15 | xxx | 24 | 24 | 27 | 30 | 45 | 54 | xxx | xxx |
| xxx | xxx | 0 | 0 | xxx | xxx | 0 | xxx | xxx | xxx | 15 | 18 | xxx | xxx | 45 | xxx | xxx |
| 0 | xxx | 30 | 12 | 0 | 0 | 27 | 6 | xxx | 15 | 22 | 18 | 21 | 36 | 45 | xxx | xxx |
| xxx | xxx | 0 | 0 | xxx | xxx | 0 | xxx | xxx | xxx | 6 | xxx | xxx | xxx | xxx | xxx | xxx |
| xxx | xxx | 0 | xxx | xxx | xxx | 0 | xxx | xxx | xxx | xxx | xxx | xxx | xxx | xxx | xxx | xxx |
| 0 | xxx | 39 | 21 | 0 | 0 | 36 | 0 | xxx | 3 | 19 | 11 | 9 | 24 | 33 | xxx | 39 |
| 0 | 0 | 55 | 37 | 0 | 0 | 52 | 3 | 0 | 0 | 32 | 24 | 6 | 26 | 42 | 36 | 36 |
| 0 | xxx | 38 | 20 | 0 | 0 | 35 | 0 | xxx | 0 | 15 | 4 | 0 | 12 | 21 | xxx | 27 |
| xxx | xxx | 0 | 0 | xxx | xxx | 0 | xxx | xxx | xxx | 0 | 0 | xxx | xxx | xxx | xxx | xxx |
| 0 | xxx | 0 | 0 | xxx | 0 | 0 | 0 | xxx | xxx | 0 | 0 | 0 | 0 | 0 | xxx | xxx |
| 0 | xxx | 46 | 28 | 0 | 0 | 43 | 0 | 0 | 0 | 23 | 12 | 0 | 0 | 3 | 0 | 0 |
| 0 | xxx | 0 | 0 | xxx | xxx | 0 | 0 | xxx | xxx | 0 | 0 | 0 | 0 | 0 | xxx | xxx |
| 0 | xxx | 0 | 0 | xxx | xxx | 0 | 0 | xxx | xxx | 0 | 0 | xxx | 0 | 0 | xxx | xxx |
| 0 | xxx | 9 | 0 | xxx | 0 | 6 | 0 | xxx | 0 | 0 | 0 | 0 | 0 | 0 | xxx | xxx |
| xxx | xxx | 0 | 0 | xxx | xxx | 0 | xxx | xxx | xxx | 0 | xxx | xxx | xxx | xxx | xxx | xxx |
| 6 | 0 | 64 | 44 | 0 | 0 | 59 | 10 | 0 | 0 | 39 | 28 | 2 | 12 | 19 | 0 | 0 |
| 0 | xxx | 40 | 22 | 0 | 0 | 37 | 0 | xxx | 0 | 17 | 6 | 0 | 0 | 0 | xxx | 0 |
| xxx | xxx | 0 | 0 | xxx | xxx | 0 | 0 | xxx | xxx | 0 | 0 | xxx | 0 | 0 | xxx | xxx |
| 0 | xxx | 40 | 22 | 0 | 0 | 37 | 0 | xxx | 0 | 17 | 6 | 0 | 0 | 0 | xxx | 0 |
| 0 | xxx | 46 | 28 | 0 | 0 | 43 | 0 | 0 | 0 | 23 | 12 | 0 | 0 | 3 | 0 | 0 |
| xxx | xxx | 0 | 0 | xxx | xxx | 0 | xxx | xxx | xxx | 0 | xxx | xxx | xxx | xxx | xxx | xxx |
| xxx | xxx | 0 | 0 | xxx | xxx | 0 | xxx | xxx | xxx | 0 | 0 | xxx | xxx | xxx | xxx | xxx |
| 0 | xxx | 0 | 0 | xxx | 0 | 0 | 0 | xxx | 0 | 0 | 0 | 0 | 0 | 0 | xxx | xxx |
| 5 | 0 | 62 | 43 | 0 | 0 | 58 | 9 | 0 | 0 | 38 | 27 | 1 | 11 | 18 | 0 | 0 |
| xxx | xxx | 0 | 0 | xxx | xxx | 0 | xxx | xxx | xxx | 0 | 0 | xxx | xxx | xxx | xxx | xxx |
| 0 | xxx | 0 | 0 | xxx | 0 | 0 | 0 | xxx | 0 | 0 | 0 | 0 | 0 | 0 | xxx | xxx |
| 0 | xxx | 47 | 29 | 0 | 0 | 44 | 0 | 0 | 0 | 24 | 13 | 0 | 0 | 4 | 0 | 0 |
| 0 | xxx | 50 | 32 | 0 | 0 | 47 | 0 | 0 | 0 | 27 | 16 | 0 | 0 | 7 | 0 | 0 |
| 0 | xxx | 43 | 25 | 0 | 0 | 40 | 0 | xxx | 0 | 20 | 9 | 0 | 0 | 0 | xxx | 0 |
| 17 | 0 | 86 | 55 | 0 | 6 | 80 | 21 | 0 | 5 | 50 | 39 | 13 | 23 | 30 | 0 | 0 |

## with Inadmissible Squares

| | | | | | | | | | | | | | | | | |
|---|---|---|---|---|---|---|---|---|---|---|---|---|---|---|---|---|
| xxx | xxx | xxx | xxx | xxx | xxx | xxx | xxx | xxx | xxx | xxx | xxx | xxx | xxx | xxx | xxx | xxx |
| xxx | xxx | xxx | xxx | xxx | xxx | xxx | xxx | xxx | xxx | xxx | xxx | xxx | xxx | xxx | xxx | xxx |
| xxx | xxx | xxx | xxx | xxx | xxx | xxx | xxx | xxx | xxx | xxx | xxx | xxx | xxx | xxx | xxx | xxx |
| xxx | xxx | 126 | xxx | xxx | xxx | xxx | xxx | xxx | xxx | xxx | xxx | xxx | xxx | xxx | xxx | xxx |
| 63 | 72 | 75 | 75 | 108 | xxx | xxx | xxx | xxx | xxx | xxx | xxx | xxx | xxx | xxx | xxx | xxx |
| xxx | 63 | 66 | xxx | xxx | xxx | xxx | xxx | 135 | xxx | xxx | xxx | xxx | xxx | xxx | xxx | xxx |
| 54 | 63 | 66 | 66 | 99 | xxx | xxx | xxx | 142 | xxx | xxx | xxx | xxx | xxx | xxx | xxx | xxx |
| xxx | xxx | xxx | xxx | xxx | xxx | xxx | xxx | 126 | xxx | xxx | xxx | xxx | xxx | xxx | xxx | xxx |
| xxx | xxx | xxx | xxx | xxx | xxx | xxx | xxx | xxx | xxx | xxx | xxx | xxx | xxx | xxx | xxx | xxx |
| 42 | 51 | 58 | 54 | 87 | xxx | xxx | xxx | 139 | xxx | xxx | xxx | xxx | xxx | xxx | xxx | xxx |
| 39 | 59 | 71 | 51 | 84 | 102 | 114 | 117 | xxx | xxx | xxx | xxx | xxx | xxx | xxx | xxx | xxx |
| 30 | 39 | 45 | 42 | 75 | xxx | xxx | xxx | 126 | 142 | xxx | xxx | xxx | xxx | xxx | xxx | xxx |
| xxx | xxx | xxx | xxx | xxx | xxx | xxx | xxx | 96 | 120 | xxx | xxx | xxx | xxx | xxx | xxx | xxx |
| xxx | 12 | 15 | 15 | xxx | xxx | xxx | xxx | 84 | 108 | xxx | xxx | xxx | xxx | xxx | xxx | xxx |
| 0 | 2 | 11 | 0 | 24 | xxx | xxx | 57 | 83 | 99 | 114 | xxx | 136 | xxx | xxx | xxx | xxx |
| xxx | 0 | 0 | 0 | xxx | xxx | xxx | xxx | 60 | 84 | 114 | 120 | 132 | xxx | xxx | xxx | xxx |
| xxx | 0 | 0 | xxx | xxx | xxx | xxx | xxx | 57 | 81 | 111 | 117 | 129 | xxx | xxx | xxx | xxx |
| xxx | 0 | 0 | 0 | 0 | xxx | xxx | xxx | 33 | 57 | 87 | 95 | 105 | xxx | 123 | xxx | xxx |
| xxx | xxx | xxx | xxx | xxx | xxx | xxx | xxx | 12 | 36 | xxx | 72 | xxx | xxx | 102 | xxx | xxx |
| 0 | 18 | 27 | 2 | 0 | 0 | 3 | 6 | 48 | 64 | 74 | xxx | 101 | 96 | xxx | xxx | xxx |
| 0 | 0 | 5 | 0 | 0 | xxx | xxx | xxx | 17 | 18 | 39 | 78 | 57 | 72 | 86 | xxx | xxx |
| xxx | 0 | 0 | xxx | xxx | xxx | xxx | xxx | 0 | 6 | 36 | 42 | 54 | xxx | 72 | xxx | xxx |
| 0 | 0 | 5 | 0 | 0 | xxx | xxx | xxx | 17 | 9 | 21 | 60 | 39 | 54 | 68 | xxx | xxx |
| 0 | 2 | 11 | 0 | 0 | xxx | xxx | 0 | 23 | 15 | 6 | 51 | 28 | 39 | 59 | xxx | xxx |
| xxx | xxx | xxx | xxx | xxx | xxx | xxx | xxx | 0 | xxx | xxx | 6 | xxx | xxx | xxx | xxx | xxx |
| xxx | xxx | 0 | xxx | xxx | xxx | xxx | xxx | 0 | 0 | xxx | 0 | xxx | xxx | 27 | xxx | xxx |
| xxx | 0 | 0 | 0 | xxx | xxx | xxx | xxx | 0 | 0 | 0 | 0 | 3 | xxx | 21 | xxx | xxx |
| 0 | 17 | 26 | 1 | 0 | 0 | 0 | 0 | 38 | 30 | 10 | 54 | 19 | 9 | 44 | xxx | 120 |
| xxx | xxx | 0 | xxx | xxx | xxx | xxx | xxx | 0 | 0 | xxx | 0 | xxx | xxx | 3 | xxx | xxx |
| xxx | 0 | 0 | 0 | xxx | xxx | xxx | xxx | 0 | 0 | 0 | 0 | 0 | xxx | 0 | xxx | xxx |
| 0 | 3 | 12 | 0 | 0 | 0 | xxx | 0 | 24 | 16 | 0 | 40 | 5 | 0 | 18 | xxx | 102 |
| 0 | 6 | 15 | 0 | 0 | 0 | xxx | 0 | 27 | 19 | 0 | 43 | 8 | 0 | 21 | xxx | 93 |
| 0 | 0 | 8 | 0 | 0 | xxx | xxx | 0 | 20 | 12 | 0 | 36 | 1 | 0 | 14 | xxx | 69 |
| 0 | 29 | 38 | 13 | 0 | 0 | 0 | 0 | 50 | 42 | 22 | 72 | 31 | 0 | 44 | 0 | 0 |

then the optimal solutions for $c_{ij}'$ are the same as for $c_{ij}$, $c_{ij}' \geq 0$ $i, j = 1$, $2, \ldots, 34$ and $c_{ij}' = 0$ for

$$x_{ij} \in \{x_{ij} \mid s_{ij} - d_{ij} \geq 90, d_{ij} \leq 495, 645 \leq s_{ij} \leq 720\} \tag{54}$$

The matrix $[c_{ij}']$ is given in Table V. From Table VI, which is just this matrix with the inadmissible squares blocked out, it is apparent that just over half the broken shifts are valid.

The five fundamental sets, corresponding to the five fundamental regions in the $d_{ij}, s_{ij}$ plane of Fig. 1, correspond to the different classes of valid broken shifts. For example, the set defined in Eq. 54 corresponds to the class of valid broken shifts with a break at least $1\frac{1}{2}$ hours, a duty not exceeding $8\frac{1}{4}$ hours (i.e., no overtime) and a spread at least $10\frac{3}{4}$ hours but not exceeding 12 hours.

For each of the classes the following results are true:

a.  suppose for some solution $X$ an exchange of afternoon tours is made between two broken shifts in the same class. If the new broken shifts also belong to this class, the total penalty payment is unaltered by the exchange.
b.  Suppose for some solution $X$ all the broken shifts are in the same class. Then $X$ is an optimal solution.

If the problem is feasible, then result *a* suggests that there could be many optimal solutions. But the determination of an optimal solution is not as straightforward as for the simpler problems. As is evident from Tables II and IV, the diagonal rosters obtained for the overtime problem and the spread do not coincide. They imply, however, that an optimal roster of the broken shift problem will include a broken shift with duty greater than or equal to 510 minutes, and a broken shift with spread greater than or equal to 718 minutes.

## Solution of the Broken Shift Problem

### Method

The broken shift problem, formulated as an assignment problem with inadmissible squares, has been solved by a *primal-dual* method based on the Hitchcock problem algorithm of Ford and Fulkerson.[9] This algorithm was modified to allow for the inadmissible squares and simplified for application to assignment problems.

The dual of the minimizing assignment problem defined by cost matrix $C = [c_{ij}]$ and admissible set $V$ is the linear program: find

$$\alpha_i, \beta_j \qquad i, j = 1, 2, \ldots, 34$$

which maximize

$$\sum_{j=1}^{34} \beta_j - \sum_{i=1}^{34} \alpha_i \tag{54}$$

subject to

$$c_{ij} + \alpha_i - \beta_j \geq 0 \quad \text{if} \quad x_{ij} \in V \tag{55}$$

Feasible solutions are $\alpha_i$, $\beta_j$ satisfying Eq. 55.

The primal-dual method is started with a feasible solution of the dual problem and the amount of computation then required to obtain an optimal solution depends on how well the initial dual solution is chosen. Two initial solutions have been used successfully.

### Initial Dual Solution A

Consider the dual problem with cost matrix $C$ defined by Eq. 6. The five matrices corresponding to the fundamental sets or classes of broken shifts are related to $C$ by transformations $c_{ij}' = c_{ij} + \alpha_i - \beta_j$. As the matrices are non-negative they represent different feasible solutions of the dual problem. If the broken shift problem has an optimal solution with broken shifts all in the one class, the corresponding initial dual solution would give an optimal solution immediately.

Computations have been carried out by starting with the matrix $[c_{ij}']$, with $c_{ij}'$ defined as in Eq. 53 and with the additional simplification that from each row the minimum element has been subtracted.

### Initial Dual Solution B

An alternative choice of dual variables is suggested by the proof of Theorem II. The variables $\alpha_i$, $\beta_j$ for the overtime problem, defined by Eqs. 36 and 37 transform the cost matrix (defined by Eq. 16) to a matrix which, according to Eqs. 38–40, is non-negative and has zeros on the leading diagonal. A similar definition of variables $\alpha_i$, $\beta_j$ for the spread problem transforms the cost matrix $C$ defined by Eq. 46 to a non-negative matrix with zero elements corresponding to the shifts $(i, j)$ in the diagonal roster. An initial dual solution is then defined by

$$(\alpha_i)_{\text{broken shift}} = 3(\alpha_i)_{\text{overtime}} + (\alpha_i)_{\text{spread}} \tag{56}$$

$$(\beta_j)_{\text{broken shift}} = 3(\beta_j)_{\text{overtime}} + (\beta_j)_{\text{spread}} \tag{57}$$

since, by Eq. 6,

$$(C)_{\text{broken shift}} = 3(C)_{\text{overtime}} + (C)_{\text{spread}} \tag{58}$$

The initial dual solution defined by Eqs. 56 and 57 can be expected to be a "good" one since it will immediately give an optimal solution if there is a feasible solution which is optimal for both the overtime and spread problems. Again, the additional simplification of subtracting from each row variable $\alpha_i$, the $\min_{ji} c_{ij} + \alpha_i - \beta_j$, is made.

## Results

The primal-dual method with a choice of initial dual solutions was programmed in Fortran for a CDC 3600 computer, and the optimal roster listed in Table VII was obtained. It is interesting to compare this roster with the two diagonal rosters in Tables II, IV. The total overtime for the diagonal roster in Table II is 22 minutes; the total overtime of the optimal roster is 53 minutes. The optimal solution for the broken shift problem is, therefore, not an optimal solution of the overtime problem. It is an optimal solution

TABLE VII.    Optimal Broken Shift Roster

| $(i, j)$ | Sign on | Sign off | Sign on | Sign off | Duty (min) | Spread (min) |
|---|---|---|---|---|---|---|
| (1, 1) | 0751 | 1245 | 1530 | 1836 | 480 | 645 |
| (2, 2) | 0806 | 1257 | 1617 | 1947 | 501 | 701 |
| (3, 3) | 0613 | 1047 | 1410 | 1740 | 484 | 687 |
| (4, 4) | 0620 | 1042 | 1405 | 1758 | 495 | 698 |
| (5, 5) | 0717 | 1122 | 1515 | 1909 | 479 | 712 |
| (6, 15) | 0625 | 1027 | 1355 | 1823 | 510 | 718 |
| (7, 6) | 0725 | 1127 | 1445 | 1847 | 484 | 682 |
| (8, 11) | 0613 | 1012 | 1345 | 1803 | 497 | 710 |
| (9, 7) | 0553 | 0952 | 1340 | 1743 | 482 | 710 |
| (10, 8) | 0734 | 1132 | 1417 | 1832 | 493 | 658 |
| (11, 9) | 0750 | 1147 | 1525 | 1941 | 493 | 711 |
| (12, 10) | 0733 | 1127 | 1430 | 1848 | 492 | 675 |
| (13, 12) | 0614 | 1003 | 1355 | 1814 | 488 | 720 |
| (14, 13) | 0647 | 1032 | 1420 | 1840 | 485 | 713 |
| (15, 16) | 0741 | 1118 | 1511 | 1941 | 487 | 720 |
| (16, 21) | 0641 | 1018 | 1405 | 1840 | 492 | 719 |
| (17, 14) | 0637 | 1013 | 1405 | 1830 | 481 | 713 |
| (18, 22) | 0704 | 1032 | 1410 | 1856 | 494 | 712 |
| (19, 26) | 0612 | 0933 | 1305 | 1803 | 499 | 711 |
| (20, 23) | 0757 | 1117 | 1450 | 1942 | 492 | 705 |
| (21, 17) | 0735 | 1047 | 1457 | 1927 | 462 | 712 |
| (22, 19) | 0634 | 0945 | 1350 | 1824 | 465 | 710 |
| (23, 18) | 0735 | 1041 | 1435 | 1906 | 457 | 691 |
| (24, 25) | 0741 | 1042 | 1440 | 1937 | 478 | 716 |
| (25, 29) | 0604 | 0903 | 1229 | 1747 | 497 | 703 |
| (26, 20) | 0621 | 0917 | 1340 | 1815 | 451 | 714 |
| (27, 30) | 0648 | 0942 | 1300 | 1822 | 496 | 694 |
| (28, 24) | 0756 | 1047 | 1450 | 1946 | 467 | 710 |
| (29, 27) | 0615 | 0903 | 1305 | 1811 | 474 | 716 |
| (30, 32) | 0654 | 0941 | 1241 | 1809 | 495 | 675 |
| (31, 31) | 0742 | 1027 | 1345 | 1912 | 492 | 690 |
| (32, 28) | 0745 | 1027 | 1315 | 1831 | 478 | 646 |
| (33, 34) | 0738 | 1012 | 1255 | 1859 | 518 | 681 |
| (34, 33) | 0808 | 1007 | 1410 | 2006 | 475 | 718 |

of the spread problem, however, as each broken shift listed in Tables IV and VII has a spread not less than 645 minutes.

## Discussion

In this paper it has been shown how an optimum broken shift roster can be obtained from a given list of morning and afternoon tours. The problem has been formulated as an assignment problem with inadmissible squares and solved using a variant of the Hungarian method. The computations were carried out on a CDC 3600 computer; the following table lists the computing times (exclusive of input and output) for problems of various sizes:

| No. of broken shifts | Computing time | |
|:---:|:---:|:---:|
| | dual solution A | dual solution B |
| 34 | 2 secs | 2 secs |
| 39 | 8 secs | 6 secs |
| 43 | 4 secs | 4 secs |
| 73 | 53 secs | 19 secs |
| 163 | 1 min 11 secs | 55 secs |
| 177 | 8 min 54 secs | 1 min 21 secs |

In all of these examples the problems were feasible, and indeed the lists of tours were constructed so that this was so. If the problem is not feasible, the method pairs as many tours as possible. In practice the rejected tours might be added to the straight shift roster.

The complete problem of determining the optimal straight and broken shifts can be formulated as an integer program in the following way. From the master timetable, pieces of work labeled $i = 1, 2, \ldots, m$ are formed and $n$ economical valid shifts are chosen and labeled $j = 1, 2, \ldots, n$. Let

$$a_{ij} = \begin{cases} 1 & \text{if shift } j \text{ contains piece of work } i \\ 0 & \text{otherwise} \end{cases}$$

A solution to the problem is represented by a vector $x = [x_j]$ defined so that

$$x_j = \begin{cases} 1 & \text{if shift } j \text{ is used} \\ 0 & \text{if shift } j \text{ is not used} \end{cases}$$

A feasible solution must satisfy

$$\sum_{j=1}^{n} a_{ij} x_j = 1, \qquad i = 1, 2, \ldots, m$$

and an optimal solution is a feasible solution which minimizes $\sum_{1}^{n} c_j x_j$ where $c_j$ is the cost of shift $j$. Although Balinski[10] has reported encouraging computational experience with similarly formulated integer programmes, the values of $m$, $n$ for bus roster problems are well outside the range of present integer programming techniques.

The minimization of the total cost of broken shifts has been formulated on a day to day basis. If, as is usual, the wages are paid weekly or fortnightly, other penalty payments based on the total work in these periods may have to be taken into account. A problem of constructing broken shift rosters on a weekly rather than a daily basis is being investigated.

The use of broken shifts together with straight shifts enables the morning and afternoon peak demands on public transport to be coped with economically. The problem of rostering personnel to match peak periods occurs in other transportation fields. For example, telephone inquiry calls to the Port of New York Authority Bus Terminal[11] rise rapidly to a maximum at about 11 a.m. and then fall off gradually. To roster all telephone operators in 8 hour shifts would be uneconomical. Therefore, shorter 5 hour shifts are used as well. In this and many other situations where the duty of a shift can take only a few fixed values and pay is proportional to hours worked, optimization consists in minimizing idle or slack time.

A complete analysis of the roster problem should not be made independently of an investigation of the timetable problem. It may happen that a slight change in the timetable might alter considerably the solutions to the roster problem, and as there is considerable flexibility in constructing a timetable to meet a demand which can only be estimated approximately, the most should be made of any freedom in order to allow the construction of an economical roster. The whole timetable and roster problem is exceedingly complex but at least the rigorous solution presented above to one small aspect of the problem should prove an excellent guide as to how one might formulate the problem and the approach to be used in its solution. Research in this direction is now being pursued.

## Acknowledgements

The authors are greatly indebted to Mr. L. C. Edie, Port of New York Authority, for sending them the reports referred to in this paper. The data concerning the bus roster was made available through Mr. P. G. Pak-Poy, Consulting Engineer, in liaison with the Municipal Tramways Trust, Adelaide. Appreciation is expressed to Messrs. J. N. Keynes (formerly General Manager, M. T. T.), F. R. Harris (General Manager), and R. Wilson (Traffic Manager) for many helpful discussions on roster problems.

# References

1. S. Vajda, "Readings in Linear Programming," John Wiley and Sons, New York, 1958, p. 85.
2. H. Feis, Het Probleem van de Bemanningsomloop bij een Transportbedrijf, *De Ingenieur*, **74**, A599-A604 (1962).
3. L. C. Edie, Traffic Delays at Toll Booths, *Operations Res.*, **2**, 107-138 (1954).
4. G. B. Dantzig, A Comment on Edie's "Traffic Delays at Toll Booths," *Operations Res.*, **2**, 339–341 (1954).
5. M. Kunreuther, Logic for Solution of the Tolls Manning Problem, The Port of N.Y. Authority Report, 1960.
6. C. Kirsch, Forecasting and Scheduling for Tolls Manpower, Port of N.Y. Authority Report, 1961.
7. G. B. Dantzig, "Linear Programming and Extensions" Princeton University Press, Princeton, 1963, p. 330.
8. S. C. Parikh and R. Wets, Optimality Properties of a Special Assignment Problem, *Operations Res.*, **12**, 139–142 (1964).
9. L. R. Ford and D. R. Fulkerson, "Flows in Networks" Princeton University Press, Princeton, 1962, p. 98.
10. M. L. Balinski, On Finding Integer Solutions to Linear Programs, *Mathematica Report*, 1964.
11. J. H. Dickins, An Operational Analysis of Telephone Information Service, The Port of N.Y. Authority Report, 1962.